Production Safety for Film, Television and Video

This book is dedicated to my mother, father, John and Victoria without whom I would never have finished writing it.

Production Safety for Film, Television and Video

Robin Small

Focal Press

OXFORD AUCKLAND BOSTON JOHANNESBURG MELBOURNE NEW DELHI

Focal Press
An imprint of Butterworth-Heinemann
Linacre House, Jordan Hill, Oxford OX2 8DP
225 Wildwood Avenue, Woburn, MA 01801-2041
A division of Reed Educational and Professional Publishing Ltd

℞   A member of the Reed Elsevier plc group

First published 2000

British Library Cataloguing in Publication Data
Small, Robin
  Production safety for film, television and video
  1. Motion picture industry – Safety measures   2.   Video
  recordings industry – Safety measures   3.   Industrial safety –
  Law and legislation – Great Britain
  I. Title
  363.1'19'778'5

Library of Congress Cataloguing in Publication Data
Small, Robin.
  Production safety for film, television and video/Robin Small.
  p. cm.
  Includes index.
  ISBN 0-240-51531-5 (alk. paper)
  1. Motion picture industry – Safety measures.   2.   Motion pictures –
  Production and direction.   3.   Television – Safety measures.
  4.   Television – Production and direction.   I.   Title.

  PN1995.9.P7 S63   00–035461
  384'.8'0684–dc21

ISBN 0 2405 1531 5

Composition by Genesis Typesetting, Rochester, Kent
Printed and bound in Great Britain by Biddles Ltd, Guildford and King's Lynn

Contents

Acknowledgements

Thank you to the following for help and advice:

- Margaret Riley, the most patient and supportive publisher. Thank you for having the vision to support the project and the patience to wait for it;
- Marie, Beth, Jenny, Margaret and Jane (the Focal Press team) for helping to get the book into print;
- Jane Mills and Barry Callaghan, two great educationalists, for inspiring and encouraging me to teach and write;
- Professor Rae Earnshaw and Ian Macdonald who kindly allowed me to teach health and safety on their courses;
- All the past and present students at the Northern School of Film and Television, Leeds Metropolitan University. Your questions and vitality filled in the gaps;
- Ali Rashid, Carlton Reeve, Ian Rosenbloom, Richard Woodcock and all the past and present students on the BA electronic imaging course at Bradford University, for allowing me to test my material on you;
- Roger Bush and the Hull School of Art and Design Research Committee for a grant towards picture costs and research material. Your patience and support was appreciated;
- Liz Knight and Linda Mason for all their help; and
- Jed Henry for starting me in the right direction.

A big thank you to the following who have loaned their valuable time and experience to help with the hazards sections. Any errors are the author's own.

- Chapter 5 Insurance: Juliet Miller, Stafford Knight Entertainment Brokers Ltd.
- Hazards 2 Animals: Jane Peers, senior personnel officer RSPCA; Liz Rutherford, Janimals 2; Peter Whitear, Cop and Dog Services.
- Hazard 3 Asbestos: Jed Henry, quality and safety advisor, Initial Deborah Services.

- Hazard 5 Building and construction sites: Jed Henry, quality and safety advisor, Initial Deborah Services; Gordon Eagle, health and safety advisor, CITB.
- Hazard 6 Chemicals and hazardous substances: Derek Paley, chemist, Film Lab North, Leeds; Ian McGowan and Kanji Patel, Todd.AO.Filmatic; Ian Rowley; Vic Earl, on-shore safety advisor, BP Exploration.
- Hazard 7 Children: Shiralee Mathews, Children's Support Services, NSPCC.
- Hazard 8 Churches, places of worship and village halls: Vin Arthey, RTS.
- Hazard 10 Confined spaces, including caving and mines: Martin Wilkes, The Visual Link, Carlisle.
- Hazard 11 Cranes, hoists, lifts, and access platforms: Jed Henry, quality and safety advisor, Initial Deborah Services; Peter Hird and Phillip Peacock, Peter Hird & Son Ltd, Hull; Tony Page.
- Hazard 13 Derelict buildings: John Allon, managing director, Sam Allon Ltd.
- Hazard 14 Diving and underwater: Roger Lamplugh, contracts manager, Northern Divers Ltd; Mr Clark, HSE Diving inspectorate.
- Hazard 15 Electricity: Barry Stephenson; George Small, MIEE; Geoff Thompson, MIEE RTS.
- Hazard 16 Explosives and pyrotechnics: Mr Kennington, Humberside Police; Dr Stephen Murray, Royal Military College; Ian Rowley.
- Hazard 17 Fire: Chubb Fire Services; Fire Services College, Moreton in the Marsh; Station Officer Gary Chew, Humberside Fire Brigade.
- Hazard 18 Firearms and weapons: Mr Kennington, firearms licensing, Humberside Police; Dr Steven Murray, Royal Military College.
- Hazard 19 First aid: Lincolnshire Air Ambulance; Harry Robinson, examinations officer, St John Ambulance, Hull.
- Hazard 20 Flying and airports: Bristow Helicopters; Michael Malarik Smith, Castle Air; Heathrow Airport Public Affairs Department; CAA-Licensing Department; David Edmonson, operations manager, Humberside Airport.
- Hazard 21 Food and catering: Mike Fish MCIEH, Environmental Health Officer, Technical Services Department, Hull City Council; Mike Coates, School of Food, Catering and Hotel Operations, Hull College; Gary Wilson, GT Caterers, Leeds.
- Hazard 22 Hot work: Jed Henry, quality and safety advisor, Initial Deborah Services.
- Hazard 23 Human factors: BECTU; Janice Turner, *Stage Screen and Radio*; *The Guardian*.
- Hazard 24 Lasers and radiation: British Nuclear Fuels; National Radiological Protection Board; David Perry, NRPB Library; Dr Donald Hughes, Radiation Protection Service, University of Leeds.

- Hazard 29 Scaffolding and heights: Clive Cureton, Scafftag Ltd; Jed Henry, quality and safety advisor, Initial Deborah Services.
- Hazard 33 Water: Robin Davies, managing director, Square Sail Shipyard Ltd.

Accident case studies and statistics

David Reeds, Durrants Press Agency Ltd
The Yorkshire Post News Library
Guy Strickland, BBC News Information
Janice Turner and Andy Egan, BECTU
Terry Williams, HSE inspector, Glasgow
Tom Jones and Duncan Milligan Thompson and Partners

Photo credits

The London Film Commission
Harvey Edginton, Borough Liaison Officer, London Film Commission
Jed Henry, Wakefield
Tony Kysh, Byker Grove, Newcastle
Michael Malric-Smith, Castle Air Ltd, Cornwall
Ian Rowley, Leeds
Tony Scott, Hull
Roger Lamplugh, Northern Divers, Hull
Jeremy Johns, London
Brian Shingles, Vine International Pictures
Peter Whitear, Cop & Dog Services, Hampshire
Gary Wilson, Gt Caterers, Leeds
Clive Cureton, Scafftag Ltd, Wales
Mike Stephenson and David Lockham, ARCO Ltd, Hull, for PPE
photographs
George Tarrib, Managing Director, Tyler Camera Systems Ltd,
California
Yorkshire Television Limited

Any illustrations used are depicting the potential hazards of particular locations and potential situations. They are not specifically examples of unsafe practice on the part of the film makers or production companies concerned and have been loaned and used in good faith by the author and publisher.

Copyright notice

Crown Copyright is reproduced with the permission of the Controller of Her Majesty's Stationery Office.

In addition, the following organizations and individuals are gratefully acknowledged for allowing me to use material in their copyright:

- Pam Beckly, HMSO Publications
- Elizabeth Gates and the editor of RoSPA journal *Occupational Safety and Health* for permission to reproduce health and safety articles in Chapter 1.
- Janice Turner, editor, BECTU journal, *Stage, Screen and Radio*
- ARCO Hull Ltd copyright for PPE pictures and information in Chapter 4.

Disclaimer

While great care has been taken in the research, compilation and preparation of *Production Safety for Film, Television and Video*, the publishers and author cannot in any circumstances accept responsibility for errors, omissions or advice given in this publication. Readers should be aware that only Acts of Parliament and Statutory Instruments have the force of law and that only the courts can interpret the law with authority.

About the author

Robin G. Small is Senior Lecturer in Television at the University of Huddersfield. He is a member of the Television Union BECTU, the Moving Image Society BSKTS and a Yorkshire Committee Member of the Royal Television Society. He has written several papers on the health and safety problems in media and film education, and has contributed a chapter on production management for *The Television Handbook*. He has undertaken consultancy work for university television departments, has guest lectured at various universities, and has advised independent production companies and training organizations.

Robin has worked in production for BBC Television, BSkyB and as an independent producer.

His first degree was in history from Lancaster University followed later by an MA in film and television production from Sheffield Hallam University.

Robin was production manager at the Hull School of Art and Design at the University of Lincolnshire and Humberside in Hull where he solved the production problems on numerous student productions including films and award winning documentaries and animations. He also lectured in media at Grimsby College.

Production safety activity has included consultation work for independent production companies and invitations to guest lecture at the Northern Film and Television School in Leeds and at Bradford University. From these he has identified the particular problems of teaching health and safety to students and freelances with little access to health and safety training.

This book takes an individual approach to hazard identification. Not all the hazards identified in each of the sections will be present in any one location or shoot. They are designed to help the inexperienced reader identify potential problems. Once hazards have been identified then a systematic approach to risk assessment through the production safety system can help to prioritize them according to risk. Each solution and control measure will be unique, therefore a hierarchy of control methods is suggested.

I sincerely hope that this book will help those in the film and television business and in educational production work. It is intended to be easy to read and a source of further information. It is not a substitute for experience but rather a complement and aid to those who may need help in best practice. Any correspondence and suggestions will always be welcome.

Robin G. Small, Nafferton, 2000
E-mail: rsmall@hud.ac.uk

Acronyms

ADC	Association of Diving Contractors
ACLG	Approved Classification and Labelling Guide
ACOP	Approved Code of Practice
ASC	Assured Safe Catering
ASL	Approved Supply List
BECTU	Broadcasting, Entertainment, Cinematograph and Theatre Union
BJAC	Broadcasting and Performing Arts Joint Advisory Committee
BSC	British Safety Council
BSI	British Standards Institution
CCP	Critical control points
CDM	The Construction Design and Management Regulations 1994
CHIP	The classification and labelling of substances dangerous for supply
CITB	Construction Industry Training Board
COSHH	The Control of Substances Hazardous to Health Regulations 1994 & 1999
CPHA	The Construction Plant Hire Association
DSE	Display screen equipment
HACCP	Hazard analysis and critical control points
HSE	Health and Safety Executive
HSC	Health and Safety Commission
HSCER	The Health and Safety (Consultation with Employees) Regulations 1996
HSW	The Health and Safety at Work Act 1984
IEE	Institution of Electrical Engineers
IOSH	Institution of Occupational Safety and Health
LEV	Local Exhaust Ventilation
LOLA	The Lifting Operations and Lifting Equipment Regulations 1998
MDF	Medium-density fibreboard
MEL	Maximum exposure level
MEWP	Mobile elevating work platform

NEBOSH	National Examination Board in Occupational Safety and Health
NONS	Notification of New Substances Regulations 1993
NRPB	National Radiological Protection Board
OEL	Occupational exposure level
PASMA	Prefabricated Aluminium Scaffolding Manufacturers' Association
PAT	Portable appliance testing
PPE	Personal protective equipment
PUWER	The Provision and Use of Work Equipment Regulations 1998
RCD	Residual current device
RIDDOR	The Reporting of Injuries, Diseases and Dangerous Occurrences Regulations 1995
RoSPA	Royal Society for the Prevention of Accidents
RPE	Respiratory protective equipment
RSI	Repetitive strain injury
RTS	Royal Television Society
SITAC	Screen Industry Training and Apprenticeship Committee
SRSCR	Safety Representatives and Safety Committees Regulations
SWL	Safe Working Load
SSW	Safe System of Work
TUC	Trades Union Congress
VDUs	Visual display units

Part One

1 Introduction

The state of health and safety practice in the film and television business has been an area of concern for some time. The Health and Safety Executive has been worried about safety standards. Several recent accidents and deaths have resulted in enforcement action, prosecutions and fines brought under the Health and Safety at Work Act 1974. The concern would appear justified as the number of actual accidents and incidents in the industry is believed to be much higher than the official statistics would show.

There is no doubt that good health and safety policies work where there is agreement and co-operation between employers and employees to remedy the situation. A positive culture creates the right atmosphere for good health and safety practice.

The majority of staff and freelances are keen to comply and improve health and safety, but there are few industry specific guidelines to follow unless you are lucky enough to still work for a large company such as the BBC or ITN. The industry union BECTU has been actively campaigning to improve this situation.

Company managers and producers can often be unsure of how to create a safety policy that will comply with legislation and yet deal with the scale and variation of production operations. Small employers are also naturally concerned about the costs of applying new health and safety legislation, much of which has resulted from European directives being implemented into UK health and safety law.

Workers, employees and unions are concerned at the growing number of health and safety hazards which they face daily and are worried about their welfare. Tutors to the growing legion of media and film students are faced with increasing numbers of productions but with no specific health and safety guidance to remedy the potentially dangerous situation.[1] The Committee of University Vice Chancellors has issued guidelines on health and safety which indicate a formal requirement for risk assessments for all student projects. It is particularly relevant to media, film and television work by students in universities, schools and colleges (Health and Safety Responsibilities of Supervisors

Towards Postgraduate and Undergraduate Students, issued by the Committee of University Vice Chancellors, October 1999).

The challenge for the industry is to create a safety umbrella underneath which everyone in the film and television business will be protected. Freelances and stringers outside the health and safety umbrella of large companies are especially at risk, along with inexperienced and untrained student programme makers.

Protection of people and prevention of accidents is the ultimate aim of good health and safety practice. Producers and directors make crucial decisions which can affect health and safety for better or worse – for example, in the choice of locations, the equipment to be used, the shooting schedule, the action in the script and who to hire. At this stage it is so important to consider how such choices would affect health and safety, identify the potential hazards, and the level of risk to those involved.

The producer is firmly in the frame when it comes to responsibility for health and safety of production operations. They are in control of the activity. However, the range of locations and activities makes the health and safety of the film and television business a complex proposition since no two productions are the same and there is certainly no such thing as a typical production.

The hazards and risks which some workers face change all the time. A camera operator can have a short-term high risk assignment working in a war zone or sustain longer-term damage to health through lifting and carrying heavy equipment every day. Other groups of workers do the same job every day and can face long-term risks to health as a result – for example editors and journalists with eye strain caused by excessive time spent in front of computer display screens. So safety assessments must look at immediate dangers without losing sight of the longer-term risks. Non-production staff must also be considered to be at risk from long-term health risks, particularly cleaners, drivers, catering staff, electricians, maintenance fitters, mechanics, plumbers and security staff, as many of these may be contract workers.

In other words, policies and preventative measures should not just focus on accidents. They should also focus more on incidents and near misses which are the warning signs of unsafe practice. Analysis of incidents and near misses to identify problem areas, dangerous machinery, unsafe situations and dangerous conditions can be a hugely important and effective management tool in accident prevention. More priority should also be given to long-term health risks.

The safety policy should identify all hazardous areas of activity and which workers are at risk. Risk assessments must also take into account freelances and contractors. The selection of competent and experienced contractors and freelances is essential to ensure safe practice. Safe systems of work should be put in place before production activity starts as health and safety should be proactive rather than just reactive. The aim of good health and safety practice is to put protection in place and to control the level of risks to acceptable levels before production activity begins. Then to monitor regularly while filming. All risks must be reduced to acceptable levels by eliminating the most dangerous completely and reducing the potentially serious to minor risk levels. All involved in the production should feel confident that they will finish the day's work in the same condition that they arrived in the morning through the establishment of a safe and controlled working environment free from significant risks.

Major areas of production operations where hazards have to be identified include the production office, the studio, the outside location, the constructed set and the premises of other people. Hazards in each of these work areas must be identified systematically, including factors such as catering, driving and stunts.

New hazards have surfaced in the last two years. For example the use of MDF in scenery and more recently mobile phones. (With regard to mobile phones, see Hazard 24, Lasers and Radiation. New reports on health risks of mobile phones have appeared including a recent study by the Polish Military Institute of Hygiene and Epidemiology in Warsaw. Due to be completed in 2005, this research shows the strongest links yet – see *Sunday Mirror*, 26 March 2000.) This means that health and safety policies must keep up with changes in technology and new working practices.

Hazards can be **inherent**. For example moving fork lifts and machinery can be potential hazards to a documentary crew in a factory. While some hazards are **adjacent** to locations such as low power lines or low flying aircraft, a lot of hazards are **introduced** by production crews as part of the production process. For example working with chemicals, explosives, electricity, lighting and scaffolding. So hazard identification involves an initial search for things that might create or contain risks.

Having identified the hazards we then decide how risky they are and identify who would be affected. Groups of people affected could include actors, contractors, employees, presenters, the public, subcontractors and visitors. This process is called a risk assessment.

Risk assessment identifies all risks. Then action can be prioritized; beginning with the highest risks first. Risk assessments should be written down and identify any individuals or groups of workers potentially at risk from immediate accidents or long-term risks to their health. The results of risk assessments and the proposed control measures must be communicated to all concerned. Risk is quite simply probability versus severity. In other words, how likely is an accident to happen? What would be the result if it did? More importantly, identify who would be affected and how? Steps can then be taken to eliminate the risk, remove it, or substitute the proposed action for something safer.

In a recent BECTU freelance survey, only 46% of contracts had risk assessments; of these, 37% were not communicated to members. Hence 63% of freelances still do not have the protection of risk assessments (*Stage, Screen and Radio*, March 2000, p. 16).

It is then crucial to communicate health and safety rules and information to all concerned through production paperwork and briefings. The formal health and safety policy and guidance for visitors, contractors and staff should be written down and given out to everybody. The central question when an accident occurs is who was in control? The producer, director, manager or supervisor?

Film and television work can involve special stunts. A proper expert will do a much faster and more professional job and make it safer than someone inexperienced or incompetent. Always check the safety record and qualifications of any contractors and those experts who you have asked to plan or control any aspect of production work. So deal with the usual first and seek advice from specialized experts for the unusual.

Figure 1.1   *Illustration taken from the cover of 'Camera Operations on Location: Guidance for managers and camera crews,' HSE, HS(G) 169, ISBN 0-7176-1346-1. Crown Copyright*

The press have an appetite for covering the unusual, spectacular and often fatal accidents involving explosions, helicopters and stunts. Huge coverage was given to the Michael Lush accident. This type of coverage disguises the longer-term risks to occupational health and safety that can affect large groups of workers in the film and television industry.

Pre-occupation with the famous has also characterized press reports of accidents in the film and television business. The newspapers covered the deaths of Brendon Lee and Roy Kinnear and the serious injury to Anthea Turner. These cases are indicative of the high levels of risk involved to those in the public eye, but they disguise the health and safety risks that can also happen to those behind the camera.

A very common type of accident concerns individuals who have been working extended shifts and then have to drive a long distance home or on to the next job. Many of us in the industry will know of, or have heard of people who have died or been seriously injured in this way. The figures for this will be classed as road traffic accident statistics and not connected to the conditions of work in the film and broadcasting industries. The official accident figures may be the tip of a much larger iceberg.

Recent concerns about the health and safety of the broadcasting and film industries has resulted in two new specialist publications concerning camera operations and diving, along with six free leaflets and guidance for freelances. These were produced by the HSE in consultation with the Broadcasting and Performing Arts Joint Advisory Committee (BJAC). The Producers' Association (PACT) have guidelines for producers and production companies.

The need for more specialized publications and guidance was recognized by the television and broadcasting union BECTU. Their journal *Stage, Screen and Radio* has highlighted many health and safety concerns and accidents. The union's lawyers have also fought compensation cases for its members who have been injured. For example, in December 1996, £327,000 was awarded in compensation to Lois Richardson, a make up artist, against Granada Television. This followed action from the union's solicitors Thompsons. After repeated failure to pay, sheriff's officers were ordered in to Granada's headquarters. Andy Egan, legal officer for BECTU, said 'We are using the full weight of the law to defend the interests of one of our members who has been injured.'

BECTU also provides free liability insurance cover for freelance members and are also considering taking the government to court to force employers to apply the working time directive conditions to freelance and short-term contract workers.

BECTU have identified new working practices as a major cause of stress and damage to the occupational health of people who are working in the film and television business. These are what we call human factors (see Hazard 23). They relate to the way work is organized and the consequent effects on the health, safety and welfare of those who take part in it.

The union identified the changes as an inevitable trend of decreasing permanent employment and the consequent growth of casualization and freelancing as damaging to the employment rights of its members.

The changes were driven by the need for a flexible and multi-skilled workforce. The trend towards more prescribed social legislation from Europe therefore was in direct contrast to some employment practices in the film and television business. These involved cuts to holiday entitlement, rest and meal breaks, cuts to overnights, single crew operation and the misuse of flexi-hours. These trends were the opposite to what is required by new health and safety legislation such as the Working Hours Time Regulations 1998. Some employers asked freelances to waive their rights to these benefits. The TUC are currently investigating employers who run bogus health and safety bonus schemes in which accidents are not reported.

These working conditions are a recipe for stress related illness. Stress factors should not be underestimated as the cause of many accidents. Unrealistic schedules and deadlines cause fatigue or illness. Stress can also lead to changes in behaviour, including the misuse of alcohol and drugs. Compensation claims for workplace stress have increased dramatically.

It remains to be seen if the current contraction of small independents and the expansion of global media groups will make it easier or more difficult for those working for them to get safer and healthier working conditions in the future and better health and safety training.

The training situation has gradually improved thanks to pioneering courses provided by Lionsgate Safety and the introduction of health and safety qualifications administered by Skillset and provided by their partners in the regional training consortiums (see Appendix 7). Skillset health and safety qualifications are called X Units. These are becoming increasingly required for certain grades of job, while producers and production managers must hold a health and safety management qualification. Many courses can be subsidized for freelances.

Professional health and safety qualifications can be obtained through examinations with BSC, IOSH, NEBOSH, IRM and RoSPA. The BBC have also launched an interactive CD-ROM safety course for the broadcasting industry. Since human factors cause nine out of ten accidents, the important role of good health and safety training cannot be stressed highly enough – especially since over 60 per cent of the industry are freelance and work outside the health and safety umbrella given to permanent employees in large organizations.

Many work for small companies with no health and safety policy and no budget for providing training. Companies are often formed for a short period of time to make a specific project and then close on completion.

A similar situation to the television and film industry today existed in the construction and building industries in the late 1970s. This sector often reached the papers in reports of terrible accidents and was seen as an unregulated collection of small-scale operations which only existed for a temporary period of time at different locations for a specific aim. The work involved the use of electricity, chemicals, plant and machinery which have a high risk factor and serious potential for accidents.

To improve the health and safety record a decision was made to put all construction activity under a specific set of health and safety rules called the Construction (Design and Management) Regulations 1994 (CDM). This was backed up by co-operation between employers, the Health and Safety Executive and centralized health and safety training provided by the Construction Industry Training Board (CITB).

Can the film and television industry learn from this example? Elizabeth Gates reports . . .

Fade to black

Television and film have an air of glamour. Health and safety, we are told, do not. As a result, health and safety issues are hard pressed to join even the final credits of a producer's cast list of priorities. Yet grim catalogues of avoidable disasters, near-misses and entrenched health hazards are steadily maintained by representatives of the Broadcasting, Entertainment, Cinematograph and Theatre Union (BECTU), the National Union of Journalists (NUJ) and Equity, the actors' union. Other concerned parties include the Producers Alliance for Cinema and Television and the Health and Safety Executive.

One of the industry's comparatively rare fatalities underscores some of the problems. In 1988, during the filming of *The Return of the Three Musketeers*, inexpert horseman Roy Kinnear mounted up and rode off to his death over wet cobbles in fading light to comply with his director's instruction to 'thunder' at speed across the Alcantara Bridge near Toledo.

At the time of a compensation claim by Roy Kinnear's family against the producer Pierre Spengler and the director Richard Lester (October 1994), the chairman of Equity's stunt committee Chris Webb said: 'Actors are very, very reluctant to make a fuss about doubles if they are put under pressure by the director. A lot of them are very game and will do anything even when they are frightened and feel coerced into it by the director. And it is hard when you are filming and they have got to find a double while running to schedule.'

But, the cost of having a double on standby would have been slight in comparison to the costs of lost production, litigation and ultimately

£650,000 damages. It would also have saved a man's life. And it can only be small comfort to his family that Roy Kinnear thereafter became a statistic which would influence good health and safety practice in film production.

But he did. Now, according to PACT's 60-page generic health and safety policy, horseriders may be supported by a horse master in their request for a double if the horse master feels that the actor's horse riding competence is inadequate.

Even so, in spite of PACT's close-grained policy document, driven by arrogance, greed or an unimaginative lack of responsibility, certain producers do not accept their employer's duties and legal obligations towards both employees and freelance sub-contractors. Inherent cultural attitudes – among employers and employees alike – encourage this management style.

Others subordinate their own concerns to the idea of the ultimate product, whether programme or film or story. 'Money on screen' takes precedence. As BECTU's Equality/Health and Safety Officer Jane Paul explains: 'Artistic effect or cost-cutting comes before health and safety considerations – or people's rights to protection from injury or ill health.

'We need to change the culture of the industry so that people feel confident about arguing for good health and safety standards without fear of victimization or of not getting another contract if they complain about poor working practices.

'But,' she continues, 'the situation has certainly been made worse by the casualization of production.'

Terry Williams, head of the HSE's Entertainment National Interest Group, believes this to be true. As he says, 'The industry – both for TV and film – now has considerable numbers of small businesses, often with fewer than five employees. The industry has moved away from the traditional employer/servant lines towards a form of employment which involves short-term contracts for services. For example, companies are set up to produce a series of programmes and then – at the end of the series – the company folds.'

Skillset, the industry training organization for broadcast film and video, established in 1993, published an analysis of employment patterns and training needs for 1993/94. In this, it identified that 'of an estimated 28 000 people working in production, technical and post-production areas:

- 13 000 are employed as permanent staff or on contracts of one year or more by companies across the industry.
- 15 000 work on a freelance or short contract (less than one year) basis.'

The freelance percentage was then believed to be 54 per cent. Now it is believed to be approximately 60 per cent. This has industry-wide health and safety implications.

Terry Williams accepts that an HSE with limited budget resources finds that the enormous turnover of personnel 'makes the provision of information and training on health and safety requirements difficult.'

HSE, however, he avers, has been and is 'doing a great deal of work on this, producing industry-specific guidances which have been developed in co-operation with the industry itself. We seek to influence the people who make use of these patterns of employment.'

Safety hotch-potch

And Jane Paul: 'The problem of several organizations working together and of groups of people working together – sometimes for only a day and not usually as a team – is a serious one. We lack good industry-wide standards, working practices vary greatly and . . . there is real confusion about who is responsible for what and who is in control of the management of health and safety on a particular production.'

In its report, Skillset flags up the health and safety training issues. It found that only one fifth of freelances reported receiving some training since starting work in the industry. Jane Paul's Manchester-based colleague Freda Chapman explained: 'This means that sometimes people are in control who have no health and safety interest – a manager promoted via a route which gave him no experience of health and safety or even a junior administrative assistant who is responsible for the logistics of getting the crew to the location but has no managerial responsibility for their health and safety when they get there'.

Localized assessments

But concerned parties believe the risk-assessment based approach to health and safety management (a legal obligation) is possible even in the most unpredictable of locations. Excuses – such as 'the situation is beyond our control' – fall on stony ground or should do so.

Freda Chapman contributed to the new HSE guidance for camera crews. In her view: 'The person commissioning the "story" has a responsibility to research that item as far as possible and pass on information which affects health and safety to whoever is commissioned, whether employed or freelance. And this, even though – on paper – freelances have a joint responsibility regarding health and safety.'

To illustrate: a fight broke out between one news team and a group of travellers. The travellers objected to the unannounced intrusion into what they thought of as their 'living room'. As Ms Chapman explains: 'This could have been sorted out in advance. Travellers have leaders who can be spoken to. The commissioner/producer should look for potential hazards like this before the crew arrive.'

Terry Williams adds: 'On arrival, a new localized assessment can be carried out by an experienced member of that crew.'

Communications about risk – written, verbal and visual – should be of a high standard. By law for example, an employer must have a health and safety policy. Where they exist – perhaps because they are written by H&S advisors – these policies always sound well-intentioned. But their communication to other levels may be suspect. Some complaints arise because good 'paper policies' never reach the people on the ground.

Poor communications

A recent case illustrating the point involves paint-spraying and hot-wire sculpting of polystyrene, a roof-gantry in a studio, a crew without masks, no localized ventilation, and no external fire escapes. The subcontractor says he can sleep at night. The studio where all this is happening has a perfectly-acceptable health and safety policy.

As Jane Paul explains: 'The communications sector, after all, has the technology not only to transmit information but also to produce it in multi-media formats. We should be in the forefront of health and safety training and information – not (as an HSE inspector told us recently) 20 years behind!'

The BBC are to be commended for their detailed generic risk assessments. Based on debriefing notes gathered earlier from returning personnel and other sources, these assessments provide background information to dangerous environments.

News gathering

News teams – whether covering the Brixton riots, Chernobyl or Afghanistan – receive health and safety information. And amid statements of risk state, hazard description and checklists of PPE, there are also a number of handy hints. For example, about to embark on an Antarctic expedition, one cameraman was informed that 'As a rule, if your nasal hairs freeze on inhalation, it's rapidly approaching –15 degrees centigrade.'

Minders and stringers offer priceless local advice. In a section on Algeria, for example, recommendations include avoiding lunching at the usual place at the usual time and always having 'a back-up plan for getting out of an area.'

One of the prime elements in safety management in these uncertain situations is the decision if necessary to abort. As Terry Williams says: 'If it is too dangerous, the crew may have to decide whether or not to go ahead. After all, we hope no-one is operating under the maxim, "The show must go on", any more.'

But BECTU rather fears people are. As Freda Chapman points out: 'For some freelances – though not all – the importance of the story outweighs the risk. But producers should not regard these risk takers as the better journalists. They shouldn't reward this sort of attitude. For example, one journalist travelled to Serbia – apparently on holiday with only an amateur camcorder. He produced some footage. The BBC sent him a memo ticking him off for not having any body armour and so on but transmitted the programme. Double standards are operating here.'

Two-man operations

Sometimes, risk is not foreseeable in the strictest sense. Freda Chapman again: 'You may be able to identify hazards in a war zone or even certain football matches. But there was one instance of a cameraman standing outside a provincial law court where someone was being tried for pinching birds' eggs. The cameraman filmed the guilty party on the way out and the guilty party landed him one.

'This sort of case, we believe, illustrates the need for a two-people-team policy. With camera work especially – squinting down the viewfinder and wearing headphones – you need an extra pair of eyes and ears to watch for, say, other situations developing such as adverse crowd reaction. You may also need an extra pair of hands to move the equipment if you have to evacuate.

'We find that the more experienced camera operators have the confidence to ask for this extra help. The less experienced don't want to be thought of as wimps or troublemakers. And news cameramen are the most macho group in the industry – it takes them a long time before they'll talk about their stresses and strains and aches and pains.'

According to the HSE, TV and film are industries poorly provided with access to occupational health services. Major employers (such as the BBC) have sophisticated departments, which Terry Williams would like to see offering occupational health care to the freelance sector. But, as yet, systematic surveillance and efficient reporting systems remain in the region of pious hope.

Occupational road risk

'We know', says Williams 'That, nationwide, under-reporting runs at a rate of about 1:3 below what it should be. In these industries it is probably even worse.'

Identifiable hazards are many: working with/near/under water and Weil's disease; public disorder/violence to staff; the condition of electrical equipment; display screen equipment generating eye problems and RSI/WRULDs among the editorial and administrative staff; COSHH including the contact dermatitis in the make-up and hairdressing departments; the choice of appropriate PPE; the provision of first aid, manual handling; stress-related disorders. Other problems may appear superficially to be non-HSE concerns such as driving, whether off-road or away from public roads or to and from 'base'. 'But' adds Terry Williams, 'as soon as driving when tired after shift work or working long hours causes stress, it becomes our concern. We compare certain chemical companies where if an employee drives more than 100 miles in a day to get to a meeting, he is offered overnight accommodation before he drives home again. What TV and film companies have yet to recognize are the hidden costs of pushing someone like this. If there's an accident because the driver's too tired, there's the cost of sick leave, replacement salary, possibly even compensation.'

There are some signs of spring in the TV/film industry. Watch this space.

Cinema verite

In the second of her features on the entertainment industry, Elizabeth Gates shows how woefully little attention is given to health and safety on set especially when big money is involved . . .

In April 1996, HM Inspector of Health and Safety Graham Witte walked onto the set of *The Saint* and found that one hundred people – including himself – had been exposed to asbestos fibres.

Swathes of dust, produced by damage to pipe lagging during the conversion of the former electricity generator into a set, were drawn into the air by special effects gear which pumps out steam to create 'smoke'.

The crew – including Val Kilmer and Elizabeth Shue – had been working for five hours on set when HMI Witte evacuated the premises and closed down production. 'This was a routine check', says Mr Witte. 'I just walked in and spotted this dust everywhere. And I thought, I know what this is! The labs confirmed it.'

In December 1996, Wycombe and Beaconsfield magistrates fined Pinewood Studios and Paramount British Pictures Limited £10,000 each. Pinewood were then obliged to spend £70,000 on the removal of all asbestos from the building. And Paramount are still licking their wounds over the hidden costs from lost production time – £10,000s per lost hour – and potential civil actions in the wake of health and safety legislation breaches.

As Mr Witte explains: 'Asbestos diseases are currently killing an estimated 3000 people a year in Great Britain. In the case of *The Saint,* it's not certain that everyone exposed will develop asbestos-related diseases but some may. And the company failed in its duty to check the building. They were well-intentioned but – due to the variable levels of advice and competence in the industry – basic risk assessments were not carried out and the company didn't realize it was not fulfilling its obligations.'

There have been other HSE proceedings.

In 1994, during the filming of *First Knight,* a mobile elevating work platform overturned, dropping a lighting technician into a lake from a height of over 30 metres. The platform supplier was successfully prosecuted.

In autumn 1996, Michael Samuelson Lighting – one of the biggest lighting companies in the British film industry – allowed 17-year-old Gwilym Hooson-Owen to use a pressure washer with exposed wires to clean out a rubbish bin. The equipment had not been properly maintained. The company was prosecuted under the Electricity at Work Regulations 1989 and fined £2000 plus costs.

These prosecutions glint like the top of an iceberg. Previously, occupational health and safety had not featured greatly in the film industry's consciousness. But now the whole concept shadows management, unions and individuals alike.

The more positive regard their situation as part of a learning curve. Roy Button, managing director of Warner Bros, for example, has adopted health and safety with visionary zeal.

'Health and safety', he says, 'is not a problem for the British film industry. It should be taken on board at the very beginning of production planning. It can speed the whole process of film-making up.'

He cites, as an example, the hours and production costs saved during his production of *The Avengers.* 'In this case, the Construction (Design and Management) Regulations helped us create a safe working environment for cast and crew when we needed to rig up a water tank – with electrics!'

The less confident are eloquent as to the disadvantages of including health and safety in their pre-planning. To illustrate: according to the management team of the James Bond films for Eon Productions, the difficulties are as follows:

Uniqueness of the industry

'In one day', they say, 'you can meet almost all possible health and safety risks, sometimes on a grand scale. We employ over 1000 people – sometimes simultaneously – in five locations across the world. Different countries produce different problems: for example, in Russia, we were checking a location for health and safety and someone ran a Geiger counter over the refrigerator. It was radio-active.'

'And each movie brings its own problems. *101 Dalmatians* involved animals and all their attendant problems – being cared for, hurt, people being bitten and so on. The Bond films are different again – big action movies. Everything changes all the time.'

Lack of continuity

The cast and crew may be brought in from all over the world, having experienced different health and safety standards in different countries.

And after a film company is disbanded – sometimes within weeks of its creation – the skeleton management teams are not happy to remain legally responsible for health and safety and potentially liable for compensation.

But in a resurgent British film industry, the producer's greatest fear is that health and safety concerns could scare off big American productions.

This could happen, they say, because of:

● concern over compliance costs
● attitude – 'Backers are influenced by cocktail party rumours concerning prosecutions.'
● production schedules and funding – 'Making a movie may last ten weeks from the delivery of the script to the delivery of ten rolls of film. Safety elements may extend that period – with no money up front.'
● the pound/dollar exchange rate.

And, as Barbara Broccoli, American producer of *Tomorrow Never Dies* points out: 'We don't want accidents. We know these people we work with. We don't want them hurt. People go to Bond movies to see real action stunts but we try hard to make it as safe as possible for the stuntmen. On one motorcycle stunt, we spent £100,000 on practices to get it right. A computer-generated jump would cost maybe £15,000 but people don't want that: not even the stunt people.'

Graham Witte is the voice of reason amidst all this clamour. He recognizes the good will emanating from Eon Productions and Roy Button. And, as he points out: 'A lot of the problem is that film people don't know they've got a problem. The problems on *The Saint* were caused by lack of awareness and Pinewood is no worse than anyone else in the industry – in fact, better than most.'

The ignorance – and the resistance to change which follows it – derives in part from lack of true statistics. Film makers believe their industry is safe. But many until recently did not even organize the maintenance of an accident book – ignoring the slips, trips, falls, cuts, bruises, burns which occurred daily. RIDDOR is beginning to have an impact.

'The HSE', Graham Witte continues, 'has been exceptionally understanding with the industry so far but the industry is now going to have to sort itself out. The regulations are not going to change and the industry must start addressing them.'

To do this, as HSE's most experienced film industry inspector, Mr Witte admits, there must be industry-specific competent advice. 'Management can't just dump health and safety on someone with no health and safety training. And in low budget movies, management must be competent.'

With his unquestionable personal commitment, Roy Button at Warner Bros is anxious: 'I'm filled with apprehension at the thought of bogus health and safety consultants moving in and offering misguided advice. There's nowhere else for the smaller to middle-sized companies to go.'

This is largely true. Sources of advice concerning industry-specific occupational medicine – such as occupational health departments – generally do not exist, although Roy Button thinks Warner Brothers may have one at its London headquarters. Health surveillance is unheard of.

All concerned parties favour industry-specific training which, they believe, could trigger the required culture change.

But most companies are created for production of specific films and there is a strong reliance on the freelance sector.

This brings its own problems. In its 1993/4 report, the industry training organization for broadcasting, film and video, Skillset, identified that only one fifth of freelances had received some form of training in health and safety at some time since starting work in the industry. Of these:

- only 40 per cent had had a course (post-production/camera/lights/ sound)
- 40 per cent had viewed videos (research/writing/production/support/producers/directors)
- 33 per cent (in camera/lights and in art) received training on the job.

The Broadcasting, Entertainment, Cinematograph and Theatre Union (BECTU) have grasped the nettle, developing health and safety courses, supported by the Skillset Freelance Training Fund.

The HSE is also involved in discussions with local colleges which may run courses, leading to graded industry-specific health and safety qualifications.

But the problem for both BECTU and HSE is that freelances are mobile, not always available and not always willing to spend their scant leisure time and money on health and safety training.

Roy Button is approaching the problem from a different angle. A member of the board of the Special Effects Guild – a trade grouping – he has encouraged the introduction of a grading system which leads to a qualification. At each level, a health and safety element is included. And – as these levels are attached to a pay scale – a knowledge of health and safety is ultimately rewarded.

But, in general, Mr Button maintains the pious hope that the health and safety culture he wishes to create at Warner Bros will be carried elsewhere by a constantly mobile workforce.

At Pinewood Studios, Terry Thurston is the Studio Manager of the 100-acre site. He is responsible for 140 permanent staff with potentially 3000 'others' on site on any given day. Mr Thurston would agree with Roy Button: 'The solution would seem to be the education of individuals. You could use a cascade training approach although very few at the top know about health and safety. But this is one of the most difficult industries to inform. There is no one body. There are 10 crafts guilds but none of their representatives sit on the council. It's difficult to find the key people.'

Graham Witte also feels this is a major shortfall.

And none of the top organizations seem prepared to take the necessary lead in pooling their shared wisdom or benchmarking good practice. As Eon's management team points out: 'Those who are active in the industry find it difficult enough to meet for lunch – never mind set up and run an organization.'

The HSE strategy has been – both as enforcers and advisers – to concentrate on the basics, gradually educating the industry into the ethos of health and safety management systems.

'The law has to be upheld', Mr Witte admits, 'but we (the HSE) are practical people.'

Spiralling pay levels – current rates are thought to be about £700 for a 50-hour week – also make it improbable that these specialist technicians – working in isolation in the film industry – will ever seek work elsewhere. And the health and safety culture change which occurred in the UK building industry threatens to leave them untouched.

As Eon production supervisor responsible for the daily organization of health and safety on set, Callum McDougall, explains: 'Eon has always had a history of safety consciousness, operating an open door system whereby people who are worried about something risky can come and talk to us – without penalty.'

'But, although we provide personal protective clothing – in accordance with the regulations – hard hats, for example, they may not use them. As soon as you walk away, they take them off.'

Graham Witte is sympathetic but firm. 'In practical terms, if PPE is provided with full instruction as to use and if management can prove that and if an individual chooses to flaunt the regulations, we would accept that the management had done all that was reasonably practical to "enforce" its policy.

'But you've got to make sure it's the right type or people won't wear it. Designs vary to solve these problems. And it works – look at the construction industry'.

Another area of concern is the risk attached to working at a height. Vast structures are created and dismantled daily. For *Tomorrow Never Dies*, in the 'empty space' of a massive Pinewood studio a newly-designed warship deck complete with Exocet missile is standing ready. But behind what appears on screen, is the cathedral-like structure of the scaffolding.

In the recent past, this would have been designed with scale models. These would then have been passed on to construction managers with little knowledge of current safety standards and no health and safety input. Under pressure, to gain access, riggers, lighting technicians, even cameramen may have removed handrails.

For example, a set for Stephen Spielberg's *Saving Private Ryan* – the first film to be classified under CDM – involved the creation of a bombed-out French village complete with river. A prohibition notice was served for unsafe scaffolding.

As the HSE said at the time, 'There were no handrails so work had to stop.'

But now production supervisors such as Callum McDougall have begun to insist that 'people think before they do something which may cause an accident. Five years ago,' he says, 'we didn't think like that.'

The insurance industry also has a role to play here. Stonehouse Conseillers, for example, arrange insurance cover for short television and film commercials. They cater for specific health and safety risks.

As their spokesman, Matt Lawford, says: 'We are educating our clients into thinking of hazards and accepting that higher cover will cost. What usually happens is that the script is forwarded to the insurers and rated regarding health and safety – such as the use of helicopters or animals. We must advise them of the risks involved. For example, there was a margarine manufacturer who wanted to use a black panther in an advertisement. In accordance with insurers' instructions, the scene was shot with a Perspex guard in place, a vet with tranquillisers on set and this, after the animal's history, career, age and experience had been investigated.'

Another company apparently moving in the right direction is JAK Productions at Leavesden Studios, where the new *Star Wars* film is under production. Here the scaffolding is tagged, handrails in place, hazardous materials properly stored and the workplace – a former Rolls Royce aircraft hangar – clean and tidy.

David Brown, the production manager, is fluent about the great strides health and safety consciousness is making in the industry and on his own particular production. In spite of the initial costs of compliance, he says, 'it saves money long term in terms of sickness absence and court cases. It also means a clear conscience. We have an obligation regarding the well-being of the people in our employ.'

In spite of the unique problems of this unique industry, there are discernible signs of a health and safety cultural revolution.

Just after these articles were written an accident happened on the set of *Tomorrow Never Dies*. On 25 April 1997, 84 year old Peter Stuart (stand in for Q) had a narrow escape from death when a remote stunt car failed to stop at 60 mph and hurtled towards him. The plucky pensioner tried to jump out of the way but he was hit and knocked unconscious, narrowly escaping death. He was in hospital for five weeks and now has a chronic knee condition. The stunt car had been tested several times that morning but one of the brakes had failed.[2] This would indicate that even with the most stringent precautions accidents can still happen. But the implementation of best health and safety practice can systematically reduce the risk levels in the industry to a safer and acceptable level.

There are three main reasons for good health and safety practice. Firstly a moral argument. Somebody close to you could be killed or seriously injured. The effects of an accident at work on the victims' families can be devastating, especially if they are the main bread winner (see 'My son fought so hard to live', *Woman's Weekly*, Alison Legh-Jones, February 2000, pp. 20–1).

The second reason is legal. You can be prosecuted, fined and imprisoned if you or your company commit a negligent act resulting in pollution, serious injury, manslaughter or death. The third reason is financial. Accidents and injuries at work can have a huge financial impact on the company concerned. Consider the effect on profits from the following: loss of production time; replacement costs of injured personnel; replacement of damaged buildings, equipment and machinery; increased insurance premiums; loss of management time spent in investigating the accident; loss of time spent reporting it; loss of time spent defending a prosecution or damages claim; money spent in legal expenses defending a court action; court costs; potential fines and possible compensation.

All these add up to a much greater bill and time spent than an effective health and safety strategy would have cost in the first place. Time and money spent on effective accident prevention makes good financial sense and is the cheaper option, especially for smaller companies who cannot afford to write off accident costs at the bottom of the annual balance sheet.

So, good health and safety practice can ensure compliance with the law, protect anyone concerned with the production and save you money as well. Bad health and safety practice puts lives at risk, is illegal and can cost far more money in the long term.

Notes

1 See 'Teaching production safety in media education', Robin G. Small, paper presented to Media 98: Institute of Education, University of London, 20–22 March 1998 and AMPE, Sheffield, 1999.
2 Personal letter to the author and *Stage, Screen and Radio*, November 1998, p. 20.

Further information

Free leaflet series

No. 1 Safety in Broadcasting Sports Events 1996
No. 2 Violence to Workers in Broadcasting
No. 3 Smoke and Vapour Effects used in Entertainment
No. 4 Working with Animals in Entertainment
No. 6 Working at Height in the Broadcasting and Entertainment Industries

HSE publications on film and television

Camera Operations on Location, HSE-HS(G)169, ISBN 0-7176-1346-1.
Electrical Safety at Places of Entertainment, HSE, GS(50), 1991, ISBN 0-11-885598-0.
Electrical Safety for Entertainers, HSE-INDG247.
Facts for Freelances, HSE-IND(G)217L.
HSE: *A Guide to Fire Precautions in Existing Places of Entertainment and Like Places*, HMSO, 1990, ISBN 0-11-340907-9.
Managing Crowds Safely, HSE-INDG142.
Media Diving Projects, HSE-L106, ISBN 0-7176-1497-2.

2 Legislation

Health and safety legislation is divided into three strands: Acts, regulations within those Acts and approved codes of practice (ACOP). These are laid down by parliament and administered by the Health and Safety Commission. The HSC is a ten-member tripartite body which oversees the work of the Health and Safety Executive.

The Health and Safety Executive has two major functions. First, it acts in an advisory capacity by giving information and advice. HSE and HMSO publications publish Acts of Parliament, approved codes of practice and regulations along with guidance notes and advisory leaflets which attempt to explain the rules and regulations and how to comply with them. The HSC has a network of local offices with inspectors and specialist officers who deal with specific industries (see Appendix 1 for list). Film and television work comes under the entertainment area.

The second role of the HSE is enforcement, ensuring that companies and individuals comply with health and safety legislation. The most important piece of legislation is the Health and Safety at Work Act 1974. HSE inspectors have considerable powers under section 20:

- They can enter any premises at any reasonable time.
- They can take with them any relevant person such as the police.
- They can request that work stops immediately pending an investigation.
- They can take photographs, notes, measurements and statements.
- They can obtain all relevant information from persons on the premises.
- They can examine or search any premises, plant, materials or equipment.
- They can examine or search and obtain any relevant documents, disks or records.
- They can take samples and conduct tests.
- They can request the availability or assistance from any person if it is necessary.

HSE inspectors have powers to issue *prohibition notices* under section 22. An inspector may serve a prohibition notice if any activity is being, or is about to be carried out and involves the serious risk of personal injury. The prohibition notice states the inspector's opinion and specifies the matter giving rise to the risk. It will also state any statutory provision being contravened. The notice will forbid a particular activity or the use of a specific process or machine. It can be served on an employer, an employee, a machine or a process.

HSE inspectors under section 21 can also issue an *improvement notice* which will demand that specified requirements are put in place within a time limit. An immediate ban on prohibited or dangerous activities can be made until such time as the offending practice is rectified and safeguards put in place. In extreme cases they can request the courts to impose a remedy order.

Companies and individuals who do not comply with the Acts and who breach the regulations may face criminal or civil prosecution by the HSE for breaking their statutory duty to organize health and safety at work and provide a safe working environment for their workers. The HSE inspectors can decide to prosecute offending individuals or company directors or both.

In less serious cases the inspectors may go through the lower magistrates' court. Civil law failure to comply with statute law and other authoritative publications such as approved codes of practice, codes of practice, guidance notes and British Standards may be used as evidence of negligence. The penalties are stipulated in section 33 of The Health and Safety at Work Act 1974.

In the magistrates' court for breaches of sections 2–6 of the Health and Safety at Work Act 1974 can incur a fine of up to £20,000. For failure to comply with an improvement or prohibition notice, the court can fine you up to £20,000 or six months imprisonment or both. For breaches of other regulations the maximum fine is £5000.

For very serious offences the HSE can prosecute the case through the higher crown court. If the case is serious enough for the crown court (usually a case involving manslaughter, serious injury, pollution or death) then this will be a higher criminal case for breaches of either Acts of Parliament or regulations. The HSE will usually opt to pursue a case for negligence or prosecute for breach of The Health and Safety at Work Act 1974. For serious breaches of sections 2–6 of the Health and Safety at Work Act 1974 or any regulations the penalty is unlimited fines or a minimum of two years' imprisonment or both.

The most important point to consider is that the burden of *proof is reversed* in health and safety legislation. Usually in criminal cases the defendant is innocent until found guilty. It is up to the prosecution to prove beyond all reasonable doubt the guilt of the defendant. However in prosecutions brought by the Health and Safety Executive under the Health and Safety at Work Act 1974 it is up to the accused to prove that it was not 'reasonably practicable' to do more than was in fact done. Under section 40 of the Act it shall be for the accused to prove that it was not possible to do more to protect the health and safety of those injured as a result of negligence or omission.

Also under section 16 of the Health and Safety at Work Act 1974 every approved code of practice has a special legal status. If any Act is breached then an approved code of practice can be used as admissible evidence to prove negligence or omission. It would then be up to the defendant to prove that they have satisfactorily complied with the requirements of the code of practice in some other way.

Company directors, producers, section managers and supervisors of staff have to accept their legal responsibilities for health and safety at work of everybody. This includes actors, employees, freelances, presenters, subcontractors, members of the public and visitors. Section 37 states that where an offence by a body corporate is proven to have been committed with the consent, agreement or neglect on the part of the managing director, director, partner, secretary or other similar office of a company then that person shall be guilty of the offence and shall be liable to proceedings in court.

At the end of the day the crucial factors will be: Who is in control of the activity? Who is legally responsible for health and safety and omitted to do something? Who was negligent? These responsibilities for health and safety result from the main piece of legislation in this country – The Health and Safety at Work Act 1974.

The Health and Safety at Work Act 1974

The Health and Safety at Work Act 1974 makes statutory obligations for the health and safety of all at work. It is divided into sections, each of which are binding under law and prosecutable for breaching. The main points are listed below.

Section 1: This is concerned with the scope of the Act.

This is to secure the health, safety and welfare of persons at work, and also to protect those not at work against risks arising from work activities. Specific coverage is also given to the control of explosives, dangerous chemicals and pollution.

Section 2: This concerns the duty of care of the employer to employees.

It includes the requirement for a written safety policy and consultation:

It shall be the duty of every employer to ensure, so far as is reasonably practicable, the health, safety and welfare at work of all employees. These include:

1 The provision and maintenance of plant and systems of work that are safe and without risk to health.
2 The provision for the safe use, handling, storage and transport of articles and substances.
3 The provision of information, instruction, training and supervision.
4 The provision for any place of work under the employer's control to be maintained in safe condition, including safe access and exits.
5 The provision and maintenance of a working environment which is safe and without risk to health, and with adequate facilities with regard to welfare.

It shall be the duty of every employer to prepare and, as often as may be appropriate, revise a written statement of a policy with respect to the health and safety at work of employees and the organization and arrangements for the carrying out of the policy, and to bring statements and any revision of it to the notice of all employees (see also Chapter 3).

The employer shall provide for the appointment of a safety representative by a recognized trade union from amongst the employees.

It shall be the duty of the employer to consult with safety representatives with a view to the making and maintenance of arrangements which will enable the company and employees to co-operate effectively in promoting and developing measures to ensure the health and safety at work of the employees and in checking the effectiveness of such measures.

Employers shall establish, if requested by two or more safety representatives, a safety committee to keep under review health and safety measures at the workplace.

Section 3: This concerns the duty of employers to non-employees.

Employers and self-employed persons have a duty to ensure that their activities, in so far as it is reasonably practicable, do not endanger persons not in their employment including contractors and subcontractors and in certain prescribed cases may be required to give information to the general public concerning any potential hazards to health and safety. An example would be on sets and location provide security fences, site monitoring and security to prevent sabotage from trespassers.

Section 4: This concerns the duty of occupiers.

Those persons in control of premises have specific duties in relation to those who are not employees but use non-domestic premises made available to them.

It shall also be the duty of each person who has to any extent control of premises to ensure, so far as is reasonably practicable, that the access to and exits from the premises and any plant or substances within them are safe and without risk to health and safety.

Section 5: This concerns emission of noxious or offensive substances.

Persons who have control of prescribed classes of premises where they carry on a trade, business or undertaking (whether for profit or not) where noxious fumes are involved must use the best practicable means of rendering the fumes harmless if they are discharged. This includes premises emitting substances that may cause a nuisance by their smell.

NB This could particularly apply to paint spray shops and emissions from chemical effects.

Section 6: This concerns the duties of manufacturers and suppliers, importers and designers (as amended by the Consumer Protection Act 1987).

It shall be the duty of any person who designs, manufactures, imports or supplies any article or substance for use at work to:

- Ensure, so far as is reasonably practicable, that the substance or article is safe and without risk, when it is set, used, cleaned or maintained by a person at work.
- Carry out, or arrange for the carrying out of such testing and examination as may be necessary for the above.
- Take necessary steps to secure that persons supplied are given adequate information about the use of the article or substance at work to ensure that it will be safe and without risk to health all such times mentioned above and during dismantling or disposal.

The above information must be updated as required.

It shall be the duty of any person who undertakes the design of any article or manufactures any substance for use at work to carry out the necessary research into risks to health and safety.

It is the duty of any person who erects or installs any article for use at work to ensure that it is erected and installed in a way that, when used, it is safe and without risk to health and safety.

NB Section 6 has particular relevance to the activities of designers, prop suppliers, suppliers of stunt equipment, scaffold suppliers and erectors, smoke pyrotechnic and special effects designers and suppliers.

Section 7: This concerns the duty of the employee.

It shall be the duty of every employee, whilst at work, to take reasonable care for the safety of him/herself and other persons who may be affected by his/her acts or omissions at work.

It shall be the duty of every employee, whilst at work, to co-operate with his employer so far as is necessary, for his employer to comply with any relevant statutory provision.

Section 8: This concerns sabotage.

There is a duty not to interfere or misuse. No person shall intentionally or recklessly interfere with or misuse anything provided in the interests of health and safety.

NB An example would include letting off a fire extinguisher as a prank.

In addition to the Health and Safety at Work Act 1974, further health and safety legislation developed further bringing in specific legislation for particular hazards. These are dealt with in the appropriate hazard section:

- The Control of Substances Hazardous to Health Regulations 1998 (COSHH), Regulations for Chemicals (see Hazard 6: Chemicals and hazardous substances)
- The Lifting Operations and Lifting Equipment Regulations 1998 (see Hazard 11: Cranes, hoists, lifts and access platforms)
- The Noise at Work Regulations 1989 for Noise (see Hazard 27: Noise)
- The Construction (Design and Management) Regulations 1994 for building and construction. These are very applicable to the design of sets, stages and venues (see Hazard 5: Building and construction)
- The Electricity at Work Regulations 1989 (see Hazard: 15 Electricity)
- The Control of Asbestos at Work Amendment Regulations 1998 (CAWR) (see Hazard 3: Asbestos)

The influence of European law began to be felt towards the end of the 1980s. There had been a reluctance to adopt it because of its perceived social slant. However the requirement for European harmonization resulted in a second tier of legislation which became law from 1 January 1993. These new regulations follow the European directive and are known as the 'six pack'. They are:

(1) The Workplace Health, Safety and Welfare Regulations 1992

The regulations require the provision of a safe and healthy workplace in terms of lighting, heating, washing facilities, sanitary conveniences, traffic routes and safety glazing. Particularly pertinent to the welfare facilities and safety of temporary locations.

(2) The Provision and Use of Work Equipment Regulations 1998

These require the provision of work equipment which is safe and also information and training for its use in a safe manner. Work equipment should also be regularly maintained and serviced with records made for inspection. Examples would include a light being PAT tested (portable appliance tested) or a cherry picker having a proper test certificate.

(3) The Personal Protective Equipment at Work Regulations 1992

These regulations require the careful selection and provision of suitable and appropriate personal protective clothing and equipment and its proper maintenance and use. All equipment must carry the CE European safety mark (see Chapter 4 Personal protective equipment).

(4) The Manual Handling Operations Regulations 1992

These regulations impose an overriding duty to avoid manual handling unaided (lifting) but where this is not reasonably practicable, to assess the risks and make suitable arrangements to reduce them to an acceptable level through weight reduction and proper training in lifting techniques (see Hazard 25: Manual handling and lifting).

(5) The Health and Safety (Display Screen Equipment) Regulations 1992

Requires employers to assess work stations in relation to the operators using them, and to ensure that all components of the workstation – desk, chair, computer screen, keyboard etc. – conform to British Standards. The working environment must also meet established criteria in respect of lighting, reflections, glare, heat, humidity etc. The operators must be provided with a suitable eye care programme including a free vision test (see Hazard 32: Visual display screens).

(6) The Safety Representatives and Safety Committees Regulations 1977 (SRSCR) and the Health and Safety (Consultation with Employees) Regulations 1996 (HSCER)

Employees belonging to a recognized trade union have a legal right to be represented on matters effecting their health, safety and welfare by representatives nominated by the union. This right is established by the Safety Representatives and Safety Committees Regulations 1977 (SRSCR).

The employees also have a right to request the establishment of a safety committee if this is requested by two or more recognized trade union representatives. Employers must comply with this request within three months. These regulations covered employees of a recognized trade union but this left a hole in the safety net for non-union employees.

This was covered by the passing of the Health and Safety (Consultation with Employees) Regulations 1996 (HSCER). This requires that non-union staff also have the right to be consulted on health and safety matters under section 2. This consultation process is needed for the introduction of any measure at the workplace which may substantially affect their health and safety. These include:

- The arrangements for nominating 'competent persons' to assist on health and safety matters.
- The arrangements for the planning of health and safety training.
- The introduction of new technology or processes that have health and safety consequences.
- The arrangements for complying with new health and safety legislation.
- The views of non-union employees must be considered before making any health and safety decisions.

There are also additional responsibilities for safety committees, safety representatives and consultation with employees under the Management of Health and Safety at Work Act 1992 regulation 4a, 6(1) and 7(1)(b). These requirements for consultation are reinforced by regulation 3 of the Health and Safety (Consultation with Employees) Regulations 1996.

Employees' representatives will include the recognized trade union nominated health and safety representatives and one representative from each major area of work. If required the staff may request you to organize a ballot to elect health and safety representatives.

Advice on how to do this can be obtained from the following government approved organizations.

The Electoral Reform Ballot Services Ltd, Independence House 33 Clarendon Road, London N8 0NW. Tel: 0181–365–8909
The Industrial Society, Robert Hyde House, 48 Bryanson Square, London W1H 7LN. Tel: 0171–262–2401
Unity Security Balloting Services Ltd, 130 Minories, London EC3N 1NT.

Further socially based legislation including the Working Time Regulations 1998 (see Hazard 23: Human factors) have been brought in and many major pieces of legislation will be amended and reviewed to bring UK health and safety law in line with European directives by the year 2000 and beyond.

YORKSHIRE TELEVISION

SAFETY INFORMATION FOR VISITORS

SAFETY

Yorkshire Television places a high priority on all matters affecting the Health & Safety of our employees and visitors. To help us in this objective, please comply with the following guidelines and instructions which are designed to ensure your personal safety whilst on the premises.

- Wear your visitor badge at all times

- Do not enter any restricted areas or touch the controls of any machinery or equipment unless authorised to do so.

- Note any specific requirements displayed and act appropriately.

- Emergency or medical services may be summoned by telephoning extension 444.

- If you have an accident or feel unwell, you should report to the First Aid Room in the TV Centre.

FIRE PROCEDURE

- Continuous sounding of sirens/bells indicates an emergency and you should leave the building by the nearest available exit as quickly and calmly as possible.

- *DO NOT USE THE LIFTS*

- Remain with your host or follow other YTV employees to their assembly point and await further instruction.

- Do not re-enter the building until instructed to do so by Security.

- If you discover a fire, break the glass of the nearest fire alarm point.

- *DO NOT TAKE PERSONAL RISKS*

SMOKING

The Company Smoking Policy must be observed at all times. Smoking to be restricted to designated smoking areas only.

EMERGENCY CONTACTS

Health & Safety Office	Ext 7450
Security Office	Ext 7360
First Aid Room	Ext 7070
Site Services	Ext 7350
Insurance & Legal matters	Ext 7126
Personnel	Ext 7066

GRANADA MEDIA
PART OF GRANADA MEDIA

Figure 2.1 Example of safety information for visitors. Courtesy Yorkshire Television Limited

The Management of Health and Safety at Work Regulations 1992

Management obligations were reinforced by the passing of the Management of Health and Safety Regulations 1992. These reinforced the requirement for proper management systems to control health and safety. In other words these regulations make explicit what was already implicit in the Health and Safety at Work Act 1974. Namely the duty to identify workplace hazards and eliminate them if possible and, if not, to assess the risk presented by them and control them to an acceptable level.

There is an obligation to make proper written risk assessments. The assessment should be reviewed periodically, particularly if the nature of the work or risk changes. The risk assessment must be suitable and sufficient for identifying the hazards, assessing the level of risk and identifying the measures that need to be put in place. Employers with five or more employees must record the significant findings of the risk assessments and record their arrangements to implement remedial measures.

Any remedial measures identified must be implemented. Employers must establish procedures for dealing with serious and imminent danger situations identified in the risk assessment. This is particularly relevant when filming dangerous scenes or in dangerous locations. The safety guidelines should tell employees and others how to evacuate quickly and safely in the event of an emergency.

Employees should be given understandable information on matters including health and safety risks, preventive measures and emergency procedures. They should also receive health and safety training. Separate requirements regulate the need to inform visiting employees, visitors, temporary workers, the public and contractors who may visit you by invitation.

In order to comply with the regulations, you must be able to provide written evidence of your effective management of health and safety at work. The simplest solution to this requirement is to write and implement a proper health and safety policy which contains a systematic approach to production safety.

Further reading

A Guide to the Health and Safety at Work Act 1974, 5th edition, HSE L1, ISBN 0-7176-0441-1.
The Management of Health and Safety at Work Regulations 1992, Approved Code of Practice, HSE L21, ISBN 7176-0412-8.
The Provision and Use of Work Equipment Regulations 1998, Guidance on Regulations, HSE L22, ISBN 0-7176-0414-4.

The Manual Handling Operations Regulations 1992, Guidance on Regulations, HSE L23, ISBN 0-7176-0411-X.

The Workplace Health Safety and Welfare Regulations 1992, Guidance on Regulations, HSE L24, ISBN 0-7176-0413-6.

The Personal Protective Equipment at Work Regulations 1992, Guidance on Regulations, HSE L25, ISBN 0-7176-0415-2.

The Health and Safety Display Screen Equipment Regulations 1992, Guidance on Regulations, HSE L26, ISBN 0-7176-0410-1.

The Health and Safety (Consultation with Employees) Regulations 1996, Guidance on Regulations, HSE L95, ISBN 0-7176-1234-1.

Safety Representatives and Safety Committees ('brown book', third edition) Approved Code of Practice and Guidance on the Regulations, HSE L87, ISBN 0-7176-12201.

Health and Safety Law – A Trade Unionist's Guide, Labour Research Department, 78 Blackfriars Rd, London SE1 8HF.

3 Health and safety management

Section 3 of the Health and Safety at Work Act 1974 stipulates that every employer with five or more staff must have a written health and safety policy. For those small companies without a policy guidance is available from the HSE (see Essentials of Health and Safety at Work, ISBN 0-7176-0716-X and A Guide to Preparing a Safety Policy Statement for Small Business, HSE c100/10/95, ISBN 0-7176-0424-1). Also useful is John Ridley's *Risk Management* published by Butterworth-Heinemann and Allan St John Holt's *Principles of Health and Safety at Work*, IOSH Publishing.

This should be read along with the approved code of practice for The Management of Health and Safety at Work Regulations 1992. Then a full production safety system can be prepared which complies with your legal obligations and which protects your employees and others. The aim is to have a complete system kept in a health and safety file for inspection and record keeping. In the event of an accident you then have written proof of your compliance with the law.

How to write a basic safety policy

First, prepare a general declaration based on your obligations under the Health and Safety at Work Act 1974. This can be put on the front of your 'production safety system form', given out to anybody engaged in a production and forms the first part of your written policy. This is essentially a written policy statement to confirm that you have read and understood your obligations to everyone as regards health and safety, and it will be signed by the managing director and producer. A general summary statement can be used as the front of your production safety system form.

Second, the policy should determine exactly who is responsible for health and safety arrangements within the company or production. In other words how your health and safety policy is organized and controlled. This is person specific. It must start with the name and address of the person with overall and final responsibility for health and safety. This is either the owner of the company or the managing director.

HEALTH AND SAFETY AT WORK

To   : All members of the cast and crew

Date   :

Production :

HEALTH AND SAFETY AT WORK ACT 1974 – BASIC GUIDELINES

1. The company recognizes as a primary responsibility its statutory obligations for the safety and well-being of all its employees and other persons at locations where company business is being carried out. In fulfilling this responsibility the company will act, so far as is reasonably practicable, in accordance with Section 2 HASAW Act 1974, to ensure the health, safety and welfare of all persons, including persons not employed by the company who may be affected thereby;

BY a) The provision of plant and systems at work that are safe and free from health risks.

b) Arrangements for ensuring safety and absence of risk to health in connection with the use, handling, storage and transport of articles or substances.

c) The provision of such information, instruction, training and supervision as is necessary to ensure the health and safety at work of all the employees.

d) The maintenance at every location under the management's control is a condition that is safe and free from risk.

e) A provision of a working environment that is safe and free from risks to health with adequate facilities and arrangements for the welfare of employees at work.

2. All employees of the company under Section 7 of HASAW Act 1974 have a responsibility for their personal safety and also have a duty of care to their fellow employees. Each employee's responsibilities include:

a) The duty to comply with the safety instructions and directions laid down by their management.

b) A duty to use properly the means and facilities provided for safety and health at work.

c) A duty to refrain from the wilful misuse or interference with anything provided in the interests of health, safety and welfare and any actions that might endanger him/herself or others.

d) The duty of all employees in authority to ensure that the necessary safety instructions given.

3. (PRODUCTION COMPANY NOMINATED PERSON, ie THE HEALTH AND SAFETY OFFICER)

is the executive responsible to the production company for the effective implementation of the health and safety policy during the production. He/she will co-ordinate all health and safety procedures and ensure with heads of departments that the relevant codes of practice and all statutory provisions are adhered to.

4. (Production company) will bring to the notice of its employees the health and safety policy of a third party when the Production Company is using production facilities at a third party location.

5. It shall be the company's duty to conduct undertakings in such a way as to ensure, so far as is reasonably practicable, that persons not in the company's employment who may be affected thereby, are not exposed to risks to their health and safety.

6. ALL ACCIDENTS must be reported to the production office and an accident report must be completed and handed to the health and safety officer for onward transmission to the insurers and the HSE.

Figure 3.1   *Example of health and safety declaration*

Then it must specify exactly who is responsible for overall super-vision of health and safety for the company. This is usually the health and safety manager or the manager of a building. On a location or set this will be the executive producer as they are in overall control of the production activity and in education it will be the tutor. The aim of the health and safety policy is to create a safety umbrella that covers everybody.

These people will be ultimately responsible for drawing up the policy and for implementing it. They are also responsible for making sure that everybody knows about it and are properly trained. So while ultimate responsibility for health and safety rests with the company directors, the day-to-day management can be organized through a safety officer and heads of each section or department. For example, health and safety on location may be implemented by a nominated production safety officer named on the form. S/he will be responsible for ensuring that the health and safety policy is carried out once it has been drawn up by senior management. A written health and safety policy should have a proper chain of organization and definition of responsibilities.

In television and film production the heads of the camera, sound, design, scenery, props, lighting, electrical and floor management teams will also carry out risk assessment for their own areas so that the safety umbrella covers everybody concerned with the production. Set up your policy, organize your managers, inform your staff and plan and set standards. The health and safety policy and your safety standards should be measurable, achievable and realistic.

Employers must also have employers third party and public liability insurance cover (see Chapter 5 Insurance). Health and safety arrange-ments must also include by law adequate first aid measures, fire safety precautions and proper safety signing. There must also be a written system for reporting and recording accidents and incidents.

First aid

Minimum measures must include providing a first aid container and trained, qualified first aiders. The size and number needed will depend on the number of people at work and the nature of the work itself. Customary practice includes provision of unit nurses, doctors and field ambulances.

The location and names of these appointed first aiders including telephone numbers must be provided throughout the location on green safety signs. Provision must also be made to maintain the first aid container and to report any accidents. If in any doubt contact the local branch of St John Ambulance and read the HSE approved code of practice – The Health and Safety (First Aid at Work) Regulations 1981, Approved

Code of Practice, HSE L43, ISBN 0-7176-0617-1 – and First Aid Training and Qualifications, HSE, ISBN 0-7176-1347-X along with the 8th edition *First Aid Manual* as used by St John Ambulance, St Andrew's Ambulance and The British Red Cross (see Hazard 19: First aid).

Fire

Employers must make sure that fire precautions comply with The Fire Precautions (Workplace) Regulations 1997. There are six basic things that you must do:

1 Assess the fire risks in the workplace. Then draw up a fire risk assessment and take action to ensure that it covers the following:
2 Check that a fire can be detected in a reasonable time and that people can be warned.
3 Check that people who may be in the building or location can get out safely to a muster point. A system of knowing who was in the building is essential.
4 Provide reasonable fire fighting equipment for each type of fire.
5 Check that those in the building know what to do if there is a fire. This includes fire drills and provision of proper fire safety signing.
6 Check and maintain your fire safety equipment.

Minimum fire prevention measures must include a means of escape, means of giving warning and a means of fighting the fire. It is essential to provide all staff, subcontractors and visitors with proper information about fire alarms and fire escape routes including muster points. These should be clearly marked, along with the location of fire alarms and fire extinguishers. Fire alarms and extinguishers must be properly maintained, as must any other fire equipment such as smoke alarms, hose reels, etc.

Fire extinguishers must conform to the new Euro Standard EN 3/BS 7863. These use pictograms and symbols to indicate the class of fire they may be used on. All staff should be made aware of their location. Staff must also be trained in their proper use. Suitable and sufficient numbers of extinguishers for each fire hazard must be provided. (Don't forget to include catering, chemical, electrical, vehicles and workshop areas when assessing needs.)

Don't forget to make sure that fire cover is provided on location. Most base buildings, public auditoriums and temporary venues will also need a current fire certificate under The Fire Precautions Act 1971. If in any doubt about fire precautions contact your local fire brigade. (See Hazard 17: Fire, and Fire Precautions in the Workplace, ISBN 0-11-341169-3.)

Safety signs

The Health and Safety (Safety Signs and Signals) Regulations 1996 require that employers must use safety signs wherever there is a risk to health and safety which cannot be controlled by other means. The regulations enforce the European directive (92/58/EEC) to standardize signage throughout the European Union.

Employers must make sure that signs are properly understood by employees. Signs, especially fire, first aid and warning signs, should be properly maintained and adequately lit. Signs must contain a pictogram. Text-only signs are not acceptable. Also safety signs must be of a specified type. All emergency signs, fire warning and first aid signs must comply with BS 5499 Part 1. These will be red for fire and green for emergency information.

Figure 3.2 *An example of a fire warning sign*

Employers are now legally bound to provide safety signs wherever there is a risk. Sign functions will be either prohibition/stop signs which are red, warning/caution signs which are yellow, and blue signs which are mandatory action.

Information about fire safety, first aid, disabled access and emergency procedures must also be given to all visitors and subcontractors. Information for staff can be given out in a staff booklet.

Accident reporting (RIDDOR)

In 1985 came a requirement to report any accidents or serious diseases at work. The Reporting of Injuries, Diseases and Dangerous Occurrences Regulations 1985 (RIDDOR) are known as the Reporting Regulations. All

ACCIDENT BOOK

1 About the person who had the accident	2 About you, the person filling in this book	3 About the accident
▼ Give full name ▼ Give the home address ▼ Give the occupation	▼ Please sign the book and date it ▼ If you did not have the accident write your address and occupation	▼ When it happened ▼ Where it happened

Name
Address
 	
Postcode
Occupation
	Your signature Date
	
	          / /
	Address
	
	Postcode
	Occupation
		Date Time
		  / /
		
		In what room or place did the accident happen?

Name
Address
 	
Postcode
Occupation
	Your signature Date
	
	          / /
	Address
	
	Postcode
	Occupation
		Date Time
		  / /
		
		In what room or place did the accident happen?

Name
Address
 	
Postcode
Occupation
	Your signature Date
	
	          / /
	Address
	
	Postcode
	Occupation
		Date Time
		  / /
		
		In what room or place did the accident happen?

Name
Address
 	
Postcode
Occupation
	Your signature Date
	
	          / /
	Address
	
	Postcode
	Occupation
		Date Time
		  / /
		
		In what room or place did the accident happen?

Figure 3.3   *Pages from an accident book.* © HMSO

serious accidents, injuries and occurrences must be reported to the HSE under the Reporting Regulations. This enforced the requirement for an accident book to be maintained by firms who employ ten or more people. Accident books are available from HMSO, (Form BI 510).

All serious accidents and injuries must be reported on a Form F2508. Serious diseases must be reported on a Form F2508A.

Serious injuries are defined as those which result in:

- death,
- a major injury,
- any injury that results in that person having 3 days' absence or more from work,
- an injury to the member of the public that requires an ambulance,
- finally, an injury that results in an overnight stay in hospital.

	Reporting of Injuries, Diseases and Dangerous Occurrences, RIDDOR 1985	
4 About the accident - what happened	For the Employer only	
▼ Say how the accident happened. Give the cause if you can. ▼ If any personal injury say what it is.	Please initial the box provided if the accident is reportable under RIDDOR	
How did the accident happen?_____		
	Employer's initials	
How did the accident happen?_____		
	Employer's initials	
How did the accident happen?_____		
	Employer's initials	
How did the accident happen?_____		
	Employer's initials	

Figure 3.3 *Continued*

HSE Health & Safety Executive

Health and Safety at Work etc Act 1974
The Reporting of Injuries, Diseases and Dangerous Occurrences Regulations 1995

Report of an injury or dangerous occurrence

Filling in this form
This form must be filled in by an employer or other responsible person.

Part A

About you
1 What is your full name?

2 What is your job title?

3 What is your telephone number?

About your organisation
4 What is the name of your organisation?

5 What is its address and postcode?

6 What type of work does the organisation do?

Part B

About the incident
1 On what date did the incident happen?

2 At what time did the incident happen?
(Please use the 24-hour clock eg 0600)

3 Did the incident happen at the above address?
Yes ☐ Go to question 4
No ☐ Where did the incident happen?
  ☐ elsewhere in your organisation – give the name, address and postcode
  ☐ at someone else's premises – give the name, address and postcode
  ☐ in a public place – give details of where it happened

If you do not know the postcode, what is the name of the local authority?

4 In which department, or where on the premises, did the incident happen?

F2508 (01/96)

Part C

About the injured person
If you are reporting a dangerous occurrence, go to Part F.
If more than one person was injured in the same incident, please attach the details asked for in Part C and Part D for each injured person.

1 What is their full name?

2 What is their home address and postcode?

3 What is their home phone number?

4 How old are they?

5 Are they
  ☐ male?
  ☐ female?

6 What is their job title?

7 Was the injured person (tick only one box)
  ☐ one of your employees?
  ☐ on a training scheme? Give details:

  ☐ on work experience?
  ☐ employed by someone else? Give details of the employer:

  ☐ self-employed and at work?
  ☐ a member of the public?

Part D

About the injury
1 What was the injury? (eg fracture, laceration)

2 What part of the body was injured?

Continued overleaf

Figure 3.4 *Report of an injury or dangerous occurrence. © HSE*

3 Was the injury (tick the one box that applies)

☐ a fatality?

☐ a major injury or condition? (see accompanying notes)

☐ an injury to an employee or self-employed person which prevented them doing their normal work for more than 3 days?

☐ an injury to a member of the public which meant they had to be taken from the scene of the accident to a hospital for treatment?

4 Did the injured person (tick all the boxes that apply)

☐ become unconscious?

☐ need resuscitation?

☐ remain in hospital for more than 24 hours?

☐ none of the above.

Part E

About the kind of accident

Please tick the one box that best describes what happened, then go to Part G.

☐ Contact with moving machinery or material being machined

☐ Hit by a moving, flying or falling object

☐ Hit by a moving vehicle

☐ Hit something fixed or stationary

☐ Injured while handling, lifting or carrying

☐ Slipped, tripped or fell on the same level

☐ Fell from a height

How high was the fall?

☐☐☐ metres

☐ Trapped by something collapsing

☐ Drowned or asphyxiated

☐ Exposed to, or in contact with, a harmful substance

☐ Exposed to fire

☐ Exposed to an explosion

☐ Contact with electricity or an electrical discharge

☐ Injured by an animal

☐ Physically assaulted by a person

☐ Another kind of accident (describe it in Part G)

Part F

Dangerous occurrences

Enter the number of the dangerous occurrence you are reporting. (The numbers are given in the Regulations and in the notes which accompany this form)

Part G

Describing what happened

Give as much detail as you can. For instance

- the name of any substance involved
- the name and type of any machine involved
- the events that led to the incident
- the part played by any people.

If it was a personal injury, give details of what the person was doing. Describe any action that has since been taken to prevent a similar incident. Use a separate piece of paper if you need to.

Part H

Your signature

Signature

Date / /

Where to send the form

Please send it to the Enforcing Authority for the place where it happened. If you do not know the Enforcing Authority, send it to the nearest HSE office.

For official use

Client number   Location number   Event number

☐ INV REP ☐ Y ☐ N

Figure 3.4 *Continued*

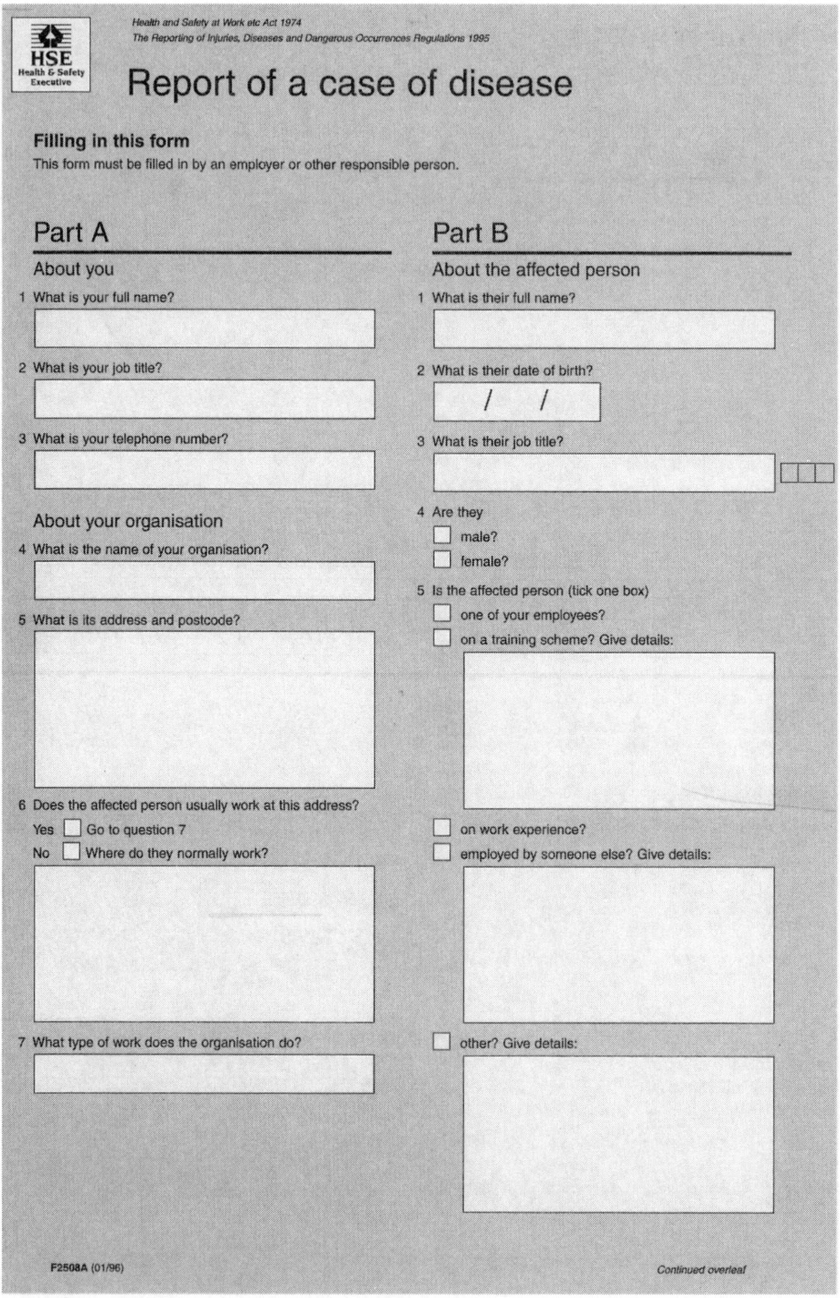

Figure 3.5   *Report of a case of disease.* © HSE

Part C

The disease you are reporting

1 Please give:

- the name of the disease, and the type of work it is associated with; or

- the name and number of the disease *(from Schedule 3 of the Regulations – see the accompanying notes).*

2 What is the date of the statement of the doctor who first diagnosed or confirmed the disease?

    /   /

3 What is the name and address of the doctor?

Part D

Describing the work that led to the disease

Please describe any work done by the affected person which might have led to them getting the disease.

If the disease is thought to have been caused by exposure to an agent at work *(eg a specific chemical)* please say what that agent is.

Give any other information which is relevant.

Give your description here

Continue your description here

Part E

Your signature

Signature

Date

    /   /

Where to send the form

Please send it to the Enforcing Authority for the place where the affected person works. If you do not know the Enforcing Authority, send it to the nearest HSE office.

For official use

Client number

Location number

Event number

☐ INV REP ☐ Y ☐ N

Figure 3.5 *Continued*

Examples could include eye damage, head wounds, amputations, electrocution, a serious fall, being hit by a vehicle, being trapped by moving machinery, drowning, contact with a harmful substance, asphyxiation, attack by an animal, gun wounds, fire burns or explosive injury.

Areas of high risk in film and television work would include stunt work, filming in danger zones, electrical work, diving work, driving, working at height on cranes and roofs, a scaffolding collapse, lasers or radiation burns, rigging and scenery construction.

Internal reporting of near misses and incidents is especially important in order to identify hazards before they cause harm.

Serious diseases must be reported on form F2508A. Examples would include asbestosis, the bends, contamination, food poisoning, leptospirosis/Weil's disease, psittacosis, radiation sickness, skin disease/dermatitis and zoonotic infections. Activities in film and television work where these could be contracted include building and maintenance work, contact with animals, chemicals, disused sites, diving, food and catering, hairdressing and make-up artists, model makers, overseas travel, plumbers, radiation work and vehicle maintenance.

Bad health at work and stressful conditions can lead to incidents and accidents so your production safety system should also focus on health issues including long-term risks. For further information read Good Health is Good Business: An Employer's Guide, HSE MISC-130.

Constructing a production safety system

The best way to do this is by adopting a written systematic approach to production safety – a production safety system. This must be backed up by a good flow of information to all staff engaged in production. A member of staff in each area should be nominated as a safety representative and consult with management about how to carry out operations in a safe and healthy working environment. The production safety system should incorporate the following points:

Stage 1: Hazard identification

Identify hazards in each area and record significant findings. A hazard is a source of possible harm. Identifying hazards which have the potential to cause harm can be done at several key control points (first the ideas/proposal stage, then the script stage, during location finding and recces, and at the shooting script stage, prop finding and scenery construction). Hazard identification is a process of anticipation. It may help to take notes and photographs on your site visits and obtain plans and maps of buildings and locations. Also ask local experts, owners and surveyors.

There are four main types of hazard. Hazards can be inherent, introduced, proximity, or weather induced.

- **Inherent hazards** are those which are already there, for example farm animals, asbestos, children and water.
- **Introduced hazards** are those you bring in, for example chemicals, cranes, lighting, explosives.
- **Proximity hazards** are those near your location, for example power cables, a slope or low flying aircraft.
- **Weather-induced hazards** i.e. drop in temperature/ice, poor visibility etc.

Now use the hazard list on the form in Appendix 5 (page 462) and tick which are present and which are not for each location and activity. Then deal with the ones that are identified. Having identified any hazards, the second step of evaluating them by a process called risk assessment can now be taken.

Stage 2: Risk assessment

Having identified potential hazards carry out a written risk assessment to determine the actual level of risk involved. Enter your findings on the form in Appendix 6 against each hazard.

A risk is the chance of something happening versus the level of harm it would cause if it did happen. Use a simple risk rating system to evaluate the risk level of each hazard, graded from high to low (low being a near miss or graze, high being a multiple fatality). Simple risk rating systems should balance the level of risk versus the probability of it happening. In other words the degree of potential harm versus the actual chance of it happening.

Degree of risk:	A	B	C	D	E	(high to low)
Probability:	1	2	3	4	5	(high to low)

Examples:	A1 is a very high risk with a high probability of death or injury such as a pyrotechnic stunt.
	A5 is a very high risk with low probability such as a securely caged wild animal.
	B2 is a high risk with high probability such as working on water or at height.
	C3 is a medium risk with medium probability such as welding or manual handling.
	E2 is a low risk with high probability such as a slip or trip hazard.

STEP 1

Hazard

Look only for hazards which you could reasonably expect to result in significant harm under the conditions in your workplace. Use the following examples as a guide

- slipping/tripping hazards (eg poorly maintained floors or stairs)
- fire (eg from flammable materials)
- chemicals (eg battery acid)
- moving parts of machinery (eg blades)
- work at height (eg from mezzanine floors)
- ejection of material (eg from plastic moulding)
- pressure systems (eg steam boilers)
- vehicles (eg fork-lift trucks)
- electricity (eg poor wiring)
- dust (eg from grinding)
- fumes (eg welding)
- manual handling
- noise
- poor lighting
- low temperature

STEP 2

Who might be harmed?

There is no need to list individuals by name - just think about groups of people doing similar work or who may be affected, eg

- office staff
- maintenance personnel
- contractors
- people sharing your workplace
- operators
- cleaners
- members of the public

Pay particular attention to:

- staff with disabilities
- visitors
- inexperienced staff
- lone workers

They may be more vulnerable

STEP 3

Is more needed to control the risk?

For the hazards listed, do the precautions already taken:

- meet the standards set by a legal requirement?
- comply with a recognised industry standard?
- represent good practice?
- reduce risk as far as reasonably practicable?

Have you provided:

- adequate information, instruction or training?
- adequate systems or procedures?

If so, then the risks are adequately controlled, but you need to indicate the precautions you have in place. (You may refer to procedures, company rules, etc.)

Where the risk is not adequately controlled, indicate what more you need to do (the 'action list')

STEP 5

Review and revision

Set a date for review of the assessment (see opposite).

On review check that the precautions for each hazard still adequately control the risk. If not indicate the action needed. Note the outcome. If necessary complete a new page for your risk assessment.

Making changes in your workplace, eg when bringing in new
- machines
- substances
- procedures
may introduce significant new hazards. Look for them and follow the 5 steps.

Figure 3.6 *Five steps to risk assessment. Step 4 is to record your findings of Steps 1, 2 and 3 on a form you may devise. See the production safety forms given in Appendix 6. © HSE*

Note that the risk factor can be reduced to safe working levels if the task is carried out by an experienced competent person using a work method statement and properly supervised. For example, a high risk pyrotechnic stunt can be carried out safely if a proper supervisor is used to plan and carry the effect out. Similarly, high risk diving work can be carried out safely if experienced contractors and divers are employed. Working with electricity or scaffolding can be high risk but the risk can be reduced to acceptable levels if qualified and experienced electricians and scaffolders are used.

Lastly a lower-risk, high-probability task such as working at night can be made less risky if the activity is properly lit and high visibility clothing is provided and worn.

Make your risk assessment person-specific. Look at each hazard or hazardous activity and ask, **who** would be at risk? This could be a group of workers, for example riggers or make-up artists, or it could be specific individuals, for example a camera operator or actor.

Then each head of department, in consultation with the producer, should draw up their own health and safety plan for their own area and conduct risk assessments for their production activities. (See Hazard 16, p. 258 for an example of a risk assessment and Appendix 6 for a risk assessment form.)

To make this task easier divide health and safety responsibilities into specific areas with supervisors for each one. By doing this you are establishing a chain of responsibility. Divide your operations up into sections that reflect the type of work you do: camera, sound, lighting, costume, make-up and wardrobe, maintenance, scenery design and construction, transport, special effects, catering, security and stunts.

Identify and break down these operations into separate activities which may involve risk. For example chemicals, driving, electrical, lifting, manual handling, display screens and noise. Most importantly, identify who is doing this work and who would need to be protected. Risk assessments should be activity based but person specific.

As mentioned in Chapter 1, risk assessment is not as widespread as it should be and where they are conducted the results are not being communicated. A written risk assessment will only be a paper exercise unless you then take active steps to enforce the findings in reality, starting with the weakest points of the production safety chain (see Five Steps to Risk Assessment, HSE, IND(G)163-Rev.; A Guide to Risk Assessment Requirements, HSE, IND(G) 218.)

Stage 3: Take action

Having identified the risks, take action starting with the most dangerous activities and the weakest points.

Plan ahead and put precautions in place before production activity starts. The aim is to protect particular people from hazards specifically identified on your form by active risk reduction action (see Health Risk Management, HSE, HS(G)137, ISBN 0-7176-0905-7).

Written safe systems of work must be put in place for any risky activity. Start with the high risk ones which would affect the most people and then deal with the minor risks. Identify and take into account all the significant factors that can affect the health and safety of everybody concerned and reach a conclusion about how to manage and improve by implementing effective control measures.

Stage 4: Select control measures

The correct selection and implementation of the most appropriate control method is crucial to how successful your control measures will be. Start with the most effective method of eliminating the greatest hazard and highest risk to the greatest number of people.

In particular instances it may be appropriate to select more than one control measure. Consideration should be given to which is the most effective at reducing the level of risk. The aim should always be to choose the correct method which reduces the level of risk to a safe working level. Consideration should also be given to the most cost-effective measure.

However, the organization and arrangements you make to enforce your policy will transform it from writing to actuality. The actions taken should include all or some of the following:

A   Choose a safer alternative if the risk is too high.
B   Substitute the activity or substance with a safer one.
C   Eliminate the risk altogether by getting rid of it.
D   Prevent anybody from proximity to risk by sealing off.
E   Use guard rails, fences and enclosures to segregate.
F   Adopt a safe working system, e.g. for loading, lifting, etc.
G   Select and use appropriate equipment. Always follow the operating instructions and ensure regular maintenance and testing. Use a qualified and experienced operator.
H   If in doubt seek expert advice before proceeding.
I   Obtain this from premises owners, stunt arrangers, etc.
J   Check the expert's credentials and insurance.
K   Draw up a special working plan with your expert.
L   Get extra advice from HSE, unions, experienced staff.
M   Check on changeable factors such as the weather/new ideas or a change in personnel or location.
N   Re-assess the risks and your plan in relation to M.

O   Make sure all staff, subcontractors and performers have written health and safety information and a proper briefing prior to filming.
P   Secure the set or location by permit systems and security.
Q   Establish controls for the introduction of chemicals, electrical equipment, gases, guns and explosives. Don't forget to include controls for subcontractors, caterers, performers and visitors.
R   Ensure staff are properly trained and informed.
S   Make sure all activities are properly supervised by experienced and trained supervisors.
T   Provide proper protective equipment.
U   Make sure it fits and is worn in all danger areas.
V   Put in place proper insurance cover (including office).
W   Consult and inform others affected by your activities.
X   Ensure emergency equipment and plans if something goes wrong.
Y   Record your action plan and review it regularly to keep pace with changing needs, circumstance, production size and new legislation.
Z   Record near misses and incidents. Use these to identify problem areas.

Stage 5: Select right tools for the job

A number of key decisions have to be made in order to ensure proper management of health and safety for a production environment. The first is the proper selection of equipment. Always use a reputable hire company. Always make sure that you are given the operating instructions along with copies of any test certificates and insurance documents. Keep these in your health and safety file. Select the right tools for the job and ensure they are PUWER 98 compliant.

Stage 6: Select competent staff and contractors

Ensure that any operator is qualified and experienced to do the job you are asking them to do. For example, armourers, crane operators, divers, pilots, pyrotechnic operators, scaffolders and sea captains. Check credentials with the professional body. For example actors who can carry out stunt work are listed in Equity's Spotlight Stunt Register. Ensure you provide them with correct information on the task required and the location. Also obtain copies of their licences and qualifications. Keep these in your health and safety file.

A major headache for production companies is the selection of competent contractors. The first step is to make a risk assessment of the job you wish them to do. How difficult is it? What level of experience do

WAYNE MICHAELS

Joined Register 1981

Height	6 ft
Weight	12 st 7 lbs
Chest	42 in
Waist	34 in
Hips	36½ in
Leg, Inside	31 in
Arm, Inside	21½ in
Shoes	8
Collar	16 in
Hat	7 ⅞ in
Hair Colour	Brown
Eye Colour	Hazel

Credits:
 Stunt Co-ordinator:
  The Man Who Knew Too Little
  Prince Valiant
  Restoration
  Shadowlands
  The Madness of King George
  Four Weddings and a Funeral
  Tomorrow Never Dies (Doubled Pierce Brosnan)
  GoldenEye (Doubled Pierce Brosnan)

Capabilities:
 High Falls (100 feet plus), Dives, Heights, Free
 Fall Parachuting, Wire Work, Cars, Bikes,
 HGV 1, All Horse Work, Fire, BSAC Diver,
 Trampoline, Trampette, Air-Ram, All Fight
 Work, Fencing, Abseiling.

Acting Experience:
 Film, Television, Theatre and Commercials.

Special Skills:
 Opening Title Sequence of GoldenEye (seven
 hundred feet world-record dive from the Lugano
 Dam, Switzerland), Aerial Stunts, High Falls, Sky
 Diving, Boat Jumps, Rope and Wire Work, Specialist
 Rigging and Fire Stunts.

Personal Equipment:
 Full array of Stunt, Safety and Rigging Equipment.

Stunt Co-ordinator with worldwide experience.
Innovative and original.

Figure 3.7 *Equity Stunt Register entry. © Spotlight Stunt Register and Equity*

you need to get the task completed safely? This will determine the level of competence required. It is best to select a contractor who belongs to the relevant professional body (for example Sitac for scaffolding or a Food Hygiene Certificate for a catering operative). In work involving electrical and gas installation or work with explosives this is a legal requirement. However, membership of the relevant professional body does not by itself form a sound basis for the determination of competence. Previous experience may be a more valuable guide. So it is sensible to draw up a list of checks and questions which will enable you to prove in the event of an incident that you made the best efforts to select a competent contractor. Written answers by a responsible person in the potential contracting company or individual should be made to the following questions:

1 Please give details of the size of your company, the nature of your operation and your experience in the relevant areas.
2 Please give details of your company's safety policy (including health and safety responsibilities within the company, e.g. safety manager and supervisors). Attach a copy of your policy or relevant sections of it.
3 Give details and attach copies of all risk assessments carried out under the Management of Health and Safety at Work Regulations 1992, Control of Substances Hazardous to Health Regulations 1999 and relevant control measures for work involving confined spaces, diving, explosives, firearms, flying, lasers, pyrotechnics, scaffolding, stunts and water.
4 Please give details of all relevant insurance policies.
5 Please provide at least three example of similar work carried out, including the name of the organization you worked for and contact details of the responsible person who may be able to supply references.
6 Please supply details of accreditation to BS 5750, ISO 9000 and other professional standards.
7 Give details of health and safety training provided to employees, and any necessary additional training/qualifications for this contract. Include qualifications of key employees such as divers and pilots, etc. Please supply details of your emergency procedures for your employees including fire, first aid, evacuation procedures, medical screening and PPE.
8 Please give details of nominated individuals and competent persons who will be responsible for this specific contract. Please give details of any work that will be subcontracted and your selection criteria for subcontractors.
9 Provide a work method statement and plan for your intended task including health, safety and supervisory arrangements.

10 Provide details of any plant and machinery which require safety certificates and trained operators.
11 Please give details of accident and incident statistics within your organization.
12 Please give details of any enforcement action taken against the company (its predecessors or individuals working for it).
13 Please give details of membership of any trade and professional organizations.

Satisfactory answers to the above should form the basis for your selection and these should be written down and recorded as the basis for your appointment. Following appointment of the competent contractor, the client must then monitor the contractor's health and safety performance and discharge their own responsibilities to provide a work method statement and a safe working environment. The client must also identify particular hazards and provide information to contractors about their own safety rules and regulations. The selection of contractors should always be made on the basis of competency and experience backed up by a safe system of work agreed in advance. Further information can be obtained from HSE, Managing Contractors, A Guide for Employers, ISBN 0-7176-1196-5.

Stage 7: Communicate health and safety information

Ensure that all staff are aware of any health and safety hazards, especially if they are working on the premises of others and in dangerous locations. Essential information must be given out to all concerned with the production before filming starts. This could include health and safety information and notes from other organizations. Back up written information by a briefing before filming begins. Operate a safe system of work and use a written work method statement to lay out how a particular job should be done. Circulate this to everybody concerned and use a health and safety noticeboard.

Stage 8: Seek advice from experts and specialists

Engage specialists and experts to help you undertake any dangerous or difficult work. Make sure that contributors who supervise or carry out stunts carry the right insurance. Exchange written risk assessments before filming begins, especially for diving work, flying and pyrotechnics. Avoid changing plans at short notice and brief all crew and participants carefully first. Supervisors and stunt artists should also be experienced in film and television work. In the event of an accident the onus will be on you to prove that you took all reasonable steps to check that they were experienced, competent and bona fide.

Stage 9: Provide education and safety training

Eliminate errors by proper education and training. If necessary send staff on short courses for fire prevention, first aid, manual handling and safety. Send specialists on courses for machinery and tools such as cranes, fork-lifts, MEWPs, scaffolding and wood working. Keep proper training records and update them regularly. Keep unqualified staff away from dangerous areas such as confined spaces, working at height, working with chemicals, gases, explosives and electricity. Employ a permit to work scheme or similar controls and issue the proper personal protective equipment, tools and communications for the job.

Stage 10: Establish a safety culture

Health and safety should become part of everyday working practice and not seen as something apart. Health and safety should not be thought of as an additional extra expense but as a normal cost item of every production budget. Establishing this culture requires two things. First, establish a simple, easy-to-use production safety system that can be used by everybody and establish a safety culture which views incidents and accidents as a failure which could cost lives and money. Good health and safety practice can ensure compliance with the law, protect anyone concerned with the production and save you money as well. Bad health and safety practice puts lives at risk, is illegal and can cost far more in money in the long term. So provide and explain your health and safety policy and the reasons for the production safety system. Get your staff involved and committed by stressing the benefits to them. Consultation is a legal requirement under The Health and Safety (Consultation with Employees) Regulations 1996. Under the Health and Safety at Work Act 1974 section 2, the employer must consult with safety representatives of a recognized trade union and establish a safety committee.

Second, use examples of other organizations who do this already and give examples of accidents that can happen. This helps to establish that it can be done and that accidents do happen unless active prevention measures are taken.

A positive health and safety culture works on competence, control, co-operation and communication.

Competence means making a proper assessment of the skills needed to do each job properly and safely. Provide the training and instruction for staff to obtain competence. If necessary use outside training and experts to help you provide courses, such as Skillset and regional media training consortia along with first aid and fire training. Support staff with information cards, books and videos.

Control means identifying risky operations and making sure that they are properly planned and supervised by experienced and competent staff who command respect and who are qualified to manage the task. Establish control systems including permits to work and safe systems of work. Control subcontractors and visitors. Fence off locations and provide proper security. Always check on how tasks are being performed and perform daily safety checks of locations, studios and sets.

Co-operation means consulting with your staff on how work should be organized and identifying the right people and systems to do each job safely. Encourage feedback and a positive reporting culture to improve safety standards via safety representatives and safety committees.

Communication means providing information about potential risks and hazards. Provide written safety guidelines and a work method statement. Pass on information and ensure that verbal safety briefings are established every day and before any new or especially risky operation. Also make sure that health and safety signs are provided and a health and safety notice board established. Copy urgent safety notes to everybody concerned with the production and send it out with schedules. Ensure that all staff can keep in contact with efficient communications such as phone, fax, pagers, mobiles, etc., with the production base office.

The crucial steps in the management of accident prevention are:

1 Stop and actively observe the full range of production activities. Take time to listen to your staff and be receptive. What are their jobs? What do they work with and who works together?
2 Put people at their ease by establishing positive communication and constructive concern. How can you help? What do they need?
3 Establish an atmosphere of relaxation by explaining what you are doing and why.
4 Think through the stages and processes necessary for each job.
5 Ask yourself and visualize the worst accident that could happen – hazard identification. Make notes about each process, location and intended action.
6 Ask yourself and identify who it could happen to and those most at risk.
7 Assess the chances of it happening and the level of risk – risk assessment. Praise aspects of safe behaviour and criticize unsafe behaviour.
8 Study accidents reports and incidents. Identify causes – ask why they happened.
9 Plan and present solutions and corrective actions. Work method statements and safety plan.
10 Change behaviour and environments. Increase the level of information, supervision and training.

11 Put into your solutions action by doing something about them.
12 Seek expert advice and help where necessary.
13 Keep up to date with legislation, keep up site visits and review your policy.

Conclusion: the health and safety file

Keep written records of all your actions in a health and safety file, including the results of the initial hazard identification, risk assessment and a record of the necessary preventative measures. This should be formulated into a coherent **work method statement**. This is a statement of how the work will be done, including details of the tools to be used, the timing, work schedule and who will supervise and carry it out. The next document is called a **health and safety plan**. This is an action plan for how your crew will be protected from any risks which you have already identified. The health and safety plan should set out how the risky work will be done and how accidents will be prevented. This includes details of segregation methods, permits to work, substitution strategies, the protective equipment to be used and who will supervise the stages of the job in a safe and logical order. The health and safety file should contain:

1 A copy of your health and safety policy statement. A plan of how your health and safety is controlled.
2 Details of how health and safety is organized. This must include: fire precautions, safety signing, first aid precautions (this information must also be provided for visitors), accident reporting and insurance, details of safety representatives and minutes of safety committee meetings. Staff records must include medical information and health monitoring. Training records and safety information sheets should be kept for all staff.
3 A list of who is responsible for each area of operation and supervisors.
4 A list of each area and the process and activities which take place.
5 A hazard identification sheet for each base area and each location.
6 A risk assessment of each intended activity and scripted action.
7 An action plan to control the level of risk and eliminate them. This should include work schedules and method statements.
8 Details of any insurance required.
9 Details of any experts used including certificates and qualifications.
10 Details of any plant or machinery with test certificates.
11 Details of any drivers and operators with qualifications.

12 Details of any electrical equipment with safety test records.
13 Details of any chemicals stored, the quantity and data sheets (COSHH log).
14 Details of any explosives stored, the quantity and safe storage procedures.
15 Details of any subcontractors and their tools, chemicals, plant and staff.
16 Details of safety advice cards given to subcontractors and contributors. Details of written risk assessments and work method statements by supervisors and subcontractors.
17 Details of all permits to work.
18 Details of all VDU testing and manual handling assessments.

These steps should help you to construct a workable and effective health and safety policy.

Further reading

Allan St John Holt, *Principles of Health and Safety at Work*, 5th edition, IOSH Publishing, ISBN 0-901-357-219.

John Ridley, *Safety at Work*, 5th edition, Butterworth-Heinemann, ISBN 0-7506-0746-7.

The Management of Health and Safety at Work Regulations 1992, Approved Code of Practice, HSE L21, ISBN 0-7176-0412-8.

Essentials of Health and Safety at Work, HSE, ISBN 0-7176-0716-X.

A Guide to the Reporting of Injuries, Diseases and Dangerous Occurrences Regulations 1995, HSE L73, ISBN 0-7176-1012-8.

First Aid At Work – The Health and Safety (First Aid) Regulations 1981, Approved Code of Practice and Guidance, HSE L74, ISBN 0-7176-1050-0.

The Health and Safety (Consultation with Employees) Regulations 1996, Guidance on Regulations, HSE L95, ISBN 0-7176-1234-1.

Safety Representatives and Safety Committees, Approved Code of Practice and Guidance on the Regulations ('brown book', third edition), HSE-L87, ISBN 0-7176-12201.

4 Personal protective equipment

The legislation covered in this chapter includes:

The Personal Protective Equipment at Work Regulations 1992
The Provision and Use of Work Equipment Regulations 1998
The Health and Safety at Work Act 1974
The Merchant Shipping (Life Saving Appliances) Regulations 1986

On 6 February 1993 a stunt man plunged to his death. Ted Tipping fell thousands of feet into woods after his parachute failed to open during the stunt performed for the BBC 1 series 999.

Personal protective equipment (PPE) remains the last link in the safety chain. Protective equipment should only be used if all other means to eliminate the risk factor from hazards have been taken. Protective equipment is a last resort, not a cheap alternative to proper preventative measures.

The variety of PPE in the film and television business varies with the variety of risk situations encountered. Everyday situations may require foot, head and ear protection along with the need for visibility clothing. However there will also be the need for specialist protective equipment such as the bullet-proof vest for the journalist in a war zone or a safety harness for a stunt at height. So when making an assessment of what PPE is needed, take into account everyday operations and the unusual one-offs for which specialist advice may be needed.

There are circumstances where the use of PPE is not only a sensible precaution but also a life-saving protective measure. For example a life-jacket when working near water or a hard hat when working at height. The key to having the correct PPE is making the correct selection of appropriate equipment to the situation, making sure that people at risk have the protective equipment to hand, that it fits correctly, and is worn at all times when either a mandatory sign or level of risk dictates that this should be done.

The Personal Protective Equipment at Work Regulations 1992 require employers to assess the health and safety risks to employees in the workplace, and where appropriate to issue suitable PPE. Since July 1995 all PPE bought or sold in the European Union has to display a CE mark.

This means that the PPE conforms to European standards. It is an offence for employers to buy PPE which is not CE marked. So manufacturers must ensure that their PPE products are approved to carry the mark and employers and managers must ensure that PPE equipment has a CE mark when they purchase it. There are three categories of European PPE:

- Grade 1: Simple equipment.
- Grade 2: Intermediate safety equipment, and
- Grade 3: Complex life-saving equipment.

The European Commission has just published a list of harmonized standards for PPE (*Official Journal of the European Communities*, c338/2 6.11.98).

Figure 4.1   *The CE mark*

There are also British standards for certain types of equipment which will eventually harmonize with those of other EU countries. So any equipment purchased and issued must carry the CE mark and conform to the relevant EU and British standards for that piece of equipment. For example ear defenders are BS/EN 24869–1 and ISO 4869–1.

All PPE must fit the person who is wearing it. This is particularly important for dust masks and respiratory equipment. For example, under the new asbestos regulations, all respiratory equipment must have a fit test to make sure that the face mask is moulded individually for the person who has to wear it. Each operative then carries a fit test certificate for their own PPE. A copy is also kept for safety monitoring records.

The correct type of PPE must also be issued for each person and the nature of the task that they are performing. For example life-jackets have different standards and will vary according to the sea conditions and the weight of the person. Similarly, fall arrest harnesses will vary in strength and different ones are needed for work at different heights and the load they will support. Always seek advice from the maker and supplier and give them as much detail as you can about the activity for which you intend to use the PPE.

Staff must have proper training in the use of PPE, especially for stunt harness work, working at heights and diving equipment. The stunt arranger or supervisor must brief those concerned about the correct use and operating instructions. Verbal briefings should always be backed up by a copy of the manufacturer's instructions for safe use.

The protection which PPE can afford can be rendered useless if the staff concerned do not wear them when needed. For example taking off ear defenders for two minutes in a high noise environment can nullify the effects of wearing them and result in hearing loss or damage. Staff regulations should make it a disciplinary offence not to wear the correct PPE when the need is identified.

Supervisors and managers must encourage a culture of wearing PPE. Warning signs should indicate mandatory PPE areas such as hard hat areas and high noise zones.

MA85   200 x 300
MA86   400 x 600

Figure 4.2   *Warning sign. © ARCO Ltd, reproduced by kind permission*

It is important to take note of any PPE requirements when working on the premises of other people. It is also essential to anticipate PPE requirements for location work and crew cars should carry a basic PPE issue kit. Extra PPE precautions will also be necessary in bad weather conditions and dangerous terrain. Other situations were proper PPE is required include working at height, working at night, location finding in derelict sites, working in war zones, working near water and working in confined spaces. Don't forget to assess studio requirements and electrical safety equipment such as cable ducts, safety working tags and PAT testers.

Specific regulations require the mandatory wearing of PPE. The Construction (Head Protection) Regulations 1989 require head protection to be worn on all construction sites. Schedule 3 and 4 Regulation 6(3)c and 6(3)d of the Construction (Health, Safety and Welfare) Regulations 1996 lay out the compulsory need for safety harnesses and fall arrest devices on working platforms or working at height. The Noise at Work Regulations 1989 require mandatory ear protection at noise levels above 90dba.

Respiratory protective equipment (RPE)

The use of respiratory equipment is required in hazardous areas under the COSHH Regulations 1994 and 1999 and the Control of Asbestos Regulations 1998. Respiratory PPE works either as a filter face mask or as a face mask/suit fitted with a clean air pump. These are called negative RPE or positive RPE respectively.

Negative RPEs have filters that filter contaminated air before it is inhaled by the wearer. These RPEs can be either simple filtering respirators or powered respirators. Simple filtering respirators come in three main types: disposable filtering face-pieces, half-masks with filters and full face masks with filters. Powered respirators come in four main types: blouses; hoods, helmets and visors; half-masks; and constant flow.

Positive RPEs are of three major types: simple compressed air supplied equipment, fresh air hose equipment and breathing apparatus. This equipment provides uncontaminated air for breathing from an independent source.

- Simple compressed air equipment comes in four types: blouses; hoods, helmets and visors; half-masks; and constant flow.
- Fresh air hose equipment comes in three types: unassisted, manually assisted and powered assisted.
- Breathing apparatus comes in two types: compressed air line apparatus or self-contained breathing apparatus. Compressed air lines are demand type with or without positive pressure. Self-contained systems work on a closed/open circuit with compressed air/oxygen mixture.

Positive RPE should always be used in environments where the occupational exposure levels (OELs) are exceeded or there is risk from gas or toxic fumes. Disposable respiratory face filters should conform to EN 149. Compressed air breathing systems must conform to EN 132. Filter respirators must conform to EN 136.

Respiratory protective equipment should be used for any environment or task which may contain or release dangerous dust or fumes. These include asbestos, demolition work, metalwork, spraying and wood working. Consult your supplier for the most appropriate type. Consider first if the risk is from a dust, gas or particles. Then select the correct type of RPE. The different types are:

- Disposable filters and face-piece respirators. These take filters FFP1, FFP2 and FFP3.
- Half mask respirators with filters. These take filters P1, P2 and P3.
- Full face mask respirator with filter. These take filters P1, P2 and P3.

ARCO Freeflow SL Selector Guide

INDUSTRY	CONTAMINANT	P1SLV	P2SLV	P2SLV	P2SLV welding	P3SLV
Woodworking	Softwood	•	•	•		•
	Hardwood		•	•		•
Foundries	Metallic Dust		•	•	•	•
	Metallic Fume			•	•	•
Welding	Metallic Fume			•	•	•
Agriculture	Spraying		•	•		•
	Grain Stores	•	•	•		•
	Animal Feeds		•	•		•
Mining/Quarry	Quartz/Si dust	•	•	•		•
	Granite/sandstone	•	•	•		•
	Limestone dust	•	•	•		•
Textiles	Cotton dust	•	•	•		•
Brickworks	Brickdust	•	•	•		•
Insulations	Glass fibre	•	•	•		•
	Rockwool	•	•	•		•
	Mineral wool fibre	•	•	•		•
Auto refinishing	Grinding			•	•	•
	Buffing	•	•	•		•
Laboratories	Chemical Powders	•	•	•		•
Potteries	Clay dust	•	•	•		•
Shipbuilding	Grinding			•	•	•
Pharmaceuticals	Tablet Powders	•	•	•		•
Chemicals	Chemical Powders	•	•	•		•
Food Processing	ingredient Dusts	•	•	•		•
Animal Husbandry	Skin, fur, feathers	•	•	•		•

Figure 4.3 *ARCO Freeflow selector guide. © ARCO Ltd, reproduced by kind permission*

- Powered respirator with helmet or hood. These take filters THP1, THP2 and THP3.
- Finally powered respirators with full face masks. These take filters TMP1, TMP2 and TMP3.

Workers who intend to use RPE must be medically fit to do so. Staff should be screened for breathing problems and asthma. All RPE must be properly maintained with good seals. Staff who wear glasses or who have facial hair may compromise the seal of the RPE system and pose a risk to their health. All staff who conduct work with RPE should have regular health monitoring and screening with the records kept for inspection.

Hand protection

Hand protection is covered by section 4 of The Personal Protective Equipment at Work Regulations 1992 and gloves are designed in three categories of risk:

- simple design for minimal risks but frequent use
- intermediate design for risks greater than the ordinary, and
- complex gloves designed for special uses which would otherwise result in irreversible injury or damage.

Special gloves should be used for electrical work and welding. Protective gloves should also be worn for handling chemical and hazardous substances.

Staff who deal with long-term exposure to chemicals such as cleaners, hairdressers, make-up artists and painters should use disposable gloves to prevent dermatitis. In certain situations advanced barrier creams and skin care products could be used instead.

Eye protection

Section 4 of The Personal Protective Equipment at Work Regulations 1992 requires mandatory wearing of eye protection in hazardous areas, for example when welding. Eye protection has four main categories: safety spectacles, eye shields, safety goggles and face shields. Each type is suitable for different levels of risk and guidance should always be obtained regarding the correct type to use for the identified hazard. For example British Standard and CE eye protection must be worn for work with class 3b and class 4 lasers.

Eye protection must be BS 2092. This includes the lens and the housing. However, special housing applies for certain types of hazard. Impacts have two grades: BS 2092 Grade 1 and BS 2092 Grade 2. For liquid drops and chemical splashes BS 2092 Grade C applies. For dusts BS 2092 grade D applies. For gases BS 2092 Grade G applies. For molten metals BS 2092 Grade M applies. Some eye protection features combinations of the above so it is important to get the right grade of protection for the type of risk.

Safety spectacles are similar to regular glasses but made with tougher lenses. Safety spectacles can incorporate side shields to provide extra protection. These should be BS 2092 basic and Grade 2.

Eye shields are heavier than safety spectacles and come as a frameless one-piece moulded lens. They can be worn if required over the top of normal prescription glasses. These should be BS 2092 Grade 2.

Safety goggles are made with flexible plastic frames and come with an elastic headband. The lenses are usually replaceable and provide protection from all angles as the edges are always in contact with the face. These should be BS 2092 Grade 1 or 2.

Figure 4.4 *Laser goggles. © ARCO Ltd, reproduced by kind permission*

Face shields are much heavier and bulkier than the other types of eye protection. The eyes are not fully enclosed so protection is not given against gases or dusts. Specialist face shields exist for welding. These should be BS 2092 Grade 1 to protect the eyes and face from liquid splashes or molten metal. Welding face shields protect the eyes, face and neck against ultraviolet radiation. Different filters should be used for gas or electric arc welding operations. The filters should be BS 679, 1989, GW for gas welding without flux, GWF for gas welding with flux and EW for electric welding.

All forms of eye protection must be kept clean so that normal vision is possible. This is very important as impaired vision could be highly

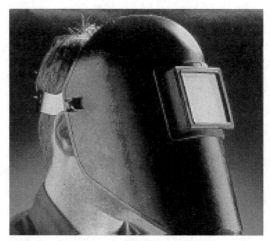

Figure 4.5   *Welding face shield. © ARCO Ltd, reproduced by kind permission*

dangerous during welding or similar work. Hygiene is also an issue as eye protection should be individual and only worn by the person it is supplied to. All eye protection should be properly cleaned and disinfected after use. Workplace eye injuries can be particularly devastating so it is essential that the need for eye protection is identified and the proper protective eye equipment is supplied and worn at all times in hazardous areas and during risk operations.

Safety belts and harnesses

Safety belts, harnesses and fall arrest devices must comply with BS 1397/EN 361. Such devices fall into the following categories: pole belts, general safety belts, chest harness, general purpose safety harness and the safety rescue harness. They may be supported by the use of suitable fall arrest devices which should be used whenever the risk of a fall or becoming trapped is identified. So work in confined spaces, near water and at height are all situations where safety harness and fall arrest devices are necessary.

Pole belts are specifically intended for lines work and should be used for no other purpose. They are not fall arrest devices but only for work positioning/restraint. They must comply with EN 358 and are also known as pammenter and petrie belts.

The **general safety belt** is attached to safety lanyards fixed to anchorage points. The maximum drop should be 120 cm. It must comply with EN 361.

The **chest harness** has a chest belt and shoulder straps to support the torso. It is designed to support a person's weight and hold them in the event of a slip or fall. The fall would be limited to 2 m. It must comply with EN 361.

The **general purpose safety harness** has extra support around the thighs and shoulders. This type of support is often built into safety or survival suits. These are recommended for situations where maximum movement is required and they restrict the fall to 2 m. It must comply with EN 361.

The **safety rescue harness** is intended for those working in confined spaces or deep holes. It is intended to be used as a rescue device so that the person can be withdrawn quickly in the event of an incident. It must comply with EN 361.

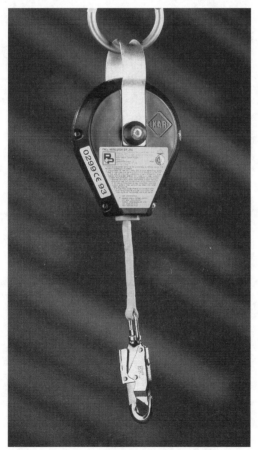

Figure 4.6 *Fablock fall arrest webbing. © ARCO Ltd, reproduced by kind permission*

(a)

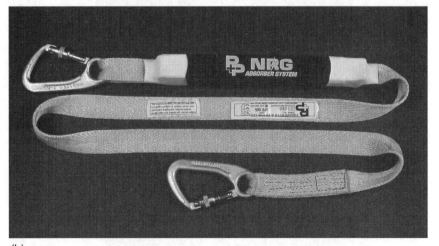

(b)

Figure 4.7   *(a) ARCO Arrester safety harness and (b) ARCO lanyard.* © *ARCO Ltd, reproduced by kind permission*

These types of harness can be used with fall arrest devices. These are ropes with energy absorbing shock reels and pulley systems. All fall arrest devices must comply with EN 360. Lanyards must comply with EN 355. Karabiner clips and fixings must comply with EN 362. Equipment must also be secured by safety lines when working in the air, near water or at height.

Water safety

The Merchant Shipping (Life Saving Appliances) Regulations 1986 lay down the type of safety harness and rescue lines for use on or near water. These are also approved by the National Water Council. The four standards of life-jackets are:

- N50/EN 393: These are buoyancy aids only and are for use by good swimmers in sheltered water conditions, where help is close at hand. They will not hold the face of an unconscious wearer clear from the water. They are also unsuitable for children.

Figure 4.8 *Worksafe 275N life-jacket. © ARCO Ltd, reproduced by kind permission*

- N100/EN 395: These are life-jackets for use in inland waterways and relatively sheltered water conditions. These will not turn an unconscious wearer face upwards if that person is heavy or wearing sodden clothing.
- N150/EN 396: These are suitable for use in all waters. These will turn most unconscious wearers face upwards unless they are wearing heavy foul weather clothing.
- N275/EN 399: These are suitable for extreme weather conditions and all waters. They are intended for the average adult and will turn an unconscious wearers face upwards under almost all circumstances.

Secumar and Stearns are reputable manufacturers of life-jackets. Water safety should also include life-lines, distress signals, hard hats and survival suits.

Head protection

All head protection should be EN 397/BS 5240. This standard lays down a minimum requirement for energy absorption, impact resistance, fire resistance and lateral deformation. Note there will shortly be a new European standard for high performance industrial safety helmets featuring side impact protection. While hard hats with chin straps are essential when working at height, bump caps (EN 812/BS 4033) can be worn in areas of restricted headroom. Most helmets are designed to protect the wearer from the impact of a falling object.

The type required will depend on the nature of the task. For example, some protective helmets come fitted with ear defenders. Some come fitted with chin straps, and yet others come fitted with a broad peak. Hard hats without peaks are better for people who need good all round visibility such as a camera operator. The Construction (Head Protection) Regulations 1989 make it compulsory for safety helmets to be worn in all civil engineering and building sites. Safety helmets should be properly fitted and be properly stored and maintained when not in use. Any marked or damaged helmets must be replaced. Climbers' helmets must conform to BS 4423 and horse riding to BS 6473.

Safety footwear

These should be worn where there is a risk of foot damage, either through heat or impact. Situations where foot protection is necessary include manual handling, lifting, set construction, working with chemicals and hazardous substances and when working in derelict sites.

Safety footwear should conform to EN/BS 345/346 with protective toe caps for safety and riggers' boots and anti-acid and heat protective properties for wellingtons and safety shoes.

Visibility clothing

High visibility clothing should be worn in all situations involving night work or poor visibility conditions. Clothing should conform to EN 471 and can take the form of vests, jackets or protective suits. Visibility jackets are needed for working in extreme conditions or when working near moving vehicles. For example when filming in docks and factories. They should also be worn when filming beside motorways, bus stations, railways and airports. Visibility clothing should also be worn when filming in remote areas and adverse weather conditions. In such conditions the clothing must not only be capable of being seen but also of being warm and water proof.

Other safety equipment

Torches should also be carried along with emergency first aid kits and communication equipment in the event of an accident or getting lost. GPS satellite position tracking devices can be useful along with a compass and a proper map. Communication and location equipment can be lifesaving and is often vital PPE for extreme location work. For hot work outdoors, protective hats, glasses and sun cream should be used.

Protective hats, aprons and gloves should be used for food preparation.

Lone workers should always carry lone worker alarms and location finders and managers can make effective use of location probes to detect hidden cables and pipes. Electricians and plumbers may find these useful along with electrical testers and safety tagging systems.

Gas detectors are essential for confined space working, underground working and derelict sites.

Use a pocket symbol seeker to identify hazardous substances, drums, ammunition and chemicals. Lastly don't forget to have proper fire and first aid precautions backed by an emergency plan and communications.

The Provision and Use of Work Equipment Regulations 1998 require the provision of work equipment which is safe and also information and training for its safe use. Work equipment should also be regularly maintained and serviced with records made for inspection.

So always make sure that your PPE is suitable, properly maintained, regularly serviced and that staff are trained in the safe use of PPE. Above

(a)

(b)

Figure 4.9   *(a) Mentor PGD2 Portable Gas Detector and (b) CAT (Cable Avoiding Tool). © ARCO Ltd, reproduced by kind permission*

all, where no alternative exists, ensure that all PPE safety areas are identified by mandatory warning signs and that staff adhere to regulations and wear what you provide. PPE stores can issue equipment on a form for external and location productions after a PPE risk assessment has been carried out to identify the level of risk and the appropriate need for PPE.

Further reading

Personal protective equipment at work

The Personal Protective Equipment at Work Regulations 1992, Code of Practice and Guidance on the Regulations, HSE L25, ISBN 0–7176–0415–2.
A Short Guide to the Personal Protective Equipment at Work Regulations 1992, HSE IND(G)174(L).

Head protection

HSE Construction Information Sheet SS29, Personal Protective Equipment, HSE, IND(G)111(L).
Personal Protective Equipment Safety Attitude Guide, The British Safety Council.
Respiratory Protective Equipment: A Practical Guide for Users, HSE, HS(G)53, ISBN 0–1188–5522–0.
Selection of Respiratory Protective Equipment Suitable for Use with Wood Dust, HSE information sheet, Woodworking sheet no. 14 (WWS 14).

PPE suppliers

ARCO, PO Box 21, Waverley House, Waverley St, Hull HU1 2SJ
Tel: 01482–327678

ASPLI Safety Ltd, 211 Hunslet Rd, Leeds LS10 1PF
Tel: 01132–2461550

Barrow Hepburn Sala Ltd (fall-arrest devices and safety harness)
4 Old Mill Rd, Portishead, Bristol BS20 9BX
Tel: 01275–846119

British Safety Council: National Safety Centre
70 Chancellors Rd, London W6 9RS
Tel: 0181–741–1231

British Standards Institution
BSI Standards, 389 Chiswick High Rd, London W4 4AL
Tel: 0181–996–7111

Castle Associates (sound meters)
Salter Rd, Scarborough, North Yorkshire YO11 3UZ
Tel: 01723–584250

Dustraction Ltd (dust extraction systems)
PO Box 75, Mandeville Road, Oadby, Leicester LE2 5ND
Tel: 0116–271–3212

Guardian Safety Products (chemical storage)
Portsilo Ltd, Huntingdon, York YO3 9RP
Tel: 01904–624872.

Health Care and Emergency Services Ltd (safety gloves and resistant clothing)
Unit 5 Station Rd, Birnam, by Dunkeld, Perthshire, Scotland PH8 0DS
Tel: 01350–727170

Jallatte Technical Footwear Ltd
Centre House, Rookery Lane, Alridge, Walsall, West Midlands WS9 8NN
Tel: 01922–743336

Protector Technologies (respiratory devices)
Pimbo Rd, West Pimbo, Skelmersdale, Lancashire WN8 9RA
Tel: 01695–50284

Reid Marketing Ltd (symbol seeker ISBN 0695570595)
60 Moor Street, Ormskirk, Lancashire L39 2AW
Tel: 01695–570595

Royal Society for the Prevention of Accidents (RoSPA)
Edgbaston Park, 353 Bristol Road, Birmingham B5 7ST
Tel: 0121–248–2000

Sabre Gas Detection (gas detectors)
Protector Sabre Matterson House, Ash Rd, Aldershot, Hampshire GU12 4DE
Tel: 01252–344141

Scafftag Ltd (scaffold tagging and safety systems)
Wimborne Rd, Barry, Vale of Glamorgan, Wales CF63 3DH
Tel: 01446–721029

Walk-Overs Ltd (cable ducting)
14 Windermere Way, Thatcham, Berkshire RG13 4UL
Tel: 01635–865774

5 Insurance

The Employer's Liability (Compulsory Insurance) Regulations 1998

Film and television insurance is tailor made to suit the requirements of each production. There is no such thing as a typical production, and hence no typical policy! Film making creates demands for insurance coverage which are not readily met by standard policy wordings.

Each policy will be different, with special cover included and particular activities excluded. The first essential step is to consult a specialized entertainment broker who can discuss your needs and put together a package for you. They are always very helpful and will provide brochures on request. A list is provided at the end of the chapter. Insurance must be in place before production activity begins, so always discuss insurance needs with your broker well in advance.

Check that the dates on your Certificate of Employer's Liability Insurance match the whole production activity. In other words make sure that you are covered! This check also applies to territorial limits. If scenes involve filming outside the UK make sure that this is covered as well. Saving money by having limited insurance cover is an increasing trend for production companies who want to use an exotic location for one scene but don't want to pay the extra premium involved.

The first basic legal requirement in the UK is employer's liability. All employers are required under the Employer's Liability (Compulsory Insurance) Regulations 1998 to take out an employer's liability insurance policy. Employers must now keep copies of their Employer's Liability Certificates for a minimum period of 40 years. This covers the production company or contractor in respect of its legal liability for the injury, death, illness or disease of any employees resulting from their employment. Basically a legal liability will exist if negligence on the part of an employer can be demonstrated. For example, not having a health and safety policy or making a breach of the Health and Safety at Work Act 1974.

This policy must begin before anybody is taken on and continue until the last employee has been paid off. The policy must include any short term contract workers or occasional contributors, as the definition of an employer of an individual is one that has the individual under its direction and within its control.

Any stunt arrangers, pyrotechnic operators, armourers, pilots and divers must also carry their own specialized cover. Also any subcontractors must cover their own employees. This is because at some point they direct or carry out production operations under their own control including members of the production company. Therefore, they should carry out a risk assessment of their own activities and provide their own liability cover. For example, caterers must have employer's and public liability cover. Production polices must cover the use of subcontractors. The employer's liability certificate must be displayed in the location site office and base building.

The second basic insurance is called public liability cover. This policy indemnifies the production company against all third-party claims including personal injury and property damage. In other words the company is exempt from legal liability to anybody not employed by the company for death, bodily injury and property damage claims. It is essential that you obtain your public liability cover from the same broker as your employer's liability. If this is not done the potential for disputed claims will be created. This is why such policies are often called combined or joint liability cover. Public liability cover is often bought in a joint policy with employer's liability cover in a policy called 'film producer's combined liability production cover'. The level of risk will escalate depending on how much activity takes place in the public domain and how expensive the location being used.

The third basic insurance is third-party property damage cover. This indemnifies the production company for the loss or damage to any property that is in the care, custody or control of the production company. For example accidental damage to a location or hired antique items.

Another standard cover is equipment all risks. This covers equipment owned by you, usually against all risks up to the total replacement value of the equipment owned by the production company. Principal exclusions include confiscation by customs or security officials, wear, tear and deterioration, faulty manipulation of apparatus, mysterious disappearance (losses discovered only through stock-taking), theft by employees and damage during maintenance; losses from unattended vehicles will generally be subject to certain specific security conditions.

Cover can include electrical and mechanical breakdown, as well as specialized cover for aerial and water work. Theft cover may be restricted to forcible and violent entry. In the event of breakdown cover can be obtained for replacement equipment. Equipment can usually be covered for specific territorial locations.

Insurance cover can also be obtained for any hired-in equipment. This is often called all risks of physical loss and/or damage (hired equipment).

The policy provides an all-risks cover for a stated sum insured and covers all productions in any policy year.

Make sure your policy also includes cover for loss of use. This is cover for the loss of rental income to the hire company if their equipment is stolen or damaged. A minimum figure would usually be £30,000 over three months.

Policies can now include computer equipment. Hired equipment all-risks insurance can be taken out as annual cover based on the level of hiring charges or the number of productions you mount in any one year. An annual hired equipment policy is usually cheaper than taking out cover with hire companies every time you need equipment. The 'quick fax' of your policy can also speed things up as hire companies will insist on this before releasing equipment and can often insist on you taking their own cover. These will have excess levels. Don't forget to check the insurance requirements for hired equipment such as boats, cranes, planes, fork-lifts, MEWPS and plant such as generators, etc. Very often a condition of hiring specialized equipment is that the user has properly trained operatives to carry out the task.

Film and production insurance is often sold as a 'six-pack' called film producer's indemnity cover. This will include the following: pre-production indemnity and cast insurance, film producer's indemnity, consequential loss, abandonment risk extension, errors and omissions, and finally negative and tape stock insurance.

Pre-production indemnity cover indemnifies the production company against the additional costs that would be incurred if the production is held up or abandoned because of an accident, sickness or death of a specified person during shooting or beforehand. Good examples of this would include a leading director or main star in a feature film. Another example in documentary could include the director or main contributor. As some productions are pre-sold on the basis of a particular star or director, this cover is essential if they are forced to withdraw or delay their contribution through no fault of their own. It is usual to include an abandonment clause for extreme situations when a contributor is deemed irreplaceable. Such policies will usually involve medical checks and may contain specific clauses that forbid key members from undertaking risky activities or travelling together.

Film producer's indemnity will usually include cover against accident, illness and death to the insured person. Insurance can sometimes be obtained to include extra expenses incurred. For example **consequential loss cover** would be provided for extra expenses incurred due to the breakdown of a vital piece of equipment such as a camera or generator. This cover can be extended to any factor which would delay shooting and cause overrun. A good example would be the loss of an expensive set which would set the production back.

Commercial producer's indemnity provides the most extensive cover possible in respect of additional costs incurred during commercial film production, including any additional expenditure incurred due to an event insured under this policy over and above the budgeted costs. An insured event is any interruption, postponement, cancellation or abandonment of a production due to any cause beyond the production company's control and not excluded by the policy conditions. Cover is not provided for war, insolvency, radiation or nuclear explosion, adverse weather, insufficient light, unacceptable quality or content of the production, death or disablement of any person on whom the production substantially depends when engaged in either flying, hazardous feats, or performance (unless notified to the insurers) loss arising from the use of animals and any cause within the control of the production company, although some of these exclusions can be 'bought back'.

Negative and tape stock insurance provides coverage against loss or damage of master tapes and the extra re-shooting costs involved if this happens. This could be due to camera faults, being lost in transit or accidental damage during processing or transfer. It is essential that the policy is extended to include losses caused by faulty raw stock, faulty camera and processing risks. This is so the policy covers the negative through all its stages from raw stock to projection print. Such policies do not cover errors of judgement in exposure, lighting or sound recording, or from the use of incorrect types of camera lens, filters and wrong choice of raw film stock. Policies do not include either cover against war, nuclear contamination and losses caused by security checks at airports and confiscation of shot documentary material by police overseas.

The loss of original material would incur massive further cost so a contingency must be made against this. A good example would be of tapes being wiped by X-ray machines at airports. Such policies may include an immediate requirement to copy in order to reduce the risk. Film stock policies can be extended to include video/digital and audio tape.

Errors and omissions insurance can be included which indemnifies the producer and production company from any accidental extra legal costs. This could include third-party claims for possible slander, libel, defamation, infringement of copyright, plagiarism, invasion of privacy, incorrect use of formats, titles and ideas. This cover must be in place before first photography and will last through distribution, exhibition and exploitation in any medium. It is essential to take legal advice on this especially for exposé documentaries and fiction films based on real people or events.

Many productions will also carry a requirement for all-risks cover on sets, wardrobe and props. This will cover all such items against damage, fire and theft. This will include hired items or ones which are being constructed specially for the purpose. Special cover may be needed for props used in stunts and any firearms or weapons.

Major exclusions include mysterious disappearance of props, wardrobe items and antiques since these items are often only missed at the end of a production. Vehicles including planes, boats and cars can be included as long as they are static props. If they are action/moving vehicles then special insurance must be purchased and the legal requirements of normal motor or aircraft insurance must be adhered to.

Large films will also carry cover for cash in transit and fidelity guarantee. This is to guard against theft and fraud. Specific employees in key financial positions can be specifically covered such as production accountants and production managers.

Most productions must also carry union film insurance to cover employees for personal accident cover. If filming overseas this will be extended to include cover for cast and crew against sickness, personal accident and provide temporary cover for life insurance, medical expenses and loss of baggage.

Office insurance should be specially taken out to include production activity. Normal office policies will not insure some factors found in a production office – for example large amounts of computers, video equipment and cash. Get a special policy drawn up to cover your office for film production including protection of artists and third parties.

Note that all insurance policies are underwritten based on an accurate and truthful account of the facts given in the policy proposal. Any policy will be invalid if the information relevant to the likely risks has not been given. Submit a copy of the shooting script for your insurers to check any special risks. These include work with animals, children, people over 65, guns, explosives, fire, action vehicles, boats and planes. Similarly most policies will not cover negligence or accidents caused by alcohol and drug abuse or incidents caused by known medical conditions especially epilepsy and pregnancy. Policies will not cover travel by plane, stunts and the carriage of actors in private cars. Always check your policy exclusions and brief your crew accordingly. Don't forget to include medical insurance and emergency repatriation medical cover when filming overseas.

All relevant facts should be given and any changes notified in writing. For example, policies will have territorial limits and date restrictions that conform to the production period and geographical location of the production. Notify any changes to your broker immediately.

Directory of insurance brokers

Aegis Insurance Brokers Ltd
Thrale House, 44–46 Southwark Street, London SE1 1UN
Tel: 0171–397–5081

Allan Chapman & James
652 The Crescent, Colchester Business Park, Colchester, Essex CO4 4YQ
Tel: 01206–505040

John Ansell and Partners (specialist diving insurance brokers)
Overseas House, 19–23 Ironmonger Row, London EC1V 3QN
Tel: 0171–251–6821

Aon Entertainment Risk Services
Pinewood Studios, Pinewood Rd, Iver Heath, Bucks SL0 0NH
Tel: 01753–658200

John Charcol (media and entertainment)
10–12 Great Queen St, Holborn, London WC2B 5DD
Tel: 0171–611–7000

Arthur Dobson (Brokers) Ltd
219–225 Slade Lane, Levenshulme, Manchester M19 2EX
Tel: 0161–225–9060

Entertainment Insurance Brokers Ltd
1 Kingly St, London W1R 6HU
Tel: 0171–287–5054

Heath Fielding International Ltd
133 Houndsditch, London EC3A 7AH
Tel: 0171–234–4000

Bain Hogg
Digby House, Causton Road, Colchester, Essex CO1 1YS
Tel: 01206–577612

Hogg Robinson Pas Ltd
17 Burley Way, Leicester LE1 3BH
Tel: 0116–251–1555

Hanover Park Commercial
Greystoke House, 80–86 Westow St, London SE19 3AQ
Tel: 0181–771–8844

RHH-Albert G Ruben Insurance Brokers
Braintree House, Braintree Rd, Ruislip, Middx HA4 0YA
Tel: 0181–841–4461

Rollins Hudig Hall Entertainment
Admin Block, Pinewood Studios, Pinewood Rd, Iver, Bucks SL0 0NH
Tel: 01753–654555

SLE Worldwide
1 Minster Court, Mincing Lane, London EC3R 7AA
Tel: 0171–283–1033

Stafford Knight Entertainment Insurance Brokers
18 London St, London EC3R 7JP
Tel: 0171–265–1717

Stevenson Price Insurance Brokers Ltd
134 Tooley St, London SE1 2TU
Tel: 0171–407–2396

Sutton Winson
St James House, Grosvenor Road, Twickenham, Middx TW1 4AJ
Tel: 0181–891–4021

Part Two

Hazards

Hazard 1: Agricultural locations

In Europe it is estimated that over 18 million injuries including 3600 fatal accidents occur in agriculture each year.

HSE newsletter, No. 87, Feb. 1993

The legislation

The Agriculture (Field Machinery) Regulations 1962
Control of Substances Hazardous to Health Regulations 1988, 1992 (COSHH)
The Health and Safety (First Aid) Regulations 1981
The Health and Safety at Work Act 1974
The Management of Health and Safety at Work Regulations 1992
The Manual Handling Operations Regulations 1992
The Noise at Work Regulations 1989
The Personal Protective Equipment at Work Regulations 1992
The Health and Safety (Safety Signs and Signals) Regulations 1996
The Wildlife and Countryside Act 1881

The risks

- animals
- asbestos
- chemicals
- children
- communication
- confined spaces
- contamination
- deep tanks
- derelict/unsafe structures

- dust/respiration
- electricity
- elevators
- exposure to cold
- exposure to heat
- foot damage-nails etc.
- fire
- head risk – falling objects
- isolation of location
- machinery
- manual handling
- moving vehicles
- noise
- poor visibility/night work
- silos
- slips, trips and falls
- stacks
- vermin risk
- working alone
- working at height

Those most at risk

Countryside programme crews, regional magazine crews, news and drama crews. Especially those working alone and children.

To the city dweller, agricultural locations appear Arcadian and benign. However, farms can be potentially dangerous working environments as they have many inherent risks of their own and agricultural activity is carried out most hours of the clock. Introducing production activity into an already hazardous environment multiplies the risk factor.

The unfamiliar nature of the agricultural environment increases this risk factor, so always recce them first once permission has been sought from the owners. Then carry out a risk assessment. A crew or performers should never be 'sent in to film' on a potentially dangerous agricultural location; simply not bothering to find out the risks constitutes gross negligence and becomes a high risk to the health and safety of your crew.

At this point stop and consider if a safer alternative location is available? Do you really need to use this particular farm location at all? Deciding to go somewhere else could be safer and cheaper.

Make sure you have a separate and adequate health and safety budget to take all the necessary precautions and protective measures. Pay particular attention to the special risks of isolation and working alone. Staff should always carry a lone worker's safety alarm.

Ask yourself and identify in writing who would be affected if you decide to film in a high risk agricultural environment: public, crew, employees, contractors? What measures and precautions should be taken to see that there is no risk to anybody's health and safety? The biggest cause of fatalities on farms is from moving vehicles, so extra care and visibility is essential during filming to eliminate this risk. Only trained operators should use agricultural machinery and make sure all crew are wearing high visibility clothing and that the location has adequate lighting.

Any significant risk to health and safety should be detected on the recce as part of the hazard identification and a risk assessment made to identify any danger. For example, check access points, gates and footpaths. Then the correct procedures should be followed to eliminate or control the risk before any filming activity is undertaken. A health and safety method statement should be produced to deal with any assessed risk and lay out exactly what procedure to follow for any identified hazard.

Your legal liability will depend on if you actually own, manage, control or temporarily occupy the premises. Under the Management of Health and Safety at Work Regulations 1992 it is important to determine the contractual relationship between the location owner, production company and crew: are they freelance or employed?

The HSE have also identified children as especially at risk in agricultural locations and have issued a special set of guidelines about the dangers (HSE-AS10). These should be read if planning to use children for filming on a farm location. Children should be warned from entering any danger areas and properly supervised at all times. No child under thirteen years should ride on or drive any tractors or farm machinery. Children should not enter oxygen deficient store areas such as silos, grain sheds, slurry stores, cesspits or tanks. They must not enter any pen inhabited by an animal. They should not be allowed to do any manual handling or come into contact with any chemicals (see also Hazard 7: Children).

Country based programmes such as *Peak Practice*, *Heartbeat* and the James Herriot series are very popular and farming topics such as blacksmiths and agricultural shows are often good material for news items. Farms are likely to be a popular location for drama and factual programme makers despite the high risks involved. These can be either risks inherent to the farmyard itself or from the terrain in which it is located.

The risk from an isolated location increases from factors such as altitude of location, poor access, poor communication and poor weather.

This is an uncontrolled environment and the risk from exposure would increase dramatically on marsh/moor land/mountain farms, especially if you are shooting a long way from habitation. Check the site first for factors such as access/drainage/wind protection. Remember that a sudden change in the weather could turn a safe location into a dangerous one.

Make sure you provide adequate shelter/toilet and wash facilities, light/heat and food on site in accordance with section 2 of the Health and Safety at Work Act 1974 relating to the proper welfare of employees in a workplace situation.

Elevation increases the risk of stress and fatigue of having to move any equipment to the site. Manual handling issues arise because of the likely distance involved and the terrain, e.g. gates/fences/narrow paths. Also watch out for slips, trips and falls caused by slippery surfaces, pot holes, rabbit holes, mole hills, etc.

Make sure that equipment is kept to minimum or is as light as possible. Ensure that enough carrying equipment is available for manual handling and lifting. Allow extra time in the shooting schedule for this and making sure that you can de-rig and return well before dark. Have emergency lighting available.

Another factor to consider is the physical fitness of the crew, contributors and actors to carry out what you are asking them to do, such as move camera equipment and generators or imitate demanding rural sequences. You should also consider the effect your activity would have on neighbouring land or animals.

Make sure your vehicles are road-worthy with spare tyre/tow rope/ spare petrol/and suitable for the terrain (HSE-AIS-11). Have a good, accurate map and a contact number for the location. Check on the weather conditions and take plenty of warm clothing. Extra protective clothing required would include waterproofs, hard boots and wellingtons, hard hats, gloves and visibility jackets.

Make sure that you have first aid kit which is more comprehensive than usual because of the isolated location, and an agreed emergency procedure if you remain out of contact for more than an agreed safe period.

In case of emergency, always carry a compass, distress flare and waterproof torches. Take back-up communication which will work in the terrain with spare and fully charged batteries. If in doubt seek advice from local experts such as farmers, park authority, emergency services and mountain rescue. Try to avoid working alone (see also Hazard 12: Dangerous terrain).

Inherent risks

In farmyards there are certain risks inherent within the structures of the buildings and the animals, plant and machinery which they contain. Always seek permission from the farmer or landowner first. Seek their advice as they will be familiar with the risks on their property. Good advance warning means they can also make sure that all animals and farm guard dogs have been contained during filming. Obey the country code and always close gates. Beware of the unique hazards presented by animals who may be frightened by your activity, especially during the mating season or when with young. Avoid the use of bright lights and loud noises.

Make sure you are aware of any dangerous animals such as bulls and keep equipment clear of pens and vehicle pathways. Avoid filming at busy periods where large scale animal movements are likely such as feeding and milking times (see also Hazard 2: Animals).

Make sure you are aware of the fire risks from introducing hot lights and electrical equipment into an environment which has a lot of straw dry grain and wood. Take adequate fire precautions and seek advice about the location of any fire hazards. Never smoke and drop matches or cigarette ends. Avoid filming and undertaking low flying, driving or crane operations during stubble burning as visibility is poor and the fire risk is high.

Working at heights to get good shots is tempting, with stacks, silos and ladders offering a choice of dangerous situations. Farm buildings often have fragile roofs therefore the risks from working at height are great without prior knowledge of the load bearing capacity and taking precautions to secure yourself and the equipment.

Cameras should be secured with safety lines and anybody working at height should have a safety line/harness/fall-arrest device and a hard hat. Crawl ladders or duck boards should be used after the loading capacity of the roof has been checked. Nobody should walk below the area and warning signs should indicate that filming is taking place. Take special care about filming on straw bale stacks which can fall or be toppled by hoists or cranes.

A sensible precaution would be to have at least one team member watching out for hazards and to protect the camera operator while filming as camera operators may be partially sighted or sound operators partially hard of hearing when undertaking concentrated filming. Hence they are more at risk and unable to take avoiding action from falling debris/moving farm machinery or animals.

There is a risk of falling debris from semi-derelict buildings which is another hard hat situation. Floors may be rotten with a risk of falling through. Derelict buildings may also contain chemical or petrol deposits.

The floor may also have nails, glass and exposed electrical cable. Make sure you have the right footwear and that staff have had tetanus jabs, particularly for puncture wounds from barbed wire.

Beware of cross-contamination from chicken and turkey deposits. Also from pigeons, vermin deposits and rats. Pregnant women should not be allowed to come into contact with mammals who have recently given birth as there is a risk of zoonotic infections which can cause miscarriage in humans. This is a very high risk in an agricultural location and potential crew, actors or participants should be warned about this (HSE-AIS2).

Never enter prohibited or controlled areas where there is risk of cross infection or contamination, such as pig breeding units, without complying with the personal protective clothing regulations. To reduce the risk of cross infection, always wear wellington boots that can be hosed down and take a shower and wash your hands after working with or near animals. Always obey warning signs relating to infection control for chicken and pig breeding units. Cattle and rats carry risks of leptospirosis (HSE-INDG84 and AIS5 and AIS19). Occupational health risks from working closely with animals or their environment should be properly assessed including the risk of any allergies.

Exposure to asbestos could also be a risk, especially in derelict buildings (see Hazard 3: Asbestos). Never clamp lights to pipes as they might contain asbestos, high pressure gases or liquids.

Slurry pits, cesspits and tanks are usually oxygen deficient and toxic. These storage areas can contain nitrogen dioxide and other gases (HSE-AIS9 and AIS15). Other potentially toxic locations include fowl manure and mushroom compost. Use a portable gas analyser such as an Extox to detect the presence of any gas and carry a Gasbadge personal gas alarm to detect and warn of the presence of gas and toxic fumes. Deep tanks may give off overpowering toxic fumes so breathing apparatus should be used and never work alone in this situation. Carry a lone worker's safety alarm.

Dry crop storage areas such as silos, feed bins, fruit and grain stacks are usually oxygen deficient to preserve the contents. Therefore there is a high risk of asphyxiation. Never try to open shutes or gates as the contents are heavy and can bury you very quickly.

Grain stacks and silos are especially dangerous. Never enter these as the contents act like quicksand and will kill you very quickly if you fall in. Harvesting situations, potato and grain stores have the risk from dust and pollen which could require the use of respiratory protectors and suits (HSE-AIS3 and INDG140).

Particular crops such as yellow rape seed may be risky for asthma sufferers. Since 1983, 623 cases of occupational asthma have been caused by exposure to grain dust and flour. Always wear the proper respiratory protective equipment and masks. Management should also monitor workers with asthma and not expose them to dusty situations and hot work.

Dusty situations also contain the risk of fire and explosion from electrical equipment and smoking, especially after spells of dry weather or prolonged storage.

Farms have chemicals and gases covered by the COSHH regulations (HSE-AIS28 and AIS16). These should be stored properly and do not introduce other chemical hazards or ignition risks near chemical storage areas (see Hazard 6: Chemicals). Beware of and do not move or open unmarked drums of chemicals. They could be very dangerous. Do not expose yourself or others to fumes or toxic substances. Wear protective clothing in the vicinity of sheep dips, pesticides and chemical spraying. Beware of spray drift from adjacent crop spraying activities. Do not smoke or use electrical equipment in the vicinity of chemical stores, drums or containers. Farm machinery such as sprayers have chemical residue which may contaminate you and tractors have petrol and diesel fumes which can be explosive and toxic.

Always work with a competent electrician as farm locations have high voltage power supplies and power take-off shafts (HSE-AIS17 and AIS24). Never work across phases and check any socket or supply first with a circuit tester before trying to connect any electrical equipment. Try and use stepped down transformers and fit all equipment with circuit breakers. Make sure you site all electrical and hot equipment away from fire hazards. Beware as well of low-slung, high-voltage lines if you are working at height/using a long boom/crane or high-sided vehicle especially at night (HSE-AIS8 and MISC049). Make sure you locate equipment and cables a safe distance from any animals and protect them behind barriers and cable ducts. Beware of contact with electric fences around pens and fields. Farm machinery is high risk on account of its power and the potential to become trapped. So avoid loose clothing and always have someone watch your back. Keep a good distance between yourself and working machinery, especially moving pea viners, balers, combines, and trailers. Avoid working near rotary flail hedge-cutters and chain saws. Farm machinery is often very noisy and can cause ear damage so ear protection must be worn near moving machinery, vehicles and hoists.

Be alert for switches which may activate machinery by accident. Never try and operate anything yourself. Make sure you understand safety signing and keep out of prohibited areas. Do not tamper with any taps, valves or shutes. Wear the correct goggles in proximity to working machinery. Always be alert for moving vehicles such as tractors/tankers/ lorries and fork lift trucks. Never be tempted to use farm vehicles to film from without proper advice and supervision. They can be very dangerous and should not be used to film from or be used as working platforms without proper overloading and overturning risks being assessed. Tampering with strange levers can cause accidents. Beware of farm vehicles such as pea viners and combines with extended blades and arms which could knock over lighting and scaffolds. Take extra care at night to make sure you are visible to moving farm vehicles and comply with the traffic regulations for farm vehicles and abnormal loads. if in doubt contact your local police abnormal loads officer or the NFU. Make sure you have high visibility clothing, especially in poor visibility and night conditions. Beware of slip and trip hazards due to uneven surfaces, frozen water and waste. Make sure that you wear high visibility clothing and warm jackets, especially during the winter period and while filming at night, as the visibility reduces and the temperature drops. When filming at night always make sure that you have adequate lighting and back-up torches. Never go unaccompanied into animal pens or fields which contain animals. Seek advice from the farmer or keeper before attempting any filming, especially during culling or lambing season. Agricultural sites are a classic example of an inherently dangerous location with many dormant hazards, therefore care should be taken when filming and a proper risk assessment made before commencing. A health and safety method statement should be produced to deal with any identified risk and lay out exactly what procedure to follow for any potential hazards in liaison between the farmer and safety officer.

Further reading

Robert J. Koester, *Outdoor First Aid*, (Zou 3) and Robert J. Koester, *Wilderness and Rural Life Support Guidelines* (Wil 2), both available from Emergency Response Publications, 5 Shelly Court, South Zeal, Okehampton, Devon EX20 2PT, Tel: 01837–840102.

Prevention and Control of Dust Explosions, RC12, 1991, available from the Loss Prevention Council, Melrose Avenue, Borehamwood, Hertfordshire.

The HSE have published approximately 40 different free guides to different health and safety aspects on farms. Consult section 3.14 in HSE free publications catalogue.

Preventing Accidents to Children in Agriculture, Approved Code of Practice and Guidance Notes, HSE COP24, ISBN 0-11-883997-7.
Code of Practice for the Safe Use of Pesticides on Farms and Holdings, HSC/ MAFF HMSO, ISBN 0-11-242892-4.
Guidance on Storing Pesticides for Farmers and Other Users, HSE-AIS16, 1996.
Pesticides 1999, Pesticides Safety Directorate, ISBN 0-11-243048-1.
HSE, Farm Wise – Your Guide to Health and Safety, 1992, ISBN 0-11-882107-5.
HSE, Grain Dust, 1993, ISBN 0-11-882101-6.

The Occupational Zoonoses, HSE Books, 1993, ISBN 0-11-886397-5.
A Guide to Producing a Farm COSHH Assessment, HSE leaflet IACL81.
The Health and Safety (Safety Signs and Signals) Regulations 1996, HSE 1996, L64,
  ISBN 0-7176-0870-0.

Contact organizations

ATB-Landbase (formerly Agricultural Training Board)
Customer Services Unit, National Agricultural Centre
Kenilworth, Warwickshire CV8 2LG
Tel: 01203–416178

British Agrochemicals Association
4 Lincoln Court, Lincoln Rd, Peterborough PE1 2RP
Tel: 01733–349225

The Country Landowners' Association
16 Belgrave Square, London SW1X 8PQ
Tel: 0171–2350511

The Countryside Commission
John Dower House, Crescent Place, Cheltenham, Gloucestershire
GL50 3RA
Tel: 01242–521381

The Environment Agency
Rie House, Waterside Drive, Bristol BS32 4UD
Tel: 01454–624400

The Forestry and Arboricultural Safety and Training Council (FASTCO)
231 Corstorhine Rd, Edinburgh, Scotland EH12 7AT
Tel: 0131–314–6193

The Forestry Commission of Great Britain
231 Corstorhine Rd, Edinburgh, Scotland EH12 7AT
Tel: 0131–3343047

The Forestry Contracting Association Ltd
Dafling, Blairduff, Inverurie, Aberdeenshire, Scotland AB51 5AL
Tel: 01467–651595

Ministry of Agriculture Fisheries and Food
Safety Unit, Hook Rise South, Surbiton, Surrey KT6 7NF
Tel: 0181–330–8075

HSE Agricultural National Interest Group Unit
Stoneleigh, Kenilworth, Warwickshire CV8 2LZ
Tel: 01203–696518

National Association of Agricultural Contractors
Huts Corner, Tilford Rd, Hindhead, Surrey GU26 6SF
Tel: 01428–605360

National Farmers Union
164 Shaftesbury Avenue, London WC2H 8HL
Tel: 0171–331–7200

RSPCA Headquarters
Causeway, Horsham, Sussex RH12 1HG
Tel: 01403–264181
For advice, contact Chief Veterinary Officer or Inspectorate
Department.

National Parks Authority

Ten National Parks in England and Wales; contact information offices:

Brecon Beacons National Park
7 Glamorgan St, Brecon, Powys, Wales LD3 7DP
Tel: 01874–62443-Ex-238

Dartmoor National Park Authority
Parke, Bovey Tracey, Newton Abbot, Devon TQ13 9JQ
Tel: 01626–832093

Exmoor National Park
Exmoor House, Dulverton, Somerset, TA22 9HL
Tel: 01398–323665

Lake District National Park
Murley Moss, Oxenholme Rd, Kendal, Cumbria LA9 7RL
Tel: 01539–724555, × 236

Northumberland National Park
Eastburn, South Park, Hexham, Northumberland NE46 1BS
Tel: 01434–605–555

North Yorkshire Moors National Park
The Old Vicarage, Bondgate, Helmsley, N. Yorkshire YO6 5BP
Tel: 01439–770657

Peak Park Joint Planning Board
Aldern House, Baslow Rd, Bakewell, Derbyshire, DE45 1AE
Tel: 01629 816200

Pembrokeshire Coast National Park
County Offices, St Thomas Green, Haverfordwest, Dyfed, Wales
SA61 1QZ
Tel: 01437–764591

Snowdonia National Park
Penrhyndeudraeth, Gwynedd, Wales LL48 6LS
Tel: 01766–770274

Yorkshire Dales National Park
Hedben Rd, Grassington, Skipton, North Yorkshire BD23 5LB
Tel: 01756–752748

Hazard 2: Animals

In October 1994 the family of the actor Roy Kinnear won £650,000 in damages after the actor fell off a horse and died of his injuries during the filming of *The Return of the Three Musketeers* in 1988.

The legislation

The Protection of Animals Act 1911
The Performing Animals (Regulation) Act 1925
The Cinematograph Films (Animals) Act 1937
The Dangerous Wild Animals Act 1976
The Health and Safety at Work Act 1974
The Management of Health and Safety at Work Regulations 1992
The Personal Protective Equipment (PPE) at Work Regulations 1992
The Wildlife and Countryside Act 1881

The risks

- audience
- bites/scratches
- children/elderly/pregnant women
- contamination
- death
- inexperience
- leptospirosis/Weil's disease
- phobia
- psittacosis
- the public
- serious injury
- multiple injuries
- stunts
- venomous injury

Those most at risk

Countryside programme crews, fiction film actors, regional magazine crews, news crews, veterinary and wildlife programme makers. Special risks to audiences, pregnant women and the disabled.

Animal programmes have always been popular viewing with documentaries about circuses, police dogs, shire horses and vets, not to mention programmes such as Crufts, *One Man and his Dog* and show jumping. The risk involved in working with animals can vary from being trampled on to being bitten. The risk can come from programmes where animals are an integral part of the action, for example programmes about circuses, farms, horse racing and wildlife.

The risk can also be unexpected, for example earlier this year BBC cameraman Peter Powell was attacked and bitten by a Rottweiler belonging to the late MP Alan Clark.

The scale of the risk is not always commensurate with the size of the animal, for example the placidity of a large shire horse compared with the venomous capacity of a small snake.

The use of the animal could be quite simple, for example a single shot of a rabbit or an actor walking his dog up a driveway. In simple cases, assistance and advice may not be necessary, but if the use of the animal is more complex then consultation before production activity begins between the producer and the experts is necessary.

In practice this means prior consultation with an experienced and reputable agency. This allows the agency to select the correct animal and handler for the action which the director requires, rather than attempting shots which may be impossible. Always make sure that the agency is licensed and has the correct insurance cover (for example, against bites and knocking over equipment). This should include insurance for any vehicle which the agency may introduce onto the set. Never cut corners by using a friend's or an untrained animal. If you pay peanuts you get monkeys! An experienced agency will save you time and money in the long run.

A properly trained animal is not the same as an animal experienced in doing film work, which requires intense concentration and the ability to perform a precise repetitive action or noise. In other words, getting an animal to reproduce something it does in real life is a staged emulation not simple reproduction. So make sure you record the rehearsal – it may be your best take due to the unpredictable nature of animals when confronted with a new or strange environment.

Figure H2.1　© *Cop and Dog Services*

Employ a proper handler (not the owner) to carry out commands. Directors should realize that animals are not props and have no doubles, so they should not be called until required to minimize waiting time and have proper rest periods, especially in hot conditions. Directors who are used to perfection may well not get perfectly reproduced sequences with animals if their demands are unrealistic. The director should also make sure that any actors which they use are experienced with working with that particular animal and have no phobias or allergies.

Consult the RSPCA headquarters (see Contact organizations at the end of this section) in the first instance for advice on the proposed use to make sure a control plan is prepared which takes into account the safe welfare of the animal and the suitability of the use to which it is proposed. This should be approved and the correct information circulated to all concerned with the production.

The RSPCA may well feel that the presence on location of an inspector is necessary for consultation and advice. A local veterinary surgeon may be needed and the keeper or supplier of the animals must be fully qualified and trained to handle the animal concerned with proper arrangements made for its welfare and the heath and safety of the crew and members of the public.

Producers who contemplate the use of animals in productions should understand the rules and legislation which will apply to them.

Producers must always inform the environmental health office of their local authority before a dangerous animal is contracted for a production. These are animals listed under the Dangerous Wild Animals Act 1976 and a list is available from your local environmental health office. You need a licence to use a dangerous or wild animal and a vet must be present on set.

Under the Protection of Animals Act 1911 it is illegal to inflict pain or suffering to any animal. Any film which intends to imitate or suggest this also has to inform the local authority. Any film which has actually done so can be prosecuted under the Cinematograph Films (Animals) Act 1937. Producers should be especially careful not to suggest cruelty or mistreatment to animals in programmes for children. Never attempt to try and drug, sedate or tranquillize an animal. This is illegal and strictly prohibited by the Royal College of Veterinary Surgeons.

The risks involved with animals can be very high. They can vary from falling off a horse to being attacked by a wild animal. The risk can be either due to the type of animal you are going to use or what you trying to do with it. There is also the effect this may have on the animal translated into behaviour likely to injure third parties such as actors, crew or audience. This is a particular danger when there is risk to members of the public. Always reduce the number of crew, onlookers and the public to a minimum and increase the number of handlers and keepers to ensure good health and safety, especially when filming with wild animals. Only the handler should control and come into contact with the animal.

Any bites, scratches or injuries should be reported immediately. Keep any animal which bites, or scratches with its mouth, teeth or claws away from faces and hands. Any crew and handlers must have the correct vaccinations and inoculations before the production begins. Always wash your hands after working with animals to prevent cross-infection with food or work surfaces.

Producers should always check that they have the correct insurance and that any dangerous animals are supplied by a licensed keeper or authorized supplier who carries proper insurance. If an animal is being used for stunts, the keeper should be an approved stunt arranger and the participants approved stunt artists. For example any drivers for carriage or sleigh stunts or horse riders should be fully qualified and insured.

Never involve members of the public in an animal stunt or use untrained animals supplied by a member of the public. Make sure that the animals are the best trained and securely contained. An individual risk assessment should always be made and an individual control plan worked out. A health and safety method statement should be produced to deal with any identified risk and it should lay out exactly what procedure to follow for any identified animal hazard.

If you are working with dangerous or wild animals, the supplier and keeper should have a dangerous and wild animals licence, under the Dangerous Wild Animals Act 1976. The supplier and trainer of the animal should be experienced and qualified. Always submit in advance a script and floor plan of the intended use with details of camera and lighting positions. The location of presenters, crew and the public in relation to the animal should always be marked. The supplier and keeper should then perform their own risk assessment and any changes built into the script and the control plan. Once this has been agreed no sudden changes should be made without proper consultation of all concerned with health and safety.

The control plan should be made in advance and written into the risk assessment along with the advice of any experts such as keepers/vets/ supplier/stunt arrangers and zoological staff. The RSPCA have issued their own guidelines on the use of animals in filming which should be consulted before proceeding.

Animals should have the correct cage which is large enough to ensure their health and welfare and yet provide protection for the public. The correct muzzle and harness should be used to satisfy legal requirements and ensure control of the animal with no danger to the public or the good welfare of the animal. The animals should have the necessary veterinary safeguards, inoculations, grooming and certificates. If in doubt seek advice from an expert or the RSPCA about the correct inoculations, housing and harness. When animals are in transit, proper bedding, ventilation, food and water should be provided with rest breaks to reduce stress to the animal. The control plan should take into account the nature of the animal and what you are going to do and take into account the health and welfare of the animal along with the location risks.

All the crew, audience and presenters should be familiar with this plan in advance of filming and an emergency procedure should be in place. Closed set notices should be in place and extra handlers in place before filming begins. Try to avoid animal action with an audience. If necessary record this section first before the audience is allowed in. The crew should also be provided with the correct personal protective clothing such as safety suits, visors, boots and gloves. Everybody should be briefed by the keeper about what to avoid and how best to pacify the animal, for example, avoid sudden movement, noises and light. Beware of risk from the audience, music, power tools, cars or planes. Remember that some animals have acute hearing and that an air conditioning system which is hardly detectable to human ears may be distressing to a cat.

Any actors or presenters working with animals should be properly briefed and qualified. Actors who do animal stunts can be found in Equities Spotlight Register of Stunt Performers. Check to see if they hold membership of a relevant society. They should be given a copy of the script, the intended use, activity and a copy of the control plan at an early stage. If necessary a 'double' who is a qualified handler should be used where any significant risk exists.

The set, studio or location should be closed with a permit-to-work system in place. Warning notices should read 'Danger, work with dangerous animals in progress'. Precautions may also have to be taken to prevent any dangerous animal escaping.

Filming time should be kept to a minimum and the animal properly fed and watered to avoid it becoming too hot and antagonistic. Always ensure the room is cool and that the animal has a clean water supply. Film early morning in the morning in summer where possible to reduce the risk of heat. It is best to keep any animal in a separate and quiet rest place until needed. Then rehearse quickly and efficiently keeping studio time (and so stress time to an animal in an unfamiliar environment) to a minimum. Ample protection for the audience should be in place in the form of adequate barrier protection and escape routes. The audience should have a proper briefing about what is going to happen and the evacuation procedure. Special attention should be paid to the likelihood of danger or risk to any contributors or audience who are elderly/young/handicapped. Their low capacity to escape or avoid danger quickly is a higher risk especially where fast moving animals are concerned. Beware of this risk, especially in programmes about or which may involve guide dogs. Make sure disadvantaged members of the public or contributors have a chaperone and are placed as near to an exit as possible. If necessary, appoint a member of the floor management team and ushers with special responsibility for anybody identified at high risk by the risk assessment.

You should also make sure that no members of the intended crew or audience have a particular phobia about the type of animal you are going to film. Contamination risk problems can come from a number of areas, for example disease through being bitten, so make sure all your crew and presenters have recent tetanus and polio jabs. Pregnant women should not be allowed to come into contact with mammals who have recently given birth as there is a risk of zoonotic infections which can cause miscarriage in humans.

Avoid contamination and infestation risk through contact with the animal or its bedding. Use protective equipment and gloves. Ideally any straw or bedding should also be fire-proofed in accordance with safety regulations for design and scenery. Alternatively where fire proofed bedding could cause poisoning to the animal, extra fire precautions would have to be put in place in agreement with the fire authorities.

There is a contamination risk from pigeons, which can pass on psittacosis, and from other birds' droppings. This can be a risk to crews working on roofs, scaffolds, in confined lofts, public squares and parks. This can be particularly concentrated in pigeon lofts and sea cliffs or where large concentrations of birds are present such as aviaries. All surfaces must be disinfected and staff involved should wear the correct personal protective equipment.

Beware of contamination from micro-organisms, especially from rats which can pass on leptospirosis (other rodents can't). This is known as Weil's disease and is caught via rats' urine and passed on through contaminated water, cuts, bites or scratches. This last hazard is extremely dangerous and is an ever present high risk in any production that is filming in/near water. Current affairs and news crews should be aware of the risk near drains and sewers and leisure film crews on water locations. This risk is also present in derelict buildings and farms. This risk should be identified during the location finding process and protective equipment made available. Make sure all crew have had recent inoculations and tetanus jabs. A vaccination is available against Weil's disease and a spray can be used after infection is suspected. Never underestimate the strength of large animals and the speed of small animals when frightened. Even apparently tame domestic pets can be dangerous if provoked and tend to defecate when frightened. Therefore try and use a concealed camera where possible and keep as much distance as possible by the use of a specialized lens. If undertaking specialized wild life filming, employ experienced guides and minimize risks. Take advice from experts in that area and keep a supply of antidotes and blood. Beware also of weather risks from isolated outdoor locations. Farm or wild animals can be dangerous in their own environment and are an inherent hazard of the location, while animals and animals stunts which are brought onto sets or into studios or locations are an introduced hazard. Both are high risk situations for the film crew and third parties. Make a proper risk assessment of any overflying activity over animals that can cause panic or distress.

Horses are used a lot for films and television. If a horse stunt is contemplated, the producer should perform a risk assessment and consult experts. Some members of the Equity Stunt Register are qualified to perform or supervise horse stunts. These members have passed and hold current certificates in one of the following: the Grade 3 award from the British Horse Society; the Grade 4 award from the Riding Club; the 'A' test standard of the Pony Club; or the Equity Stunt Register horse riding qualification.

Never ask an unqualified actor or member of the public to ride a horse, drive a horse-driven vehicle or perform a horse stunt.

Always make sure that the terrain is level and free from hidden obstructions or ditches when the site for a horse stunt is selected.

Enough pick-up and outriders should be employed to round up stray animals and emergency preparations put in place in the event of a runaway or fall. Proper first aid and more advanced medical facilities should be in place along with protected edges and fall bags. Make sure the area selected is a closed set with good barrier protection to keep out members of the public. Barbed wire fences should have rubber caps. All weapons should be props. Avoid the use of an area where there might be the risk of a stampede as a result of sudden noise from an aircraft or the proximity of other horses. Always use trained horses for the intended purpose such as jumping or racing. For wagon chases, always ensure that the horse can run free before crash simulations and use a breakaway rail for fence accidents.

Never use spurs, reins or whips to try and get a horse to perform and never trip a horse to try and obtain a fall. Always ensure proper feeding, watering and safe corralling for the welfare of the horse. If in any doubt consult the RSPCA or the British Horse Society.

Always carry out a thorough recce and perform a risk assessment before undertaking any filming which involves animals. If you decide to go ahead, consult the experts and control the risks by putting measures in place to protect yourself and members of the public.

Further reading

RSPCA Guide: The Use of Animals in Filming, A Guide on Basic Procedure (produced jointly by the RSPCA and the British Film and Television Producers' Association, 1985) available free.

The Occupational Zoonoses, HSE Books, ISBN 0-11-886397-5.

HSE, Zoos: Safety, Health and Welfare Standards for Employers and Persons at Work, Approved Code of Practice and Guidance Notes, 1985, COP 15, ISBN 0-11-883811-3.

Working with Animals in Entertainment, HSE information sheet, Entertainment Sheet no. 4, 1996.

BBC Guidelines, Working with Animals.

Contact organizations

The British Horse Society
Stoneleigh Deer Park, Kenilworth, Warwickshire CV8 2XZ
Tel: 01926–707700

The British Film and Producers' Association
162–170 Wardour St, London W1V 4LA
Tel: 0171–4307700

Cop and Dog Services
25 Gunners Park, Bishops Waltham, Hants SO32 1PD
Tel: 01489–893028

Equity Stunt Register, British Actors Equity
Guild House, Upper St Martins Lane, London WC2H 9EG.
Tel: 0171–379–6000

The Federation of Zoos
Zoological Gardens, Regent's Park, London NW1 4RY
Tel: 0171–586 0230

Janimals:2
13 Manor Rd South, Esher, Surrey KT10 0PY
Tel: 0181–398–2425

Ministry of Agriculture Fisheries and Food
Hook Rise South, Surbiton, Surrey KT6 7NF
Tel: 0181–330–4411

RSPCA Headquarters
Causeway, Horsham, Sussex RH12 1HG
Tel: 01403–264181
For advice, contact Chief Veterinary Officer or Inspectorate
Department.

Royal College of Veterinary Surgeons
Belgravia House, 62–64 Horseferry Rd, London SW1P 2AF
Tel: 0171–222–2001

Royal Zoological Society of London
Tel: 0171–722–3333

Hazard 3: Asbestos

In December 1996, Pinewood Studios (UK) and Paramount Pictures (UK) were fined £10,000 plus costs for exposing 100 actors and crew to potentially lethal asbestos dust. During the shoot, asbestos pipe insulation was unwittingly disturbed by members of the film crew at a disused electricity generating building. The case highlights the need for adequate risk assessments before any work is undertaken.

Stage, Screen and Radio, Feb. 1997 p. 6

RPS Thompson Ltd has been fined £3500 with costs of £2664 after it admitted causing its subcontractor to breach asbestos regulations and for failing to protect persons not in its employment against risks from exposure to asbestos. The prosecution followed an incident in November 1997 when asbestos was discovered in pipework in Elstree Studios.

Health and Safety Bulletin, May 1999, p. 3

The legislation

The Asbestos (Licensing) (Amendment) Regulations 1998
The Asbestos (Licensing) Regulations 1983
The Asbestos (Prohibition) Regulations 1992
The Asbestos Products (Safety) Amendment Regulations 1987
The Asbestos Products (Safety) Regulations 1985
The Control of Asbestos at Work (Amendment) Regulations 1998 (CAWR)
The Control of Asbestos at Work Regulations (Amendment) SI/1992
The Control of Pollution (Special Waste) Regulations 1980
The Chemical (Hazard Information and Packaging) Regulations 1993
The Road Traffic (Carriage of Dangerous Substances in Packages, etc.) Regulations 1986
The Construction (Health, Safety and Welfare) Regulations (CHSWR) 1996

The Environmental Protection Act 1990
The Health and Safety at Work Act 1974
The Management of Health and Safety at Work Regulations 1992
The Personal Protective Equipment (PPE) at Work Regulations 1992
The Reporting of Injuries, Diseases and Dangerous Occurrences
Regulations 1995 (RIDDOR)

The risks

- exposure
- inhalation
- death

Those most at risk

Film and drama actors and crews, news crews and documentary film makers. Special risk for builders, electricians, lighting crew, location finders/managers, production managers and studio operations, vehicle maintenance fitters and documentary film makers making films about asbestos.

Special risk: accidentally disturbing un-encapsulated and hidden asbestos, particularly in insulating board and pipes.

Asbestos is a mineral fibre which was used in building and insulation material in the 1930s '40s and '50s. During the 1960s it was recognized as a source of asbestos cancer called mesothelioma. The increasing risk of asbestos was raised by documentary film makers (*First Tuesday*'s exposé of the Turner and Newall case). Akin to coal dust related cancers, mesothelioma is a time bomb ticking away inside the victim. It can grow for up to 12 years before becoming clinically detectable. This process can be latent for 30 years. The sharp fibres become embedded in the victim's lungs. Survival after diagnosis is usually between 3 and 12 months. Some 1000 deaths occur in Britain each year.

Care should be taken while filming as asbestos can also contaminate camera equipment.

New laws came into force in February 1999. These were the Asbestos (Licensing) (Amendment) Regulations 1998 and the Control of Asbestos at Work (Amendment) Regulations 1998. These increased protection for people working with asbestos following research from professor Julian Peto, a leading epidemiologist with the Institute of Cancer Research. Carpenters and electricians were identified as the largest group of workers at risk.

There are three main types of asbestos – containing either blue, brown and white fibres. Diseases caused by it are usually called asbestosis. Asbestos is usually safe until disturbed and exposed to the air. The risk from asbestos is very high during demolition work as unidentified concentrations of asbestos can be disturbed. From 24 November 1999, a Europe-wide ban was put on the use of white asbestos (chrysotile). Advice should be sought on the use of safe substitutes.

Asbestos can kill, and it can kill you. The risk of exposure to asbestos should be detected on the recce as part of the hazard identification and a risk assessment made to identify any danger. Then the correct procedures should be followed to eliminate or control the risk before any filming activity is undertaken. Immediate action should be taken to seal off the area and measures should be taken to prevent access. Erect warning signs at all access points, then contact an ACAD registered contractor. They will conduct a bulk air-sampling test to determine the following:

- What immediate action should be taken? Don't disturb it or let any one get near it by proper warning signs and barriers.
- Use a licensed contractor to conduct test sampling.
- What concentration is it? Identify control limits and action level.
- Who would be affected? Public, crew, employees, contractors.
- What measures and precautions should be taken to see that there is no risk to anybody's health and safety? Encapsulation, licensed removal, personal protective clothing, safe disposal.

The presence of asbestos is hard to identify as its appearance can be changed by surface coatings and heat. Asbestos is often hidden underneath surface material as it was often used as an insulation material or as fire-proof cladding. Working with insulating board, in particular, has been identified as high-risk work and been brought under the Asbestos (Licensing) Regulations 1983. Asbestos can be found in insulation materials like pipes and lagging, and also in motor vehicle brake linings, clutch linings, gaskets and the seat padding of motorbikes and scooters. Therefore motor vehicle fitters and garage staff can be at risk from the use of asbestos products. Non-asbestos brake linings are now available but these are not as effective at stopping heavy vehicles.

Asbestos was also used as a fire retardant. Therefore asbestos can be located in boilers, pipework, ceilings and heating plant.

Locations to beware of asbestos and where a high risk factor of exposure to asbestos can be found are churches, hospitals, schools, ships and power stations. Disused buildings can be a very high risk as the asbestos may have lain dormant for many years until your production activity disturbs it.

Asbestos was also used in building materials such as plaster and cement. This means that asbestos may be a risk in any building built or refurbished prior to the mid-1980s. Hence, disused cement manufacturing plans, factory sites, pipework and behind cladding are particularly prime locations. The main uses were insulation and sprayed coating, insulating board and asbestos cement, so other locations where asbestos might be found include older school buildings, hospitals, and any area which may have needed acoustic or thermal cladding including church bell towers, sound studios, stages, heating pipework and workshops in broadcasting and film production buildings.

If you suspect a location may contain asbestos, inform the location owner immediately. If in any doubt, assume that asbestos may be present until you can prove that it is not. Under the Control of Asbestos at Work Regulations 1987 and the Control of Asbestos at Work (Amendment) Regulations 1998, the employer and owner of the premises must make sure nobody can get near to it by sealing the area and putting warning signs up. Warning signs indicate the hazard and keeping people out prevents further risk.

Your legal liability will depend on if you actually own, manage, control or temporarily occupy the premises. Under the Management of Health and Safety at Work Regulations 1992 it is important to determine the contractual relationship between the location owner, production company and crew. Are they freelance or employed? It is obvious that a crew or performers should never just be 'sent in to film' on a potentially dangerous location, especially when there is an asbestos risk. In this situation, simply not bothering to find out constitutes gross negligence and possess a high risk to the health and safety of your crew.

A bulk air sampling test should be made to detect asbestos. This usually takes about 45 minutes and should only be carried out by a competent contractor. The employers or owner/occupiers must identify the presence of asbestos and inform the enforcing authority of any concentration of asbestos fibre present in the location. Employers and self-employed owners or occupiers of premises may do this without a licence. However, it is better to use competent HSE approved and licensed contractors to do any kind of asbestos detection and removal work. The air test is sent to a NATLAS or NAMAS (National Accreditation for Measurement and Sampling) approved laboratory.

From 1999, all laboratories carrying out asbestos related work will need to be accredited to EN45001 standard from the UK accreditation service. A report is produced which takes about seven days. NAMAS publish a directory of accredited asbestos sampling laboratories. The laboratory will produce an air monitoring report to indicate if there is any risk from exposure to asbestos and the level of risk present.

If this report is related to surveillance of employees, contractors or public health, the results summary must be kept for 40 years as part of occupational health records and at least for a minimum of five years in all other cases. In this respect asbestos can be a proximity hazard as the effects go beyond the immediate vicinity and can affect a large number of people. Producers and production companies can be exposed to compensation claims if actors, crew or the public are put in a location which has asbestos. Not knowing is no defence in law.

Once the analysis has been made, you can determine what action can be taken depending on the duration of the work, the level of concentration and the type of asbestos involved.

The three types of asbestos are:

- crocidolite (blue),
- amosite (brown), and
- white asbestos.

If possible you should get more original information about what type it is from the manufacturer or contractor who put the asbestos in the location.

The location risk assessment should show the location of any asbestos (preferably on a clear plan) with details of sampling tests and what measures you are going to adopt to contain the risk and prevent it from spreading (sealing is the first option): either from direct action or subsidiary action, as strict controls are placed on the wet stripping and disposal of asbestos waste, including any laundry and protective clothing worn by asbestos workers or contractors. Asbestos waste should be properly sealed and indelibly labelled. Its disposal must be made in accordance with the Control of Pollution (Special Waste) Regulations 1980 and the DOE Asbestos Wastes Management Paper no 18. A special consignment note for the carriage and disposal of hazardous wastes should be used and a notification of intention to dispose made to the hazardous wastes department of the local county council. Regulation 13 states that the carrier, disposal authority and site owner must keep a register of all hazardous waste for at least two years. Names of authorized carriers of asbestos waste can be obtained from the National Association of Waste Disposal Contractors (NAWDC) or the Asbestos Control and Abatement Division (ACAD).

The contractor must perform this risk assessment. Competent contractors are HSE licensed and are members of ACAD. If in doubt ask for a copy of their licence. If they are not licensed then the HSE must be notified at least 28 days in advance of an intention to work with asbestos and under the Control of Asbestos at Work Regulations 1987 you should notify the authorities of the name, address and telephone number of the notifier and their usual place of business, the type and maximum quantity of asbestos to be handled and their manufacturing origin, what activities this will involve, where the asbestos will be handled and the start date of the work.

A written control plan should identify what steps will be taken to reduce the exposure levels to the lowest reasonably practicable level through the use of respiratory equipment. All employees should be given proper information and training in the use of protective equipment. Any risk to the health of your employees or subcontractors should be identified and removed.

Those most at risk from asbestos are:

- lighting crew who may use clamps on walls and pipework;
- electricians who may disturb old insulation and fixings;
- stunt arrangers and scenery artists who are modifying vehicles, handling materials and altering locations;
- maintenance and building repair staff in broadcasting buildings, premises and studios are at high risk from accidental exposure to asbestos dust by disturbing hidden concentrations of the fibre which are un-marked on building plans.

A prime example is encapsulated asbestos located in studio grids and walls. Workers should be unable to physically access these locations.

Always seek advice from a competent contractor first as they are licensed to handle asbestos. Asbestos is a prime example of a dormant inherent hazard that becomes a very high risk if activated by negligent activity. Asbestos can kill if undetected, so always adopt a cautious approach and seek advice from the experts.

Further reading

The Asbestos (Licensing) (Amendment) Regulations 1998, ISBN 0-11-080279-9.
Asbestos Exposure Limits and Measurement of Dust Concentrations, HSE EH10, 1995, ISBN 0-7176-0907-3.
A Guide to the Asbestos (Licensing) Regulations 1983, L11, HSE Books, 1991, ISBN 0-11-885684-7.
Asbestos Dust – The Hidden Killer – Essential Advice for Building Maintenance, Repair and Refurbishment Workers, HSE, 1995, IND(G)187(L).

Asbestos – Exposure Limits and Measurement of Airborne Dust Concentrations, HSE Guidance Note EH10, 1995.

The Asbestos (Licensing) Regulations 1983.

Asbestos and You, leaflet HSE IND(G)107(L), 1996.

Academy, journal of ACAD division of the Thermal Insulation Contractors' Association (TICA).

Asbestos Use in Buildings, SHE9, 1993 (available from the Loss Prevention Council, Melrose Avenue, Borehamwood, Hertfordshire).

British Asbestos Newsletter, published monthly, contact Laurie Allen, Tel: 0181–9583887.

The Control of Asbestos at Work Regulations 1987 (CAWR), HSE SI/1987 No. 2115, ISBN 0-11-078115-5.

The Control of Asbestos at Work Regulations, L27 (amendment), SI/1992–3068, ISBN 0-11-025738-3.

Chrysotile Asbestos, World Health Organisation 203, UNEP, ILO/WHO, ISBN 92 4-157203-5.

Health and Safety in Construction, HSE, 1996 (HSG-150), pages 75–77, ISBN 0-7176-1143-4.

HSE's Methods for the Determination of Hazardous Substances, MDHS 39/4 Asbestos Fibres in the Air.

Managing Asbestos in Workplace Buildings, IND(G)223L leaflet, HSE, 1996.

NAMAS Directory of Laboratories Accredited by NAMAS for Asbestos Sampling and Testing (D25).

CITB Health and Safety Publications Catalogue 1997 (available from the Construction Industry Training Board (CITB), Publications Department, Bircham Newton, King's Lynn, Norfolk PE31 6RH, Tel: 01553–776677; also series of leaflets, books, training videos and computer packages).

Construction Site Safety GE700/11 1996 revision, Section 11 asbestos and CITB asbestos hazards video

Contact organizations

Asbestos Control and Abatement Division (ACAD)
Charter House, 450 High Rd, Ilford, Essex IG1 1UF
Tel: 0181–514–2120

Asbestos Removal Contractors Association
Friars House, 6 Parkway, Chelmsford, Essex CM2 0NF
Tel: 01245–259744

Asbestos Information Centre Ltd
PO Box 69, Widnes, Cheshire WA8 9GW
Tel: 0151–420–5866

Construction Industry Training Board (CITB)
Bircham Newton, King's Lynn, Norfolk PE3 6RH
Tel: 01553–776677

Initial Deborah Services
10 South Parade, Wakefield, W. Yorkshire WF1 1LS
Tel: 01924–378222

European Asbestos Removal Association (EARA)
Tel: 0031–302588969

HSE, Asbestos Licensing Unit, c/o HSE Occupational Health and
Environment Unit (OHEU)
Belford House, 59 Belford Rd, Edinburgh EH4 3UE
Tel: 0131–247–2135

HSE HM Factory Inspectorate, Asbestos Licensing Unit
Magdalen House, Stanley Precinct, Bootle, Merseyside L20 3QY

The Institution of Civil Engineers
1 Great George St, London SW1P 3AA
Tel: 0171–222–7722

The Institution of Structural Engineers
11 Upper Belgrave St, London SW1X 8BH
Tel: 0171–235–4535

NAMAS Executive National Physical Laboratory
Teddington, Middx TW11 0LW

National Association of Waste Disposal Contractors
Mountbarrow House, 6–20 Elizabeth St, London SW1 9RB
Tel: 0171–824 8882

Occupational and Environmental Diseases Association
Mitre House, 66 Abbey Rd, Bush Hill Park, Enfield, Middx EN1 2QH
Tel: 0181–360–8490

Protector Technologies Group
Mattesol House, Ash Rd, Aldershot, Hampshire GU4 4DE
Tel: 01252–344141

Thermal Insulation Contractors' Association (TICA)
Charter House, 450 High Rd, Ilford, Essex IG1 1UF
Tel: 0181–514–2120

The United Kingdom Accreditation Service
21–27 High St, Feltham, Middx TW13 4UN
Tel: 0181–917–8400

Hazard 4: Audiences

On 25th March 1997 Granada TV were ordered to pay £327,000 plus costs after a make-up artist's career was ended as a result of being knocked over by a six foot three, 17-stone wrestler carrying out a pre-arranged but unannounced scuffle. The artist was knocked over as the wrestler ran off the set.

Stage, Screen and Radio, April 1997, p. 17

The legislation

The Construction (Health, Safety and Welfare) Regulations 1996
The Construction (Design and Management) Regulations 1994
The Health and Safety at Work Act 1974
The Health and Safety (First Aid) Regulations 1981
The General Access Scaffold 1982
The Management of Health and Safety at Work Regulations 1992
The Occupiers Liability Act 1957
The Occupiers Liability Act 1984
The Health and Safety (Safety Signs and Signals) Regulations 1996

The risks

- access
- animals
- cables
- chemicals
- elderly/blind/deaf/inexperienced
- electricity
- emergency access and evacuation
- fire

- heights
- insurance
- lasers
- noise
- panic
- scaffolds/rostra
- slips/trips/falls
- strobes
- stunts
- weather

Those most at risk

Members of the public in studio audiences, third party premises used for television activity and uncontrolled temporary locations.

Special risks: disadvantaged members of the public, fire, scaffolds and weather.

Any significant risk to health and safety of audiences should be detected as part of the hazard identification, and a risk assessment made to identify any danger. Then the correct procedures should be followed to eliminate or control the risk before any filming activity is undertaken. A health and safety method statement should be produced to deal with any assessed risk and should lay out exactly what procedure to follow for any identified hazard.

Your legal liability will depend on if you actually own, manage, control or temporarily occupy the premises. It is important to establish the contractual relationship between all parties involved in a production, including the location owner.

Members of the public or an audience can't be simply 'invited in to watch or take part in filming' in a potentially dangerous studio or temporary outside broadcast location. In this situation simply not bothering to find out if any risk exists constitutes gross negligence and poses a high risk to the health and safety of the public. Failing to carry out a proper risk assessment is a prosecutable offence.

Working with audiences often takes place in a studio where members of the public are invited onto company premises. The owners and operators of the premises have a responsibility under the Health and Safety at Work Act 1974 (section 4) and the Management of Health and Safety at Work Regulations 1992 for their welfare.

Who would be affected? Public, crew, employees, contractors. What measures and precautions should be taken to see that there is no risk to anybody's health and safety?

Figure H4.1

A basic requirement is the provision of third party and public liability insurance. Also fire insurance cover (see Chapter 5: Insurance). The policies should be framed near the main entrance or in the company office. The Occupiers Liability Acts 1957 and 1984 lay down the legal responsibility of owners or operators of premises towards the health and safety welfare of visitors. Audiences are classed as visitors because they have been invited by the owners of the studio to attend a recording, rehearsal or performance. Therefore the owners should take all reasonable precautions against known risks such as fire and inherent hazards to protect the public. These precautions can be expressed in a number of steps taken to ensure compliance with common law against reasonably foreseeable dangers. The owner can do this by making sure the public is aware through warnings and by installing precautions to avoid serious injury or death.

Measures that can be taken include that the premises should have an up-to-date fire certificate and a local authority licence. The legal public capacity of the studio audience should never be exceeded and seating rostra should never be overloaded. Staff should be trained in first aid and St John Ambulance should be in attendance for any public performance. All crew should be briefed about emergency evacuation and fire procedures.

Emergency exits and access points should be wide enough and strong enough for the number of people needing to use them. When making your calculation, don't forget performers, crew and presenters as well as the audience. The rules and calculations can be found in *A Guide to Fire Precautions in Existing Places of Entertainment and Like Places* (HMSO, 1990, ISBN 0-11-340907-9).

Managers should ensure that fire exits and escape routes are never blocked and appoint fire wardens to each location who are trained in the correct use of fire fighting equipment, basic first aid, and the correct evacuation procedure. There should always be enough fire wardens for the total present on the location (not just the audience) and the number of fire exit routes. Great care should be taken so that any emergency evacuation is carried out safely, without causing mass panic.

Fire extinguishers should always be prominently displayed and tested regularly. There should be more available than the basic fire authority minimum recommendation and enough of each type to deal with electrical, wood or chemical fires. All fire extinguishers should be CE marked and rated at BS EN 3 from January 1997.

Fire exits should be clearly marked. All fire signs should be on a red background and comply with BS 5499 Part 1 and BS 5378. These indicate the location of fire fighting equipment, fire alarms, fire hose reels and extinguisher locations. All fire exit signs are green and yellow and should conform to BS 4599 and EU Directive 92/58/EEC. Fire information signs should be large enough to read clearly and be luminant.

Emergency lighting must be provided for all gangways, access points, exits, footpaths, vehicle roadways (especially where pedestrians can cross) steps, emergency exits, warning signs and fire/first aid equipment locations. The location should also have smoke detectors/sprinklers and a proper fire alarm and warning system. Any fire incidents and precautionary measures must be recorded in a workplace fire safety log book.

Smoking should not be permitted (except as part of a production when it is carefully controlled) and no smoking signs should be displayed. All scenery, props and costumes should be fire-proofed. Fire evacuation drill should be explained to the audience before recording begins and the exits indicated. If a special risk of fire has been identified (such as a fire stunt, pyrotechnic effect or COSHH hazard) then the fire authorities should be informed and should be in attendance.

The Safety Signs Regulations 1980 insist that all fire prevention equipment should be properly marked. Fire exit and no smoking signs should be clearly visible and illuminated. The emergency signs should have battery/alternative power back-up in event of an electrical supply failure. Emergency lighting should also have a standby supply which cuts in automatically. Any risks or prohibited areas should be clearly indicated. Fire gangways should be clearly marked on the floor and fire doors indicated. Rostra should be edge-painted white and yellow and have fire exits indicated on the floor (see Hazard 17: Fire).

Any audience seating must be safe and built in accordance with the Construction (Design and Management) Regulations 1994. This insists that they are designed correctly, with safety features built in to make them safe for the audience.

Temporary seating must also satisfy regulations governing scaffolding and height. Audience seating is also regulated by entertainment and venue regulations of the local authority. Any temporary structures require a proper plan with loading and emergency measures indicated to be submitted before a public safety licence is issued.

The safety of audience seating can come under the Working at Height Regulations. Kick boards must be in place and steps should be painted to avoid trips. Proper edge protection guard and hand rails must be in place in all constructions above 2 m. Gangways should be wide enough and nobody should be allowed to sit in the aisles.

Studio technical managers should ensure that the public are not at risk from any of their activities. Cable runs should have proper ramps or ducts to avoid trips and falls. Cables and equipment should be placed so that there is no contact with electricity. No working at heights should be allowed once the public have access to the studio and gantry equipment should be secured with access locked. All lamps and suspended equipment must be secured by safety chains and clamps.

All camera positions and cranes must be safe and the audience properly protected. The floors must also be dry before public access is allowed, to avoid slip accidents. All inherent risks of the studio or premises should be identified and protective measures put in place before an audience is admitted.

When an audience is admitted the management should ensure that enough ushers and floor management supervision is available and they are properly trained in emergency procedures. They should all be given a copy of the company's health and safety policy and any special regulations for the studio environment. Fire wardens trained in the use of fire extinguishers should be appointed and a sufficient number of extinguishers for the total numbers present (not just the audience) and for each fire escape route and exit.

There should also be a sufficient number of trained first aid wardens – Health and Safety (First Aid) Regulations 1981 – and sufficient first aid equipment available. St John Ambulance should be consulted about the right precautions and may be present along with a doctor if special risks are anticipated.

Adequate communications and a proper chain of responsibility are essential for the staff to work as a team during an emergency so a health and safety method statement should be produced to deal with any identified risk and lay out exactly what procedure to follow for any identified audience hazard. Steps should be taken to conduct an emergency evacuation without causing mass panic. A risk assessment of the audience should be made with special chaperoning and ushering provided for any blind, deaf, elderly or young in the audience.

Risks to an audience can also be introduced from the activity the audience are going to watch as well as from those inherent in the building. The audience could be exposed to special risks from the content of the intended recording. Therefore a proper risk assessment should be made of the programme activity and content in relation to the audience, for example the risk of phobia or attack from an animal. There is an asthma risk from smoke effects which is a chemical risk under the COSHH regulations. All chemicals should be locked in a secure compound away from any exposure or fire risk (see Hazard 6: Chemicals).

Other risks to the audience include noises over 85 dB(A); these require ear protection under the Noise at Work Regulations (see Hazard 27: Noise). Stroboscopic or laser effects are especially dangerous to epileptic people and can damage eyesight (see Hazard 24: Lasers and radiation), any sudden noise or effect such as pyrotechnics and thunder flashes should be explained before the activity commences.

Beware of the risk factor from excess heat caused by studio lighting. Make sure audience, crew and performers get sufficient rest periods, especially during periods of hot weather. These risks are common to music or light entertainment programmes.

Members of the public should not take part in any stunts or dangerous activity. Management should also ensure that no activity in the programme content would put the audience at risk or cause panic such as guns, firearms, pyrotechnics or water. All stunts should be properly supervised by an expert stunt supervisor and all guns or explosives should be securely locked away from the audience in a fire-proof compound in a secure container or box. Studio audiences are a classic example of an introduced hazard into a controlled premises. A proper risk assessment should be made and precautions put in place before they are invited to enter.

External and temporary locations

Television production activities also encounter audiences in controlled locations outside studios. For example road shows (*Antiques Road Show/Mastermind*, agricultural shows, and live concerts) – if these activities take place inside the premises of others then it is essential to obtain copies of the health and safety policy of that organization. You should also obtain a floor plan with the fire exits, access points, power supplies and emergency procedures clearly marked. Always seek permission of the owner to use the property.

A proper recce should be carried out to make sure fire precautions and safe electricity supplies are in place. If in doubt, establish your own control measures to make sure all fire and first aid regulations are conformed to. All the crew and participants should be briefed on the safety policy, fire/first aid precautions and evacuation procedures. In event of an emergency, the safety regulations for the location should be followed and appropriate protective equipment worn.

The risk of filming on the premises of third parties is especially high for factual and documentary film crews (for example, building sites, chemical plants, mines and prisons). Always follow the advice of appointed safety representatives and assume the location is not safe until you can prove that it is by doing a hazard identification and risk assessment to complement that of the location operators.

Location drama shoots, outside broadcasts and sports events often take place in temporary locations established for the purpose. The design and management of such sites fall under the Construction (Design and Management) Regulations 1994 which should mean that designers, managers and operators of temporary public locations should design and manage the site to prevent any risk to audience health and safety. So a proper risk assessment should be made and hazards identified so that any risks are eliminated or controlled and protective measures put in place, especially in relation to risks inherent in the design of the location and the production activities within it. Any project lasting over 30 days should be notified to the HSE on an HSE notification of project form.

Riggers should hold a qualification from the Construction Industry Training Board (CITB) and hold an SITC Advanced Riggers and Scaffolders Ticket. All scaffolders and electricians must be properly experienced and qualified for the task management are asking them to perform. All work should be properly designed and supervised, with health and safety risks made a priority.

Special attention should be paid to access risks in temporary locations or the premises of others when an audience is present and could panic in an emergency situation. Fire exits should be checked and adequate gangways and exits should be wide enough to allow quick exit for the size of the audience in the event of a fire or emergency. These should be properly indicated by signs and illuminated with emergency back-up lighting. Never obstruct fire exits with cables or equipment. *A Guide to Fire Precautions in Existing Places of Entertainment and Like Places* (HMSO, 1990, ISBN 0-11-340907-9) should be consulted in the planning stage.

Fire wardens trained in the use of fire extinguishers should be appointed and a sufficient number of extinguishers for the total numbers present (not just the audience) and for each fire escape route and exit. All fire extinguishers should be CE marked and rated at BS EN 3 from January 1997.

Fire exits should be clearly marked. All fire signs should be on a red background and comply with BS 5499 Part 1 and BS 5378. These indicate the location of fire fighting equipment, fire alarms, fire hose reels and extinguisher locations. All fire exit signs are green and yellow and should conform to BS 4599 and EU Directive 92/58/EEC. All fire information signs should be large enough to read clearly and be luminant.

There should also be a sufficient number of trained first aid wardens – Health and Safety (First Aid) Regulations 1981 – and sufficient first aid equipment available.

Temporary locations are especially vulnerable to bad weather. Make sure the surface is safe in the event of rain with proper drainage and roofs. Check that all emergency access and exits have solid roadways and will not become a sea of mud if it rains. Make sure all electrical installations are protected from rain and ground water. External locations become doubly dangerous at night.

Separate entrances into the site should be made and kept clear for emergency vehicle access. No car parking should be allowed close to the site and emergency exits should be separate from emergency access lanes or active vehicle entrances. If the site is designed properly the audience can exit quickly and safely while incoming emergency service access can take place without risk. Never ask actors, crew or audiences to come into a location with only one exit or entrance point. Try and avoid working in narrow or confined locations. Narrow streets and churches are particularly dangerous. A full risk assessment should be made and all access points should be clearly marked on the site plan.

A special risk on temporary sites comes from the proper provision of water. Make sure that the water supply is adequate for the amount of people and that it is safe to drink. There should be three totally separate supplies, one which is safe for drinking water and catering, one which is for emergency and fire use, and one of which is for toilet and sewerage use. The sewerage and toilet arrangements must be large enough to cope and cater for men, women and disabled people, with separate facilities for crew, performers and catering. They must be cleaned and comply with public health and environmental regulations.

The storage of the waste must comply with COSHH and the disposal of the waste must comply with the Disposal of Hazardous Waste and Water Pollution Regulations and not simply flushed into the nearest drain or stream.

There is a risk of damage to temporary water pipes from cuts or pulls. Make sure pipes are protected and clear of any vehicle or equipment movements. Also ensure that any taps or connectors cannot be opened by members of the public to prevent loss or flooding. Ensure that you know the location of the nearest fire hydrant and that a separate back-up water supply is available for fire and emergency use only.

The water supply should also be kept well away and downhill from any electrical supply and may need an adequate pump to distribute it (with a standby back-up if this fails). Electrical supplies and equipment should be properly installed and maintained (Electricity at Work Regulations). Ensure that any electrical supply is either up hill from or isolated above on-site water supplies and groundwater. Electrical supplies should be properly installed and phased, with correct fuses. Never cross, connect or touch separate three-phase supplies. Always try and use stepped down low voltage equipment fitted with circuit breakers and PAT tested. Electrical supplies should be routed away from vehicle lanes and public access points in ducts or conduits. Terminals and switches should be secure and isolated from the public. Keep cables out of the reach of audiences and the radius of moving equipment. An adequate electrical back-up supply should cut in on a trip in the event of generator or mains failure. A battery operated emergency lighting supply should also be installed (see Hazard 15: Electricity).

Audiences should be protected from the weather and warm protective clothing must be provided in extreme cases in exposed locations. Night operations can be especially hazardous and staff should be issued with visibility clothing and emergency torches. Audience areas should be brightly illuminated and access/exit areas should have emergency back-up lighting.

Care should be taken that no risk to the audience will arise from camera or cable placements and that no risk exists from falling or faulty equipment. Lights and suspended equipment should be secured by clamps and safety chains and safety nets should be suspended and attached to catch falling tools, equipment or staff.

The audience should be kept well back behind barriers and clear from any extended cranes/jibs or moving dollies. Lights or lighting stands should be well secured with proper safety chains, weights and gauze. In the event of them falling they should be secured or have an adequate free fall area which protects the public or any participants.

Scaffold towers or cranes should be clear of any audience location and sited on firm ground. Proper attention should be taken about erecting any camera towers or temporary rostra. Riggers and scaffolders should be CITB qualified. Camera towers are usually supplied mobile towers with system or proprietary ready-made sections designed and supplied by the contractor. Manufacturers and suppliers of prefabricated aluminium tower proprietary scaffold systems should be members of PASMA. Such scaffolds should be built and designed in accordance with BS 1139 Part 3 1994 (HD1004) and European standard EN 4711. The maximum height of aluminium tower scaffolds should be three and a half times the base inside and three times the base outside. Erectors of prefabricated aluminium scaffolding towers should have passed a PASMA course. You should always check the operator's licence and the rigger's certificate and identity card before operations begin. Never use an unqualified or inexperienced contractor.

For further information consult the PASMA operator's code of practice (see Hazard 11: Cranes, hoists lifts and access platforms, and Hazard 29: Scaffolding and heights).

Barrier protected runs should be made for flying arms or Steadicam operations with no public access. Film action, stunts and performances behind guard rails and protective barriers. Make sure protective equipment is available. Crew and invited audiences should also be protected from noise hazards inherent in live concert situations (see Hazard: 27 Noise).

Camera positions in audience locations must be safe with no risk from height, movement or electrical supply. Camera positions should have proper guard rails and edge protection in case of falling equipment. If a high risk to the audience from height exists, secure any equipment with safety lines and make sure operators have a safety harness. Camera positions should also be barrier protected and secure from public access. A full risk assessment should be made in advance and equipment and camera locations clearly marked on a site plan which should also indicate electrical supplies, water services and chemical placement.

The temporary site design should also take into account adequate hygiene provision such as water supply and toilets. Catering may have to be provided (which complies with food hygiene and environmental health regulations) and sufficient shelter available for the audience in the advent of bad weather to cater for their welfare. The audience should also have sufficient breaks during the recording.

Audience and crew should be protected from any danger inherent in the filmed activity such as car stunts or animal stunts. Never involve members of the public or unqualified people to perform or take part in stunts or special effects. Use a properly trained stunt supervisor or pyrotechnic card holder.

Special advice should be taken regarding any stunt, and members of the public kept off limits for the duration. Attempted car stunts or speed stunts in wet weather or poor visibility are particularly dangerous and high risk to audiences and members of the public.

To ensure audience safety make sure any studio premises or temporary location is adequately controlled and designed. Potential hazards should be identified and precautionary measures taken to eliminate the danger.

The risks to the audience arising from any film activity in the studio or on location should also be assessed and either eliminated or sufficient precautions put into place well in advance so that any risks to audience safety have been identified and removed. A health and safety method statement should be produced to deal with any identified risk and lay out exactly what procedure to follow for any identified audience hazard (see also Hazards 2 (Animals), 6 (Chemicals and hazardous substances), 8 (Churches, places of worship and village halls), 15 (Electricity), 17 (Fire), 24 (Lasers and radiation), 29 (Scaffolding and heights) and 31 (Sports grounds) which also contain risks for audiences).

Further reading

- Design Guide for the Fire Protection of Buildings, DG1, 1996
- *Guide to Fire Safety Signs,* Ian Jerome
- Water Supplies for Fire Fighting Systems, TBN6, 1996

The above are available from: The Loss Prevention Council, Melrose Avenue, Borehamwood, Herts WD6 2BJ, Tel: 0181–207–2345.

J.F. Whitfield, *A Guide to the 16th Edition IEE Wiring Regulations,* 1991, EPA Press (Pocket Reference)

J.F. Whitfield, *A Guide to Electrical Safety at Work,* 1992, EPA Press.

T.E. Marks, *Handbook on the Electricity at Work Regulations 1989,* 2nd edition, 1994, William Ernest.

Electricity in the Workplace Bookset, Vol. 2: Portable Appliance Testing, Megger Instruments Ltd.

A. Smith, *The Handbook of Electrical Installation Practice,* 1996, Blackwell.

Health and Safety in Construction, HSE, 1996, HSE HS(G)-150, ISBN 0-7176-1143-4.

A Guide to Fire Precautions in Existing Places of Entertainment and Like Places, HMSO, 1990, ISBN 0-11-340907-9.

Hot Work-RC7/1994 (available from the Loss Prevention Council, Melrose Avenue, Borehamwood, Hertfordshire WD6 2BJ, Tel: 0181–207–2345).

The Provision of Welfare Facilities at Transient Construction Sites, HSE, 1996, Construction Information Sheet No 46.

The Construction (Design and Management) Regulations 1994, Approved Code of Practice L54, HSE, 1995, ISBN 0-7176-0792-5.

Managing Crowd Safety in Public Venues, HSE, CRR53/1993, ISBN 0-71760708-9.

Managing Crowds Safely, Leaflet INDG142.
Safety in Broadcasting Sports Events, HSE-ETIS 1-C100.
Slips, Trips and Falls, HSE, ISBN 0-7176-11450.
The Health and Safety (Safety Signs and Signals) Regulations 1996, HSE 1996 L64, ISBN 0-7176-0870-0.
Cris Hannam, *An Introduction to Health and Safety Management for the Live Music Industry*, 1997, Production Services Association Pocket Book Volume 1, ISBN 0-9530914-06.

Contact organizations

Fire Services College
Moreton in the Marsh, Gloucestershire GL56 0RH
Tel: 01608–650831

Guild of Location Managers
37 Woodeaves, Northwood, Herts HA6 3NF

HSE Information Centre
Broad Lane, Sheffield S3 7HQ

Institution of Fire Safety
PO Box 687, Croydon CR9 5DD
Tel: 0181–654–2582

The National Association of Scaffolding Contractors
18 Mansfield St, London W1M 9FG
Tel: 0171–580–5404

National Entertainment Safety Association (NESA)
Contact Tony Bond
Tel: 01202–524426

Prefabricated Aluminium Scaffold Manufacturers Association Ltd (PASMA)
PO Box 1828, West Mersea, Essex CO5 8HY
Tel: 01206–382666

Production Services Association
Hawks House, School Passage, Kingston upon Thames, Surrey KT1 3DU
Tel: 0181–392–0180

The Professional Lighting and Sound Association
7 Highlight House, St Leonards Rd, Eastbourne, E. Sussex BN21 3UH
Tel: 01323–410335

Production Managers Association (CoPACT)
45 Mortimer St, London W1N 7TD
Tel: 0171–331–6000

St John Ambulance
16 Grosvenor Crescent, London SW1X 7EF
Tel: 0171–235–5231

Hazard 5: Building and construction sites

Although employing less than 10 per cent of the country's workforce, the construction industry accounts for 25 per cent of all injury accidents.

CITB, Construction Site Safety, GE 700–9 1996 revised

The legislation

The Control of Asbestos at Work Regulations 1987 (CAWR)
The Control of Asbestos at Work Regulations (Amendment) SI/1992
The Construction (Head Protection) Regulations 1989
The Construction (Health Safety and Welfare) Regulations (CHSWR) 1996
The Lifting Operations and Lifting Equipment Regulations 1998
The Construction (Design and Management) Regulations 1994
The Health and Safety at Work Act 1974
The Management of Health and Safety at Work Regulations 1992
The First Aid at Work Regulations 1981
The Manual Handling Operations Regulations 1992
The Personal Protective Equipment (PPE) at Work Regulations 1992
The Provision and Use of Work Equipment Regulations 1998
Reporting of Injuries, Diseases and Dangerous Occurrences Regulations 1995 (RIDDOR)
The Health and Safety (Signs and Signals) Regulations 1996

The risks

- access
- air tools
- asbestos

- confined spaces
- cranes
- deep excavations
- drowning
- electricity/power tools
- fire
- working at heights
- hoists/lifts
- manual handling
- noise
- power equipment
- powered access platforms
- plant
- scaffolding

Those most at risk

Location camera and sound crews and location managers, performers, riggers and lighting crew.

Special risk: access, electricity, manual handling, working at heights.

Building and construction sites are dangerous locations and can kill. Directors like using them for realistic locations and often to get good camera vantage points from positions of height afforded by cranes and scaffolds in congested urban locations.

However, it is important to realize that construction sites are inherently dangerous unless proper health and safety management is in place. It may be prudent to consider a safer alternative location.

Ask yourself who would be affected? Public, crew, employees, contractors. What measures and precautions should be taken to see that there is no risk to anybody's health and safety? The producer should be responsible for producing a framework of responsibility and written guidelines which all crew and employees should follow. Make sure that you have adequate insurance cover in place by checking the position with the contracting company before filming begins. Conduct a site survey and search first to ascertain any risks. This is a requirement under BS 6187 for demolition work.

Always proceed with caution as a derelict building may contain many risks that are hidden until your search reveals them. Never conduct a site search alone or unaccompanied. Carry a lone worker's safety alarm. Use a proper locator to find out the presence of hidden live utility services. Your search should identify the structural elements of the building and their condition.

If the risks are too great or the site is too dangerous to be made safe, opt for an alternative. This can be cheaper and safer in the long run.

Any demolition or building work in derelict buildings comes under the Construction (Design and Management) Regulations 1994. The HSE guidance notes for demolition and derelict buildings, GS29 Parts 1–4, insist that a premises-specific risk assessment should always be carried out as an essential part of the preparation and planning process.

The results of the risk assessment and the necessary preventative measures should then be put into a coherent work method statement called a health and safety plan for how your crew will be protected from any risks which you have identified. The health and safety plan should set out how the work will be done and who will do it. This includes details of the timing, work schedule, the equipment to be used and who will supervise the stages of the job in a safe and logical order.

Beware of proximity hazards to the public from dust, noise and vibration and make sure that the public cannot get onto your site during hazardous activity or at night.

The site should be fenced off and lit properly with safe access and exits. All preventative measures to ensure site safety and prevent injury to the public must be put in place before any work is undertaken. Any staff, members of the public, actors and contractors who come on to the site must be given a site induction which includes emergency procedures, location of fire exits, fire extinguishers and muster points, first aid precautions and the details of any risks found during the site search and risk assessment. Everybody should be given accurate information of the risks and what precautions and protective equipment to comply with. Safety signs should indicate these at the site entrance, backed up by a site-specific health and safety rule book.

Managers and producers must ensure that all staff are given accurate information, and are properly trained and competent for the work they have been asked to do and that all work in derelict buildings is properly supervised. Any demolition work must be notified to HSE on a notification of project form 10 (rev). This should also be used for any construction work or project lasting more than 30 days or 500 person days.

The form gives information about the client, planning supervisor, principal contractor, site address, local authority, and details of the work to be carried out and which contractors are undertaking it.

Any work, safety and maintenance records must be entered into a health and safety file. This is a legal requirement under the Construction (Design and Management) Regulations 1994. The file should contain details of any hazards which may have to be removed or contained if they present a significant risk to the health and safety of your crew or cast.

Any significant risk to health and safety should be detected on the recce by the production/location manager as part of the hazard identification and a written risk assessment made by the producer to identify any danger. For example working at height, the risk of falling into deep excavations, movement of heavy materials by manual handling and plant/crane operations. The correct procedures should be followed to eliminate or control this risk before any filming activity on a building or construction site is undertaken. A health and safety method statement should be produced to deal with any assessed risk and lay out exactly what procedure and action plan to follow for any identified hazard.

Your legal liability will depend on if you actually own, manage, control, operate or temporarily occupy the construction or building site premises. Under the Management of Health and Safety at Work Regulations 1992 and the Construction (Design and Management) Regulations 1994, it is important to determine the contractual relationship between the location owner, production company and crew. It is obvious that a crew or performers should never just be 'sent in to film' on a potentially dangerous construction site location, especially when there is a very high risk. In this situation simply not bothering to find out constitutes gross negligence and poses a high risk to the health and safety of your crew.

Building sites (like agricultural locations) are an inherently dangerous location with very high risks. The building and construction site owners and operators should have produced a health and safety method statement and framework of responsibility to deal with any identified risk and lay out exactly what procedure you and your crew should follow for any recognized building or construction site hazard. For example mandatory adherence to warning, prohibition and safety signs and the wearing of personal protective clothing. Some larger sites and companies will have their own written safety rules and guidelines. Make sure you and your crew have read these in advance and understood how to comply with them.

Permission should always be obtained in advance and make sure staff have the correct site access identity passes. Always report to the site office and contact the foreman. Obtain from them a proper health and safety briefing of the risks particular to that site and the evacuation procedure. Anybody entering a building site should wear the proper protective equipment indicated by the warning signs at the entrance. A minimum standard would include boots, eye and ear protection, hard hats, gloves and safety overalls.

Site managers should brief you on the health and safety risks of the site. Always follow their advice and co-operate fully with their safety instructions. Obey warning signs and safety signals. Wear protective equipment – it could save your life. Site managers should have passed a CITB construction site managers safety certificate and site management safety training scheme. They should also have passed the CIOB's safety modules.

Avoid doing a recce alone or at night. Make sure you are accompanied by an experienced and qualified site manager or supervisor. Always make sure that site security know who you are and what you are there for. Make sure that any of your intended activities on the building and construction site do not contravene section 7 of the Health and Safety at Work Act by endangering your crew, contractors or the public.

Be aware also of the risk from demolition or controlled explosions on site. Always check at the site office and make sure operating staff know you are present. This is also a special risk in quarries and derelict buildings. Always make sure you can be contacted in case of dangerous operations or emergencies.

Site access and parking can often be a considerable distance from the main entrance so be aware of the manual handling implications for moving your equipment over difficult surfaces with lots of trip hazards.

Beware of foot hazards such as cables, broken glass, rusty nails and wire and slip hazards such as ice, water and chemical residue.

Manual handling accounts for 20 per cent of all accidents in the construction industry. Therefore, under the Manual Handling Operations Regulations 1992, you should assess the manual handling task to reduce any risk that may be inherent in your activity. If possible avoid manual handling by finding another way to move the equipment or materials. Factors to consider are the nature of the task itself. What loads you are intending to move. What weight you are intending to lift or move. Can one person do this safely? If not, do you have sufficient crew and equipment to do it safely? Are your crew trained in safe manual handling? Are they experienced in doing this kind of work? How far are you intending to move the object?

Consider the terrain and environment, height and surface you are intending to move across or over, then the capability of the individual or group doing the lifting depending on age, sex, fitness, physique and training. A simple way to cut the risk of manual handling is not to do it at all. Or if an object has to be moved, can you divide the weight or break it up into smaller more manageable loads?

The assessment must identify these factors and draw up an action plan to reduce the risks by taking appropriate steps to protect crew and employees. The first step would be to send your crew and employees on a manual handling course so that they know the safest way to lift and move equipment. For example, avoiding stooping and twisting movements with heavy loads. Learn how to lift kinetically and avoid back strain.

The second step is to make sure that all manual handling operations such as loading and unloading are properly supervised by a qualified, experienced and competent supervisor. Third, management must ensure that protective hard cap boots, gloves and back supports are used. Fourth, staff should be trained in the safe use of lifting equipment and make sure that this is available with trolleys to move equipment. Fifth, management must ensure that enough crew are available to undertake the lifting in a safe way so that the load is spread and no-one is trying to lift and carry heavy objects by themselves.

Avoid manual handling when you can. If you have to, and a risk exists, take precautions and implement measures to reduce that risk such as using mechanical lifting equipment and trolleys. Your crew should all have completed a manual handling course and been given adequate training about how to lift safely and avoid injury (see Hazard 25: Manual handling and lifting).

Beware of fast moving plant vehicles/lorries and cranes. Never try to operate unauthorized lifts/cranes/vehicles or conveyers.

A sensible precaution would be to have at least one team member watching out for hazards and to protect the camera operator while filming as camera operators may be partially unsighted or sound operators partially hard of hearing when undertaking concentrated filming and so they are more at risk and unable to take evasive action from moving machinery/plant and falling debris.

Beware of the risk from falling objects always wear head protection. Ground hazards such as glass and nails require foot protection. Make sure your crew have had vaccinations against tetanus. Protective clothing should be worn to guard against the risk of rat bites. Extra caution should be taken to guard against the risk of leptospirosis from contaminated water. Beware of buried and overhead electrical cables.

Specific safety equipment may be necessary to combat risks to eyesight ears or respiratory organs. Never smoke on building sites as there are usually inflammable materials such as wood/petrol and oils.

There could also be the risk of exposure to chemical hazards. If necessary a proper COSHH risk assessment should be carried out first. There is a particular risk from air lines/compressors and gas. A proper recce should also detect any asbestos risk. This could be particularly likely during building demolition, repair or maintenance work on base or third party premises (see Hazard 3: Asbestos and Hazard 6: Chemicals and hazardous substances).

All electrical equipment on construction sites is 110 volts to reduce the danger of electrocution. Do not bring 240V equipment onto the site. Make sure all your equipment is fitted with a residual current device (RCD) and that your cables and plugs are PAT tested and in good condition. All electrical equipment should bear the CE mark, be to BS 2769 and be double insulated to BS 2754. Never place your cables near footpaths, water outlets, in trenches or vehicle access paths (see also Hazard 15: Electricity). All electrical installation and repair work should be properly supervised and the electricians who carry the work out should properly trained and qualified.

Another risk comes from deep excavations and trenches (see Hazard 10: Confined spaces). Always keep well away from the edges and avoid slipping or falling over the edge. Avoid working at night or in bad visibility or rain, especially with slippery conditions such as ice or mud.

The site operator should have fitted barriers at least 1.5 m from the edge to avoid the risk of falls or collapses. Do not be deceived by shallow trenches. At least seven deaths a year happen in trenches which are less than 2.5 m deep. One cubic metre of soil weighs 1 tonne, which would be enough to bury you alive. Also the longer the trench has been open, the greater the risk of collapse.

If you must film near the edge be aware that the risk of your weight and your equipment combined may be too heavy and cause a collapse, especially after a prolonged period of excessive rain or dry weather. Be especially careful of placement of heavy lights, dollies, cranes, cameras and scaffolds and any movement of crew or actors that may involve backwards or unsighted motion near the edge of an excavation.

So make sure that you and your equipment are properly secured by safety lines and fall arrest devices to prevent yourself or any equipment falling in. Any cranes, hoists, scaffolds or dollies with camera equipment should be assessed for weight and kept at least 1.5 m from the edge by a stop device. Do not park heavy crew buses, catering vans or links vehicles near the side of deep excavations as the prolonged pressure may trigger a slip or collapse.

If the edge of the site is near water or the deep excavation has filled with rain, beware of an additional risk from drowning to anybody that may fall in. Additional protective equipment and measures would be necessary in this situation such as provision of buoyancy aids and rescue equipment (see Hazard 33: Water).

Access is also restricted so there is a danger of becoming trapped and having your escape route cut off, so make sure proper access ladders and emergency exit procedures are in place. Beware of serious risk posed by sudden flooding or egress of water.

Noise can also be amplified in a confined space so be aware of any risk to hearing. This could also come from heavy plant and machinery so make sure your crew have adequate ear protection.

Always carry out a gas test before any activity in a confined space begins and ensure regular monitoring. There can be a build-up of underground methane with a serious risk of fire, especially near old mine workings or rubbish tips. Never film alone in a confined space and always have somebody else in close attendance and working communication as there is a serious risk from fumes and lack of oxygen. Beware of contact with old gas pipes or electrical cable. Beware of any leakage from LPG cylinders or your special effects containers as gas will sink to the lowest point of the trench, forming an explosive concentration. Beware of smoking or employing any electrical equipment where there is a risk of explosion or fire. Similarly do not use any petrol/diesel generator or engines to power equipment adjacent to anybody working in a confined space as it can cause a build-up of toxic fumes. Precautions should include extra ventilation and respiratory equipment. Never try and pump oxygen in as this can be highly explosive in a confined space.

Fifty per cent of fatal accidents in the construction industry occur as a result of falling from height. The HSE and BECTU's London production division had a meeting on 3 October 1996 which identified working at heights as one of the major risks of the film and television industry.

Construction location risk assessments should highlight this and make sure that filming activity at height is not entertained unless stringent precautions have been taken (see Hazard 29: Scaffolding and heights). Always ask if the shot can be obtained in another way, for example a nearby building or the use of a MEWP.

These include the provision of secure platforms and safe working areas and the availability of safety equipment such as hard hats and safety harness and other fall arrest devices (see Chapter 4: Personal protective equipment). All rigging and scaffolding installation and repair work should be properly supervised and the riggers and scaffolders who carry the work out should be CITB qualified and experienced.

The risk involved in working at height on building sites can come from a number of different areas. The most simple and common risk is that of falling objects such as bricks, bolts or tools. Falling sharp objects can inflict fatal injuries by a rapid gain in velocity, so make sure your crew wear adequate head protection. Steps should also be taken to protect those below by securing yourself and any equipment by sufficiently strong secure lines and safety harness. This is a particular risk if building works overhang or are adjacent to public streets. Warning signs should be placed below and should read 'danger working at height' to indicate that a risk exists and nobody should walk underneath. Also create a safe exclusion zone to protect third parties.

Make sure that all tower scaffolds and constructions are safe before attempting to use them. They should be erected and dismantled by a qualified and competent contractor. The scaffold should be the right type for the intended work activity. There are five major types:

1 putleg
2 independent
3 birdcage
4 mobile tower constructed with tube fittings and wheels
5 mobile tower with system or proprietary ready-made sections designed and supplied by the contractor.

Manufacturers and suppliers of prefabricated aluminium tower proprietary scaffold systems should be members of PASMA. Such scaffolds should be built and designed in accordance with BS 1139 Part 3 1994 (HD1004) and European standard EN 4711. For further information consult the PASMA *Operator's Code of Practice*.

Tower scaffolds should always be tied to a permanent structure and weighted to avoid toppling or being blown over. The maximum height of aluminium tower scaffolds should be three and a half times the base inside and three times the base outside.

The design will depend on the task in hand and the weight which the scaffold will support. It should be constructed out of proper materials in accordance with HSE GS42 guidance notes. Beware of any scaffold that is not braced or tied and built with rusty, bent or defective tubes. The scaffold should be able to support the intended weight and not be blown over or topple.

Site suitability is also a key factor. Is the structure placed on a hard, level site? Has it rained or been excessively dry? Are the internal ladders and exits constructed safely and secure? Are the feet wide enough and implanted properly? Never construct a scaffold close to power lines and cables, working cranes, the edge of an excavation or hillside or near a busy traffic or pedestrian thoroughfare.

It is essential that any scaffolding is erected by a licensed and authorized contractor. Any construction should have a 7 day scaffold inspection report and the contractor should supply a handover certificate. The construction should also have a scaffolding tag indicating it has been inspected and safe. A green tag and edge caps should indicate that it is safe – if it hasn't got these, don't use it.

A red tag indicates that it is still being built or not inspected and passed for use. There should be no access allowed to a partially constructed or dismantled scaffold. Warning signs should be in place and barriers erected to deny access until the work is completed.

Scaffolds should be built with proper internal ladders and hoists for equipment. It is vital to ensure good access and quick egress in the event of an emergency. The timber boards should be in good condition and strong enough for the intended weight.

Double guard rails at least 910 mm above the edge and toe boards at least 150 mm high should be fitted to all working areas to prevent falls of personnel and equipment. If necessary fit a safety net and barrier as well for extra protection. If working on a sloping roof of more than 10 per cent, fit catch barriers with two 430 mm boards and guardrails with toeboards. All poles should have edge caps for protection. Warning signs should be placed below and should read 'danger working at height' to indicate that a risk exists and nobody should walk underneath. Also create a safe exclusion zone to protect third parties.

Cranes, hoists or powered access platforms should not be used until they have been checked to see if they can support the intended load and that they have been inspected with a current inspection certificate.

The supplier/hirer should have public, employers and third party liability insurance cover. The operator should also be experienced in film work and licensed. If self-employed, they should possess public and third party liability cover (see Hazard 11: Cranes, hoists and lifts and access platforms).

A health and safety method statement should be produced to deal with any identified risk and lay out exactly what procedure to follow for any identified building or construction site hazard before production activity on such sites begins. These sites are usually inherently high risk and introducing production activity increases the risk factor. Look out in particular for risks from working or activity at height. A proper risk assessment and hazard identification should be made and stringent precautions taken to avoid any danger to the health and safety of your crew. Make sure they have proper personal protective equipment and have been briefed by the site management.

Extra care should be taken to do this when building or construction activity is introduced to normally safe environments such as your production base where these risks are unfamiliar. Particular caution should be taken when crews are sent out at short notice to construction sites without the time to conduct a proper risk assessment. This is when construction site accidents are waiting to happen.

Further reading

V.J. Davies and K. Tomasin, *The Construction Safety Handbook*, 1997, Thomas Telford Publishing (Tel: 0171–987–6999).

R.W. King and Roland Hudson, *Construction Hazard and Safety Handbook*, 1985, order code Bk3478, British Safety Council, 70 Chancellors Rd, London W6 9RS (Tel: 0181–741–1231).

Construction Industry Publications Catalogue 1998.

Fire Prevention on Construction Sites, 3rd edition, FSB9/1995. Available from the Loss Prevention Council, Melrose Avenue, Borehamwood, Herts WD6 2BJ (Tel: 0181–207–2345).

HSE – Health and Safety in Construction, HS (G) 150, HSE Books, 1996, ISBN 0-7176-1143-4.

Entry into Confined Spaces, HSE, 1994, GS-5 (Rev), ISBN 0-7176-0787-9.

Accidents to Children in Construction Sites, HSE, 1989, GS7, ISBN 0-11-885416-X.

Electrical Safety on Construction Sites, HSE, 1995, HSG(141), ISBN 0-7176-1000-4.

Noise in Construction, HSE, 1993, IND(G)127L.

Tower Scaffolds, HSE, 1987, GS 42, ISBN 0-11-883941-1.

HSE Site Safe News (published twice a year), Sir Robert Jones Memorial Workshops, Units 3 and 5–9, Grain Industrial Estate, Harlow St, Liverpool L8 4XY.

HSE – The Health and Safety (Signs and Signals) Regulations 1996, HSE, 1996, L64, ISBN 0-7176-0870-0.

BS 6187 – Code of Practice for Demolition Work.

Also series of HSE guidance notes in Plant and Machinery series: PM Nos 1–81 give specific guidance about particular construction hazards relating to site, plant and machinery operational safety.

SP130, Site Guide. Site Safety 1996 available from the Construction Industry Research and Information Association, 6 Storey's Gate, Westminster, London SW1P 3AU.

A. Smith, *The Handbook of Electrical Installation Practice*, 1996, Blackwell.

J.F. Whitfield, *A Guide to Electrical Safety at Work*, 1992, EPA Press.

T.E. Marks, *Handbook on the Electricity at Work Regulations 1989*, 2nd edition, 1994, William Ernest.

The items in the bullet list below are available from the Construction Industry Training Board (CITB) publications department (series of leaflets, books, training videos and computer packages): CITB, Bircham Newton, King's Lynn, Norfolk PE31 6RH, Tel: 01553–776677.

- Health and Safety Publications Catalogue 1997.
- Construction Site Safety Notes and Section 9, Manual Handling, 7th revised edition, 1996, (book GE700).
- Safely Does It (video O38).
- Subcontractors and You (book LJC03).
- A Guide to Practical Scaffolding (book CE509).
- Mobile Crane Operator's Safety Guide (book CJ502).
- Safe Start – Construction Site Safety Handbook (book GE 707) 1995, ISBN 0-902-02974-6, CITB.
- Safe Start: Supervisor's Safety Check Card and Training Notes (CITB FTR 007/C).

Prefabricated Aluminium Scaffold Manufacturers Association Ltd (PASMA), *Operator's Code of Practice*, 4th edition, January 1994.

Contact organizations

The Association of Building Engineers
Jubilee House, Billing Brook Rd, Weston-Favell, Northampton NN3 8NW
Tel: 01604–404121

The Chartered Institute of Building
Englemere, Kings Ride Ascot, Berkshire SL5 8BJ
Tel: 01344–23355

Building Employers Confederation
Federation House, 82 New Cavendish St, London W1M 8AD
Tel: 0171–580–5588

Construction Industry Research and Information Association
6 Storey's Gate, Westminster, London SW1P 3AU
Tel: 0171–222–8891

Construction Plant Hire Association (CPA)
28 Eccleston St, London SW1W 9PY
Tel: 0171–7307117

Construction Industry Training Board (CITB)
Bircham Newton, King's Lynn, Norfolk PE3 6RH
Tel: 01553–776677

Federation of Civil Contractors (FCEC)
Cowdray House, 6 Portugal St, London WC2A 2HH
Tel: 0171–404–4020

Federation of Manufacturers of Construction Equipment and Cranes
Ambassador House, Brigstock Rd, Thornton Heath, Surrey CR7 7JG
Tel: 0181–665–5727

Federation of Master Builders
14 Great James St, London WC1N 3DP
Tel: 0171–242–7583

HSE Construction National Interest Group
Mr A. Sheddon, HM Principal Inspector of Health and Safety
1 Long Lane, London SE1 4PG

HSE Construction Policy Division
Rose Court, 2 Southwark Bridge, London SE1 9HS

The Institute of Quarrying
7 Regent St, Nottingham NG1 5BS
Tel: 01159–484035

The Institution of Civil Engineers
1 Great George St, London SW1P 3AA
Tel: 0171–222–7722

The Institution of Structural Engineers
11 Upper Belgrave St, London SW1X 8BH
Tel: 0171–235–4535

Prefabricated Aluminium Scaffold Manufacturers Association Ltd
(PASMA)
PO Box 1828, West Mersea, Essex CO5 8HY
Tel: 01206–382666

Royal Institution of Chartered Surveyors
12 Great George St, Parliament Square, London SW1P 3AD
Tel: 0171–222–7000

Hazard 6: Chemicals and hazardous substances

The legislation

The Control of Substances Hazardous to Health Regulations 1999 (COSHH)

The Chemicals (Hazard Information and Packaging for Supply) (Amendment) (No. 2) Regulations 1999

The Classification, Packaging and Labelling of Dangerous Substances Regulations 1984

Occupational Exposure Limits EH40 1999

The Highly Flammable Liquids and Liquefied Petroleum Gases Regulations 1972

The Road Traffic (Carriage of Dangerous Substances in Packages etc.) Regulations 1986

The Carriage of Dangerous Goods (Amendment) Regulations 1999

The Health and Safety (Safety Signs and Signals) Regulations 1996

The Pressure Systems and Transportable Gas Containers Regulations 1989

Those most at risk

Cleaners, designers, film processing workers, location and production managers, painters, plumbers and air conditioning workers, scenery painters, scenery construction artists, spray shop workers, special effects artists, wig makers and beauticians. In short, anybody handling or coming into contact with chemicals.

Special risks: absorption/sudden or prolonged exposure, dermatitis, explosion and fire, inhalation.

The handling, identification, labelling, storage and use of chemicals and hazardous substances are regulated by specific pieces of legislation. The Control of Substances Hazardous to Health Regulations 1999 (COSHH) and Chemicals (Hazard Information and Packaging for Supply) (Amendment) (No. 2) Regulations 1999 (known as CHIP 99 (2)) place a duty on employers and workers to identify any hazardous substances which may be used as a part of any process or activity. Substances covered by the COSHH regulations include anything toxic, corrosive, acidic, or irritant. They also cover maximum permitted levels of dust and regulate the level of micro-organisms. COSHH regulations cover chemicals, gases and substances which have set exposure limits that must not be exceeded.

By May 2001 a new European directive 98/24/EC regarding the protection of the health and safety of workers from the risks related to chemicals at work will be adopted and may amend current legislation.

Chemical hazard in film and television work may be integral to the type of work, for example film processing. It could be produced as a result of a process or chain reaction, for example a smoke effect. It could be introduced by a third party such as a caterer or scenery artist. The hazard could already be inherent to your premises or that of a third party, for example in your scenery construction workshop or in a refinery. The hazard could also be dormant in a derelict location.

Chemical hazards can have two widely differing features:

1 Either a swift and violent chain reaction caused by exposure to air, through contact or mixture with another incompatible substance, through spillage, or by contact with a heat or ignition source which will cause a fire.
2 Or a slow but often more deadly prolonged exposure to chemical hazards as an everyday part of the work. This can cause long-term skin disease such as dermatitis, and, in serious cases, cancers, breathing and lung diseases and poisoning.

Therefore the range of risks which the producer must identify and control under the COSHH regulations can vary from the risk of a massive explosion causing large loss of life very quickly to the long-term health risk caused by prolonged exposure over a period of time to a specific group of staff.

COSHH means the control of substances hazardous to health and failure to comply with the regulations can expose people to risk and is therefore an offence under the Health and Safety at Work Act 1974. To comply with the COSHH regulations producers must identify all hazardous substances as part of the risk assessment and put in place control measures to prevent exposure/explosion/absorption/contamination.

FIRE HAZARDS

Main hazards

27   The main hazards from the storage of flammable liquids are fire and explosion, involving either the liquid or the vapour given off from it. Fires or explosions are likely to occur when liquid or vapour is released and comes into contact with a suitable ignition source, or alternatively, when a heat or fire source comes into contact with the container.

28   Common causes or contributory factors of such incidents include:

(a) lack of awareness of the properties of flammable liquids;
(b) operator error, due to lack of training;
(c) inadequate or poor storage facilities;
(d) hot work on or close to flammable liquid containers;
(e) inadequate design, installation or maintenance of equipment;
(f) decanting flammable liquids in unsuitable storage areas;
(g) exposure to heat from a nearby fire;
(h) dismantling or disposing of containers containing flammable liquids.

Combustion of liquids

29   Combustion of liquids occurs when flammable vapours released from the surface of the liquid ignite (see Figure 1).

30   The extent of a fire or explosion hazard depends on the amount of flammable vapour given off from a liquid which is determined by:

(a) the temperature of the liquid;
(b) the volatility of the liquid;
(c) how much of the surface area is exposed;
(d) how long the liquid is exposed for; and
(e) the air movement over the surface.

31   Other physical properties of the liquid give additional information on how vapour/air mixtures may develop and also on the potential hazards. These physical properties include:

(a) flashpoint;
(b) auto-ignition temperature;
(c) viscosity;
(d) lower explosion limit; and
(e) upper explosion limit.

Flashpoint

32   Flashpoint is defined as the lowest temperature at which a liquid gives off vapour in sufficient quantity to form a combustible mixture with air near the surface of the liquid under specified test conditions. Generally, a liquid with a flashpoint below the ambient temperature of the surroundings will give off sufficient vapour to mix with the air and be ignited. Liquids with a flashpoint greater than ambient temperature are less likely to give

Figure H6.1   *Fire hazards description.* Source: The Storage of Flammable Liquids in Containers, *2nd edition, 1998, HSE, HSG51, ISBN 0-7176-1471-9.* © HMSO

FUEL
Flammable gases
Flammable liquids
Flammable solids

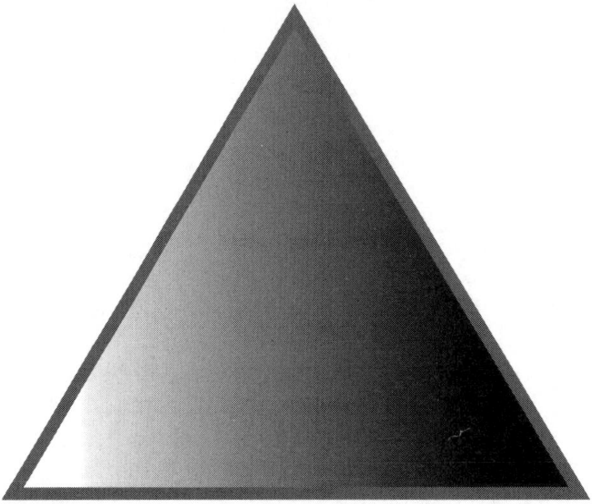

OXYGEN
Always present in the air
Additional sources from
oxidising substances

IGNITION SOURCE
Hot surfaces
Electrical equipment
Static electricity
Smoking/naked flames

Figure 1   The fire triangle

off a flammable concentration of vapour unless they are heated, mixed with low flashpoint materials or released under pressure as a mist or spray. The lower the flashpoint of a liquid, the higher the risk.

Viscosity

33   The viscosity of the liquid is also significant as it determines how far any spilt material will spread and therefore the size of any exposed surface.

Health hazards

34   Flammable liquids can pose a health hazard if they are ingested, come into contact with skin or eyes, or their vapours are inhaled. For example, methanol is toxic as well as flammable. Information on the health hazards of a particular liquid, and on any specific precautions required, should be obtained from the material safety data sheet (MSDS) or from the supplier. The Control of Substances Hazardous to Health Regulations 1994[14] require employers to assess the health risks from exposure to hazardous substances and the precautions needed. Paragraphs 37–39 give further details on health precautions.

Figure H6.1   *Continued*

Employers have a legal duty to identify situations where workers may come into contact with hazardous substances which are a danger to health and to take steps to prevent exposure or adequately control it.

The risk may come from the nature of the substance itself – for example phosphorus. It may come from the way in which the substance is used – for example mixing one chemical with another to produce an effect. The risk may come from the amount of the substance somebody is exposed to and for how long. In other words a small quantity of a very dangerous substance can cause a health risk if spilled. Similarly a very large quantity of a minor toxic substance can cause a health risk if the quantity is large enough or it is used over a prolonged period of time.

The key to control of chemical hazards is substitution; in other words find out if a safer alternative is available (see *Seven Steps to Successful Substitution of Hazardous Substances* in Further reading), then dilute the substance to make sure you use the minimum quantity required. Don't store large quantities of hazardous substances: those that are stored should be kept well away from heat sources, ignition risks and other substances. Reduce the handling time to a minimum and the number of people involved – this will reduce the risk but not remove it altogether.

Not doing it at all will remove the risk all together. Consider the safest option and if you don't have the budget to proceed safely don't do it at all. Afterwards is too late.

To comply with the COSHH regulations producers must assess the risks by asking the following questions. What is the substance we want to use? Is it dangerous by itself? Is it dangerous when mixed or exposed to air? Is the quantity we are intending to use dangerous? How should it be labelled? What are the correct ways of storing it? What is the safest way to use it? Who is at risk from using it? What is the maximum time they should be allowed to come into contact with it? How do we protect them? How do we dispose of it safely afterwards? All these factors should be considered in a COSHH risk assessment.

The risk assessment is a written control plan that is drawn up by management with the help of specialist experts that dictates how you are going to work safely. This will depend on what you are working with, where you are working, and who is doing it.

Ten steps for a COSHH risk assessment

For a proper COSHH risk assessment the following ten steps should be followed. First identify the properties of all hazardous substances you intend to work with. Make a list of these – called a COSHH file. Then deal with each one separately by entering each one on a COSHH hazard form.

Then enter all the information about each hazard on the form and later devise a strategy for dealing with each one.

Information on substances and their properties can be found in *Saxe's Dangerous Properties of Industrial Materials*. Information on substances can also be obtained from the HSE's EH40/97 list, called COSHH data sheets. Product information must be given by the manufacturer and supplier. Make sure you ask for and obtain this information as asking anybody to work with an unidentified chemical is an offence and a health risk.

Second, once you have identified the substance and know its properties you should decide on what precautions are needed. To begin with, let everyone else know what the substance is by proper labelling. Then store the substance in the correct containers and in a separate secure compound. This isolates the substance from fire risks and contact with other hazards.

Third, once the substance is correctly identified, labelled and stored, a control plan should be put in place to reduce the risks caused by your intended use. This involves the use of the substance in the correct quantity and making sure control measures such as proper first aid/fire precautions are in place. The proper written safety procedures should be followed if a substance is accidentally spilled or released into the air.

The process should be enclosed with proper ventilation and extraction. This ensures that the working environment is controlled and safe. No smoking should be allowed.

Fourth, guidance on the length of time anybody is allowed to be in contact with the substance should be followed. This is where anybody working with a substance is at risk through inhalation. The COSHH regulations stipulate the substances with maximum exposure levels in Schedule 1 and the HSE produce a list of substances with limited occupational standards. Guidance is available in HSE EH40/97 about these.

The guidance should be followed and producers or managers should ensure that the maximum exposure limits (MELs) and the limits for any particular kind of work, called occupational exposure standards (OESs), are not exceeded.

Fifth, monitoring any exposure that might be a risk to health should be recorded. In other words producers and managers must keep records of which staff are at risk, what they are at risk from and for how long (see *Monitoring Strategies for Toxic Substances* in Further reading). Supervisors or production managers must be informed of this responsibility.

This is easier in a base building where permanent staff are constantly around but more difficult in a film and television environment where freelance staff on short-term contract work and temporary locations are involved. Happily the HSE have drawn up some special guidelines to help successfully monitor transient workers (see HSE guidance COSHH and Peripatetic Workers).

The sixth action to be taken is a proper surveillance of the health risks. Where an employee or subcontractor is engaged in one of the processes listed in Schedule 5 of the COSHH regulations or where employees are linked to a substance that can cause a particular disease then regular health monitoring of all employees engaged in this work must be carried out. This is so that any long-term adverse effects on health can be monitored, recorded and detected – for example monitoring the health of employees engaged in work which involves diesel fumes, petrol vapour or paint spray (asbestos and lead are covered by separate regulations). Workers engaged in this type of work should have regular health checks.

Regular checks should be made for damage to eyes, nose, lungs, skin and hands. These records must be kept for forty years under the COSHH (Amendment) Regulations. For guidance on how to set up a health surveillance and record system, see Health Surveillance Under COSHH, Health Risk Management and Health Surveillance of Occupational Skin Disease, all listed in Further reading.

The seventh action is for managers and producers to provide the proper information and guidance to employees and the public about COSHH hazards. They must make sure that information is up-to-date and accurate. It must be made available to anyone at risk. Information about chemicals and gases must be supplied on a safety data sheet by the manufacturers and this should be given to any contractors or staff.

The data sheet should be read before handling the contents of any cylinder or drum. The data sheet reference number must be duplicated on any product label. If a data sheet is not supplied, you should request a copy before use.

The data sheet contains information under 16 different headings:

1 product name and manufacturer's name and address
2 description of gas/chemical and identification code
3 hazard identification code
4 first aid measures if staff are exposed to the contents
5 fire fighting measures to be taken
6 accidental release measures action
7 handling and storage information
8 exposure limits and personal protection information
9 physical and chemical properties of substance
10 stability and reactivity information
11 toxicological information
12 ecological information
13 disposal instructions
14 transport information

15 regulatory information
16 any other information.

Proper training and instruction must be provided to anybody involved in COSHH related work. One way to do this is to draw up a company COSHH code of practice and draw up a health and safety policy statement. This should outline employees' responsibilities and the rules they should follow (see Guide to Preparing a Safety Policy Statement for a Small Business, HSE c100/95). Employers and managers must make sure that employees and the public are provided with proper personal protective equipment and that all work tools and safety equipment are properly maintained, safe and compatible. All dangerous COSHH work should be properly supervised by an experienced, qualified and competent supervisor appointed for the purpose.

The eighth action is to make sure that all spillages and accidents are reported. Any exposure, escape, explosion, fire or accident should be reported under the Reporting of Injuries, Diseases and Dangerous Occurrences Regulations 1995 (RIDDOR). Use an HSE report of an injury or dangerous occurrence form (F2508/F2508A). Injuries caused by flammable gas should also be reported on a report of flammable gas incidents and dangerous gas fittings (F2508G). Employers should maintain an accident and incident record book (HSE form B1–510) and encourage the reporting of unsafe behaviour and environments.

The ninth action is the safe disposal of any hazardous chemical or substance after you have used it or any waste residue created as a result of any process. The disposal of hazardous chemicals and waste must be made in accordance with the Control of Pollution (Special Waste) Regulations 1980. A special consignment note for the carriage and disposal of hazardous wastes should be used and a notification of intention to dispose made to the hazardous wastes department of the local county council. Regulation 13 states that the carrier, disposal authority and site owner must keep a register of all hazardous waste for at least two years. Names of authorized carriers of hazardous waste can be obtained from the National Association of Waste Disposal Contractors (NAWDC). Never pour hazardous chemicals down drains as this could contaminate the water supply.

The final action is to continuously review and record the preceding nine steps as legislation and regulations may change. The assessment should be carried out on site and the supervisor should update it if the nature of the working conditions or the task changes. Remember everyone should be made aware of the changes. A lot of accidents happen because the work method changed but nobody was told. Producers and managers should make sure that all COSHH files are updated and that a proper risk assessment is carried out for each location, action and process.

	Category of danger	Symbol letter	Indication of danger	Symbol (orange background)
Physico-chemical	Explosive	**E**	Explosive	
	Oxidising	**O**	Oxidising	
	Extremely flammable	**F+**	Extremely flammable	
	Highly flammable	**F**	Highly flammable	
Health	Very toxic	**T+**	Very toxic	
	Toxic	**T**	Toxic	
	Harmful	**Xn**	Harmful	
	Corrosive	**C**	Corrosive	
	Irritant	**Xi**	Irritant	
	Sensitising	**Xn**	Harmful	
		Xi	Irritant	
	Carcinogenic *Categories 1 and 2*	**T**	Toxic	
	Category 3	**Xn**	Harmful	
	Mutagenic *Categories 1 and 2*	**T**	Toxic	
	Category 3	**Xn**	Harmful	
	Toxic for reproduction *Categories 1 and 2*	**T**	Toxic	
	Category 3	**Xn**	Harmful	
Environmental	Dangerous for the environment	**N**	Dangerous for the environment	

Figure H6.2   *CHIP 99 (2) chemical danger symbols.* Source: *HSE, CHIP 99 (2) for Everyone.* © *HSE*

Identifying and labelling of chemicals

Identify any chemical hazards and list them on a COSHH assessment form. Always try and substitute them for something less hazardous.

All chemicals should be only those on the approved supply list.

Inform your safety officer before introducing any chemical onto a site, building or location as this may alter your insurance cover. Check with your safety equipment supplier that you have the correct protective equipment.

Any harmful substance has to be properly labelled and marked under the COSHH and Health and Safety (Signs and Signals) Regulations. Employers should make sure that any hazardous substance which is introduced by suppliers or contractors is properly labelled with square orange warning signs to indicate a COSHH health hazard. The main classifications are:

1 Explosive
2 Irritant
3 Highly flammable
4 Harmful
5 Oxidizing
6 Toxic
7 Corrosive.

Make sure any supplier or subcontractor informs the safety officer of any hazardous substance they are planning to use or bring onto location, for example metal fabrication work, special effects and gas used for mobile catering, heating or diving. Producers and contractors should always request a safety data sheet which should be given to anybody handling or using a substance.

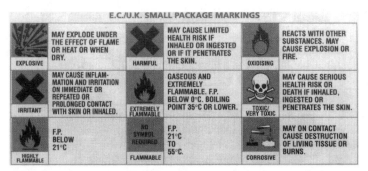

Figure H6.3 *Seven chemical symbols signs.* Source: Symbol Seeker, *Reid Marketing Co.*

Danger labels are triangular and give specific content warning in sixteen different classifications:

- Compressed gas
- Poison gas
- Flammable gas
- Flammable liquid
- Flammable solid
- Spontaneously combustible
- Dangerous when wet
- Oxidizing agent
- Organic peroxide
- Harmful – stow away from foodstuffs
- Toxic
- Corrosive
- Multi-load
- Oxygen
- Marine pollutant
- Other dangerous substance.

Chemical hazard labels can be identified with the *Symbol Seeker* (ISBN 0-6955-7059-5). Appropriate warning posters and labels can be obtained from your safety signs supplier.

All chemical drum and compressed gas container labels must comply with the Health and Safety (Signs and Signals) Regulations 1996 and comply with BS 5378 and EU standards. Yellow caution signs should indicate to staff any risk. Red circular signs should stop and prohibit access or specific activity and blue circular signs should indicate mandatory action such as the wearing of appropriate personal protective clothing. Green triangles indicate safe exit routes. Through the proper identification, labelling and warning signs staff should be aware of any hazardous substance. Beware of any drum or cylinder which has no marking or label. This risk may exist in derelict sites and waste dumps. If in doubt, do not touch, move or open.

The correct storage of hazardous chemicals and substances

To prevent and control the risk of exposure any chemicals/gases or materials should be stored for a maximum period of twelve months in separate secure compounds at least 3 metres away from site boundaries and 2 metres away from other cylinders. Compounds should be marked with content warning and fire warning labels. Emergency exits should open outwards and the compound should be properly ventilated and out of direct sun light and other heat sources. Emergency lighting should be installed and any bulbs or electrical supplies must be flameproof and have intrinsically safe gas tight fittings.

A proper record should be kept of all chemicals and gases being stored and when they enter or leave a site. They should be booked in and out and stock must be rotated to prevent deterioration.

Never smoke near chemicals or introduce the risk of fire by storing chemicals near to paper, wood or plastics. No smoking signs and highly flammable signs should be visible with labels to indicate the content and flash point of any stored substance.

The storage of all inflammable liquids and gases is subject to the Highly Flammable Liquids and Liquefied Petroleum Gases Regulations 1972. Drums must conform to BS 814 and storage building and cupboards to BS 476. Storage cupboards must hold a maximum of 50 litres and be fire resistant for at least 30 minutes. Cylinders should be stored upright (unless the data sheet specifies otherwise) and strapped securely.

Use proper chemical resistant pallets and make sure the surface is level. Liquefied petroleum gas (LPG) cylinders should never be stored in rows of more than six. Never store gas which is heavier than air on raised platforms or near ditches, drains, pipes, sewers or water courses.

Do not store hazardous chemicals in inappropriate containers such as white spirit/paraffin containers, coffee jars or similar. Use the correct sealed container and the correct label for identification. Careful thought should be given to the storage of large amounts of paint, thinners and spirits. These should be kept cool and separate.

Fire precautions for chemicals and hazardous substances

Make sure that proper fire prevention precautions are in place with the correct extinguishers and sand buckets. All fire fighting equipment must be safe in itself, regularly serviced and correct for the task required.

All fire extinguishers should be CE marked and rated at BS 5423. From January 1997 all extinguishers should conform to European safety standard and BS EN 3 and be CE marked. All new extinguishers can retain a small colour panel for easy identification. The panel will indicate the contents by colour and a symbol will indicate the class of fires which the extinguisher may be used on.

There are four classes of fire:

- Class A: water, paper, cloth.
- Class B: flammable liquids and fats.
- Class C: flammable gases.
- Class D: electrical hazards.

FIRE STORAGE REQUIREMENTS FOR CHEMICALS

1   HM Chief Inspector of Factories has issued Certificate of Approval No 1 for storerooms, process cabinets or enclosures, workrooms, cupboards, bins, ducts and casings, which are required to be fire-resisting under the Highly Flammable Liquids and Liquefied Petroleum Gases Regulations 1972. The main requirements for cabinets, enclosures, storerooms, ducts and casings are summarised below. These should form the basis for construction of fire-resisting enclosures, whether or not the specific Regulations apply.

2   Cupboards, bins, cabinets and similar enclosures

The materials used to construct each side, top, floor, door and lid should:

(a) if tested in accordance with BS 476 Parts 20 and 22 (or previously Part 8) be capable of satisfying the integrity requirement of that test for at least 30 minutes;

(b) provide an internal surface to the enclosure with a surface spread of flame and heat release classification of Class 0 (as defined in Approved Document B issued in connection with the Building Regulations 1991);

(c) be fastened together in such a manner, using fastenings (including any hinges) that are of high melting point (in excess of 750°C), that:
   (i)   the entire enclosure, if tested in accordance with BS 476 Parts 20 and 22 (or previously Part 8), would not come apart for at least 30 minutes;
   (ii) the joints are made, bonded or fire-stopped to prevent or retard the passage of flame and hot gases;
   (iii) the structure is sufficiently robust that its integrity will not be impaired by any reasonably foreseeable accidental impact;

(d) be sufficiently durable that if coated with residues from any spillages, that these can be removed without impairing the structure's fire resistance.

3   Storerooms

The following requirements do not apply to external doors, external windows and external walls, any opening provided for ventilation, or any tops or ceilings of single-storey buildings and top-floor rooms, unless these components are within the separation distances to the vulnerable features previously specified (see section on Separation) and not otherwise protected:

(a) Every enclosing element, that is to say every wall (including every door or window therein), floor (other than a floor immediately above the ground), and any ceiling plus its associated floor, should if tested in accordance with BS 476 Parts 20 and 22, and as appropriate Part 21 (or previously Part 8) be capable of satisfying the integrity and insulation requirements of the test, and as relevant the load-bearing capacity requirement.

(b) The internal surfaces of all walls and ceiling/roof should be capable of achieving at least Class 1 if tested in accordance with BS 476 Part 7 (surface spread of flame).

(c) Doors should be self-closing from any position.

(d) Joints between elements of construction should be made, bonded or fire-stopped to prevent or retard the passage of flame and hot gases.

Figure H6.4   *Fire storage requirements for chemicals.* Source: The Storage of Flammable Liquids in Containers, *2nd edition, 1998, HSE, HSG51, ISBN 0-7176-1471-9. © HMSO*

(e) The structure should be sufficiently robust that its fire resistance will not be impaired by any reasonably foreseeable accidental impact.
(f) The materials of construction used should be sufficiently durable that if coated with residues from any spillages, that these can be removed without impairing the storeroom's fire resistance.

4 Ducts, trunks and casings

(a) Ducts, trunks and casings should be such that if tested in accordance with BS 476 Parts 20 and 22 (or previously Part 8) they would be capable of satisfying the integrity requirement of that test for at least 30 minutes.
(b) They should provide an internal surface to the enclosure with a surface spread of flame and heat release classification of Class 0 (as defined in Approved Document B issued in connection with the Building Regulations 1991).
(c) They should be supported and fastened in such a manner, using supports and fastenings that are of high melting point (in excess of 750°C) that:
   (i) the structure plus its supports, if tested in accordance with BS 476 Parts 20 and 22 (or previously Part 8) would not collapse or come apart for at least 30 minutes;
   (ii) the joints are made, bonded or fire-stopped to prevent or retard the passage of flame and hot gases;
   (iii) the structure is sufficiently robust that its integrity will not be impaired by any reasonably foreseeable accidental impact.
(d) They should be sufficiently durable that if coated with residues, that these can be removed without impairing the structure's fire resistance.

Figure H6.4 *Continued*

There are four major types of new fire extinguisher:

1 Water or hydrospray – for wood/paper/fabric fires only. The panel colour is red. For Class A fires only. Do not use on electrical or chemical fires.
2 Foam spray (AFFF) – burning liquid fires only. The panel colour is cream. For Class A and B fires only. Do not use on electrical fires.
3 Dry powder – for burning liquid and electrical fires only. The panel colour is blue. For Class A, B, C and some electrical fires only (ideal for carrying in vehicles).
4 Carbon dioxide (CO_2) – for burning liquid and electrical fires only. The panel colour is black. For Class B and electrical fires only (ideal for computers, generators and lights).

NB Halon (BCF) extinguishers were coloured green and were used for burning liquid and electrical fires only. However all halon extinguishers should have been replaced by 1999 as the CFCs they contain damage the environment.

Signs for fire extinguishers should be to BS 7863 to indicate the contents. Do not use the wrong type of fire extinguisher for a particular kind of fire. This can create a violent reaction or cause electrocution. Make sure all staff are trained in the correct extinguisher type to use and receive proper instruction on how to use them. Above all make sure that there are enough types of extinguisher for each category of fire risk and in sufficient quantity. All fire extinguishers should be properly serviced and maintained at least once a year in accordance with BS 5306 part 3, 1985. Remember to provide fire extinguishers of the appropriate type in all your production vehicles and kitchens.

Make a risk assessment about appropriate fire fighting precautions and draw up a containment and evacuation plan in the event of a fire/spill or exposure (see Hazard 17: Fire). Any fire incidents and precautionary measures must be recorded in a workplace fire safety log book.

Designers and scenery construction workers should take fire risks into account when planning or storing sets. All wood and material must be flame-proofed and treated with flame-retarding paints. Standards include wood BS 476 Part 7 class 1; fibreglass BS 476 Part 7 class 1; drapes BS 5687 Part 2; carpets BS 4790.

Set designers and constructors should also avoid the risk of explosion from direct heat sources such as sunlight, electrical sparks, welding activities and lights during the construction and use of scenery on set and during storage or maintenance work.

No smoking must be enforced in preparation areas and wood must be stored away from inflammable materials and chemicals. Beware of the explosion risk from concentrations of dry wood dust in saw shops and construction bays. This would be increased by dry weather and spillages of paint and thinners. In the event of a chemical spillage, prevent access until the area is safe. Anybody entering must wear protective equipment including gloves, boots, suits, eye protection and respiratory masks. Then spread Rench-Rapid or similar absorbent to soak up any oils or chemicals. The residue and waste should be disposed of safely and the area checked for fumes before access is permitted.

Metal workers and welders should beware of fumes and the explosion risk from fabrication work. They should wear eye protection and hand protection and beware of working in hot conditions for too long.

Adequate fire precautions and evacuation procedures should be in place including smoke detectors, fire alarms and sprinklers.

Batteries used to power film equipment contain chemicals and can give off dangerous fumes if overcharged or overheated. Always store in a separate area at a safe temperature and maintain according to the manufacturer's instructions. Always charge batteries in an open environment to reduce the risk of chemical explosion. Never smoke or use naked flames in battery maintenance areas. Any lights in battery charging areas should have intrinsically safe gas-tight fittings when there is a risk of explosion.

The handling and movement of dangerous chemicals and substances

The manual handling of chemical or hazardous substances should only be undertaken after a proper identification has been made since some substances are highly unstable and require special moving procedures.

Bulk liquids, chemicals and gases are usually very heavy so proper lifting equipment would be needed to prevent the risk of back or lifting injuries. The Manual Handling Regulations specify the correct lifting procedures (see Hazard 25: Manual handling and lifting). Make sure the containers are secure and the lifting equipment is powerful enough to do the job.

Unstable chemicals and compressed gas should not be moved without the right containers and under expert advice (see *A Guide to Transportable Gas Containers Regulations 1989* and Approved Code of Practice).

Before handling or exposing chemicals make sure it is safe to do so and always wear appropriate protective clothing such as gloves, eye protection, boots, and appropriate respiratory equipment. The need for these should be identified as part of the risk assessment and is required by the Personal Protective Equipment at Work Regulations 1992. Staff should be given protective equipment to prevent inhalation/absorption/swallowing/burning/contamination and asphyxiation. Special protective creams should be used to prevent dermatitis. Maximum exposure levels should not be exceeded and the storage and handling procedures should be outlined on COSHH data sheets obtained from the supplier and manufacturer.

Chemicals and hazardous substance risks in film and TV work

Broadcasting and film work can contain chemical and hazardous substance risks from four main types of activity which place particular staff in high health risk situations.

The first risk is to location managers, production managers, crews and actors working on the occupied locations of third parties. This can be fiction or documentary activity outside of base but where the site, building or location have an occupier and owner. Such locations are often unfamiliar and have particular risks of their own.

If you are going to work on somebody else's workplace such as a refinery, plant or manufacturing unit where COSHH hazards are ever present, you should submit a work plan in advance for approval and a list of tools and equipment you are going to use. Always follow the in-house safety rules, emergency procedures and obey personal protective equipment regulations. In other words you come under the control of the owner or operator of the location who must supply you with health and safety information.

Producers and supervisors must make sure that information is communicated and followed in the same way as if you were filming on your own location. However you must carry third party and public liability cover and make sure that any equipment you introduce is safe.

Farming, agricultural and rural programmes have a special COSHH risk of exposure and contamination from pesticides and chemicals used on agricultural locations. Check with the farm owner/operator first (see Hazard 1: Agricultural locations).

Documentary and news crews should assess the risk presented by programme access to manufacturing sites, chemical plants, refineries, transport/tanker depots, petrol and gas stations, oil rigs, sheet metal and welding locations, shipyards and chemical gas storage depots. Always inform the site owner/operator of what you intend to do and what equipment you are going to introduce. They can then draw up a proper risk assessment in advance.

Contact the health and safety officer for the plant and obtain a copy of the health and safety rules and emergency procedures for that site. Circulate these to your crew and get a proper briefing from the site health and safety officer before entering. Follow the PPE Regulations and wear the correct protective equipment. Always use local qualified knowledge. Any risk assessment should be carried out on site and the supervisor should update it if the nature of the working conditions or the task changes. Everyone should be made aware of the changes. A lot of accidents happen because the work method changed but nobody was told. The problem is one of information, communication and supervision.

The second major area of risk comes from derelict locations. Chemical and hazardous substance exposure risks extend to programmes about hazards. For example, a documentary crew making a programme about the risks of asbestos might be at risk from asbestos themselves if filming on the site. Derelict sites make tempting locations for fiction films because the lack of owners or occupiers means they are often cheaper and more atmospheric. However this very lack of an occupier can mean that safety information is non-existent and that the location is a minefield of dormant COSHH risks waiting to be activated by your production along with other biological hazards such as discarded needles and condoms to be found on derelict sites (see Hazard 13: Derelict buildings).

Location managers and production managers should be aware of chemical hazards on initial site visits and a full risk assessment and hazard identification should be made. If possible get accurate and experienced local knowledge to help you and get copies of old site plans from the former occupier. These will help you to locate hazards such as disused gas pipes, electricity cables, sewage and waste pipes or storage tanks.

COSHH risks are very high in derelict plants and factories, waste ground and urban demolition sites, building sites, abandoned mines and quarries as chemical and hazardous substance risks are inherent to the location – for example, the risk from methane, radon and other gases inherent under contaminated land, waste tips and mines. Use a portable gas analyser to detect the presence of gas.

Call the nearest fire authority and gas company if you suspect gas seepage (emergency numbers are in *The Phone Book*), avoid smoking and beware the risk of explosion and fires. Do not disturb walls, floors and pipes as these may contain polluted and unstable chemicals or asbestos used as lagging. Use a competent and experienced chemical/waste contractor to clear the site and perform a proper COSHH risk assessment before sending anybody in to recce the site. Make sure that they have adequate personal protective clothing and good communications. Never send them alone or ask them to enter into any confined space where hazardous fumes may be present. Never assume that because a building is derelict that it has no hazards. Always assume that such locations are dangerous and unsafe until you can prove that they are not. The problem is one of identification and protection.

The third major risk comes from introduced activity. This means chemicals or substances which may be brought onto site or location as part of the programme-making activity or as a result of it. The hazards can be introduced intentionally or unintentionally. The major problem here is one of control as nobody may know that the hazardous chemical or substance is present and therefore no precautions have been taken.

Particular attention should be paid to what substances might be introduced by contributors or third parties to programme content. Never introduce strange or unmarked containers onto the location and make sure the substances are correctly labelled and securely stored away from fire risks. Inform your safety office before introducing any chemical on to a site, building or location.

Make sure any supplier or subcontractor informs the safety office of any hazardous substance they are planning to use or bring onto your location. For example, metal fabrication work, special effects and gas used for mobile catering, heating or diving. Another example would be temporary chemical toilets and sewerage facilities on temporary locations. Any hazardous chemical present in the workplace should be recorded in the COSHH register with data and product information. The chemical should be stored correctly and the maximum occupational exposure levels observed.

Producers and directors should identify at an early planning stage any intentionally introduced hazard which they intend to use. Examples would include chemicals in health or scientific programmes both in the studio and on location. This could include lasers, radioactive and nuclear hazards (see Hazard 24: Lasers and radiation). Lifestyle programmes can be at risk from demonstration products such as lead paint for DIY programmes and gas for cooking programmes.

While fiction films can introduce firearms, pyrotechnics and smoke effects (see Hazard 16: Explosives and pyrotechnics, and Hazard 18: Firearms and weapons), use of scenery and stunts are all high risk activities under the COSHH regulations and must be identified on the COSHH risk assessment.

Longer-term risk to health and with more deadly effects can come from every-day base station activities such as cleaning, maintenance of buildings and vehicles, film processing, scenery construction and painting, model making, hairdressing and make-up, metal fabrication and handling newsprint.

The effects of such exposure are very slow and long-term causing respiratory/asthma, skin diseases and cancers. Health of workers who may suffer long-term exposure to hazardous substances should be regularly monitored and the records kept.

In-house COSHH assessments should use a separate coloured form for each type of COSHH hazard and clearly identify the type of hazard, the location, who is at risk and the precautions. These should be kept along with the COSHH register of each chemical hazard and its properties.

Always ask, can the job be done a better way? And can a safer substitute be used?

Film processing and laboratory work carries a heavy risk of long-term exposure to chemicals and the premises where this is done would have a high risk of fire and explosion. Film graders should be aware of any risk from handling film stock and processing chemicals. All laboratory personnel should be trained in proper procedures and safety precautions for handling chemicals.

This includes storage areas, processing rooms, cleaning and inspection rooms. Eye irritation and dermatitis are major hazards associated with handling photographic processing chemicals. Film processing workers should be aware of the potentially toxic fumes from chemical solutions which can be an irritant. Solutions should always be mixed correctly in safe quantities and staff should wear proper PPE such as gloves, suits, eye protection and breathing apparatus. Staff should be trained in the safe storage, mixing and handling of any chemical substances and such work should be properly supervised and carried out by experienced and competent people.

Film cleaning uses a lot of 1,1,1-trichloroethane as a solvent before telecine transfers. The use of 1,1,1-trichloroethane is strictly regulated by the Montreal Protocol and restricted. This is because it destroys the ozone layer and can induce dangerous anaesthetic effects on any user. Laboratories should switch to perchloro-ethylene which is safer. However, film cleaning operatives should still wear proper protective equipment and work in properly ventilated areas. Film stock storage areas carry a high fire risk and should be properly ventilated. The storage of antique nitrate film is strictly prohibited and confined to a special licensed MOMI (Museum of the Moving Image) archive in Berkhampstead. Film[1] researchers should be aware of the risk of fire and exposure to chemicals when handling film stock. Similar risks could also apply to film camera operators and film editors who handle negative and processed stock on a regular basis.

Scenery designers should take special care that they don't expose construction staff, the public, audiences, crew, scenery removal staff and actors to risk of exposure from hazardous materials used in sets. The construction of sets and scenery are covered by the Construction (Design and Management) Regulations (CDM) which insist that any built construction should be properly designed with safety built in. This means that any structures should not be made with large quantities of hazardous substances and that the COSHH Regulations apply to the materials used in their preparation.

Painters are at very high risk from lead paints and solvents. Paints which contain isocyanates are very dangerous to anybody suffering from asthma, hay fever or lung problems. Maximum exposure levels and occupational exposure standards should be followed for any paint or toxic substance. Exposed skin should be kept to a minimum and be protected by barrier cream. Painters should read the manufacturer's safety data sheet and product advice sheet for the correct use of the paint. Eye protection and impervious gloves should be worn. Conduct painting in well ventilated areas and avoid breathing fumes by wearing suitable respiratory protection. Always clean your hands afterwards.

Proper training should be given to avoid accidents and spillages. In the event of a chemical spillage, prevent access until the area is safe. Anybody entering must wear protective equipment including gloves, boots, suits, eye protection and respiratory masks. Then spread Rench-Rapid or similar absorbent to soak up any oils or chemicals. The residue and waste should be disposed of safely and the area checked for fumes before access is permitted.

Avoid the use of asbestos, glass and lead. Scenery construction staff should wear the right protective equipment including eye, ear and hand protection – especially when welding, using power tools, lathes and saws. All electrical equipment should be properly tested and controlled by a master electricity cut-off switch. All machinery should have proper guards fitted and working areas should have correct extraction and ventilation. All tools should be stored properly and only used by experienced and competent staff unless proper supervision is in place.

Carpenters and woodworkers should be aware of dust hazards and chemical hazards from paints and thinners, especially when constructing large-scale sets and rostra from soft wood. One particular hazard that has recently been identified is the amount of fine dust and formaldehyde fumes given off by working with MDF, described by Ray Lockett of BECTU as the asbestos of the 1990s.

The risk from MDF only became clear when workers with prolonged exposure to it began to fall ill. As dust related diseases take 20 years to develop, the risk from a product that is 25 years old will only now start to be seen. Normal procedures would recommend that masks and respiratory equipment should be used with proper ventilation. Dusts masks should be CE/EN149 with an FFP3 filter.

MDF fibres, however, are very small and pass through normal dust masks. Moreover, the UK recommended exposure level for formaldehyde at 2ppm is 20 times higher than Europe or the USA. Proper masks and improved dust extraction in workshops would help to reduce the risk but this costs money. The formaldehyde gas given off is colourless and is emitted after manufacture for several months. The solution here is to buy MDF which is bonded with safer resins. Again this is more expensive. So in a climate of tight financial controls the outlook for rapid improvement in the risk from MDF is not good.

Model makers should be aware of the risks from working with glass fibre glues, polystyrene moulding and plaster work. These have particular fumes and handling problems and should be properly supervised and ventilated with the proper protective equipment and advice given about maximum exposure levels. Use water based fillers for glass fibre (see Hazard 30: Scenery and props).

Fibreglass in particular has been used for many years in sets, scenery, props and models. It is polyester based and gives off bad fumes which can be explosive. This has led to rising insurance costs as the risks from solvents and fumes became clearer. The use of a safer substitute such as jesmonite is recommended.

Make-up artists, wig artists, beauticians and hairdressers have a high risk of contact dermatitis. The risk factor is 36 times higher than the national average in these occupations.

All scenery construction areas, wood shops, model making areas and metal work preparation areas should be kept separate, with proper extraction such as a Plymovent fume extraction system. Proper ventilation should provide clean air and adequate fire precautions must be taken. The combination of protective clothing, gas and hot weather can raise working temperatures to dangerous levels. This is called hot work and conditions should be constantly monitored to ensure that recommended working times and break periods are enforced.

Maintenance, plumbing and cleaning staff are also exposed to chemicals on a daily basis and the risks should be properly identified and precautions put in place as the most common agents associated with contact dermatitis are soaps and cleansers.

Vehicle maintenance staff are exposed to risks from petrol and diesel fumes on a regular basis with an attendant risk of lung damage. New guidance has been produced by the HSE on the control of diesel exhaust fumes (Control of Diesel Engine Exhaust Emissions in the Workplace HSG 187, ISBN 0-7176-1662-2).

Journalists and research staff handle quantities of newsprint which can be absorbed into hands over a long period of time. The problem is overlooking the risk in everyday activities and monitoring them effectively.

Section 6 of the COSHH Regulations says that 'an employer shall not carry on any work that is liable to expose any employees to any substance hazardous to health'.

Management should monitor everyday, long-term work situations as well as one-off, special situations and construct an effective plan to control chemical and substance hazards by performing a proper COSHH risk assessment. This means putting into place identifying labelling, storage, preventative, control and protective measures to reduce risk from such exposure during production activity. This should be backed up by clear communication and proper supervision in an effective chain of responsibility.

Note

1 For a good description of the hazards of nitrate film, see Lobban Grant, The Restoration Business, *Image Technology* (BSKTS journal), May 1997 volume 79, no. 5, pages 26–8.

Further reading

The Control of Substances Hazardous to Health Regulations 1999 (COSHH), HSE SI 437, ISBN 0-11-082087-8.
The Chemicals (Hazard Information and Packaging for Supply) (Amendment) (No. 2) Regulations 1999, (CHIP 99 (2)), HSE-SI 197, ISBN 0-11-080410-4.
The Approved Classification and Labelling Guide, 4th edition, HSE, ISBN 0-7176-1726-2.
The Approved Supply List, 5th edition, HSE, ISBN 0-7176-1725-4.

The Carriage of Dangerous Goods (Amendment) Regulations 1999, HSE SI 303, ISBN 0-11-080470-8.

HSE Toxic Substances Bulletin (TSB), published by HSE Books, PO Box 1999, Sudbury, Suffolk CO10 6FS (subscription £15 a year for three issues).

Approved Codes of Practice: Control of Substances Hazardous to Health and Control of Carcinogenic Substances (including Control of Substances Hazardous to Health Regulations 1988) (4th edition) HMSO L51993, ISBN 0-11-882085-0.

Control of Substances Hazardous to Health Regulations 1994, Approved Code of Practice, HSE, 1995, ISBN 0-7176-0819-0.

A Step By Step Guide to COSHH Assessment, HSE 1993, HS(G)97, ISBN 0-11-886379-7.

The Storage of Flammable Liquids in Containers, HSE-HSG51, 2nd edition 1998, ISBN 0-7176-1471-9.

The Carriage of Dangerous Goods (Amendment) Regulations 1998, SI 2885, ISBN 0-11-079850-3.

The Chemicals (Hazard Information and Packaging for Supply) (Amendment) Regulations 1998, SI 3106, ISBN 0-11-079931-3.

The Chemicals (Hazard Information and Packaging for Supply) Regulations 1994: CHIP 2 For Everyone, HS(G)126, ISBN 0-7176-0857-3.

Monitoring Strategies for Toxic Substances, HMSO, EH42, 1989, ISBN 0-11-885412-7.

EH40, Occupational Exposure Limits 1999, HSE, E40/99, 1999, ISBN 0-7176-1660-6.

Health Surveillance Under COSHH – Guidance for Employers, HMSO, 1990, ISBN 0-11-885447-X.

Surveillance of People Exposed to Health Risks at Work, HSE, HS(G)61–1990, ISBN 0-1-885574-3.

Health Surveillance of Occupational Skin Disease, HSE, MS/24, 1991, ISBN 0-11-885583-2.

Health Risk Management, HSE-HS(G)137 ISBN 0-7176-0905-7.

Lift Trucks in Potentially Flammable Atmospheres, HSE, HS(G)113, 1996, ISBN 0-7176-0706-2.

Read the Label (How to Find Out if Chemicals are Dangerous), HSE, HS IND(G)186, HSE, 1995, ISBN 0-7176-0898-0.

A Short Guide to Personal Protective Equipment at Work Regulations 1992, HSE 1995, ISBN-IND(G)-147L.

Solvents and You, HSE-IND(G)93(L).

Health Hazards to Painters, HSE-IND(G)72(L).

Five Steps to Risk Assessment, HSE-1994-IND(G)163L.

European Agreement Concerning the International Carriage of Dangerous Goods By Road (ADR) and Protocol of Signature, UN, ISBN 0-11-941712-X.

The Construction (Design and Management) Regulations 1994, Approved Code of Practice 154, HSE 1995, ISBN 0-7176-0792-5.

Safety of Pressure Systems and Transportable Gas Containers Regulations 1989, Approved Code of Practice, HSE, 1989, ISBN 0-11-885514-X.

A Guide to Safety of Pressure Systems and Transportable Gas Containers Regulations 1989, Approved Code of Practice, HSE, 1989, ISBN 0-11-885516-6.

Guide to the Classification and Labelling of Explosives Regulations 1983, HSE, 1983, ISBN 0-11-883706-0.

Seven Steps to Successful Substitution of Hazardous Substances, HSE-HS(G)110, ISBN 0-7176-0695-3.

Smoke and Vapour Effects used in Entertainment, HSE Entertainment Sheet No. 3, ETIS(3).

Also series of HSE guidance notes in Chemical Safety series: nos 4, 6, 8, 9, 11, 15, 16, 18, 21, 22 give specific guidance about handling and storage of specific chemicals.

Howell, Jeff, Are we playing with fibre? *Independent on Sunday*, 28 September 1997, p. 9 (article on the MDF risk).

P.G. Urben (editor), *Brethericks Handbook of Reactive Chemical Hazards,* 2 vols, Butterworth-Heinemann, Oxford.

John Barton and Richard Rogers, *Chemical Reaction Hazards,* 2nd edition, Institution of Chemical Engineers, 1997, ISBN 0-85295-341-0.

Code of Practice for Pyrotechnics and Smoke Effects, Association of British Theatre Technicians, 47 Bermondsey St, London EC1 3XT, ISBN 0-11-341072-7.

Dictionary of Substances and their Effects, Royal Society of Chemistry, Cambridge.

J.F. Whitfield, *A Guide to Electrical Safety at Work,* 1992, EPA Press.

Robin Garside, *Electrical Apparatus and Hazardous Areas,* 2nd edition, 1994, Hexagon Technology Ltd.

A.C. Bronstein and L. Currance, *Emergency Care For Hazardous Materials Exposure,* 2nd edition, 1994, code EME-8, Emergency Response Publications, 5 Shelly Court, South Zeal, Okehampton Devon EX20 2PT, Tel: 01837–840102.

Peter B. Cook, *Occupational Health Hazards (A Practical Guide to COSHH),* 1989, code BK-6581, British Safety Council, 70 Chancellors Rd, London W6 9RS, Tel: 0181–741–1231.

Library of Fire Safety, *Volume 1: Fire Safety Handbook* and *Volume 2: Fire and Hazardous Substances.* Available from the Fire Protection Association, Melrose Avenue, Borehamwood, Hertfordshire WD6 2BJ, Tel: 0181–207–2345.

CEA Classification of Materials and Goods, CEA2, 1996.

Fire Protection of Stores Containing Hazardous Substances, CEA1, 1996.

● Spraying and Other Painting Processes Involving Flammable Liquids and Powders, RC14/1989.

● Storage and Use of Flammable Liquids, RC20/1990.

● Storage, Use and Handling of Common Industrial Gases in Cylinders (excluding LPG) RC8/1992.

The three items above are available from the Loss Prevention Council, Melrose Avenue, Borehamwood, Hertfordshire WD6 2BJ, Tel: 0181–207–2345.

Saxe's Dangerous Properties of Industrial Materials, 3 volumes, 9th edition, 1996, ISBN 0-4420-20825-2, Van Nostrand Reinhold.

Symbol Seeker, Reid Marketing Co., 60 Moor St, Ormskirk, Lancs L39 2AW, Tel: 01695–570595

W. Chapman, *Workshop Technology, Volume 1,* 5th edition, 1972, ISBN 0-7131-3269-8, *Volume 2,* 4th edition, 1972, ISBN 0-7131-3272-8, Edward Arnold.

A.C. Davis, *The Science and Practice of Welding, Volumes 1 and 2*, 10th edition, 1993, ISBN 0-5214-3566-8, Cambridge University Press.
Equity Spotlight Register of Stunt Action Co-ordinators and Performers.
BECTU joint industry special effects grading scheme.

Contact organizations

Association of British Theatre Technicians
47 Bermondsey St, London SE1 3XT
Tel: 0171–403–3778

British Actors Equity Association
Guild House, Upper St, Martins Lane, London WC2H 9EG
Tel: 0171–379–6000

BECTU
111 Wardour St, London W1V 4AY
Tel: 0171–437–8506

British Agrochemicals Association
4 Lincoln Court, Lincoln Rd, Peterborough PE1 2RP
Tel: 01733–349225

British Compressed Gases Association
14 Tollgate, Eastleigh, Hampshire SO53 3TG
Tel: 01703–641488

The Society of Chemical Industry Health and Safety Group
14–15 Belgrave Square, London SW1X 8PS
Tel: 0171–235–3681

The Chemical Hazards Communications Society
C/O D. Waight, 3m UK Plc, PO Box 1, Market Place, Bracknell, Berkshire RG12 1JU
Tel: 01908–653658

The Chemical Industries Association
Kings Buildings, Smith Square, London SW1P 3JJ
Tel: 0171–834–3399

Dustraction Ltd
PO Box 75, Manderville Road, Oadby, Leicester LE2 5NE
Tel: 0116–271–3212

Health Education Authority
64 Burgate, Canterbury, Kent CT1 2HJ
Tel: 01277–455564

The Institution of Chemical Engineers
Davis Building, 165–189 Railway Terrace, Rugby CV21 3HQ
Tel: 01788–578214

Jesmonite Technologies Ltd
The Old School, Stanton Lacy, Near Ludlow, Shropshire, SY8 2AE
Tel: 01584–856–585

Liquefied Petroleum Gas Association
Alma House, Alma Rd, Reigate, Surrey RH2 0AZ
Tel: 01737–224700

National Association of Waste Disposal Contractors
Mountbarrow House, 6–20 Elizabeth St, London SW1 9RB
Tel: 0171–824 8882

National Chemical Emergency Centre
AEA Technology plc, F6, Culham, Abingdon, Oxon OX14 3DB
Tel: 01235–463060

The Royal Society of Chemistry
Burlington House, Piccadilly, London W1V 0BN
Tel: 0171–437–8656

Hazard 7: Children

The legislation

The Health and Safety (Young Persons) Regulations 1997
The Employment (Young Persons) Regulations 1997
The Children and Young Persons Act 1933 and 1963
The Children (Performances) Regulations 1968
The Education Act 1944
The Factories Act 1961
The Health and Safety at Work Act 1974

Special risks: filming in schools, inadequate barriers supervision, confined spaces, moving equipment and fatigue.

Film and television production can come into contact with children in a number of ways: directly employing them in productions as actors, as forum participants, as guests taking part in a programme, or when programmes are made on locations where children are likely to be, such as schools. Programme types include *Children in Need*, *Grange Hill* and *Ready, Steady Cook*. Producers and directors should beware of simulating dangerous activity or behaviour in children's programmes as children are excellent copiers of adult behaviour.

Any employer of children must carry out a risk assessment of that work before employing a young person. This must be properly recorded and passed on to the parents or guardians of any young person below school leaving age.

Location managers should be aware of the attraction television location activity can have for young children and should ensure that production sites are safe and secure from unauthorized access. If necessary, issue a warning notice with details of the proposed activity to local schools and play groups.

Children are legally defined as those below the minimum school leaving age in England and Scotland. Under the Children and Young Persons Act 1963, potential employers of children must obtain a licence to do so from the local authority of that location which takes about 21 days. Any child who is to perform for six days in any six-month period needs a medical examination and must be certified fit before a licence is granted.

Child actors from an EU country need a licence from the local authority in which their work takes place. Child actors from outside the EU require a work permit. Children on work experience are deemed to be employees for the purposes of health and safety legislation.

Employers of children must comply with the regulations governing their health and safety. These govern how many hours a child can work, up to a legal maximum of five consecutive days in any week and 80 days in any one year, going down depending on their age (rehearsal days don't count in calculating this). Children without a licence can work a maximum of 4 days in 6 months and cannot miss school without a licence.

Maximum location attendance times for 13–16-year-olds are an 8 hour day with the longest continuous recording or rehearsal period being 1 hour and 3 hours 30 minutes respectively.

The regulations also lay down minimum time for meal breaks (1 hour) and rest periods (15 minutes). Production managers should ensure that their schedules reflect these times and do not exceed them. A child is not permitted on any premises or location outside permitted hours.

Local authorities can also enact their own bye-laws and regulations concerning children, and production managers should check with the relevant local authority before agreeing a contract of engagement.

Children under the age of 12 are prohibited from training for or taking part in any dangerous stunt. For those over 12 a special licence to be trained for performances of a dangerous nature has to be obtained from the local authority under the Children and Young Persons Act 1933 section 24 (note also special rules for children in agricultural environments).

The education of children while being employed in film and television production work is also governed by the Children (Performances) Regulations 1968 which insist that the local authority issuing a child performing licence has also to approve of teaching provision. Teaching must take place in minimum blocks of 30 minutes up to a total of 3 hours a day inside normal permissible hours. A private tutor may be provided. On location the rules are more relaxed, insisting on a minimum of 6 hours education a week (up to 5 hours in any one day) aggregated over a four-week period.

Figure H7.1　*Filming on* Byker Grove. © Byker Grove

Chaperones must be provided by the production company if the children's parents or teachers are not present. The company must employ one chaperone for every twelve children. Chaperones must be approved by the local education authority and must always keep the children in their charge in sight.

Floor management should ensure extra supervision as children can move fast and are inquisitive by nature, so careful watch on them is necessary to ensure they are not at risk from moving equipment or can hide in confined spaces. Protect any access to roof spaces, cables, roads and chemical storage areas.

Children should have proper rest and meal breaks. Always take into account the extra stress of travelling time and keep this to a minimum.

Production managers should ensure that extra caution is taken if filming in conditions of extra heat or cold. Make provision for food, drinks and protective clothing. Make sure the children, audience, crew and performers get sufficient rest periods, especially during periods of hot weather. Studio lights can produce very hot conditions which can cause stress for children as pre-puberty children are unable to regulate their body temperature as well as adults. This means that they should be protected from the sun during exterior work as they are much more susceptible to melanomas and skin cancer than grown-ups.

Producers should also beware of the heat hazards for children's performers who may be wearing confined suits under hot studio lighting when playing characters like bears, Mr Blobby and Teletubbies. Accommodation for children should be separate from adult accommodation with toilets, hot water and rest facilities. Children are not usually permitted to work nights.

Production companies must keep employment and medical records of children employed by them (including a special hazard and risk assessment for any location involving children and any proposed activity within it) for at least six months after the production has finished. The records should also include details of any chaperones, teaching records and details of any personal protective equipment and welfare provisions.

Special provision should be made where necessary for personal protective equipment which will fit the age of the children who need it.

There is a special risk to children when filming in schools, playgroups or playgrounds. Permission should be obtained in writing from the head teacher and local education authority giving details of proposed production activity. Parental consent for any participants should also be obtained. Production companies granted permission to work in schools should carry specialized third-party and public liability cover.

Care should be taken about manual handling of equipment. Avoid heavy equipment movement and parking movements during lesson breaks and play times when large numbers of children will be moving around the site under minimal supervision. Route cables above doorways and gangways to avoid trip hazards. Keep all working equipment behind protective barriers and maintain free fall areas for all lights which should be supervised and out of reach. Liaise with teachers at all times and avoid the introduction of any hazardous stunts or chemicals.

Special risks to children exist on construction sites and farms. These locations are especially dangerous and present high risk temptations to children. Think twice before considering introducing children to these environments and consult the special guidelines.

Any risk to the health, safety and welfare of children either in or adjacent to production activity should be detected on the recce as part of the hazard identification and a risk assessment made to identify any danger. Then the correct procedures should be followed to eliminate or control the risk before any filming activity is undertaken with the correct legal requirements complied with and recorded.

Further reading

Preventing Accidents to Children in Agriculture, Approved Code of Practice and Guidance Notes, HSE COP24, ISBN 0-11-883997-7.
Accidents to Children in Construction Sites, HSE, 1989, GS7, ISBN 0-11-885416-X.

Electrical Safety in Schools, GS/23, HSE, 1990, ISBN 0-11-885426-7.
Workplace (Health, Safety and Welfare) Regulations 1992, Guidance for the
    Educational Sector, HSE, ISBN 0-7176-1049-7.
The Health and Safety (Training for Employment) Regulations 1990.
Young People at Work, HSE HS(G)165, ISBN 0-7176-1285-6.
Managing Health and Safety on Work Experience. A Guide for Organisers, HSG
    199, ISBN 0-7176-1742-4.

Contact organizations

British Actors Equity
Guild House, Upper St Martins Lane, London WC2H 9EG
Tel: 0171–379–6000

Department of Education and Employment
Sanctuary Building, Great Smith St, London SW1P 3BT
Tel: 0171–925–5000

National Society for Prevention of Cruelty to Children (NSPCC)
National Centre, 42 Curtain Rd, London EC2A 3NH
Tel: 0171–825–2500

Hazard 8: Churches, places of worship and village halls

The legislation

The Control of Asbestos at Work Regulations 1987 (CAWR)
The Control of Asbestos at Work Regulations (Amendment) SI/ 1992
The Electricity at Work Regulations 1989
The Health and Safety at Work Act 1974
The Management of Health and Safety at Work Regulations 1992
The First Aid at Work Regulations 1981
The Manual Handling Operations Regulations 1992
The Personal Protective Equipment (PPE) at Work Regulations 1992
The Provision and Use of Work Equipment Regulations 1998
The Reporting of Injuries, Diseases and Dangerous Occurrences Regulations 1995 (RIDDOR)
The Construction (Health, Safety and Welfare) Regulations 1996
The Health and Safety (Safety Signs and Signals) Regulations 1996

Special risks: access, asbestos, audiences, cold, derelict churches, electrical systems, fire, heights, noise, scaffolds.

Production activity in churches can carry a high risk as places of worship which are listed buildings are exempt from the Health and Safety at Work Act and certain fire precautions as the fabric of the building cannot be altered. Production activity can also take place in either working or derelict churches which have separate risks attached to them.

Churches which are used as working buildings can vary in age, shape, size and location. In fact, the buildings are as individual and varied as the practices and beliefs of the different religious communities who use them as places of prayer and worship. Never try to film in a place of worship or film a religious ceremony without permission. Act with sensitivity and respect the customs and sacred nature of these places. Avoid filming during services without prior permission, during holy days or religious holidays and respect the special requirements of monasteries and synagogues. Respect periods of silence and fasting. Avoid filming funerals and other private moments of prayer.

Contact the local incumbent, priest, minister or official and liaise closely with the local authorities responsible for the running and upkeep of the building. Check first on your insurance position as the introduction of production activity (especially in listed buildings) will increase the insurance risk to the owners from fire and accidental damage. Always check with your insurance to make sure that you are covered for special risks and that you have the necessary third-party, public and employer's liability cover.

Conduct a proper recce first to assess any risks, especially where these locations may be unfamiliar. Do this on a quiet and appropriate day. Look out for problems with access, height, electricity and fire.

The level and type of risk in working churches will depend on the nature of the production activity. Fiction and drama shoots like to use places of worship for filming baptisms, funerals and wedding scenes. Documentary activity could include making a film about nuns or the life of a Hindu temple. News and local current affairs programmes may interview controversial clergy or chronicle the activities of a bell ringing club, while ghost and horror film makers like to use locations with religious significance. Then again your programme may be coverage of a service with a large invited audience. Precautions and preventative measures, including the correct insurance, should be in place before production activity starts. Before proceeding always ask, is this shot or location necessary? And can it be done safely? Could it be done in another way? For example, use the church exterior rather than the interior or use library film.

Churches which are still used must be protected from the fire risks which your production will introduce to the location. Never smoke or drop cigarette ends. Lighting crew should be aware of the risks of fire from church buildings which contain a lot of inflammable flags, woods, vestments and curtain materials, especially during Christmas services and Harvest festivals. Never place lighting close to any inflammable substances and keep a clear free fall area for any lights erected at height.

There is also a risk of fire presented by candle flames and lanterns catching equipment, chemicals, costumes or set dressings used in a production. These materials should be flame-proofed and stored away from heat sources. Materials and set dressings should be placed at a safe distance from any fire or ignition hazard. Extra fire precautions should be taken as the risk of asphyxiation is very high because some older churches may be poorly ventilated with very few doors. The correct fire extinguishers conforming to EN3 standard must be provided and extra fire blankets and sand buckets placed adjacent to any hazard. A special emergency water supply should be tested and be available for use to combat non-electrical or chemical fires. A COSHH or fire assessment may have to be performed in a church or temple with burning incense.

Filming in churches often involves working at heights where a high risk exists because vantage points such as galleries, bell towers and steeples often provide good location shots of surrounding areas and are popular with directors. A particular risk may come from lightning strikes as they provide easy earth points and care should be taken to avoid filming on towers or steeples during stormy weather or bad visibility. Avoid working alone or unsupervised while at height and ensure good communications to those on the ground in case of a sudden hazard or emergency. Carry a lone worker's alarm. If necessary consult climbing or steeplejack experts who have experience of undertaking work at height in these locations.

Access to tower or subterranean areas is often confined and narrow – for instance, stone stairs and ladders. These must be checked for their condition and make sure that any roof access ducts and ladders can support the weight required. In popular public places such as cathedrals, special attention should be made to avoid a risk to the public or audience by warning notices indicating work at height and a safe area should be created below, where no access is permitted while activity is taking place. Crew should always wear hard hats, visibility jackets and fall arrest lifelines as protective equipment when working at height. If any doubt exits, safety nets should be in place and lifelines and safety harness provided to arrest falls from personnel or equipment.

Producers should identify on their risk assessment any risks from manual handling heavy equipment or cameras, especially to high towers or steeples with narrow stairs or ladders. If any significant risk is involved, use an alternative such as an external crane or internal hoist to lift equipment rather than carry it.

Producers should make sure that any camera or lighting crew working at height have an alternative emergency escape route such as an access platform or emergency escape chute if prolonged filming is going to take place at height with only one exit. Working platforms and access scaffolds should be constructed safely by a qualified and experienced scaffold company or access tower provider. Care must be taken to make sure that working platforms are suitable to take the combined weight of crew and equipment. Proper edge protection, kick boards and guard rails should be in place to protect anyone working on or below such platforms.

Camera positions should be constructed safely, taking into account weight factors on balconies or walkways. Special attention should be given to clearance risks from moving jibs or cameras coming into contact with projecting stonework, flags, suspended lanterns and monuments.

Churches are often thought of as quiet locations but a particular noise risk can happen in churches with the placement of crew near to bells or an organ. Ear protection should be provided if recording these or if filming in a bell tower. The noise will be considerably louder and vibrate in the roof. Care should be taken to avoid placing cables or equipment near clocks as these have moving parts which may become suddenly active so crew should be alert to this if filming in a confined space adjacent to a clock tower.

Care should be taken if filming in confined crypts, catacombs or basements to make sure that sufficient air supply exists and no fire or ignition risk is present. Use a portable gas analyser to detect any risk. A high vermin risk is also likely in these locations so wear protective clothing including boots, overalls and gloves. Ensure good communications to the ground crew exists with a visual light indicator when filming in confined locations.

Producers and electricians must be aware of the potential problems of electrical supply in churches. They could be out of date and in older buildings there may be very few sockets. A qualified electrician should inspect and test the mains board, fuses and sockets for loading capability and electrical safety. Use a socket tester to check electrical safety before plugging any equipment in – afterwards is too late. If any doubt exists about the safety of the electrical supply, install your own low-voltage system (110 V) and make sure you provide a back-up generator and emergency lighting.

The supply should never be overloaded and do not use two separate phases. To join them is extremely dangerous. To avoid this, do not use extension leads to join supplies from one side of a corridor to the other or to run supplies from one floor of a building to another, or to run supplies from one building to another. Keep electrical supplies physically separate and with a large gap between them which cannot be crossed accidentally.

Cables should be fitted with RCDs and routed away from gangways and exits to avoid trip hazards and damage from manual handling operations. Care should be taken to avoid placing electrical cables or powered equipment near the bottom of rains sprouts, taps and guttering as sudden rain could introduce a water hazard into your electrical system, rendering it highly dangerous.

Cables should not be placed near any fire hazards such as heating pipes or candles. Tall lights and production equipment including camera positions should be behind safety barriers to protect the public, and safety signs should clearly indicate any hazards and emergency exits.

Derelict churches are particularly dangerous and should only be used with caution as they contain old electrical cables, glass, falling masonry, and the hazards associated with derelict property such as vermin and needles in urban locations. Not to mention hidden cellars, rotten woodwork and dangerous towers.

A very high risk is the presence of asbestos in pipes, walls, belfries and organ cladding. Electricians, riggers and lighting crew should be aware of the exposure risk from asbestos through accidental exposure when clamping lights or attaching structural supports (see Hazard 3: Asbestos and Hazard 13: Derelict buildings).

Access and emergency exits are often a problem in old churches. Great care should be taken to identify any access problems during the recce, such as single narrow stair access to a tower or to an underground crypt. A full access risk assessment must be made. Derelict church buildings may only have one door or exit which would be a very high risk if you are planning to have actors or an audience. There would only be one means of escape which is an unacceptable risk where a high fire hazard exists. The doors may also be permanently locked or poorly maintained. Other hazards may be located behind them such as inflammable rubbish, chemical storage or a drop below. Some doors may end in a dead end or simply be blocked off.

Derelict churches are usually old and often isolated buildings which have a lot of attendant risks. The buildings can be in a poor state of repair with loose stonework and rotten wood. There is a risk of glass and masonry debris falling from height. Special checks should be made to inspect the structure to assess the risks of potential damage caused by vibration from lighting and scaffolding operations or from the movement of machinery and plant. Seal off dangerous areas and erect safety nets for fall hazards. Special care should be taken to check the safety of the electrical supply and the proper fire precautions must be in place. Always seek permission and always conduct a thorough recce to identify any hazards before you start, as disused churches contain the usual risks of derelict buildings.

Village halls

Television productions will often seek to use village and church halls as temporary locations. For filming, this can bring extra risks as many venues are not designed to cope with the extra hazards which production work can bring. This is especially true when the productions require a lot of equipment or have the requirement for an audience.

A key problem is access and installation. Access points are usually limited and this could create manual handling problems. Extra trolleys and trained lifters may be needed. Any electrical installation work to effect a temporary supply must comply with the Electricity at Work Regulations 1989 and should be carried out by a qualified electrician. Care should be taken to ensure that the supply is not overloaded and that safe and sufficient emergency lighting is provided. All portable electrical appliances must be properly PAT-tested and safe to use. All sockets, plugs and cables should be checked for damage and not used if potentially dangerous.

Extra catering facilities may have to be brought in and all food preparation must comply with the food hygiene regulations for the safe preparation and serving of food to avoid cross-contamination and food poisoning. Extra fire precautions must take into account the extra risks imposed by the catering and electrical facilities. The fire precautions must comply with the requirements for temporary small premises (see *Fire Precautions in Existing Places of Entertainment and Like Premises*, HMSO, ISBN 0-11-340907-9, Chapter 10, pages 134–45). These cover single storey halls with an auditorium of 200 m^2 or less and a maximum capacity of 300 people.

The safety of the public is the responsibility of the manager or licensee and s/he must be in charge of and present on the premises during the whole time that they are open to the public. S/he must also be kept free from work which would prevent them from being immediately available in the event of an alarm of fire.

Licensees or managers must consult the local licensing magistrates for permission to hold the event and obtain a temporary licence. If this is granted it will contain information regarding the maximum allowed audience and must contain a written fire evacuation plan drawn up in consultation with the local fire authority. Any premises which are hired out by a voluntary committee or organization must nominate someone to be responsible for obtaining the entertainment licence and for being responsible for safety arrangements. The hirer must be over eighteen and sign a written undertaking to accept responsibility for being in charge of and on the premises at all times when the public are present. They must also make sure that all conditions of the entertainment licence relating to management and supervision of safety are met.

Attendants trained in fire procedures must be present. The minimum legal requirement is one for every 250 people: however more are required if the audience will contain significant numbers of children, elderly or disabled people. There must be sufficient fire extinguishers for the size of the audience and the nature of the fire risk. Care should be taken to identify any fire risk from storage areas such as lofts or basements. All fire exit signs must comply with BS 5499 Part 1 and self-luminous signs with Part 2. Emergency lighting must be installed that complies with BS 5266 so that the audience can never be plunged into total darkness.

Before filming at a village hall or similar location, make a thorough on-site inspection of the premises first. Make notes to identify any hazards, paying particular attention to fire precautions, audience welfare arrangements, restricted headroom, ventilation, safe access and egress, electrical safety, parking and insurance.

Further reading

The Church of England Yearbook: 1996, Church House Publishing 1996, published in UK, 466 pp.
The Jewish Yearbook: 1997, edited by Stephen Massil. Vallentine Mitchell 1997, 400 pp.
The Multi-Faith Year Book, edited by Paul Weller, University of Derby and the Inter Faith Network.

Contact organizations

Baptist Union Corporation
Baptist House, PO Box 44, 129 Broadway, Didcot, Oxfordshire OX11 8RT
Tel: 01235–512077 or contact local minister/church secretary

Catholic Media Office
39 Eccleston Square, London SW1V 1BX
Tel: 0171–8288709 or contact local priest

Church of England: each Anglican parish or cathedral is independent. Contact the priest or dean of chapter direct. Addresses can be found in the *Church of England Year Book*

Church of Scotland
General Trustees, 121 George St, Edinburgh, Scotland EH2 4YR
Tel: 0131–225–5722

Church of Wales
39 Cathedral Rd, Cardiff, Wales CF1 9XF
Tel: 01222–231638

Churches Conservation Trust
83 Fleet St, London EC47 1DH
Tel: 0171–936–2285

The Board of Deputies of British Jews
Commonwealth House, 1–9 New Oxford St, London WC1A 1NF
Tel: 0171–543–5400
or use *The Jewish Yearbook* which lists all synagogues in the UK. No
filming allowed Friday nights, Saturdays or Jewish festivals

The Methodist Church Property Division
Central Buildings, Oldham St, Manchester M1 1JQ
Tel: 0161–236–0752

The Society of Friends
Friends House, 173 Euston Rd, London NW1 2B1
Tel: 0171–663–1055

The United Reformed Church
86 Tavistock Place, London WC1H 9RT
Tel: 0171–916–2020

Hazard 9: Civil unrest and war zones

Sixty-three journalists were killed worldwide in 1993.

Cameraman Edward Henty was killed in the City of London bomb blast and cameraman Mohamed Amin by a sniper in Ethiopia.
Stage, Screen and Radio, November 1994, page 9.

The legislation

The Health and Safety at Work Act 1974
The Management of Health and Safety at Work Regulations 1992
The First Aid at Work Regulations 1981
The Personal Protective Equipment (PPE) at Work Regulations 1992
The Reporting of Injuries, Diseases and Dangerous Occurrences Regulations 1995 (RIDDOR)

Special risks: death, physical injury, chemicals and explosives, intimidation, kidnapping.

The particular risk to broadcast staff from riot and situations of civil unrest are usually faced by news, current affairs and documentary crews and journalists or reporters. These high-risk situations can occur in the UK or abroad. When overseas, the crew undertake the risk in order to obtain exclusive pictures of an unfolding story such as Northern Ireland or Chechnya. On the other hand, a risk can be present suddenly in a seemingly benign situation. The key to a safe situation is to have a prepared plan of action if something goes wrong.

The Foreign and Commonwealth Office publish the Foreign Office Advice Against Travel List. This is a constantly updated list of countries which are very high risk.

The level of risk should be identified first, on a proper recce or by a reliable local contact on the ground. In other words the risk of violence should be assessed, before filming, in the production planning stage. Key figures here are the heads of news gathering, commissioning editors and producers who have the information first and take the decision for filming to begin. As they control the activity they must be responsible for stating that it is safe to proceed and what precautions to take.

The best aid to safety on the ground is keeping up-to-date information about the situation and being able to react quickly to unfolding events which may change a previously safe location into a very dangerous one. You should always ensure that you have good local knowledge and an escape route if trouble develops – in other words, if violence cannot be controlled, then put safety first.

It is also possible to encounter violence when filming on locations such as housing estates and at sports grounds. The most common risk is the threat of violence from people who do not want their activities recorded, such as political protesters or active criminals such as drug pushers in high-risk city areas.

If you do get attacked then withdraw quickly and any non-consensual injuries should be recorded, treated and reported if they result in death, major injury or cause an absence of work for three days. This is a requirement of the Reporting of Injuries, Diseases and Dangerous Occurrences Regulations 1995 (RIDDOR).

Protest situations can vary from preventing building projects such as the Manchester Airport runway and the Newbury bypass to preventing settlements in Israel. Always avoid being confrontational yourself by acting calmly and avoid getting too close to your antagonists. Avoid prolonged eye contact and loud words. The safer option is compromise or leave quickly.

In riot or protest situations you should always seek advice from the police operational emergency control centre and local community leaders in touch with the situation and the mood of the crowd. In each case an individual risk assessment should be made of the risks and precautions taken.

Very often during a riot or civil disturbance the threat could also come from the government forces trying to prevent protest who do not want their regime's activities shown in a bad light. There is also the risk of violence from government forces if an important opposition figure is giving you an interview. Avoid filming identification features such as house numbers and car number plates or any obvious clues of the location.

An assessment should be made about what side of the fence physically you are going to film from and from what source or direction the threat of violence is likely to come. Will it come from the authorities, their opposition or both?

Very often injuries can occur when being caught between two violently opposed sides in a confrontational situation. There is then a serious risk of physical assault, riot gas and water cannon. There is also a serious danger from rubber bullets and rifle fire. Always wear a helmet and a flak jacket.

Remember that in a war situation a camera picked up by the sun pointing from a window can provide a tempting target for a sniper. Turn off your tally light and turn down the viewfinder. Don't smoke either as this can be picked up by an infra-red sniper sight. Don't film at night as the light from the camera can be picked up.

Try to avoid camera placement in recently vacated firing positions as you may be the next target. Remember they have been vacated for a reason, either because an attack is imminent or because they have become too dangerous. Beware of the COSHH hazards presented by chemical and biological attack or tear gas grenades.

Never assume that a situation which was safe will still be safe when you return, for example it may have been mined or booby trapped. Imagine the hazards of making a documentary about mines in northern Iraq or Bosnia.

So always arrange a trusted and expert local fixer who knows the area and the dangers within it. This choice can be crucial as you may be trusting your lives to this person. Always pass on this vital local information to others who may need it and avoid a routine that would encourage kidnappers. Keep your equipment hidden as this can be held to ransom as well. If necessary, secure the protection of private security to protect you.

Make sure you have good communications which cannot be overheard or detected and that the operating frequencies will not trigger mines. Ensure you can all speak the same language and have pre-arranged warning signals. Never work alone and always have someone to watch your back – with a driver on standby in case you have to evacuate quickly.

Assess if it is better to have an unmarked or marked vehicle. A four door vehicle can be easier to get out from in a hurry. Always carry a spare jack, tyres, pump, spark plugs and leads. Don't forget petrol, oil and water to avoid grinding to a halt in a remote or dangerous situation.

Driving with the window open and the radio off will allow you to hear gunfire. If your car is dirty then you have a better chance of seeing if it has been tampered with. Always park out of sight and ready for a swift exit by pointing it in the right direction. In a war or riot zone it may be much safer to leave any vehicle behind in a safe place and proceed on foot for a faster exit. In a war zone beware of hidden mines on road edges.

Avoid suspicious driving such as sudden stops and U-turns near security check points or soldiers. Avoid wearing green and khaki or anything that might look like a military uniform.

Try to film from concealed positions which are above the street level and which give a safe but excellent vantage point. If not, keep your recording equipment hidden or use a miniature or hidden camera. If by filming you may endanger yourselves or escalate a dangerous situation, withdraw quickly. Always have an alternative means of escape.

If necessary, form a broadcasting pool with other agencies and share footage from one source to minimize the risk. Always make sure you wear appropriate protective equipment including hard hats, vests and body armour. First aid training is an essential skill as you could be in a life saving situation. News crews often attend battlefield first-aid training courses run by the British army to get experience of treating serious injuries under fire. You should always carry a supply of fresh water. Always carry an emergency first-aid kit and a supply of uncontaminated blood. Have proper medical insurance which will evacuate you quickly in an emergency situation and include the cost of being flown home by air immediately. Make sure that your inoculations are correct and up-to-date for the country you are visiting.

Getting proper insurance cover for war and riot zones is almost impossible. It is either too expensive or specifically excluded from the policy conditions. Check that your employer's liability cover will stretch to dangerous situations. This should also apply to travelling to and from such places and cover for your equipment. Some companies will cover you if you have attended and passed a hazardous environment safety training course run for the Institute of News Safety by Lionsgate Safety Training, Centurion Risk Assessment Services and Ake Ltd.

In a dangerous situation of civil unrest there is no substitute for experience and teamwork backed up by good information and communication. Think on your feet and always watch your back.

Remember, if the risk is too great, say no until the situation is safe.

Further reading

- C. John Eaton, *Essentials of Immediate Medical Care*, ISBN 0-443-04575-5.
- Jon Wiseman, *The SAS Survival Guide*, Collins Gem, Ref. SAS2.
- Jon Wiseman, *The Urban Survival Handbook*, Ref. Urb1.

All three books available from: Emergency Response Publications, 5 Shelly Court, South Zeal, Okehampton Devon EX20 2PT, Tel: 01837–840102.

For an excellent article on survival skills courses, please read: Gillian Sanders, The skills of survival, *UK Press Gazette*, 14 January 2000.

Camera Operations on Location. Guidance for Managers and Camera Crews on News Gathering, Current Affairs and Factual Programming. HSE, HSG169, ISBN 0-7176-1346-1997.
Facts For Freelances, HSE, IND(G)217L 1996.
Stuart A. Gray, *The First Aider's Pocket Companion*, Altman Books, 1995, ISBN 1-86036-000-9.
The Foreign Office Advice Against Travel List, The Foreign and Commonwealth Office.
Health Information for Overseas Travel, HMSO, 1999 edition, ISBN 0-11-32-1833-8.
International Travel and Health, World Health Organisation, ISBN 92-4-158024-0.
Kamal Ahmed, In the line of fire, *Media Guardian* 5 January 1998, p. 6.
Rani Singh, One shot at staying alive, *Media Guardian* 5 January 1998, p. 7.
Management of Health and Safety at Work Regulations 1992, Approved Code of Practice 1992, HSE, ISBN 0-7176-0412-8.
Nicola Godwin, Shooting in a war zone, *Television Buyer*, September 1993, pp. 22–7.
Pascal Don, Staying safe on location filming, *Safety Management Magazine*, November 1997 pp. 12–15.
Violence to Staff, HSE ING69, ISBN 0-7176-1271-0.
Violence to Workers in Broadcasting, HSE leaflet, Entertainment Sheet No. 2, ETIS 2 1996.

Contact organizations

The British Red Cross
9 Grovesnor Crescent, London SW1X 7EJ
Tel: 0171–235–5454

The Foreign and Commonwealth Office
Travel Advice Unit, Consular Division
1 Palace St, London SW1E 5HE
Tel: 0171–238–4503

Guild of Location Managers
37 Woodeaves, Northwood, Middx HA6 3NF

Lionsgate Safety Training
Teddington Studios, Broom Road, Teddington, Middx TW11 9T
Tel: 0181–288–7400

The Ministry of Defence
Whitehall, London SW1A 2HB
Tel: 0171–218–9000

Paramedic Rescue Services
Freepost (KT4337)
West Molesey, Surrey KT8 2BR
Tel: 0181–642–7405

Production Managers Association (CoPACT)
45 Mortimer St, London W1N 7TD
Tel: 0171–331–6000

St John Ambulance
1 Grovesnor Crescent, London SW1X 7EF
Tel: 0171–235–5231

Hazard 10: Confined spaces, including caving and mines

A company director was fined £30,000 after a worker was buried alive. It took the rescue team 36 hours to find him because the excavation was so deep. The upper part of the excavation collapsed because it was not supported. No method statement had been produced for this high risk activity.

HSE

The legislation

The Confined Spaces Regulations 1997
The Control of Substances Hazardous to Health Regulations 1999
The Construction (Design and Management) Regulations 1994
The Construction (Health, Safety and Welfare) Regulations 1996
The Health and Safety at Work Act 1974
The Management of Health and Safety at Work Regulations 1992
The Manual Handling Regulations 1992
The First Aid at Work Regulations 1981
The Mines and Quarries Act 1954
The Personal Protective Equipment (PPE) at Work Regulations 1992
The Provision and Use of Work Equipment Regulations 1998
The Reporting of Injuries, Diseases and Dangerous Occurrences Regulations 1995 (RIDDOR)
The Health and Safety (Safety Signs and Signals) Regulations 1996

The risks

- access
- asphyxiation
- explosion

- fire
- chemicals
- drowning
- electricity
- falls
- gases
- hot work
- birds
- rats
- traps
- water
- working alone

There is a high risk from working in confined spaces such as deep excavations, roof spaces, pipes, tanks and trenches. From January 1998 any work in confined spaces is controlled by the Confined Spaces Regulations 1997. An employer must be able to prove that confined space work is necessary with no alternative way of eliminating it or substituting it for something safer.

If it is necessary to proceed, work in confined space must be considered high risk and should be properly planned in advance before work begins. A confined space risk assessment should be made by the producer and an action plan drawn up in the form of a method statement which can be clearly understood and followed by the crew. Producers and managers proposing to conduct production activity in a confined space must devise and implement a safe system of work.

Work in a confined space should be properly supervised by a qualified and experienced supervisor such as a production or location manager, and, if necessary, an expert, to make sure that the action plan is followed. This should be written down on cards and given out to all concerned, then backed up by an oral briefing before filming begins. Any changes to this plan must be communicated to those who will be affected by it and a new briefing will be necessary.

All precautions and protective measures must be in place before any filming activity commences, including the correct rescue procedures should something go wrong. A confined space is an enclosed space where there will be a danger from fire, explosion, gas, a lack of oxygen and extreme heat. There will also be a danger from proximity to moving machinery and a high risk from water or entrapment in a free flowing solid.

The first safety issue in a confined space is access. Can you get out quickly in an emergency? Anybody undertaking work must have safe entrance and exit from the confined space. Since access in a confined space is restricted there is a danger of becoming trapped and having your escape route cut off – make sure proper access ladders and emergency exit procedures are in place. You should not ask anyone to undertake filming work where there is only one escape route without extra precautions and they should not be asked to work by themselves.

Never film alone in a confined space and always have somebody else in close attendance and ensure working communication because of the serious risk from fumes and lack of oxygen. Use a guardian communication system.

The second safety issue is fresh air supply. Can you breathe? The air quality must be breathable.

Always carry out a gas test using an Extox gas analyser or similar device which can detect oxygen quality and carbon monoxide levels before any activity begins and ensure regular monitoring and testing for the duration of the work.

Do not use any petrol/diesel generator or engines to power equipment adjacent to anybody working in a confined space as it can cause a build-up of toxic fumes. Precautions should include extra ventilation and respiratory equipment. Never try and pump oxygen in as this can be highly explosive in a confined space. The same risk comes from fumes, so avoid the use of petrol driven compressors or generators near a confined space.

Rust in old tanks and confined spaces eats up oxygen and brings the risk of asphyxiation. The disturbing of slurries in agricultural and chemical liquids in industrial locations can trigger the release of poisonous gases. The use of paint, coatings and thinners can release harmful vapours which could be dangerous in a confined space. An air check meter should always be used to test if a confined space is initially safe before working begins and to continually monitor it until the work has been completed.

Be especially careful of the build-up of fumes in old sewers, manholes and waste pits. Use a portable gas analyser such as an Extox and carry a gas badge personal gas alarm to detect and warn of the presence of gas and toxic fumes.

Gas can explode so the third risk in a confined space is the inherent risk of fire or explosion. There can be a build-up of underground methane in a confined space with a serious risk of fire, especially near old mine workings or rubbish tips. Any gas detection system should be able to detect flammable gases. Smoking should be prohibited and power tools must be safe. Beware of the ignition potential of hot work such as welding and repairs in a confined space.

Further advice can be obtained from the British Approvals Service for Electrical Equipment in Flammable Atmospheres.

Fire hazards in confined spaces can also be introduced so no hazards should be created by the nature of the work, for example by the introduction of inflammable materials or gases. Never smoke or use direct heat sources in a confined space. Beware of smoking or employing any electrical equipment where there is a risk of explosion or fire, especially in underground storage areas, tanks, mines and agricultural silos. Any leakage from LPG cylinders will cause gas to sink to the lowest point of the confined space forming an explosive concentration.

Beware of heat hazards, high temperatures and hot working conditions when working in confined spaces. Operatives wearing suits in confined spaces get hot very quickly, especially during periods of hot weather. Staff should be issued with a work permit to control hot work. Producers should ensure that they get proper rest periods according to the length of the work.

Above 26°C allow a minimum rest period of 20 minutes for 40 minutes work. Rest areas should be cool with plenty of fluids available (not salt water). The temperature in confined spaces should be monitored. At temperatures above 31°C, access should be for inspection purposes only and operatives should be medically monitored. Remember, the greater the number of people and the more lights and tools used, the faster the oxygen will be used up and the working temperature will rise quickly to unsafe and potentially dangerous levels.

Hidden services can be a danger in confined spaces. Especially in old factories, building sites, cellars, lofts and derelict buildings. Beware of the risk to life from electrocution, explosion and the sudden entry of water. Look out for signs of hidden services. Assume an unidentified pipe is full and that any cable is live. Use a proper locator to establish the presence of utility services' hidden pipes or cables.

Plastic pipes may not be easy to detect. Contact with old gas pipes and electrical cable can cause explosion or electrocution so put collars on all power tools to restrict the impact risk and avoid sharp points during initial drilling or digging. Consult old site maps and obtain the advice of past employees who can help to detect hidden risks early enough to take action.

A risk in confined spaces can also come from hidden water, especially in roof tanks, building sites or locations close to running water. Beware of serious risk posed by sudden flooding or egress of water from old workings or broken pipes or sewers.

A particular risk of filming in confined sewers, pipes and drains is contamination and bites from rats and vermin. Staff should always wear protective suits and breathing equipment. There is a very high risk of being bitten by vermin or contaminated by their droppings; always look out for droppings and other signs of vermin. If necessary, call in a specialist pest contractor to remove the vermin as exposure to them constitutes a high risk to the health and safety of employees and a breach of the Environmental Health Act. Make sure all your staff have had recent polio and tetanus jabs.

Contamination of water in sewers, tanks and drains by rats' urine can, in extreme cases, cause a jaundice condition known as Weil's disease. This is contracted by swallowing or inhaling contaminated water and is potentially fatal. In mild form it is called leptospirosis. The risk of leptospirosis should be fully assessed, especially in confined spaces which may have water such as mills, fish farms, warehouses and factories near canals and rivers. Never enter water without getting a water test done first at an NRA laboratory. Avoid entering water if you have cuts, especially in your feet.

Confined spaces such as roof tanks and ceilings in derelict buildings and lofts could also be contaminated by faeces and guano, specially from pigeons. A high risk to health is present and any bird droppings must be identified and removed by a specialist contractor. This is because you can contract psittacosis through inhaling the dust from bird droppings, which can give you symptoms of pneumonia and arthritis. These can last for years and in some cases it can cause fatal respiratory failure. Psittacosis is the most common and serious illness that humans can develop from birds.

Noise can also be amplified in a confined space so be aware of any risk to hearing. This could also come from heavy plant and machinery so make sure your crew have adequate ear protection.

Anybody working in a confined space should carry a lone worker's safety alarm and a stand-by should be present outside to keep watch and ensure the safety of those working inside. There should always be a safe system of work within confined spaces with a controlled permit to work system and constant communication.

Adopt a safe system of working. Have an emergency evacuation plan in place with a safe and quick means of escape in the event of an emergency. Make sure that a rescue plan is in place with trained and experienced rescuers on hand in the event of somebody becoming trapped or being overcome by fumes (very often it is untrained rescuers who can become the victims). Make sure all staff and rescue teams have the proper personal protective equipment (boots, protective overalls/ suit/hard hats, goggles, barrier cream and safety line) and that staff have swift contact to the local emergency services.

Staff and contractors should wear highly visible protective suits, hard hats and self-contained breathing apparatus (SCBA) when working in a confined space such as a roof space or manhole. The worker should be physically attached to a fall arrest lifeline attached externally to a support and a winch which will extract them quickly and safely if overcome. Make sure any lighting will not cause an explosion and will not raise the safe working temperature. Panic alert devices should be worn with a good system of communication and visibility.

Further factors to consider about work in a confined space include the size of the confined space; the size, age and medical condition of the person or persons doing the work inside the confined space; how long and for what period they are going to work there; the availability of oxygen, lighting and communication; the size and safety of equipment to be used; and any inherent hazards and risks posed by the confined location, the nature of the work and the changing conditions. The safest option is to try and find a way of doing the job without entering the confined space.

Caving and mines

The legislation

Health and Safety (First Aid) Regulations 1981, Approved Code of Practice 1993
The Management and Administration of Safety and Health at Mines Regulations 1993
The Coal Mines (Owners Operating Rules) Regulations 1993
The Coal and Other Safety Lamp Mines (Explosives) Regulations 1993
The Escape and Rescue From Mines Regulations 1995

Each mine has its own safety rules which are unique to each location due to geological and airflow factors. You should always seek advance permission from the manager and electrical engineer of the mine concerned. In consultation with HSE Inspectorate of Mines, they will help you to draw up a particular set of rules to follow. These will be unique to each visit because gas levels and geological factors are in constant flux. Crews should be given a copy of these rules and should comply with them at all times. A list of equipment and its specifications should be supplied to the mine's electrical engineer prior to the shoot for approval. Do not bring anything that is not on the approved list.

Anybody filming in a mine must pass and possess a current self-rescuer certificate. These are updated annually. This is to ensure that in the event of gas or a fall that everybody knows how to operate their own emergency supply of air. Thus it makes sense to use a crew who have a lot of experience at filming underground and who possess a current certificate.

Any crew working in a mine have to come under the close personal supervision of the mine management and must be accompanied at all times by a mine's mechanical and electrical manager. Each party member must be accompanied by a member of mine's staff on a 1:1 ratio. The crew should always follow any instructions and familiarize themselves with emergency and evacuation procedures.

When attempting to film, crews must ensure that the air is constantly monitored for gas. Pockets of methane are especially dangerous. It is advisable to use lights with gas tight fittings and remove as much ignition risk as possible in the choice of equipment you are planning to use. If in any doubt, submit details of what you plan to use to the mine's electrical manager. Always inform the mine's management if there are any last minute changes which should be avoided. In mines with particular gas risks it may be necessary to use a clockwork camera.

It may also be necessary to take extra-long-life batteries as the mine may have strict rules about changing them in fresh air conditions. Because this may involve a walk of over a mile or having to return to the surface, production managers should think carefully about the choice of battery power. If in any doubt get advice from the mine's electrical engineer.

Further reading

The hazards associated with work in confined spaces, *Croner's Health and Safety Special Report*, issue 39, January 1999.

BS 1377: Methods of Tests for Soils for Civil Engineering Purposes.

BS 5930: Code of Practice for Site Investigations.

BS 6031: Code of Practice for Earthworks.

CIRIA report 97: Trenching Practice, 1992, revision.

Avoiding Danger from Underground Services HS (G)47, HSE Books 1989, ISBN 0-7176-0435-7.

Entry into Confined Spaces, GS 5 (rev), HSE Books 1994, ISBN 0-7176-0789-9.

Safe Work in Confined Spaces: The Confined Spaces Regulations 1997: Approved Code of Practice, Regulations and Guidance, HSE Books, 1998, L101, ISBN 0-7176-1405-0.

Leptospirosis: Are You at Risk? HSE, INDG84.

First Aid at Mines. Health and Safety (First Aid) Regulations 1981, Approved Code of Practice 1993, HSE, ISBN 0-7176-0617-1.

The Management and Administration of Safety and Health at Mines; Management and Administration of Safety and Health at Mines Regulations 1993, Approved Code of Practice, HSE, ISBN 0-7176-0618-X.

The Coal Mines (Owners Operating Rules) Regulations 1993, Guidance on the Regulations, HSE, ISBN 0-7176-0621-X.

Explosives at Coal and Other Safety Lamp Mines: Coal and Other Safety Lamp Mines (Explosives) Regulations 1993, Approved Code of Practice, ISBN 0-7176-0619-8.

Escape and Rescue from Mines Regulations 1995, Approved Code of Practice, HSE, ISBN 0-7176-0939-1.

The Prevention of Inrushes in Mines, Approved Code of Practice 1993, ISBN 0-7176-06201.

The Safe Use of Portable Electrical Apparatus PM32(rev), HSE Books, 1990.

Health and Safety in Construction HS(G) 150, HSE Books, 1996, ISBN 0-7176-1143-4.

Robin Garside, *Electrical Apparatus and Hazardous Areas*, 2nd edition, 1994, Hexagon Technology Ltd.

Hot work, RC7, 1994, available from the Loss Prevention Council, Melrose Avenue, Borehamwood, Hertfordshire WD6 2BJ, Tel: 0181–207–2345.

Allan Padgett and Bruce Smith, *On-rope – Caving Safety Guide* (code ONR1), available from Emergency Response Publications, 5 Shelly Court, South Zeal, Okehampton, Devon EX20 2PT, Tel: 01837–840102.

Working in confined spaces, *Safety Management*, November 1997, pp. 38–9.

Construction Industry Training Board (CITB) Publications department: series of leaflets, books, training videos and computer packages.

Contact organizations

British Approvals Service for Electrical Equipment in Flammable Atmospheres
Harpur Hill, Buxton, Derbyshire SK17 9JN
Tel: 01298–28000

British Cave Rescue Council
Pearl Hill, Dent, Sedbergh, Cumbria LA10 5TG
Tel: 01539–625412 (Hon. Secretary Pete Allwright)

Caving councils
Five regional caving councils cover the following areas:
   Southern area (Mendips)
   Cambrian (Wales)
   Derbyshire (Peak District)
   Northern (Yorkshire Dales and Pennines)
   Devon and Cornwall

The Construction Industry Training Board (CITB)
Bircham Newton, King's Lynn, Norfolk PE31 6RH
Tel: 01553–776677

Health and Safety Executive, HM Inspectorate of Mines
St Anne's House, Stanley Precinct, Bootle, Merseyside L20 3RA
Tel: 0151–951–3636

Institution of Mining Engineers
Danum House, South Parade, Doncaster DN1 2DY
Tel: 01302–320486

Institution of Mining and Metallurgy
44 Portland Place, London W1N 4BR
Tel: 0171–580–3802

The Institute of Quarrying
7 Regent St, Nottingham NG1 5BS
Tel: 01159–484035

Mining Association of the United Kingdom
6 St James Square, London SW1Y 4LD
Tel: 0171–753–2117

The National Caving Association (NCA)
Monomark House, 27 Old Gloucester Street, London WC1N 3XX
Tel: 01335–370629 (contact Jenny Potts)

RJB Mining
Harworth Park, Blyth Rd, Harworth, Doncaster, South Yorkshire
DN11 8DB
Tel: 01302–751751

Hazard 11: Cranes, hoists, lifts and access platforms

The BBC has been charged over the death of a father of two. Electrician David Coles plunged 130ft when a gantry toppled during the filming of Casualty. Mr Coles died in hospital of multiple injuries. The BBC and equipment company Butler Powered Access were accused of failing to ensure his safety.

Daily Star, 12 December 1996

The legislation

The Lifting Operations and Lifting Equipment Regulations 1998
The Lifts Regulations 1997
The Construction (Design and Management) Regulations 1994
The Health and Safety at Work Act 1974
The Management of Health and Safety at Work Regulations 1992
The Manual Handling Operations Regulations 1992
The Noise at Work Regulations 1989
The Personal Protective Equipment (PPE) at Work Regulations 1992
The Provision and Use of Work Equipment Regulations 1998
The Health and Safety (Safety Signs and Signals) Regulations 1996
The Supply of Machinery (Safety) Regulations 1992

The risks

- access
- electricity
- loading

- working at heights
- cranes
- hoists/lifts
- manual handling
- noise
- powered access platforms
- plant
- ropes and chains
- training

Those most at risk

Lifting equipment hire companies, location camera and sound crews and location managers, performers, the public, maintenance staff, loading staff, electricians, riggers and lighting crew.

Special risk: access, lack of experience, loading operations, manual handling, maintenance, overloading, the public, ropes and chains, high wind, working at heights.

Any lifting and moving operations must comply with the Lifting Operations and Lifting Equipment Regulations 1998 which came into force on 5 December 1998. Any company which hires such equipment must also comply with the Supply of Machinery (Safety) Regulations 1992. The regulations apply to owners of companies, employers, self-employed operators and any person at work who supervises, controls or uses lifting equipment. Lifting equipment includes cranes, hoists, lifts, fork-lift trucks and MEWPs. All lifting equipment must be safe and adequate for the task. Never use lifting equipment that is not designed for the task and which exceeds the safe working load (SWL). Never attempt to carry people in lifting equipment not designed for the task. All lifting equipment must carry and be supplied with an EEC declaration of conformity.

All lifting operations should be planned by a competent person. All lifting operations should be properly supervised and carried out in a safe manner with properly qualified drivers/operators.

It is crucial to select the correct mount for any camera and the right rig for any lighting that may be suspended. Always seek advice from an expert or your supplier and give the correct information to the hire company about the weight of equipment and the number of operators so that the right type of lifting equipment can be provided.

Before beginning production activity which uses a crane, lift, hoist or powered access platform, stop and consider if a safer alternative means of achieving your work is available. For example a helicopter, rooftop or stock shot; do you really need to use this equipment at all? Why not stop and don't do the activity at all if the risk is too high and protective measures too expensive? Make sure you have a separate and adequate health and safety budget to take all the necessary precautions and protective measures before production activity begins – afterwards is too late.

As the responsible producer you should ask yourself who would be affected by this activity. Is the equipment right for the task? Who would be put at risk – the public, crew, employees and contractors? What measures and precautions should be taken to see that there is no risk to anybody's health and safety?

All lifting and powered equipment should be properly maintained, suitable for the task and safe. All lifting equipment must be inspected every year and passenger lifts every six months.

The Construction (Health, Safety and Welfare) Regulations 1996 No. 27 states that 'all plant and equipment used for the purpose of carrying out construction work shall, so far as is reasonably practicable, be safe and without risks to health and shall be of good construction, of suitable and sound materials and of sufficient strength and suitability for the purpose for which it is used or provided.'

All staff and operators should be properly qualified, experienced and competent. Regulation 28 of the Construction (Health, Safety and Welfare) Regulations 1996 states that 'any person who carries out any activity involving construction work where training, technical knowledge or experience is necessary to reduce the risks of injury to any person shall possess such training, knowledge or experience, or be under such degree of supervision by a person having such training, knowledge or experience, as may be appropriate having regard to the nature of the activity.'

Any significant risk to health and safety posed by lifting equipment should be detected on the recce as part of the hazard identification (use form in Appendix 6) and a risk assessment made to identify any danger (fill out form). Then the correct procedures should be followed and the machine safety checklist read to eliminate or control (action taken form) the risk before any filming or moving activity is undertaken. A health and safety method statement should be produced to deal with any assessed risk and should lay out exactly what procedure to follow for any identified hazard. With lifting equipment a hazard might be introduced as part of the activity you are going to do or it could be inherent to the location.

Figure H11.1 *Lifting equipment. Courtesy of Yorkshire Television Limited*

However, with lifting equipment, especially cranes, another hazard is a proximity hazard, i.e. because of the extended length and height cranes can easily come into contact with physical objects which are adjacent to the site or on the road – for example cables, bridges, railways, bus routes, aircraft and narrow access.

Great care should be taken to identify this before any movement is undertaken and a check made just before hand along the intended route and around the perimeters of the site. Another factor to consider is the weight of the crane so look out for floor hazards such as weak bridges and weak surfaces. Perhaps the biggest hazard of all is presented by inquisitive members of the public who are drawn to lifting operations like a moth to a candle. Ensure adequate security and perimeter fences. Always keep the public well back behind barriers, a considerable safe distance away from the operation.

It is obvious that a crew should never just be 'sent in to film' on a potentially dangerous piece of lifting equipment especially when there is a very high risk. In this situation simply not bothering to find out constitutes gross negligence and poses a high risk to the health and safety of your crew. On average there are approximately 17 fatal accidents a year involving cranes. The usual cause is overturning. One of the main reasons for this is the use of an unsuitable machine for the task in hand or the exceeding of the safe working load. Consult the Construction Industry Research and Information Association's publication, Crane Stability on Site.

Cranes, hoists, lifts and powered access equipment are used by television crews to move or lift heavy equipment and to use height as a vantage point for cameras, lights and stunts – especially for outside broadcasts, drama filming and sporting coverage.

Cranes

Cranes are usually mobile or lorry mounted. The main types are:

- telescopic mobile cranes (between 15 and 1000 tonnes), divided into lorry-mounted telescopic (up to 33 tonnes), rough-terrain telescopic and all-terrain telescopic (up to 95 tonnes);
- crawler cranes (between 15 and 250 tonnes);
- lattice jib cranes (between 450 and 1500 tonnes);
- lorry loaders (between 0.5 and 10 tonnes); and
- tower cranes, divided into trolley jib (45 metre tonne up to 2000 metre tonne) and the luffing jib (80 metre tonne up to 700 metre tonne).

However these are only rough guidelines and you should always consult the manufacturer or supplier and consult the handover certificate and the duty chart. Never try and modify a crane to take a heavier weight than it was designed for. Choose the correct one in the first place.

When operating on a road, the police should be notified and the road closed off with cones during movement or operations on a public highway. Lorry mounted crane operators should have a CITB CTA construction plant operator's licence.

The Construction (Lifting Operations) Regulations 1961 Regulation 26a states that the crane operator should hold a valid licence and be over 21 years of age. They should also have a medical examination every five years to quality for CTA training they must hold a LGV licence.

You should always check the operator's licence before operations begin. Never use an unqualified or inexperienced operator. Since January 1998, all crane drivers have had to pass a new EU standard test.

The cranes themselves must be correctly taxed and insured. All paperwork and examination certificates must comply with BS 7121 Part 2 for the inspection, testing and examination of cranes. You should check that the crane operator or contractor can supply a test and examination certificate F96: always check the duty chart in the cab which is specific to each crane. This gives vital information such as the SWL, maximum extension of the arm and the emergency controls to use in case of a power failure. All operating staff should be familiar with the location and operation of the emergency axcillary. Under the Construction (Lifting Operations) Regulations 1961 Regulation 28, each crane must have a valid HSE inspection and test certificate. The certificate is valid for four years and carries details of the crane's owner, maker, type, date of manufacture, identification number, registration number, maximum radius and safe working load. The crane should also be tested every 14 months.

Under the Factories Act 1961 Regulation 27, the owner/operator should also supply a 14-month insurance test certificate for a lifting machine or appliance. Any chains or lifting gear attached should be examined every six months with a certificate issued. A separate lifting gear inspection certificate is needed to check that all the chain, hooks and tackle are in safe working condition. These certificates should be kept in the cab and you should check them before operations begin. The automatic indicator should be regularly tested and a separate certificate necessary for passenger hoists. The owner/operator/contractor or hirer/ supplier must give you a valid handover certificate to indicate that the crane is in safe working condition under section 3 of the Health and Safety at Work Act: Duty and care to others.

The crane should always be on a firm and level site taking into account any recent period of rain or dry weather. The main types of site are: greenfield, beaches, construction sites, paved areas, town centre sites and shipyards. The weight of the crane relative to the supporting capability of the surface is a key factor – in other words, the ground bearing capacity. Site investigation procedures and soil examination are covered in detail by BS 5930/1377 and Annex G of BS 5975.

A thorough site and surface investigation should be carried out as an essential element of the risk assessment, along with a risk assessment of the intended route.

Surface supports such as proprietary mats, steel grillage, timber mats, concrete pads, and piled foundation are choices which you can make in consultation with the crane supplier and the site manager.

Cranes should be sited away from the edge of any deep excavation or slope. Beware of height restrictions such as archways, cables and bridges during transit. Particular attention should be paid to avoid undertaking crane movements adjacent to either roads, electrical power cables or scaffold towers. Particular attention should be paid to the location of underground weak points which could undermine a heavy crane such as service pipes, cellars and cisterns. Always allow enough time for the job at hand and build into your schedule an allowance for delays.

Any signals to conduct crane operations should be made in accordance with the Health and Safety (Safety Signs and Signals) Regulations 1996 and BS 7121 Part 1 for the safe use of cranes. Staff doing such work should

Mobile Crane Safety Checklist

Prior to work commencing check and ensure that:

- there are up-to-date test and examination certificates available for site management to inspect
- daily/weekly maintenance and inspections are carried out
- cab windows are clean and screen wipers, where fitted, are in working order
- cab and floor are clean and free from litter and tools
- before starting power unit, the crane controls are in neutral
- on starting the power unit, all gauges are reading correctly
- the safe load indicator is fully operational, and, where fitted, the automatic visible and overload indicator is working correctly and that the correct cam/programme is selected and fitted
- all other limit switches are operating correctly, e.g. over hoist, etc
- all ropes are free to operate and are not visibly defective
- where applicable, tyre pressures are as recommended by the manufacturer and tyres are free from dangerous cuts and weaknesses
- all tools and equipment are checked and stowed correctly
- fire extinguisher, if fitted, is free from visible defect and fully charged
- tracks are in good operational condition
- there are no restrictions on access, i.e., check overall dimensions of crane
- work areas are clearly visible and are adequately lighted where necessary
- ground is capable of taking loads (outriggers/crane/load/wind). If in doubt, get ADVICE from supervisor/line manager
- the approach and working areas are as level as possible
- there is adequate protection from any overhead electric lines
- if outriggers are used (blocked duties), they are set in the correct position as per crane manufacturer's instructions, locked and adequately supported
- there is ample room to swing and lift the crane jib clear of any obstructions and the rear of the crane is clear of obstructions
- weights of the loads are known, and that correct lifting gear is available
- there is a direct contact at the site available to supervise the proposed lift, e.g., a lift supervisor or slinger/signaller.

Whilst work is in progress, check and ensure that:

- loads are lifted carefully and remain within the safe radius in accordance with the crane duty chart
- the crane is operating from planned/approved positions only
- the slinger/signaller is working in correct manner
- the crane hook is positioned directly over the load. Remember to make adjustment to allow for deflection in the jib whilst lifting
- all crane motions are operated smoothly and safely
- the crane is kept at a safe predetermined distance from open excavations, etc
- when travelling with a load suspended, the manufacturer's instructions are followed, the load is carried as near to ground as possible and hand (tag) lines are used
- travel is never undertaken over uneven ground with the load suspended
- when operating near overhead electric lines, extreme care should be taken. All such lines should be treated as live, unless they are known to be isolated
- the safe load/radius indicators are always in working order if fitted
- all lifting gear is of the correct type, serviceable and used correctly
- the loads are not being slewed over persons and persons are not standing or walking under load within the intended area of operation
- when travelling on sloping ground, changes to radius are made to accommodate movement of load.

Figure H11.2 *Mobile crane safety checklist. © HSE*

be experienced and wear visibility jackets, ear protection, gloves and hard hats. They should also have some secondary means of communication with the operator.

There should be restricted access during any operations conducted under BS 7121 Part 1 for the safe use of cranes. Lifting should not take place over access points, pathways or roads. Movements should have a crane supervisor, slinger and crane driver. It is the responsibility of the management of the organization who require the load to be lifted to make sure that the task is managed safely, that the operators are qualified and that the safe working load (SWL) is not exceeded. In other words responsibility rests with the production company.

The weight of equipment being lifted should not exceed the SWL maximum, which will decrease according to the extension of the crane arm, i.e. the longer the radius of the arm, the less weight it can support before the crane falls over. All cranes have an automatic safe load indicator in the cab but the speed at which an overloaded crane will fall gives no margin for error.

Another important factor in the safe operation of cranes is the weather – especially high winds, which can have a dramatic effect on the stability of the crane and its load. Maximum wind speeds for operation are:

- tower cranes 45 mph;
- crawler cranes 31 mph; and
- mobile cranes 22 mph.

However, the wider the load, the less working margin for error – so with a wider load these figures should be reduced.

The operators should be in good and constant communication and in clear vision. Any ropes or chains used should be tested and able to support the intended load. Hooks, ropes and chains should have inspection and lifting appliances test certificates.

The management of lifting operations should be conducted safely and properly supervised. The appointed person to supervise the lifting operations must have a lifting managers' certificate. The crane driver should never be the appointed person for a lifting operation. An experienced external supervisor is always needed.

Therefore crane operations should always be a pre-planned operation with the risks assessed and the correct crane and lifting gear chosen for the task. The site and planned route should be properly assessed for inherent, introduced and proximity hazards so that the foundation is correct and the safe arrival ensured. The crane should be properly maintained and in safe working condition. It should be supplied with a handover certificate and the correct documentation. The staff operating it should be properly trained and the directing, loading and transportation should be properly supervised. The load should be stable and not exceed the SWL of the crane or the height of the arm. Particular attention should be paid to the shape and weight of the load and external factors such as high winds. Lastly the health and safety of employees, contractors and the public should be the overall consideration with no risks undertaken and all precautions including barriers, safety warning signs and personal protective equipment issued.

The CPHA and CITB mobile crane operators safety guide should be a first point of reference. Also consult the CIRIA Publication No. 131, Crane stability on site, which goes into more detail about the safe working of cranes and their operation. It is anticipated that the construction specific regulations – the Construction (Lifting Operations) Regulations 1961 – will be replaced by a consolidated set of lifting regulations covering all industries, e.g. LOLA 98.

Hoists

Hoists are often used to raise or lower equipment on outside broadcast temporary sites or up buildings where stair access is too narrow, e.g. transmitters.

The hoist should be capable of lifting the weight (SWL) which should be clearly indicated and evenly distributed. The hoist should only be controlled from one point where the operation is visible and the operator should be properly trained and have good means of communication to the top of the hoist way and any loading points. The controls should be kept locked to prevent anyone other than the qualified operator from starting the hoist. Never use the equipment hoist for moving people. A warning notice should indicate this.

The hoist should be properly constructed by trained and experienced staff according to the manufacturer's instructions. The supplier or contractor must give the receiver or operator a valid handover certificate.

The hoist platform should be in a protective cage to prevent equipment from falling out and the hoist way should be caged at any point where people might be struck, such as working platforms or windows. The base of the hoist should also be caged and access gates placed at landings and at ground level. These should be locked and only opened during loading and unloading. They should not be allowed to swing free. The hoist should be regularly tested and a weekly inspection log maintained with a full inspection every six months. Always make sure that the contractor or supplier has a full log and inspection certificate. Hooks, ropes and chains should have inspection and lifting appliances test certificates to comply with the Construction (Lifting Operations) Regulations Nos 10 and 30, 1961.

Fork-lift trucks

Fork-lift trucks are often used to move and unload film equipment from lorries. During 1995 seven people were killed and 187 were injured in fork-lift truck accidents.

The correct truck should always be selected for the job. Types include, counter-balanced front loading, reach and straddle trucks, order picking trucks with a elevating operator platform, side loading fork lift trucks, lateral stacking trucks and pedestrian controlled trucks.

Factors such as the terrain and weight of the load and how high it must be lifted should be taken into account and consultation between the supplier and the user must be a key factor in deciding which type to use. Drivers should possess a licence and insurance certificate. They should be taxed and possess a registration plate if the truck is to be used on a public road.

Drivers should be 17 or over (exceptions are horticulture and construction). To drive on a public road within 1000 yards of the workplace they must have a category b driving licence and be aged 17 for trucks up to 3.5 tonnes, 18 for trucks up to 7.5 tonnes and over 21 for 7.5 tonne and over.

Fork-lift trucks should be properly maintained and the SWL should never be exceeded. Special guidance exists for the safe operation of fork-lift trucks in potentially flammable areas such as chemical stores, refineries or near special effects.

Take special care if the truck is LPG powered as the replacement of cylinders should be done outside with no ignition source such as cigarettes, electrical sparks or lights close by. Staff should be fully trained and experienced before undertaking this (see also COSHH Regulations and government guidance note CS4 for the correct handling and storage of LPG).

The fork-lift should have a warning light or siren to warn others when it is moving. Drivers should have passed an RITB course for industrial work and a CITB course for construction work. Never allow people onto a fork-lift or undertake lifting movements with people in the vicinity.

Special guidance exists for the use of work platforms on fork-lift trucks. Avoid sudden and sharp braking movements. The fork-lift driver should take special care when travelling across access points and footpaths. Look out for electrical cables and wires when the load is raised. When moving or parking make sure you do not bump scaffold towers, camera positions or stacks.

When driving backwards take care to keep a clear field of vision and ensure that you can see in front of you when going forwards. Use the services of a banks person for wide and unusual loads.

Never leave the fork-lift parked with the keys in. Fork-lifts make tempting play targets for children. Look out for any deep potholes or steep slopes and don't raise or lower the load while moving.

Operators should always wear protective clothing such as hard hats, boots, ear defenders and gloves. For further information of safe operation for fork lift trucks consult the British Industrial Truck Association Ltd publications *Stability Awareness for Powered Industrial and Rough Terrain Lift Trucks*, 2nd edition June 1995 and the *Operator's Safety Code For Powered Industrial Trucks*, 16th edition, June 1995.

Mobile elevating work platforms/access platforms

Mobile elevating work platforms (MEWPs) or mobile access platforms are often used by film and television production companies to gain higher camera and lighting positions or to obtain access to working platforms on sets. These are often known by names such as cherry pickers but they are still MEWPs. MEWPs fall into four major types:

- scissor lift,
- mast,
- telescopic boom, and
- articulated boom.

They usually come in three types of mounting: truck mounted, self-propelled or on trailer units. Some MEWPs have been specially adapted for television work and some are suitable for rough terrain. All MEWPs should meet BS 7171 for mobile elevating work platforms and meet new EC safety standards.

MEWPs come under the Use of Work Equipment Directive 89/655/EEC. As Annex 4 of the Machinery Directive covers their use as machines which have a high risk factor, this places a responsibility on employers to ensure that workers receive adequate training on the use and maintenance of work equipment.

The owner/operator/contractor or hirer/supplier must give you a valid handover certificate to indicate that the MEWP is in safe working condition, and give details of the operating instructions, maintenance schedule, tyre pressure, emergency procedure if the arm fails and the safe working load. This is a means by which the supplier of the platform transfers obligations under the Health and Safety at Work Act, section 3, 'Duty of care to other people's employees' to the user. They should also supply a current working manual and safety instructions. Make sure the registration number and serial number of the MEWP matches that of the handover certificate and that the certificate is current.

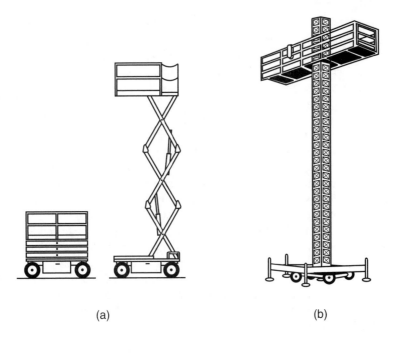

(a)

(b)

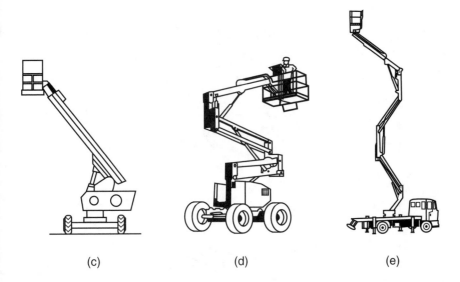

(c)

(d)

(e)

Figure H11.3 *Different types of MEWP: (a) scissor lift, (b) mast type, (c) telescopic boom, (d) articulating boom (self-propelled) (e) articulating boom (truck mounted). © Peter Hird Ltd*

Any MEWPs supplied by a contractor or hire company should have a valid road licence and insurance certificate. MEWPs should also have an electrical insulation certificate if they are being used for live electrical work or carrying electrical equipment such as lighting.

It is the responsibility of all employers who operate platforms to train their employees to an acceptable standard in order for them to meet their obligations under the Health And Safety At Work Act, section 2, 'Duty of care to their own employees'. The operator should hold a valid LGV licence and have passed an IPAF training course.

Any operator working from an access platform should have a safe working platform which can support the combined weight of operator and equipment, for example an average weight for one person would be 80 kg minimum. One person with equipment could be 120 kg minimum. The SWL should always be displayed and this should never be exceeded.

Equipment should be secured to prevent it falling and anybody working on the access platform should be secured by a safety harness to BS 1397 and fall arrest devices attached inside the platform. Never attach a safety harness to a point outside the platform. Users of MEWPs should always make sure that the ground is level and able to take the weight of the platform and its intended load.

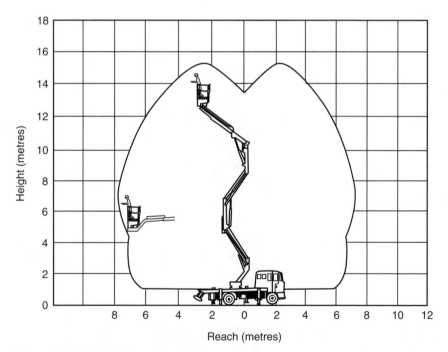

Figure H11.4   *MEWPs: safe working envelope*

Never try to add additional weights in order to increase the capacity of a truck. This is a highly dangerous practice and should not be allowed. Outrigging supports and surface base plates should be used. Any counterweight should be extended. The MEWP has a safe working envelope which should never be exceeded. This is the safe working area determined in the maximum vertical height and horizontal reach of the operating platform.

Wind force number	Description of wind	Wind effect locally	Speed mph	Speed m/s
0	Calm	Calm. Smoke rises vertically	1	0–1
1	Light air	Direction of wind shown by smoke drift, but not by wind or weather vanes	1–3	1–2
2	Light breeze	Wind felt on face. Leaves rustle. Wind or weather vanes move	4–7	2–3
3	Gentle breeze	Leaves and small twigs in constant motion, wind extends light flags	8–12	3–5
4	Moderate breeze	Wind raises dust and loose paper. Small branches move	13–18	5–8
5	Fresh breeze	Small trees in leaf begin to sway. Little crested wavelets form on inland waters	19–24	8–11
6	Strong breeze	Large branches in motion. Umbrellas used with some difficulty	25–31	11–14
7	Near gale	Whole trees in motion. Becoming difficult to walk against wind	32–38	14–17
8	Gale	Twigs break off trees. Progress is generally impeded	39–46	17–21
9	Strong gale	Chimney pots, slates and tiles may be blown off. Other slight structural damage	47–54	21–24

Figure H11.5 *Beaufort wind scale for use on land (numbers 1–9)*

The working platform should have a guard-rail and edge protection. Particular attention should be paid to constant communication and the operation of the emergency ancillary safe lowering system. It is important to keep a check on weather factors which will affect either the access platform or those working from a platform, such as fog, ice, snow and rain. Always make sure the operators have proper personal protective clothing as the wind chill factor can be dangerous. For example a ground temperature of 10°C will become 0°C in a 20 mph wind. A temperature of 0°C can become –15°C and lower, especially if the wind is stronger and the platform arm is extended.

High wind is a special risk. This should be measured from the platform top by a hand-held anemometer and checked on the Beaufort scale. The maximum speed that a platform can operate at is generally accepted as 28 mph. However, because MEWP design wind speeds are based on a 3-second gust and the Beaufort scale is based on 10 seconds, you should always use the next scale down as direct conversion would mean you are operating at an unsafe wind speed.

The wind force can be accentuated by the following factors:

● Aircraft/airports/high sided vehicles/funnelling effects of buildings. In some cases the wind speed between high sided buildings can double, so great caution should be exercised and a wind speed test carried out.
● The higher the platform the greater the wind speed can be. At 20 m the wind speed can be 50 times greater than at ground level.

Wind speed can cause the MEWP to sway, narrowing the distance between the platform and sides of buildings or cables. Therefore a 15 m gap should be maintained between the working platform and any structures. For further information consult the International Powered Access Federation (IPAF) *Guide to MEWPs*, revised edition, 1994.

Further reading

Safe Use of Lifting Equipment: The Lifting Operations and Lifting Equipment Regulations 1998, HSE L113, ISBN 0-7176-1628-2.

Do's And Don'ts With Forklift Trucks, 1995, The British Industrial Truck Association Ltd.

Stability Awareness for Powered Industrial and Rough Terrain Lift Trucks, 2nd edition, June 1995, The British Industrial Truck Association Ltd.

Operator's Safety Code for Powered Industrial Trucks, 16th edition, June 1998, The British Industrial Truck Association Ltd.

Operator's Safety Guide for Rough Terrain Lift Trucks, 6th edition, November 1997, The British Industrial Truck Association Ltd.

● BS 7121 Part 1, 1989 For the Safe Use of Cranes.
● BS 7171 Mobile Elevating Work Platforms.

Bulleted items available from British Standards Institute, 389 Chiswick High Rd, London W4 4AL.

CPA Registration Scheme for Instructors and Demonstrators in the Use of Mobile Elevating Work Platforms.

The Inspection and Testing of Elevating Work Platforms, Mobile Elevating Work Platforms Operators Safety Guide 1995, CPA/International Powered Access Federation.

European Standard for Mobile Elevating Work Platforms, EEC, PR-EN 280.

European Standard for Mast Climbing Work Platforms, EEC, PR-EN 280.

Self Propelled Truck Directive 86/663/EEC.

Health and Safety in Construction, HS(G)150, HSE Books, 1996, ISBN 0-7176-1143-4.

Rider Operated Lift Trucks, Operator Training: Approved Code of Practice and Guidelines, HSE COP 26, ISBN 0-7176-0474-8.

Safety in Working With Lift Trucks, HMSO, HS(G)6, 1998, ISBN 0-11-1440-9.

Alice Spain, Fork Lift Truck Safety, *Safety Express*, RoSPA, March/April 1999, pp. 10–11.

Lift Trucks in Potentially Flammable Atmospheres, HSE, HS(G)113, 1996, ISBN 0-7176-0706-2.

Guidance Note: Working Platforms on Fork Lift Trucks, HSE, PM28, 1981, ISBN 0-11-883392-8.

Safety in Working with Power Operated Mobile Work Platforms, HSE, HS(G)19.

Safety at Powered Operated Mast Work Platforms, HSE, (G)23.

Safety with Mobile Elevating Work Platforms: Industry Survey and Accident Review, HSE, 3.37, SIR46.

Avoidance of Danger from Overhead Electric Lines, HSE (G)GS6.

Avoiding Danger from Underground Services, HSE (G)G47.

HSE Construction Sheet No. 19, The Safe Use of Mobile Cranes on Construction Sites.

A Guide to the Lifting Plant and Equipment (Records of Test and Examinations etc.) Regulations 1992, HSE.

HSE Site Safe News, published twice yearly: Sir Robert Jones Memorial Workshops, Units 3 and 5–9, Grain Industrial Estate, Harlow St, Liverpool L8 4XY.

The Health and Safety (Safety Signs and Signals) Regulations 1996, HSE L64, 1996, ISBN 0-7176-0870-0.

Series of HSE Guidance Notes in Plant and Machinery series: Nos 1–81 give specific guidance about particular hazards relating to site, plant and machinery operational safety.

Construction Industry Research and Information Association, Crane Stability on Site, Special Publication No. 131, ISBN 0-86017-456-5.

Construction Industry Training Board (CITB):

- Health and Safety Publications Catalogue 1997.
- Construction Site Safety Notes, 7th revised edition 1996, (book, GE700).
- Subcontractors and You, (book, LJC03).
- Mobile Crane Operator's Safety Guide, CITB, revised 1994 (book, CJ502).
- Safe Start, *Construction Site Safety Handbook*, GE 707, CITB, 1995, ISBN 0-902-02974-6.

IPAF Guide to MEWPs, International Powered Access Federation, 1994.

Lifting Equipment Engineers Association, Code of Practice for the Safe Use of Lifting Equipment.

Contact organizations

Alimak Ltd
Northampton Rd, Rushden, Northants NN10 9BW
Tel: 01933–410400

Association of Loading and Elevating Equipment Manufacturers
Ambassador House, Brigstock Rd, Thornton Heath, Surrey CR7 7JG
Tel: 0181–665–5395

Bernard Brogan Ltd
Netah St, Motherwell ML1 3TF
Tel: 01698–265132

British Industrial Truck Association Ltd
Scammell House
High St, Ascot, Berkshire SL5 7JF
Tel: 01344–623800

British Standards Institute
389 Chiswick High Rd, London W4 4AL
Tel: 0181–996–9000

Building Employers Confederation (BEC)
Federation House, 2309 Coventry Rd, Sheldon, Birmingham B26 3PL
82 New Cavendish, St London W1M 8AD
Tel: 0171–580–5588

Construction Industry Research and Information Association
6 Storey's Gate, Westminster, London SW1P 3AU

Construction Industry Training Board (CITB)
Bircham Newton, King's Lynn, Norfolk PE3 6RH
Tel: 01553–776677

Construction Plant Hire Association
52 Rochester Row, London SW1P 1JU
Tel: 0171 6306868

Federation of Manufacturers of Construction Equipment and Cranes
Ambassador House, Brigstock Rd, Thornton Heath, Surrey CR7 7JG
Tel: 0181–665–5727

HSE Construction National Interest Group
Mr A. Sheddon, HM Principal Inspector of Health and Safety
1 Long Lane, London SE1 4PG
Tel: 0171–5562100

HSE Construction Policy Division
Rose Court, 2 Southwark Bridge, London SE1 9HS
Tel: 0171–7176000

Peter Hird & Son Ltd
English St, Hull HU3 2BT
Tel: 01482–227333

International Powered Access Federation
PO Box 16, Carnforth, Lancashire LA6 1LB
Tel: 01524–781393

Lifting Equipment Engineers Association
Waggoners Court, The Street, Manuden, Bishop's Stortford, Herts
CM23 1DW
Tel: 01279–816504

National Association of Lift Makers
33/34 Devonshire St, London W1N 1RF
Tel: 0171–935–3013

Hazard 12: Dangerous terrain

The legislation

The Adventure Licensing Regulations 1996
The First Aid at Work Regulations 1981
The Health and Safety at Work Act 1974
The Management of Health and Safety at Work Regulations 1992
The Manual Handling Operations Regulations 1992
The Personal Protective Equipment (PPE) at Work Regulations 1992
The Provision and Use of Work Equipment Regulations 1998
The Reporting of Injuries, Diseases and Dangerous Occurrences Regulations 1995 (RIDDOR)
The Wildlife and Countryside Act 1981

The risks

- access
- poor communications
- extreme weather
- inadequate protective equipment
- inadequate first aid equipment
- injury and exposure
- inexperience
- lack of supervision
- manual handling
- solo working

Those most at risk

Inexperienced location crews, mast and transmission staff.

Film and television programmes often make use of dangerous terrain for programme making, for example coastlines, marshland, moors, mountains, islands and national parks make attractive backdrops for feature films and specialist programmes. Outdoor sports and recreation programmes are increasingly popular including canoeing, mountaineering, skiing, walking, and windsurfing. The recreational use of dangerous terrain can lead to a familiarity and complacency when filming or programme making activity is considered. Without proper planning and precautions such areas can be death traps and very often are. They have many dangerous inherent hazards and filming activity is introducing a higher level of risk to an already dangerous location. So never go into these areas alone without thorough advanced planning. Always assume such locations are dangerous.

Producers considering programme making activity in such areas should stop and consider if a safer alternative exists, such as stock footage.

A full assessment of the risks involved should be undertaken and proper expert advice consulted before any filming is considered. Afterwards could be too late. If the risks to the health and safety of your crew are too great or you don't have the budget to put proper precautions in place, don't do it at all – this can be the safest and cheapest option. Always ask yourself – is this location really necessary and is a safer option available?

Remember that the further north, the further into winter and the higher you go increases the risks from cold and exposure. Similarly fog, rain and snow can turn an apparently benign location into a lethal one, combining cold and poor visibility. So always take these factors into account along with the weather as they dramatically increase the risks involved. The majority of accidents in dangerous terrain happen because people are not prepared, are often inexperienced and do not wear or carry the right equipment. In the wake of the Lyme Bay canoeing tragedy all activity centres must be licensed and all activities properly supervised under the Adventure Licensing Regulations 1996. Special supervision should be provided if you are planning to involve children in a dangerous terrain location or activity.

If you decide to proceed then the first step should be to obtain accurate and current information about the location from maps and other guidebooks. Rather than risk inexperienced crew to perform an initial site exploration and risk assessment why not save time and reduce the risk by two simple methods. First, find out if anyone has used the location before. The local film commission or film company library should be a good source of information. Then you can ask people with first hand knowledge of the risks what precautions they took.

Second, ask local experts with intimate knowledge of the terrain about the special risks particular to that location. Consult the local coastguard, farmers, forestry centre, gamekeepers, mountain rescue team, park rangers, pilots and weather centre about the location. They have many years of experience which will not only save you time but could also save your life.

If possible use specialist and experienced crew who understand the risks involved and how to handle an emergency situation. As well as being experienced staff should be properly briefed about particular local conditions, terrain, tides and the weather. Seek advice and make sure your planning preparation includes accurate maps, local guides and emergency procedure drawn up in consultation with the local experts and rescue authorities who should always be informed in advance. Make sure also that you have obtained permission to recce and film as a lot of land is private property.

After obtaining initial expert advice a preliminary location recce should be made to ascertain the risks involved. Never do this alone and try and use the services of an experienced local guide or expert. Check their experience and qualifications before you set off as your life may depend on their advice. Afterwards is too late to discover that they are not. Get a second opinion just in case.

Before you set off check what the weather is going to be like. Take a proper map, compass, GPS, first aid kit, flares, food, drink, waterproof torch and protective clothing. This must be visible, waterproof and warm. Minimum would be jacket, boots, hat and gloves. Take advice on this and the best type of communications to use. Check your communications will work before you set out. For example are the batteries fully charged? Second, make sure that you are not about to enter a communications blind spot where your mobile phone will not work. Also take extra batteries as cold weather will seriously shorten their working time. Make sure your vehicle is suitable for the terrain with proper tyres, a winch, water, first aid kit, communications and proper heating.

Ensure you keep a spare set of protective clothing and warm blankets in your vehicle and sufficient petrol. Always leave a map of your intended route and your contact details. Make an emergency contact list which has your number, your guide's number, and that of the nearest inhabited house and phone box. Also include the phone numbers of the police, emergency services, hospital and rescue services, along with your NI number, NHS number and blood group. Make a note also if you have any special medical condition. Leave one copy of this list with base and take another (encapsulated and waterproofed) with you. Make sure you are carrying enough money for the phone.

Management and producers should ensure that staff have the right tools and training for the job they have been asked to do. The Personal Protective Equipment (PPE) at Work Regulations 1992 and the Provision and Use of Work Equipment Regulations 1998 make it an obligation to ensure that all staff going into dangerous terrain have been provided with the proper protective equipment, specialized tools and communication equipment which must be safe, suitable and properly maintained.

A proper system for checking the number of people in your party should be in place, especially in bad visibility, and ensure that you maintain regular contact. If you are out of communication for more than the agreed period, base should contact the emergency services.

On the recce record the location with a camera and notebook taking particular care to record features such as: access – how long does it take to get there? – build this into your schedule. Where is the nearest parking spot and phone box along with the location of the nearest emergency rescue team. What is the maximum width of vehicle or number of people you can safely get onto the site? Is the site level? And is it exposed to water or wind? Where is the nearest shelter such as a mountain refuge or barn? Assess the suitability of the site for the task.

Manual handling – can equipment be moved onto the site? Will you have to use lighter or specialized equipment/do you need any special equipment to lift and move your equipment? Will you need extra help to move your equipment on and off site safely? All these factors should be built into your risk assessment.

Once a proper risk assessment has been made combining information obtained from experts and the recce, then management should turn its attention to the suitability of the staff which it wants to carry out the work in dangerous terrain. This is especially true of transmission and mast repair staff who may have to work at height and in very exposed locations such as Holme Moss or Emley Moor. A proper protection plan should be drawn up for their health and safety.

Suitability of staff – the management and producers should always make sure that anybody who is unfit, elderly, inexperienced, pregnant or with a special disability or medical condition should not be made to work in dangerous terrain or undertake manual handling. The First Aid at Work Regulations 1981 oblige employers to make sure that the staff are properly trained in first aid and that the kits are right for the task. So ensure that your crew are properly trained in first aid and emergency procedures.

The Health and Safety at Work Act 1974 places an obligation on all employers of a duty of care towards all employees so not bothering to undertake a full risk assessment of dangerous terrain and take the proper precautions constitutes negligence. For example sending out a camera operator alone into a dangerous location or not operating a daily count of staff on site. In a dangerous location a proper chain of responsibility and communication must be in place as the risk to health and safety is very high.

The Management of Health and Safety at Work Regulations 1992 place a duty on employers and producers to make sure that all work activities undertaken in dangerous terrain are properly planned and supervised and that the staff carrying out such work have been fully informed of the risks and have been properly trained in emergency procedures and the skills which they may need such as, skiing, swimming, diving, or climbing. If they do not have these make sure that any activity in dangerous terrain is properly supervised by an expert with the level of skill necessary for the task in hand. This way the producer can make sure that the filming is undertaken without risk to health and safety and that the final outcome is technically better anyway.

While the work is being carried out constant monitoring should be made of the weather and regular communication maintained. A proper control plan and emergency procedure should be drawn up along with maps and other information and circulated to all staff involved in location filming. In the event of a sudden deterioration in the weather swift retreat to a position of safety should be carried out, and in the event of a medical emergency the control plan should be implemented.

Further reading

- *ABC of Avalanche Safety,* 2nd edition, E. La Chappelle, ZHA1.
- *GPS Made Easy,* Lawrence Latham, GPS1.
- *First Aid Manual,* 6th edition.
- *Medical Handbook for Mountaineers,* Peter Steele, MED3.
- *Modern Rock and Ice Climbing,* Bill Birkett, MOD1.
- *Mountaineering First Aid,* 4th edition, MOU4.
- *Mountain Rescue Committee Handbook,* MRC1.
- *Mountaincraft and Leadership,* 3rd edition, Eric Langmuir, MOU3.
- *Outdoor First Aid,* Robert J. Koester, ZOU3.
- *The SAS Survival Handbook,* John Wiseman, SAS1.
- *The SAS Survival Guide,* John Wiseman, SAS2.
- *Staying Alive in the Arctic,* STA1.
- *Wilderness and Rural Life Support Guidelines,* Robert J. Koester, WIL2.

The above titles are available from Emergency Response Publications, 5 Shelly Court, South Zeal, Okehampton, Devon EX20 2PT, Tel: 01837–840102.

Safety in Outdoor Education, Department of Education, 1989.
So you want to go caving? Free leaflet from the National Caving Association.

Contact organizations

British Cave Rescue Council
Pearl Hill, Dent, Sedbergh, Cumbria LA10 5TG
Tel: 01539–625412 (Hon. Secretary Pete Allwright)

Caving councils
Five regional caving councils cover the following areas:
   Southern area (Mendips)
   Cambrian (Wales)
   Derbyshire (Peak District)
   Northern (Yorkshire Dales and Pennines)
   Devon and Cornwall

The National Caving Association (NCA)
Monomark House, 27 Old Gloucester Street, London WC1N 3XX
Tel: 01335–370629 (contact Jenny Potts)

The British Mountaineering Council
77–79 Burton Rd, Manchester M20 2BB
Tel: 0161–445–4747

Coastguard Agency
Bay 1/17a Spring Place, 105 Commercial Rd, Southampton, Hampshire
SO15 1EG
Tel: 01703–329401
(will give you details of local MRCC, MRSC or coastguard)

The Country Landowners' Association
16 Belgrave Square, London SW1X 8PQ
Tel: 0171–2350511

Countryside Commission
John Dower House, Crescent Place, Cheltenham, Gloucestershire
GL50 3RA
Tel: 01242–521381

The Forestry Commission of Great Britain
231 Corstorhine Rd, Edinburgh, Scotland EH12 7AT
Tel: 0131–3343047

The Maritime and Coastguard Agency
Spring Place, 105 Commercial Rd, Southampton, Hants SO15 1EG
Tel: 01703–329100

The Mountain Leader Training Board of Great Britain
Siabod Cottage, Capel Curig, Gwynedd, Wales LL24 0ET
Tel: 01690–720314

The Met Office
Information Services Unit, Sutton House, London Rd, Bracknell,
Berkshire RG12 2SZ
Tel: 01344–856681
(will give specialist advice and details of local weather centre)

National Parks Authority
Ten National Parks in England and Wales, contact information offices.

Brecon Beacons National Park
7 Glamorgan St, Brecon, Powys, Wales LD3 7DP
Tel: 01874–62443-Ex-238

Dartmoor National Park Authority
Parke, Bovey Tracey, Newton Abbot, Devon TQ13 9JQ
Tel: 01626–832093

Exmoor National Park
Exmoor House, Dulverton, Somerset TA22 9HL
Tel: 01398–323665

Lake District National Park
Murley Moss, Oxenholme Rd, Kendal, Cumbria LA9 7RL
Tel: 01539–724555, Ex 236

Northumberland National Park
Eastburn, South Park, Hexham, Northumberland NE46 1BS
Tel: 01434–605–555

North Yorkshire Moors National Park
The Old Vicarage, Bondgate, Helmsley, N. Yorkshire YO6 5BP
Tel: 01439–770657

Peak Park Joint Planning Board
Aldern House, Baslow Rd, Bakewell, Derbyshire DE45 1AE
Tel: 01629 816200

Pembrokeshire Coast National Park
County Offices, St Thomas Green, Haverfordwest, Dyfed, Wales
SA61 1QZ
Tel: 01437–764591

Snowdonia National Park
Penrhyndeudraeth, Gwynedd, Wales LL48 6LS
Tel: 01766–770274

Yorkshire Dales National Park
Hedben Rd, Grassington, Skipton, North Yorkshire BD23 5LB
Tel: 01756–752748

The National Trust, Broadcast Liaison Officer
36 Queen Anne's Gate, London SW1H 9AS
Tel: 0171–222 5097

The Royal National Lifeboat Institution Headquarters
Public Relations Office, West Quay Rd, Poole, Dorset BH15 1HZ
Tel: 01202–671133

Hazard 13: Derelict buildings

A demolition contractor is being prosecuted after a man was killed when a 13 tonne excavator and rubble fell on top of him. T. E. Scudder Limited is being prosecuted under section 2(1) of the Health and Safety at Work Act for failing to ensure the health and safety of its employee Michael Tranmore who was asphyxiated when part of the fourth floor of the Norwich Union building collapsed during demolition work in 1995.

HSE

The legislation

The Control of Asbestos at Work Regulations 1987 (CAWR)
The Control of Asbestos at Work Regulations (Amendment) SI/1992
The Control of Pollution (Special Waste) Regulations 1980
The Chemical (Hazard Information and Packaging) Regulations 1993
The Classification, Packaging and Labelling of Dangerous Substances Regulations 1984
The Construction (Design and Management) Regulations 1994
The Classification and Labelling of Explosives Regulations 1983
The Control of Substances Hazardous to Health Regulations 1999
The Health and Safety at Work Act 1974
The Control of Lead at Work Regulations 1980
The Environment Act 1995
The Management of Health and Safety at Work Regulations 1992
The First Aid at Work Regulations 1981
The Manual Handling Operations Regulations 1992
The Personal Protective Equipment (PPE) at Work Regulations 1992
The Provision and Use of Work Equipment Regulations 1998

The risks

- asbestos
- chemicals
- contaminated land
- electricity
- explosions
- falling debris
- fire
- gas and petrol
- glass and nails
- heights
- lead
- rotten floors and ceilings
- tripping hazards
- vermin
- contaminated water

Those most at risk

Crew, location managers, performers, riggers and stunt artists.

Derelict building are popular choices with location managers and directors as they often have visual atmosphere and provide good locations for fiction shoots – especially crime and horror films. Because derelict buildings are unoccupied they have no occupants to get in the way or set opening hours. This means the buildings can be set up and used continually which appears to make them cheaper.

Behind the initial superficial attraction lie a lot of dormant hazards which can make the selection of a derelict building a potentially dangerous risk to the health and safety of your crew. These risks can be expensive to put right. This is because old, disused and derelict buildings require building, demolition or site clearance work to make them safe as long periods of neglect have made the fabric unsafe. The building may have inherent risks on account of its condition and former function. In addition, hazardous materials and damage may have been introduced by vandals and fly tippers.

Contact the owners to seek permission to enter and use a derelict building or site. Get as much information as you can about the site or

Figure H13.1   *Disused factory. © Tony Scott*

building before you consider setting foot in it. If possible engage somebody who knows the location or who may have worked there. Obtain working plans to detect hidden pipes, cables and cellars. If possible obtain a copy of the health and safety file for the site or building. This is a record of the premises' history and maintenance. Get copies of old maps and land registry records.

Make sure that you have adequate insurance cover in place and then conduct a site survey and search to ascertain any risks. This is a requirement under BS 6187 for demolition work. The CIRIA have published a series of volumes giving guidance of economic and safe solutions for the remediation of contaminated land.

Always proceed with caution as a derelict building may contain many risks that are hidden until your search reveals them. Never conduct a site search alone or unaccompanied. Carry a lone worker's safety alarm. Use a proper locator to find out the presence of hidden live utility services. Your search should identify the structural elements of the building and their condition.

If the risks are too great or the site is too dangerous to be made safe, opt for an alternative. This can be cheaper and safer in the long run.

Any demolition or building work in derelict buildings comes under the Construction (Design and Management) Regulations 1994. The HSE

Guidance Notes for Demolition and Derelict Buildings GS29 Parts 1–4 insist that a premises-specific risk assessment should always be carried out as an essential part of the preparation and planning process.

The results of the risk assessment and the necessary preventative measures should then be put into a coherent work method statement called a health and safety plan for how your crew will be protected from any risks which you have identified. The health and safety plan should set out how the work will be done and who will do it. This includes details of the timing, work schedule, the equipment to be used and who will supervise the stages of the job in a safe and logical order.

Beware of proximity hazards to the public from dust, noise and vibration and make sure that the public cannot get onto your site during hazardous activity or at night. The site should be fenced off and lit properly with safe access and exits. All preventative measures to ensure site safety and prevent injury to the public must be put in place before any work is undertaken. Any staff, members of the public, actors and contractors who come on to the site must be given a site induction which includes emergency procedures, location of fire exits, fire extinguishers and muster points, first aid precautions and the details of any risks found during the site search and risk assessment. Everybody should be given accurate information about the risks and what precautions and protective equipment to comply with. Safety signs should indicate these at the site entrance backed up by a site-specific health and safety rule book.

Managers and producers must ensure that all staff are given accurate information, and are properly trained and competent for the work they have been asked to do and that all work in derelict buildings is properly supervised. Any demolition work must be notified to HSE on a Notification of Project Form 10(REV). This should also be used for any construction work or project lasting more than 30 days or 500 person days.

The form gives information about the client, planning supervisor, principal contractor, site address, local authority, and details of the work to be carried out and which contractors are undertaking it.

Any work, safety and maintenance records must be entered into a health and safety file. This is a legal requirement under the CDM Regulations. The file should contain details of any hazards which may have to be removed or contained if they present a significant risk to the health and safety of your crew or cast.

Producers who use derelict sites or buildings should beware of specific hazards such as hidden tanks, chemicals, gas, pressure pipes and concentrations of asbestos.

Asbestos can kill – and it can kill *you*. Diseases caused by it are usually called asbestosis. The risk of exposure to asbestos should be detected on the recce as part of the hazard identification and a risk assessment made to identify any danger. The problem is that asbestos is hard to detect. The presence of asbestos is hard to identify as its appearance can be changed by surface coatings and heat.

Asbestos is often hidden underneath surface material as it was often used as an insulation material, cladding or as fire proof cladding. Asbestos was also used as a fire retardant. Therefore asbestos can be located near boilers, pipework, ceilings and heating plant.

Locations to beware of asbestos and where a high risk factor of exposure to asbestos can be found are churches, ships and power stations.

Asbestos was also used in building materials such as plaster and cement. So disused cement factory sites, pipework and behind cladding are particularly prime locations. The main uses were insulation and sprayed coating, insulating board and asbestos cement so other locations where asbestos might be found include older school buildings, hospitals, and any area which may have needed acoustic or thermal cladding.

Disused buildings are a very high risk because the asbestos may have been undisturbed for many years until your production activity disturbs it. If you suspect a location may contain asbestos inform the location owner immediately. Try and obtain old building plans or contact the original constructor to see if any asbestos concentrations are marked. If in any doubt assume that asbestos may be present until you can prove that the disused location is safe

So how can you detect it without becoming at risk? Asbestos is usually safe until disturbed. The risk from asbestos is very high during demolition or alteration work as unidentified concentrations of asbestos can be disturbed. This is why alterations to convert any derelict building into a film set should not go ahead until an air sampling test has been conducted. Otherwise the risk to riggers, electricians and plumbers is very high.

Stop and consider if a safer alternative location is available? Do you really need to use this particular derelict building? Deciding to go somewhere else could be safer and cheaper. Or simply stop and don't do it. If the presence of asbestos is detected a licensed contractor should be brought in for specialist advice. Removal or encapsulation should only be undertaken by a licensed contractor and disposed of under section 62 of the CAW Regulations. Competent contractors are HSE licensed and are members of ACAD. If in doubt ask for a copy of their licence. If they are not licensed then the HSE must be notified at least 28 days in advance of an intention to work with asbestos.

Asbestos is a prime example of a dormant inherent hazard that becomes a very high risk if activated by negligent activity. Asbestos can kill if undetected – so always adopt a cautious approach and seek advice from the experts (see Hazard 3: Asbestos).

Another risk comes from aluminium, cadmium, lead or mercury poisoning – especially in disused factories, foundries or smelters. HSE have produced individual guides to dangerous substances by type (section 3.9 in HSE publications catalogue). The Control of Lead at Work Regulations 1980 control how to work with and dispose of lead.

Old transformers often contain harmful PCBs which can cause cancers. A specialist contractor should be used to remove any PCBs or to drain old fuel, chemical and waste tanks. (Any contractor should perform their own risk assessment and work method statement which should be supplied to the production company or producer contracting them.)

Because of the risks presented by a derelict site, the location should be fenced off and adequate security provided to prevent public access. Everybody on site must be booked in and out. Any dangerous areas should be cordoned off and dangerous access points blocked up or removed. Any staff or contractors should be kept clear during dangerous site removal work or during heavy plant and lifting operations.

Chemicals are another risk in derelict locations. Always perform a COSHH risk assessment if you suspect the location has chemicals. There are often derelict drums, pipes and tanks which may contain chemicals, chemical residue or chemical fumes – especially in disused factories or plants. If these are labelled the contents can be identified by a symbol seeker to see if the contents are:

1 Explosive
2 Irritant
3 Highly flammable
4 Harmful
5 Oxidizing
6 Toxic
7 Corrosive.

The labels are square orange warning signs to indicate a health hazard.

Danger labels are triangular and give specific content warning in sixteen different classifications:

1 Compressed gas
2 Poison gas
3 Flammable gas
4 Flammable liquid
5 Flammable solid
6 Spontaneously combustible
7 Dangerous when wet
8 Oxidizing agent
9 Organic peroxide
10 Harmful – stow away from foodstuffs

11 Toxic
12 Corrosive
13 Multi-load
14 Oxygen
15 Marine pollutant
16 Other dangerous substance.

Never smoke or use naked flames or sparks in the vicinity of chemical drums.

The problem with chemicals in disused sites is that they will usually have no labels. Never try to open a drum or tank as the exposure to air could cause an explosion or release a noxious fume into the atmosphere.

Never try to move them as the contents may have become unstable over time and the container may well have rotted away. Therefore the floor may be contaminated so always wear protective boots and gloves.

The disposal of hazardous chemicals and waste must be made in accordance with the Control of Pollution (Special Waste) Regulations 1980 by a licensed contractor who can clear the site for you.

A special consignment note for the carriage and disposal of hazardous wastes should be used and a notification of intention to dispose made to the hazardous wastes department of the local county council.

Regulation 13 states that the carrier, disposal authority and site owner must keep a register of all hazardous waste for at least two years. Names of authorized carriers of hazardous waste can be obtained from the NAWDC (see Hazard 6: Chemicals and hazardous substances).

Electricity is also a high risk in derelict buildings as the site may contain exposed live cables which could kill on contact. Never touch exposed cables and look out for any hidden or jutting cables on the floor, from walls or overhead. Avoid drilling into walls and floors where a hidden electrical supply may be located make sure the supply is switched off first. Afterwards is too late.

The supply itself could be unstable over time, with damaged earths. Never try and plug any electrical equipment into old sockets. Always get a qualified electrician to test the supply and if necessary bring in your own independent supply if the existing one is too dangerous. Always wear rubber shoes to avoid earthing and carry an electrical tester.

Make sure at least one person is trained to cope with electrical shocks and emergency first aid. Never try to use disused lifts, hoists or elevators. They can be death traps (see Hazard 15: Electricity). Do not turn on old ventilation plant as this could push noxious fumes, debris and vermin into the site.

Falling debris is another risk in disused buildings. Especially from chimneys, vents, windows and ceilings. Always wear head protection and try to avoid activities which generate excess structural vibration and noise as this might dislodge loose debris from the roof or glass from a window. Vibration may also come from the use of generators, plant, tools or vehicles. Proximity vibration caused by passing vehicles, planes or trains could also dislodge debris.

Always use a competent contractor to clear the site of debris and so reduce the risk of falling debris or masonry. If necessary effect repairs and secure ceilings, windows and floors. Erect safety nets with a 12 to 19 mm mesh designed to BS 3913, tested, marked and erected by a competent contractor to catch falling debris and erect safety barriers for a safe working area.

Gas and petrol are a very high risk in derelict buildings. Always check the site plan for locations of gas pipes and petrol tanks. Always turn the supplies off first. Never drill into walls, floors or pipes which may contain gas or petrol. Never use naked flames, sparks, electrical tools or smoke which may cause an explosion. Use a portable gas analyser such as an Extox and carry a Gasbadge personal gas alarm to detect and warn of the presence of gas and toxic fumes. Beware of the risk of gas such as methane and radon which can come from underground seepage. This is explosive and dangerous, especially in old mines tips, and quarries. Beware of the risk of explosion or asphyxiation from underground tanks or silos which may have leaked. If necessary get any tanks drained or removed by a competent and experienced demolition or building contractor who is used to site clearances.

Beware also of dust hazards, especially in old grain stores, saw mills, timber stores, flour mills, warehouses and silos. There can be the risk of sparks causing fire or an explosion. Take proper fire precautions (see Hazard 17: Fire) and equip your staff with respirators or masks.

Derelict buildings contain many floor hazards such as cans, bottles, glass, nails, needles, sharp metal and trip hazards such as cables. Always wear protective footwear and gloves. Make sure your crew have had recent tetanus jabs. Always move slowly and use sufficient illumination. If necessary get the floor cleared first by a competent contractor. There may be a fire risk from dry floor debris, especially old cars and carpets.

Another hazard may be the condition of the floor itself. Is it really safe and can it support the weight you are putting on it? This may be an obvious risk in upper floors, but ground floors can hide hidden drops such as cellars, inspection pits, silos and tanks.

Always consult site plans for hidden hazards and make sure site inspection staff wear proper protective clothing and are prevented from sudden drops by a fall arrest harness and safety line. The floors may have to be supported or rebuilt before they can be used safely.

Always seal off and prevent access to rotten floors. Restrict access and loading of upper floors or weak floors to a minimum.

Avoid working at heights in derelict buildings. This is dangerous enough in buildings of good condition but lethal in buildings where time and weather damage have weakened ladders, roof boards, stairs, balconies and ceilings – especially in old factories, churches, chimneys, lighthouses, theatres and windmills.

The fall might only kill you but the falling debris could kill others with falling glass, masonry or steel. Try to use someone who is experienced such as a steeplejack or demolition contractor. Always wear hard hats and safety harness and a fall arrest device. Any work over 2 m is considered to be working at heights, including scaffolding. In these circumstances a roof inspection would be safer by an external MEWP or crane rather than trusting to dangerous structures. Any lifting plant or crane operations come under the Lifting Operations and Lifting Equipment Regulations 1998.

Do not attach a scaffold or working platform for repairs, painting, camera or lighting crew to the side of a derelict building. The structure may not be able to support the weight and could fall down due to subsidence or weakness over time. Always consult a structural engineer beforehand to make sure the walls are safe and can bear the load you are asking it to support – especially in an area of known subsidence or adjacent to water.

The water supply in derelict buildings is usually contaminated. If in any doubt conduct a water test with an NRA laboratory. This is especially true of deep water in old industrial mills, chemical works or canals. Make sure staff can swim and that proper water rescue equipment is available. Never run vehicles, heavy plant or cranes along disused embankments which contain water. They may collapse under the weight, especially when parked for a prolonged period of time, and could cause serious flooding and a risk to life.

Always assume water is contaminated unless you can prove that it is safe. Never drill or conduct repair work until you know the location of disused pipes. Get the supply turned off first. A sudden inflow of water can drown or collapse floors – especially from large roof tanks where the height factor of falling water could be lethal.

The roof tanks and ceilings in derelict buildings could also be contaminated by faeces and guano, especially from pigeons. A high risk to health is present and any bird droppings must be identified and removed by a specialist contractor. This is because you can contract psittacosis through inhaling the dust from bird droppings which can give you symptoms of pneumonia and arthritis. These can last for years and in some cases it can cause fatal respiratory failure. Psittacosis is the most common and serious illness that humans can develop from birds.

Staff should always wear protective suits and breathing equipment. There is also a risk of contamination in derelict buildings from vermin.

Get a specialist pest or environmental contractor to remove any pests or vermin and clean the site.

There is a very high risk of being bitten by vermin or contaminated by their droppings. A particular risk is contamination of water by rats' urine which causes Weil's disease. This is contracted by swallowing or inhaling contaminated water and is potentially fatal. It is often known as leptospirosis (HSE-INDG84, AIS5 and AIS19). The risk of this should be fully assessed, especially in disused buildings near water such as warehouses and factories. Always look out for droppings and other signs of vermin. If necessary call in a specialist pest contractor to remove the vermin as exposure to them constitutes a high risk to the health and safety of employees and a breach of the Environmental Health Act. Make sure all your staff have had recent polio and tetanus jabs. Beware of biological risks from discarded needles and condoms.

Derelict buildings have many inherent hazards caused by disuse, lack of repair and the effects of weather and vandalism. Always assume that such locations are highly dangerous with a very high risk to the health and safety of your crew. Conduct a full risk assessment and take precautionary measures before any production activity is undertaken. Always check for emergency access and egress and provide proper fire and first aid precautions.

A full site examination should be conducted and any high risk factors identified should be removed, sealed up or repaired by competent contractors. If the disused location cannot be made safe, choose an alternative that is safer to your staff and lighter on your budget.

Further reading

- Asbestos Use in Buildings, HSE9, 1993.
- Code of Practice for the Protection of Unoccupied Buildings, CPPUB, 1995.
- Prevention and Control of Dust Explosions, RC12, 1991.

All three available from Loss Prevention Council, Melrose Avenue, Boreham-wood, Hertfordshire, Tel: 0181–207–2345.

BS 6187: Code of Practice For Demolition Work.
Lynn Wallace, Watch out for the birdie, (article on psittacosis), *The Guardian*, 9 June 1998, p. 15.
A Guide to the Asbestos (Licensing) Regulations 1983, HSE Books, L11, 1991, ISBN 0-11-885684-7.
Asbestos Dust – The Hidden Killer – Essential Advice for Building Maintenance, Repair and Refurbishment Workers, HSE, 1995, IND(G)187L.
Avoiding Danger From Underground Services, HSE, HS(G)47, 1989, ISBN 0-7176-03435-7.
Dr P. Mcmahon, Contaminated Land, *The Safety and Health Practitioner*, April 1999, pp. 20–21.

A Short Guide to the Personal Protective Equipment at Work Regulations 1992, IND(G)-147L, HSE, 1995.

Control of Substances Hazardous to Health and Control of Carcinogenic Substances (Including Control of Substances Hazardous to Health Regulations 1988), 4th edition, HMSO L51993, ISBN 0-11-882085-0.

Control of Substances Hazardous to Health Regulations 1994, Approved Code of Practice, HSE, 1995, ISBN 0-7176-0819-0.

A Step By Step Guide to COSHH Assessment, HS(G)97, HSE, 1993, ISBN 0-11-886379-7.

Control of Lead at Work, COP2, HSE, 1985, ISBN 0-7176-1046-2.

Establishing Exclusion Zones When Using Explosives in Demolition, HSE, CIS45.

Health and Safety in Demolition Work, Part 1: Preparation and Planning, HSE, GS29/1, 1988, ISBN 0-11-885405-4.

Health and Safety in Demolition Work, Part 4: Health Hazards, HSE, GS29/4, 1985, ISBN 0-11-883604-8.

Grain Dust in Non-Agricultural Workplaces, HSE-IND(G)140(L).

Protection of Workers and the General Public During the Development of Contaminated Land, HSE-HS(G)66, 1991, ISBN 0-11-885657-X.

Contact organizations

Asbestos Control and Abatement Division (ACAD)
Charter House, 450 High Rd, Ilford, Essex
Tel: 0181–514–2120

Asbestos Removal Contractors Association
Friars House, 6 Parkway, Chelmsford, Essex CM2 0NF
Tel: 01245–259744

Asbestos Information Centre Ltd
PO Box 69, Widnes, Cheshire WA8 9GW
Tel: 0151–420–5866

Association of Building Engineers
Jubilee House, Billing Brook Rd, Weston-Favell, Northampton NN3 8NW
Tel: 01604–404121

British Pest Control Association
3 St James Court, Friargate, Derby DE1 1BT
Tel: 01332–294288

Construction Industry Research and Information Association (CIRIA)
6 Storeys Gate, Westminster, London SW1P 3AU
Tel: 0171–222–8891

The Chartered Institute of Building
Inglemere, Kings Ride, Ascot, Berkshire SL5 8BJ
Tel: 01344–23355

Cleanaway Ltd
The Drive, Warley, Brentwood, Essex CM13 3BE
Tel: 01277–234567
(can remove PCBs)

Demolition Contractors
Sam Allon Ltd, Lincoln St, Hull
Tel: 01482–320051

EP Steeplejacks
Grey St, Crook, Co Durham DU15 9EB
Tel: 01388–767450

Eurotech Tankers
Unit 6, Enterprise Park, Northern Industrial Estate, Brunnel Drive,
Newark, Notts NG24 2DZ
Tel: 01636–640611
(can drain and remove contents of tanks)

Explosive Engineers Educational and Research Trust
Century Business Pk, Hansard Cl, Attleborough Fields, Nuneaton,
Warwickshire CV11 6RY
Tel: 01203–350840

Institute of Wastes Management
9 Saxon Court, St Peter's Gardens, Northampton NN1 1SX
Tel: 01604–20426

Lesters TV and Film Services
Lane End Rd, Sands, High Wycombe, Bucks HP12 4HG
Tel: 01494–448689

National Association of Waste Disposal Contractors
Mountbarrow House, 6–20 Elizabeth St, London SW1 9RB
Tel: 0171–824 8882

National Britannia
Caerphilly Business Park, Caerphilly, Mid Glamorgan CF83 3ED
Tel: 012222–852000
(pest clearance and water tank safety)

National Federation of Demolition Contractors
Resurgam House, 1a New Rd, The Causeway, Staines, Middx TW18 3DH
Tel: 01784–451775

National Federation of Master Steeplejacks and Lightning Conductor Engineers
4d St Mary's Place, Lacemarket, Nottingham NG1 1PH
Tel: 01159–558818

National Pest Control Technicians Association
45 Wilford Lane, West Bridgford, Nottingham NG2 7QZ
Tel: 01159–826651

Royal Institution of Chartered Surveyors
12 Great George St, Parliament Square, London SW1P 3AD
Tel: 0171–222–7000

Royal Society of Health
38a St George's Drive, London SW1V 4BH
Tel: 0171–630–0121
(Certificate of Pest Control)

Hazard 14: Diving and underwater

The legislation

The Diving Operations at Work Regulations 1997
The Diving Operations at Work L6 (Amendment) Regulations 1990
The First Aid at Work Regulations 1981
The Health and Safety at Work Act 1974
The Management of Health and Safety at Work Regulations 1992
The Personal Protective Equipment (PPE) at Work Regulations 1992
The Provision and Use of Work Equipment Regulations 1998

The risks

- the bends
- underwater cables
- broken communication
- river and tidal currents
- inexperience/lack of supervision
- undertow from locks/sluices/weirs
- medical emergency
- pipelines
- poor visibility
- propellers
- passing ships
- torn diving suits
- trapped feet or air line

Those most at risk

Divers, supervisors, camera operators and anyone under water.

Diving work and operations can be very dangerous and hazardous if the work is not properly planned and supervised. Diving is divided into three areas of work: inland, inshore and offshore, and into three types of dive: scuba, air or mixed gas, depending on the depth. Air diving is allowed up to depths of 50 m and mixed gas diving in depths over 50 m. Diving work is often central to the action of a film production or television programme, for example filming underwater wildlife.

A diver is also necessary when performers are in the water or when the action is on a boat and requires a performer to fall in.

The HSE recognized these risks by issuing a special code of practice for media diving operations which came into force on 1 April 1998.

Under the Diving Operations at Work Regulations 1997, all media divers must have a qualification approved by the HSE. Under the old regulations media divers did not need an HSE approved qualification. However, since 31 March 1999 experienced media divers without one must apply to the HSE Diving Inspectorate for a certificate of competence to continue working. These will specify if the diver is qualified to work scuba, surface supplied or both. Before employing a diver for media work you must check for the correct qualifications and a valid certificate.

All diving operations must also comply with the Diving Operations at Work Regulations 1997. In the event of an accident you may be prosecuted for breach of health and safety law. If it can be proved that you did not follow the relevant provisions of the approved code of practice for media diving operations, you will need to show that you have complied with the law in some other way or a court will find you at fault. This means that all media diving operations should comply with the new code of practice.

The code applies to stunt people, journalists, presenters, photographers, camera operators, sound crew, lighting crew and any unit required to dive in support of underwater media work. The code covers any media diving work within the UK 12 mile limit. After that the offshore code is required. For any diving work involving engineering work, power tools or explosives, the provisions of the inshore code must be followed for that kind of operation.

Producers should only use and engage a properly trained and qualified diver through an HSE approved diving contractor. This is a legal obligation. The contractor must hold a current HSE registration certificate for an approved diving contractor which is valid for 14 months. The HSE certificate must be signed and have an HSE registration number which is individual to the contractor. The contractor's address is also on the certificate. Producers must also check that the contractor is suitably experienced in undertaking the management of film diving work, not just diving work in general.

It is a legal offence for anyone to act as a diving contractor without HSE registration and it is illegal for any client to enter into a contract with a

MEDIA DIVING

The class of Media Diving[f] is defined as all diving inland in Great Britain and inshore diving within United Kingdom territorial waters adjacent to Great Britain (generally 12 nautical miles from the low water line) which are covered by the Health and Safety at Work etc Act 1974 (Application outside Great Britain) Order 1995 in support of:

underwater media work by "media divers". The term "media divers" includes: stunt people, journalists, presenters, photographers, camera operators, sound and lighting technicians, and the unit crew;

but does not include:

(a) the preparation of underwater locations that require engineering and construction skills or the handling or use of explosives, for which the class of Inshore/Inland Diving is required;
(b) underwater media work where closed bell or saturation diving techniques are to be used, for which the class of Offshore Diving is required; or
(c) underwater media work taking place from vessels maintaining station by the use of dynamic positioning, for which the class of Offshore Diving is required.

HSE approves the following particulars to be included in the diving operation record for the class of media diving projects.

1 Name and address of the diving contractor.
2 Date to which entry relates and name of the supervisors (an entry must be completed daily by each supervisor for each diving operation).
3 Location of the diving operation, including the name of any vessel from which diving is taking place.
4 Names of those taking part in the diving operation as divers and other members of the dive team.
5 Approved Code of Practice that applies to the diving operation.
6 Purpose of the diving operation.
7 Breathing apparatus and breathing mixture used by each diver in the diving operation.
8 Time at which each diver leaves atmospheric pressure and returns to atmospheric pressure plus his bottom time.
9 Maximum depth which each diver reached.
10 Decompression schedule containing details of pressures (or depths) and the duration of time spent by divers at those pressures (or depths) during decompression.
11 Any emergency or incident of special note which occurred during the diving operation, including details of any decompression illness and the treatment given.
12 Details of the pre-dive checks of all plant and equipment being used in the diving operation.
13 Any defect recorded in the functioning of any plant used in the diving operation.
14 Particulars of any relevant environmental factors during the diving operation.
15 Any other factors likely to affect the safety or health of any persons engaged in the diving operation.
16 Name and signature of the supervisor completing the record.
17 Any company stamp should be affixed.

Guidance

[f] See also Media diving projects: Diving at Work Regulations 1997, Approved Code of Practice, ISBN 0 7176 1497 2.
See also Diving at Work Regulations 1997, List of approved qualifications as of 14 April 1999, pp. 13–15.

Figure H14.1 *© HSE*

Figure H14.2   © *Northern Divers Ltd*

non-registered diving contractor. Diving contractors are usually members of the Association of Diving Contractors (ADC) for inshore work and the Association of Offshore Diving Contractors (AODC) for offshore work. Ask for a membership certificate and member number.

You must also check that the diving contractor has a current ADC diving contractors insurance certificate for a contacting company which should cover public/products and employers liability as well as professional indemnity. ADC/AODC contractors must have this to be members. Copies of the diving contractors certificate, ADC/AODC membership and indemnity insurance certificate should be kept on file as proof that you have taken reasonable steps to select a competent diving contractor.

Project risk assessment and the diving work plan

The producer must submit a project risk assessment to the diving contractor who must legally supply in return a diving project risk assessment. This will detail how the work is to be done, who will supervise it, any subcontractors who will be used along with a detailed dive plan.

This procedure is a legal requirement and is necessary to ensure that the diving contractor understands the diving requirements within the production while the production company is given a detailed work method statement of how the diving element will be carried out.

Contractors and client must give 21 days notification to HSE for large-scale diving work or dangerous diving work. Also for offshore work on oil or gas installations or diving work outside the UK under the Diving Operations at Work (Amendment) Regulations 1990 REG 5(C).

Any divers engaged or employed by the contracting company must be properly qualified for the work they are undertaking. Individual divers should be members of the ADC or contracted by ADC/AODC member companies. Do not be tempted to use leisure divers or inexperienced divers as people's lives might depend on the experience of your diver.

Divers need to possess at least three certificates to work. To check if they are qualified you should ask to see a copy of these. Divers' training and qualifications is covered by Regulation 10 Certificate of competence of the Diving Operations at Work (Amendment) Regulations 1990.

The first minimum qualification under the Diving Operations at Work Regulations 1981 schedule 4 which a diver must have is a HSE diving training certificate Part 3 and 4 for inshore work. Parts 1 and 2 are necessary for offshore work, unless an exemption has been granted for work in a depth not exceeding 50 m or decompression time of 20 minutes. An exemption exists for diving work for journalism.

Scuba divers need HSE diving training certificate Parts 2, 3 and 4. Part 3 is for non-decompression fish/agricultural work only and Part 4 is for aqualung/scuba divers.

The diver must also hold a second certificate. This is a divers' medical certificate which is valid for one year. This must be signed by an HSE appointed examiner/doctor to show that the diver is medically fit to carry out work and each certificate has an individual certificate number and signature of the doctor. The Employment Medical Advisor Service (EMAS) have a complete list of doctors who are authorized to do this.

The third certificate which a diver must have is a certificate of diver first aid training. This is an HSE diving first aid certificate issued by an HSE approved training body which is valid for three years. This is a compulsory requirement under the Diving Operations at Work Regulations 1990, Regulations 10a and 13a, and each certificate has an individual number. The HSE have a special unit to issue these called the Diving First Aid Certification Unit.

More than one member of each dive team should have extra training in first aid in case the only first aider is injured. This should include being able to recognize symptoms of decompression illness and provide treatment for it; being able to administer oxygen to an unconscious patient; being able to perform resuscitation techniques of artificial ventilation and external cardiac compression; being able to recognize the symptoms of shock; and being able to administer to burns, bleeding and broken bones. Proper first aid kits must be maintained and adequate for the size of the dive team, the nature of the work and the distance from emergency care.

The diver or contracting company must be able to supply evidence of these three qualifications to you before any work is started. Make copies for your file and a note of the certificate numbers. Check the validity dates and name. If necessary, check with the qualifying and issuing body that the certificates are valid. Afterwards is too late to discover that the diver is not qualified.

The diver should also produce the professional diver's log book. This is a stamped record of the number of dives and decompressions which the diver has made and acts like an MOT certificate. It should always be carried on site during working operations. Make a copy of this for your

---

Details to be included in the diver's daily record (log)

Details should be printed and in block capitals.

1 Name and signature of the diver.
2 Date to which entry relates.
3 Name and address of the diving contractor.
4 Name and signature of the supervisor(s) for that dive.
5 Location of the diving project, including the name of any vessel from which diving is taking place.
6 The maximum depth reached on each occasion.
7 The time the diver left the surface, the bottom time, and the time the diver reached the surface on each occasion.
8 Where the dive includes time spent in a compression chamber, details of any time spent outside the chamber at a different pressure.
9 Breathing apparatus and breathing mixture used by the diver.
10 Any decompression schedules followed by the diver on each occasion.
11 Any work done by the diver on each occasion, and the plant (including any tools) used in that work.
12 Any episode of barotrauma, discomfort or injury suffered by the diver including details of any decompression illness and the treatment given.
13 Any emergency or incident of special note which occurred during the diving operation.
14 Any other factor relevant to the diver's health or safety.
15 Affix company stamp after the daily record has been signed by the diver and supervisor(s).

Figure H14.3 *Details of a diver's daily log.* Source: *Media Diving Projects: The Diving at Work Regulations 1997, Approved Code of Practice, HSE L106, ISBN 0-7176-1497-2*

records. By these steps you can prove that you have checked the qualifications of your diver prior to engagement.

The diver and the contracting company must also supply the following qualifications depending on the nature of the work. The diver must have an OPITO recognized offshore survival and fire fighting course for rig work certificate which is valid for four years.

If the diver is carrying out inspection then the diver must have an underwater inspection certificate – this has a certificate number, date of the course and the address of the training institution. There are also specialist tools which have to be used for underwater work and the company must be able to produce a card and certificate to prove competence and proper tuition in the handling of specialist underwater tools such as chain saws and power hoses. Special skills are also required for underwater work involving explosives.

The diving contractor has a number of health and safety obligations under the Diving Operations at Work Regulations 1981 and the Health and Safety at Work Act 1974. Diving contractors should supply the client (in this case the production company or producer) with a personnel list and contact numbers and addresses for the diving operations. This should include the diving company, its director, the supervisor and engineer, the divers to be used and the company doctor. This is notification of a diving project.

The contracting company must appoint a supervisor for diving operations and issue the client with a certificate of appointment of a diving supervisor under the Diving Operations at Work L6 (Amendment) Regulations 1990 Regulation 5(1). This is valid for the duration of work.

The certificate should have the date of the work, the name of the client and the contract. The director of the company or head of diving operations as a competent person must sign on behalf of the company to assign a properly qualified and experienced supervisor with their name and contact details. This is to prove that the diving work is properly supervised under the Management of Health and Safety at Work Regulations 1992. A new diving supervisor's certificate will be introduced soon by the ADC and the HSE.

The supervisor as the head in the chain of responsibility must be satisfied that the divers are fit to work with no ailments, stress or depression. Divers must not dive for at least two hours after eating a full meal, and for at least thirty minutes after a snack. The supervisor must be present on site or location while diving work is taking place. If diving for more than 12 continuous hours then there must be 2 supervisors – one per shift.

The supervisor must ensure that the professional diver's log book which the diver must carry to all locations where they are employed is kept up-to-date and stamped regularly. The supervisor must also keep a full record of dives and decompressions in a record book. This diving log book is held by contractor for inspection at any time.

Each dive has an individual page entry with a specific number, rather like a ledger entry or hotel register. This page contains the date of the dive, the diver's signature, the name and address of contractor, and the location and name of the vessel or platform from which the work is taking place. The dive information recorded includes the type of dive, the maximum depth, the amount of time spent down, the time when the diver was pressurized and left the surface and the time of the diver's decompression and surfacing. The log book also lists the type of breathing apparatus used, the type of breathing mixture used and a description of the type of work undertaken and what tools were used. The log entry is stamped by the supervisor, signed and dated. The diving log book constitutes the legal record of diving work.

Particulars to be included in the diving operation record

1 Name and address of the diving contractor.
2 Date to which entry relates and name of the supervisor or supervisors (an entry must be completed daily by each supervisor for each diving operation).
3 Location of the diving operation, including the name of any vessel from which diving is taking place.
4 Names of those taking part in the diving operation as divers and other members of the dive team.
5 Approved Code of Practice that applies to the diving operation.
6 Purpose of the diving operation.
7 Breathing apparatus and breathing mixture used by each diver in the diving operation.
8 Time at which each diver leaves atmospheric pressure and returns to atmospheric pressure plus his bottom time.
9 Maximum depth which each diver reached.
10 Decompression schedule containing details of the pressures (or depths) and the duration of time spent by divers at those pressures (or depths) during decompression.
11 Any emergency or incident of special note which occurred during the diving operation, including details of any decompression illness and the treatment given.
12 Details of the pre-dive checks of all plant and equipment being used in the diving operation.
13 Any defect recorded in the functioning of any plant used in the diving operation.
14 Particulars of any relevant environmental factors during the diving operation.
15 Any other factors likely to affect the safety or health of any persons engaged in the diving operation.
16 Name and signature of the supervisor completing the record.
17 Any company stamp should be affixed.

Figure H14.4 *Details of a diving operations record.* Source: *Media Diving Projects: The Diving at Work Regulations 1997, Approved Code of Practice, HSE L106, ISBN 0-7176-1497-2*

The diving contractor must issue all divers and employees with a safety manual which complies with the Health and Safety L6 Diving Operations at Work (Amendment) Regulations 1990/1994 and the diving rules Diving Operations at Work Regulations 1981, SI 399. Schedule 1 paragraph 3(k) states that the safety guide must include decompression tables amended by Diving Safety Memo No. 5/1988 and bottom time limitations. For example, when working at 40 ft, 240 minutes, or working at 170 ft, 20 minutes. The deeper the dive, the less time must be spent underwater. Diving below 50 m requires mixed gas.

Under the Personal Protective Equipment (PPE) at Work Regulations 1992 and the Provision and Use of Work Equipment Regulations 1998, the contractor and appointed supervisor must check that diving work equipment is correct for the task, safe and regularly maintained according to the Health and Safety L6 Diving Operations at Work (Amendment) Regulations 1990 Regulations 12 and 13. Supervisors must check that all diving equipment and protective safety equipment is not only suitable but compatible, especially the correct use of mixed gas.

Diving lines should include safety lines, a winch, communications and air supply. Essential maintenance should include divers' tools such as watches, suit seals, masks, cylinders, weight belts, radios, torches and emergency knives. Never buy or use second-hand equipment as you cannot prove it is safe or compatible.

Where diving work is in depths of 50 m or more then a submersible chamber and appropriate mixed gas must be provided. The supervisor must make sure that all safety rules are understood and in place.

The company must provide training where necessary to ensure that these are understood by all employees. Employees must be trained in the safe use of first aid equipment and specialized kits are used for diving work depending on the nature of the work, the depth, the remoteness of the location and the number of people engaged. All first aid equipment must comply with the First Aid At Work Regulations 1981. Seek advice where necessary.

The diving operations site and work base should carry an emergency phone contact list including doctors and sea rescue centres.

The diving contracting company must make sure that the divers they supply are properly qualified and that the work is properly supervised and carried out safely. The client (in this case the production company or producer) must be supplied with a health and safety statement and a copy of the risk assessment and work method statement for that site and contract. These documents should be circulated to all involved with the work including the contractors/subcontractor/client/employee/diving work site/base office and production company office.

This is a written record to prove that a proper risk assessment and work method statement have been carried out and that all staff involved are aware of the risks. The assessment should be carried out on site and the supervisor should update it if the nature of the working conditions or task changes and everyone should be made aware of the changes. A lot of accidents happen because the work method changed but nobody was told.

The Diving Operations at Work Regulations 1981 SI 399 and the Diving Operations at Work (Amendment) Regulations 1990 specify the number of people required for particular kinds of work. In normal circumstances the minimum team number is four: the diver, the standby diver in the water, the diver support and the non-diving supervisor on the surface on a ship, platform or quayside.

This rule is relaxed where the water is clear and no deeper than 1.5 metres. Regulation 8(5) states that only a supervisor and diver are necessary where the diver can easily stand up. (This will of course depend on the height of the diver.) In all cases the supervisor should never dive unless a replacement is available, except in an emergency.

Regulation 8(2)(b) specifies work where a minimum team of four are needed, with three in the water and a supervisor on the surface. This is where work is either more dangerous or where heavy tools or lifting are needed. The rules state that this work includes offshore installations, submarine pipelines, poor visibility conditions, weirs, sluices, locks and where lifting appliances for materials or equipment are needed or where heavy tools are being used which would affect divers' buoyancy. Extra team members who may be needed are a tender operator, a life support technician on surface, a winch operator and extra divers or medics.

If diving work is undertaken in port or dock areas then the dock master must give written permission. If diving to repair a ship, the ship's master must give permission and special rules apply if diving from vessels. No work must be carried out from a moving vessel.

All diving work must be indicated by appropriate warning flags and boards at least 100 m up/downstream of the intended work. Access from the side or from a boat or tender must be safe. Access/exit ladders can be used in depths under 1.5 m. If over 1.5 m, a lifting device basket or bell must be used, or a submersible where appropriate.

Divers usually work with a surface supplied lifeline and communications link. The biggest danger to divers is the failure of the compressor or main air supply, which is low pressure. In the event of this failing, the high-pressure bottled back-up cylinder should be used. If this fails the diver should use the high-pressure bail-out bottle and return to the surface immediately. Air supplies, tools and batteries should always be checked before a dive.

In the event of communications failure where radios go down the divers must resort to the spare or use the appropriate hand signals approved under the Health and Safety (Signs and Signals) Regulations

1996. These hand signals should be used and the divers should return to the surface unless back-up radios are available.

Hand signals from the surface to the diver by the signal rope which are clearly understood are:

- 1 pull, are you OK?/Diver, Yes OK.
- 4 pulls come up/Diver, I want to come up.
- More than 4 pulls is an emergency.

When working with lifting equipment:

- 1 pull is stop.
- 2 pulls is hoist up.
- 3 pulls is lower on a separate rope from the diver's emergency line.

Producers should realize that diving work can be highly dangerous and diving work with filming equipment is a potentially risky activity unless experienced filming divers are used. Use head mounted cameras or specialist equipment designed for the job. Divers should always be employed if any actor or presenter is standing in running or deep water and a standby diver employed. Make sure the ship or structure you are diving from is safe. Get up-to-date information about tide times, openings of locks and sluices and ship movements. Beware of working near deepwater pipe outlets and sewage outfalls. You should also beware of working in low water temperatures which may produce a build-up of ice that can trap a diver beneath the surface. Special risks apply to filming in caves and adjacent to dangerous wildlife. Only specialist divers should be used for this. The whole operation should be undertaken by an approved contractor and properly supervised.

Producers should follow their advice and never try to use untrained or insufficient numbers of divers. For deep sea filming, filming offshore or specialist wildlife filming, an experienced specialist company or diving contractor should be consulted and used so that the risks to health and safety are reduced, contained and managed properly.

Further reading

Media diving projects

The Diving at Work Regulations 1997, Approved Code of Practice, HSE, L106, ISBN 0-7176-1497-2.

Commercial diving projects inland/inshore

The Diving at Work Regulations 1997, Approved Code of Practice, HSE, L104, ISBN 0-7176-1495-6.

Commercial diving projects offshore

The Diving at Work Regulations 1997, Approved Code of Practice, HSE, L103, ISBN 0-7176-1494-8.

ADC Monthly Newsletter, Association of Diving Contractors.

Are You Involved in a Diving Project? HSE Books, 1998, ISBN 0-7176-1529-4, pp. 5–9.

The Diving at Work Regulations 1997, SI No. 2776.

Diving at Work, Proposals for Regulations, Consultation Document, October 1996.

Offshore Safety Notices and Offshore Operations Notices, available from HSE Publications, £25 for 12 month subscription, after initial fee of £60 (provides backdated set).

Diving Standards for Assessing Divers, Part 1: Basic Air Diving, HSE, 1992, ISBN 0-11-885905-6.

Diving Standards for Assessing Divers, Part 2: Mixed Air Diving, HSE, 1992, ISBN 0-11-885906-4.

Diving Standards for Assessing Divers, Part 3: Air Diving where no Surface Compression Chamber is Required on Site, HSE, ISBN 0-11-885907-2.

Diving Standards for Assessing Divers, Part 4: Air Diving with Self Contained Equipment where no Surface Compression Chamber is Required on Site, HSE, ISBN 0-11-885908-0.

Attitudes of Divers and Supervisors to Interim Guidelines 1993, Research Report, OTH-92–373, HSE, ISBN 0-11-882070-2.

Maintenance, Inspection and Discant of Diving Bell Hoist Ropes, OTH 91–338, HSE, 1993, ISBN 0-11-886387-8.

The Diving Operations at Work Regulations 1981, as amended by the Diving Operations at Work (Amendment) Regulations 1990, HSL6, HSE, 1981, ISBN 0-11-885599-9.

The Diving Operations at Work (Amendment) Regulations 1992, Statutory Instrument No. 608, HSE, 1992, ISBN 0-11-023608-4.

Dealing with Off Shore Emergencies, HSE HS(G)142, ISBN 0-7176-1037-3.

Scuba Diving – A Quantitative Risk Assessment, CRR140, HSE 1997, ISBN 0-7176-1398-4.

Guidance Note No. 73, HSE-3, 26 Offshore First Aid.

Contact organizations

General

The Association of Diving Contractors (ADC)
The Association of Offshore Diving Contractors (AODC)
Carlyle House, 235 Vauxhall Bridge Rd, London SW1V 1EJ
Secretary: Tom Hollobone
Tel: 0171–931–0466

John Ansell and Partners (specialist diving insurance brokers)
Overseas House, 19–23 Ironmonger Row, London EC1V 3QN
Tel: 0171–251–6821

Employment Medical Advisor Service (EMAS)
375 West George St, Glasgow G2 4LW
Tel: 0141–275–3000

Environment Agency
Kings Meadow House, Kings Meadow Rd, Reading, Berkshire RG1
8DQ
Tel: 0118–9535000

Fort Bovis and Underwater Training Centre
Plymouth, Devon PL9 0AB
Tel: 01752–48021

Greenaway Marine (manufacturers of Seapro underwater camera
housings)
15/18 Basset Down Workshops, Swindon SN4 9QP
Tel: 01793–814992

HSE Diving Operations Strategy Team
3rd Floor Rose Court, Southwark Bridge, London SE1 9HS
Tel: 0171–717–6000

HSE Diving Specialist Inspectors, Central Operations Unit
122a Thorpe Rd, Norwich, Norfolk NR1 1RN
Tel: 01603–275000

HSE Offshore Safety Division Diving Inspectorate
Room 106, Ferguson House, 15 Marylebone Road, London NW1 5JD
Tel: 0171–243–5703
(HSE Offshore Safety Division has operation centres at Aberdeen for
Scottish waters and Great Yarmouth for English waters.)

HSE Diver Training Certification and School Recognition
Safety Policy Division, C2, 4th Floor, South Wing, Rose Court, 2
Southwark Bridge Rd, London SE1 9HS
Tel: 0171–717–6592

HSE Diving First Aid Certification Unit
Rose Court, 2 Southwark Bridge Rd, London SE1 9HS
Tel: 0171–717–6763

Humberside Offshore Training Centre (HOTA)
Malmo Rd, Hull HU7 OYF
Tel: 01482–820567

Marine Technology Directorate Ltd
19 Buckingham St, London WC2N 6EF
Tel: 0171–321–0674

The Maritime and Coastguard Agency
Spring Place, 105 Commercial Rd, Southampton, Hants SO15 1EG
Tel: 01703–329100

Northern Divers (Engineering) Ltd
Conservancy Wharf, Tower St, Hull HU9 1TUY
Tel: 01482–227276

Northern Diver Equipment
East Quarry, Appley Lane North, Appley Bridge, Near Wigan,
Lancashire WN6 9AE
Tel: 01257–254444

Professional Divers Section of the Association of Management and
Professional Staffs (AMPS)
Parkgates, Bury New Rd, Manchester M25 0JW
Tel: 0161–773–8621

The following information is taken from *Are You Involved in a Diving
Project?* HSE Books, 1998, ISBN 0-7176-1529-4, pp. 12–13, © HSE:

ACOPs, guidance on diving, and HSE publications
HSE Books, PO Box 1999, Sudbury, Suffolk CO10 6FS
Tel: 01787–881165

Copies of Diving at Work Regulations and other regulations
The Stationery Office, PO Box 276, London SW8 5DT
Tel: 0171–873–9090

**Technical queries about diving and information on contractors.
Information on diving first aid and diver medics**
Diving Operations Strategy Team, Health and Safety Executive,
3rd Floor South Rose Court, 2 Southwark Bridge, London SE1 9HS
Tel: 0171–717–6763/6757

Medical Queries and list of approved medical examiners of divers
Employment Medical Advisory Service, 375 West George Street,
Glasgow G2 4LW
Tel: 0141–275–3030

Queries on diving competence qualifications and addresses of competence assessors, and information on diving certification appeals process:
Diving Policy, Health and Safety Executive, 4th Floor South, Rose
Court, 2 Southwark Bridge, London SE1 9HS
Tel: 0171–717–6592

HSE Diving Inspection Teams
Responsible for inspecting premises and projects, investigating
incidents and accidents, and dealing with complaints.

Southern Area (dealing with all English and Welsh counties south of,
and including: Greater London, Hertfordshire, Bedfordshire,
Buckinghamshire, Oxfordshire, Gloucestershire, Gwent, Mid
Glamorgan, Dyfed and West Glamorgan)
Health and Safety Executive, Offshore Safety Division (Diving), Rose
Court, 2 Southwark Bridge, London SE1 9HS
Tel: 0171–717–6758

Central Area (dealing with all English and Welsh counties north of, and
including: Essex, Cambridgeshire, Northamptonshire, Warwickshire,
Gwynedd, Hereford and Worcester, and Powys)
Health and Safety Executive, Offshore Safety Division (Diving), 122a
Thorpe Road, Norwich NR1 1RN
Tel: 01603–275016

Scotland
Health and Safety Executive, Offshore Safety Division (Diving), Lord
Cullen House, Fraser Place, Aberdeen AB9 1UB
Tel: 01224–252561

Hazard 15: Electricity

Michael Samuelson Lighting has been fined £2000 following a large-scale inspection of Pinewood Studios by inspectors from the Health and Safety Executive. At Wycombe and Beaconsfield Magistrates Court the company pleaded guilty to contravening Regulation 4(2) of the Electricity at Work Regulations 1989 (EWR) in that an electrical system including a Karcher pressure washer was not maintained so as to prevent danger.

Stage, Screen and Radio

Doug James, a 55 year old cinema projectionist, died in August 1997 when he was electrocuted as he changed a light bulb.

Stage, Screen and Radio, September 1997, page 14.

The legislation

The Electricity at Work Regulations 1989
The Health and Safety at Work Act 1974
The IEE Wiring Regulations, 16th edition
The Management of Health and Safety at Work Regulations 1992
The Provision and Use of Work Equipment Regulations 1998

The risks

- death
- electrocution
- burns
- fire
- injury from trips and falls

Special risks: Frayed cables, falling lights, mixing electricity with water, earthing, damaged plugs, dangerous sockets, joining separate phases, poor maintenance.

Those most at risk

Equipment hire companies, electricians, lighting crew, the public, anybody operating or switching on electrical equipment on location or in the office.

Electricity kills. Between 1990 and 1995, 553 people were killed in electrical incidents in Great Britain. The main reasons are either faulty equipment or a dangerous supply. The HSE National Entertainment Interest Group have identified the use of electricity as an area of major concern.

The film and television industry can be a very high risk occupation partly because of the large amount of electrical appliances used. This applies equally to location sites, studios and offices. An office kettle badly earthed can kill you as easily as a large location light. So producers performing a hazard identification should pay as much attention to small items and include base premises, offices and kitchens in their assessment.

The best way to begin is to list every item of electrical equipment with the serial number, location and voltage. Allocate an individual identity number to each item of electrical equipment and make sure it is checked for safety on a regular basis and PAT tested. This checks the safety of portable electrical equipment, which is given a green sticker to indicate it is tested and safe. This way old or potentially dangerous equipment can be removed or repaired.

Any new items can be added to the list and regular PAT testing should help to eliminate the risks from damaged or defective portable equipment.

The potential loophole in this system is either members of staff, the public or subcontractors bringing untested items onto location or into base premises. Part of your health and safety management system should be a clear rule that any item introduced must be tested first. Use a PAC-500SP or similar tester which complies with the regulations. All portable items tested should have a green PAT test sticker to indicate that they have been

CHECKLIST

Listed below are typical routine electrical checks for portable apparatus, to be carried out by a suitably competent person.

Note: This checklist is intended as a guide; certain apparatus may need different or additional inspections and tests. Non-electrical checks are outside the scope of this booklet.

Equipment: _____

Make: _____   *Serial No*: _____

Item	Test	Pass condition
1 Mains lead	a) Visual inspection b) Mains plug	Insulation (BS colours) and sheath No damage Correctly connected Cable clamp gripped to sheath Correct fuse fitted
2 *Either:* mains lead connector (if lead detachable)	a) Visual inspection of inlet male connector b) Attempt to open socket without tool c) Attempt to pull cable from female connector	No damage or burning. Unopenable No movement
Or: cable clamp in equipment	a) Inspection of grommet b) Sharp pull on cable c) Rotation of cable	Cable insulation protected No appreciable movement No rotation
3 Mains on/off switch	Visual inspection	Correct operation No damage
4 Conducting case	a) Visual inspection: if marked ▣ treat as item 5 Portable appliance tester which will check resistance and pass current of at least twice the fuse rating b) High voltage insulation 500 volts AC minimum test	 Resistance of earth from apparatus to plug pin 0.1 ohm or, for loads fused at 3 amps or less, 0.5 ohm No fault indicated after 5 seconds
5 Insulating case	Visual inspection	Maker's double insulation mark ▣ visible Case undamaged
6 Accessible fuse holders (if any)	Visual inspection	No damage Removal of carrier does not permit live* part to be touched
7 Exposed output connections	a) Visual inspection b) For outputs greater than 50 volts, test short-circuit current	No voltage greater than 25 volts Short-circuit current less than 5 mA *ie live at more than 50 volts when in use

Overall result

Unit is passed/failed (*delete as necessary*)

Signed: _____   Date: _____

Figure H15.1   *PAT test record sheet*. Source: Guide to the Electricity at Work Regulations 1989. © *HSE Books*

checked for earth continuity and insulation. Any hired portable electrical equipment, cameras, lighting tools and plant must be tested by the hirer and supplied with a safety certificate. This eliminates dangerous items from circulation and controls the safety of temporary equipment.

Damaged items should be removed from circulation immediately and the cable/plug removed to prevent anybody using it by accident. A warning sticker should indicate that it is not to be used.

The electrical records of all equipment should include a repair entry for any work done and who carried it out. In the event of an accident you can prove that regular maintenance has been carried out and any persistently faulty equipment can be removed and returned to the supplier.

Electrical equipment should be visually inspected every time it is used, before it is plugged in – afterwards is too late. Use a 240V socket tester to check extension leads and sockets for earth, fuse and polarity safety. This means that you can check the safety of the supply as well as the portable equipment you are going to plug in.

Look out for damage to plugs and cables. These can be caused by poor maintenance, rough handling, moving plant or rodents. Damaged plugs must be replaced. EU standard plugs are now completely moulded and integral to the cable. Never try and repair damaged plugs, cable and fuses. This should only be carried out by a qualified electrician. Replace damaged items with new and safe replacements. Check for cable tears and holes. These could allow water inside and result in anybody touching it receiving an electric shock. Damaged cables should be replaced not repaired. Do not use made up extension cables as they can be dangerously overloaded and poorly fused.

Check for cracks on housing and plastic holders. Make sure all screws and retention nuts are in place and secure. All portable items should be checked every time they are issued and returned. A one minute visual check could save somebody's life. A test inspection should be carried out every week and a full test every month.

Cables are easily damaged so check for frays and holes where water may get in. Use cable ramps to protect cables from moving vehicles and to avoid trip hazards on access points. If possible, route cables under access points or overhead. Beware of water; if going underneath, make sure the cables are insulated in a separate pipe, and if going overhead, beware of high vehicles and crane movements. Warning signs should read 'danger overhead electrical cables'. Always fold cables carefully to avoid damage during transit and store them in a dry environment.

Fuses should always be the correct rating and checked regularly. Appliances and lights should be protected by RCDs (residual current devices) and a trip at the mains supply. To reduce the voltage to a safe working level use a step-down transformer with 110V tools or use battery powered equipment.

Electricity should never be taken from two separate phases. In most buildings and offices the supply is three phase. To join them is extremely dangerous. To avoid this do not use extension leads to join supplies from one side of a corridor to the other or to run supplies from one floor of a building to another, or to run supplies from one building to another.

Maintain batteries properly and always charge them in a well ventilated environment to reduce the risk of chemical explosion. Never smoke or use naked flames in battery maintenance areas. Any lights in battery charging areas should have intrinsically safe gas-tight fittings when there is a risk of explosion. Always replace when performing below the manufacturer's recommended specification, and follow the manufacturer's recommended storage and maintenance instructions.

Generators are used to provide main or secondary power on location sites. If being used as a main supply, always make sure a back-up generator cuts in immediately if the main generator fails.

Consult carefully with the supplier, hirer or subcontractor to make sure that the generator is adequate for the job. Remember a generator fails usually because it is not adequate for the task and somebody was trying to save money on the budget. Use the IEE Regulations 16th edition to calculate the total wattage of the equipment you are going to connect (seek advice from camera, sound, lighting and catering departments). Then make sure that the generator is capable of dealing with this easily and allow spare capacity for safety.

Read the operating instructions carefully and make sure the operator is experienced. Make sure the correct fuel is used and stored correctly at a safe distance. Beware of the risk from overnight vandalism on locations. Always check the generator every morning and test it. Never smoke when refuelling. Place the generator on a level site and securely chocked or dug in. Use a silent generator or make sure noise protection is in place.

In 1995, 121 serious electrical fires took place which cost £45 million in insurance claims. Proper fire protection should be in place in all areas where electrical fires might occur, including in vehicles. The appropriate extinguisher should be available, in this case foam for fuel fires and spills. The location of the extinguishers must be identified by proper signs. From January 1997 all fire extinguishers should conform to European safety standard EN3. Special precautions must be taken for electrical work in hazardous areas and mines.

Film lights are top heavy and should be properly secured with chains, weights and sand bags. A proper free fall area should be made with restricted access. Nobody should be allowed under rigging work.

Yorkshire Television uses a sterile zone system in which areas of studio floor are clearly marked for rigging only while LWT uses a 'permit to work' system. Avoid floor areas while rigging is taking place. Signs should read

---

Electrical equipment

Where possible you need to locate electrical equipment in non-hazardous areas. However, if such equipment needs to be located in a hazardous environment, exposed to flammable substances, it must be constructed or protected so as to prevent danger. This is a requirement of the Electricity at Work Regulations 1989[24] and might be achieved by selecting equipment built to explosion-protected standards.

Advice on selecting, installing and maintaining explosion-protected electrical equipment is given in BS EN 60079–14[25] and in a short guide published by the Institution of Chemical Engineers[26].

There are also Regulations which apply to both electrical and non-electrical equipment, the Equipment and Protective Systems Intended for Use in Potentially Explosive Atmospheres Regulations 1996[27]. However, they are aimed at manufacturers and suppliers, requiring them to ensure the equipment is safe. Such equipment should carry CE marking. From July 2003 you will have to select such equipment but, until then, you can select equipment that does not carry CE marking provided it is safe.

Protection of vehicles

Vehicles that need to operate within areas classified as hazardous zones in storage buildings or areas should be protected to an appropriate standard, to avoid ignition of flammable vapours. During storage, the highest probability of a release from a container occurs when it is being handled. An unprotected fork-lift truck may be a source of ignition in such circumstances.

Figure H15.2 *Electrical work in hazardous areas*

'danger working overhead' and access restricted to essential staff who should wear hard hats and gloves. Lights should be placed away from fire hazards such as drapes, costumes, wigs, wood and chemicals.

Rigging staff should wear gloves as lights have sharp surfaces and are often very hot. It's better to adjust and move lights when they are cold than risk serious burns. Lights should be fitted with barn doors, safety chain and safety gauze. Never switch on a light while it is pointed at anybody or look into a light when switching on in case the bulb glass explodes.

Make sure the light is properly fused and tested. The bulb should be correctly fitted and suitable for the housing. Always check the cables and plugs for signs of damage before plugging in. Small portable lights should be fitted with RCDs (rated at 30 mA with no time delay). HMIs and lights on dimmers would trip an RCD.

Beware of the weight of lights as the Manual Handling Operations Regulations 1992 insist that proper lifting techniques or equipment must be used to prevent injury. Use proper stands and make sure each light has a safe free fall area.

Office equipment should be regularly tested and suitable for the task (see also Hazard 32: Visual display screens). Computers can be tested with an adaptor from a socket tester. Check electrical safety on items which may be introduced to the set such as special effects and catering.

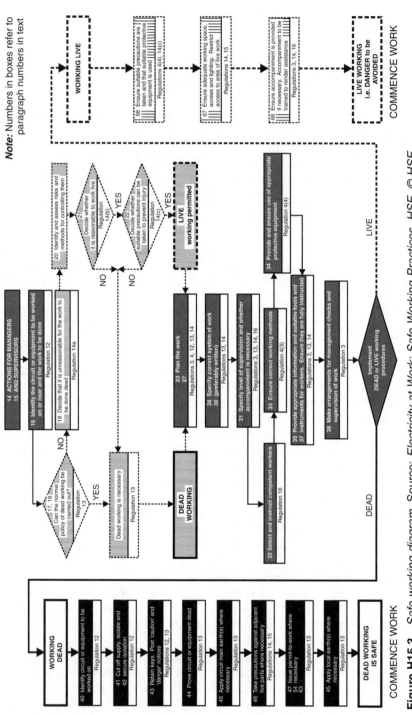

Note: Numbers in boxes refer to paragraph numbers in text

Figure H15.3 *Safe working diagram. Source: Electricity at Work: Safe Working Practices, HSE. © HSE*

Subcontractors must carry personal, third party and public liability insurance and catering equipment must conform to the food hygiene and environmental health regulations.

The Construction (Design and Management) Regulations 1994 stipulate that the design of any outside broadcast location or set which has a built in or temporary power supply must take into account health and safety factors. For example cables generate heat so the set must be properly insulated and earthed. Electricity should never be taken from two separate phases unless the design physically separates the two and makes sure that they cannot be accidentally joined. Trip devices must be kept free of moisture and dirt and protected against vibration and mechanical damage. Adequate fire protection must be built in and the correct extinguishers provided.

Beware of any situation which combines electricity and water. The combination is lethal and can kill. So always make sure adequate protection is provided against rain and groundwater. Precautions should be designed and built in on temporary locations and sets. If water is involved in any activity, perform a proper risk assessment to identify any proximity to electrical equipment or supply. This must be removed or controlled before any activity is permitted. Work may have to stop if it rains.

Producers asking staff to carry out electrical work must make sure that they are properly trained electricians and are aware of the health and safety risks involved. At least one team member should be appointed to supervise any installation work and they should be experienced and competent. Adequate personal protective clothing should be issued including gloves and rubber soled footwear.

Cables should always be safety tagged detailing any maintenance work. Always assume that a socket or power supply is unsafe until you can prove otherwise. Never just plug something in. Test the supply first as it may be dangerous, especially in old and derelict buildings or churches. Use a PAC 500SP tester or similar device to test the safety of sockets and plugs. Make sure that a qualified electrician installs a temporary supply and issues a safety certificate. Always build in time for electrical testing and safety into your schedule and never be a bright spark by asking unqualified or inexperienced staff to undertake electrical work.

Further reading

Electrical Incidents in Great Britain, HSE, 1998, ISBN 0-7176-1459-X.
The Electricity at Work Regulations 1989, SI 635, HSE, ISBN 0-11-096635-X.
Electrical Test Equipment for use by Electricians, GS38, HSE, 1995, ISBN 0-7176-0845-X.

Electrical Safety at Places of Entertainment, GS50, HSE, 1991, ISBN 011-885727-4.

Electricity at Work: Safe Working Practices, G85, HSE, 1993, ISBN 0-7176-0442-X.

Maintaining Portable Electrical Equipment in Offices, IND(G)160, HSE-1994, ISBN 0-7176-0719-4.

Maintaining Portable Electrical Equipment in Offices and Other Low Risk Environments, HSE-IND(G)236, HSE, 1997, ISBN 0-7176-1272-4.

Memorandum of Guidance on the Electricity at Work Regulations 1989, HSR 25, HSE, 1989, ISBN 0-11-883963-2.

The Safe Use of Portable Electrical Apparatus, PM32, HSE, 1990.

Maintaining Portable and Transportable Electrical Equipment, HS(G)107, HSE, 1994, ISBN 0-7176-0715-1.

Electrical Safety for Entertainers, IND(G)247l, HSE.

HSL22, Work Equipment – The Provision and Use of Work Equipment Regulations 1998, Guidance on the Regulations, HSE, 1998, ISBN 0-7176-0414-4.

IEE Wiring Regulations 16th edition, BS 7691, 1992, including Amendment No. 1 1994 (Amd-856), plus Guidance Notes Nos 1, 2, 3, 4, 5, 6. From IEE.

J. F. Whitfield, *A Guide to the 16th Edition IEE Wiring Regulations*, EPA Press, 1991, (Pocket Reference).

Brian Scaddon, *The 16th IEE Wiring Regulations Explained*, Butterworth-Heinemann, Oxford, 1998, ISBN 0-7506-4056-1.

J. F. Whitfield, *A Guide to Electrical Safety at Work*, 1992, EPA Press.

T. E. Marks, *Handbook on the Electricity at Work Regulations 1989*, 2nd edition, 1994, William Ernest.

Electricity in the Workplace Bookset: *Vol. 1: Electricity in the Workplace* and *Vol. 2: Portable Appliance Testing*, Megger Instruments Ltd.

The Institution of Lighting Engineers, Code of Practice for Electrical Safety in Public Lighting Operations.

Ken Oldham-Smith, *Electrical Safety and the Law*, 1993, Blackwell Scientific.

A. Smith, *The Handbook of Electrical Installation Practice*, 1996, Blackwell Science.

Contact organizations

Institution of Electrical Engineers
Savoy Place, London WC2R 0BL
Tel: 0171–240–1871

Institution of Lighting Engineers
Lennox House, 9 Lawford Rd, Rugby, Warwickshire CV21 2DZ
Tel: 01788–576492

Lighting Industry Federation
Swan House, 207 Balham High Rd, London SW17 7BQ
Tel: 0181–675–5432

National Inspection Council for Electrical Installation Contracting
(NICEIC)
Vintage House, 37 Albert Embankment, London SE1 7UJ
Tel: 0171–582–7746

Performing Services Association
Hawks House, School Passage, Kingston-upon-Thames, Surrey KT1
3DU
Tel: 0181–392–0180

The Professional Lighting and Sound Association
7 Highlight House, St Leonards Rd, Eastbourne, E. Sussex BN21 3UH
Tel: 01323–410335

Hazard 16: Explosives and pyrotechnics

A producer and director who worked on the BBC's live transmission of the royal tournament appeared in court today under the Health and Safety at Work Act accused of negligence. They denied failing to take reasonable care of presenter Anthea Turner over an incident where her face was burnt when two fireworks were electrically ignited.

Daily Telegraph, 25 July 1990

On one film last year sfx technician Nick Middleton was killed when an explosion went wrong. And on another production sfx supervisor Peter Dawson was badly burned following an accidental explosion in an sfx workshop.

Stage, Screen and Radio, November 1997, p. 10

The legislation

The Classification, Packaging and Labelling of Dangerous Substances Regulations 1984
The Control of Explosives Regulations 1991
The Classification and Labelling of Explosives Regulations 1983
The Control of Substances Hazardous to Health Regulations 1994 (COSHH)
The Explosives Act 1875
The Carriage of Explosives by Road Regulations 1996
The Health and Safety at Work Act 1974
The Highly Flammable Liquids and Liquefied Petroleum Gases Regulations 1972
The Road Traffic (Carriage of Dangerous Substances in Packages etc.) Regulations 1986
The Packaging of Explosives for Carriage Regulations 1991

The risks

- death
- electrical fault
- explosion
- fire
- premature ignition
- secondary fires and explosions
- serious injury
- unidentified explosives

Those most at risk

Special effects technicians, cast, crew, performers, presenters, the public, anybody in the vicinity.

Explosive materials used in special pyrotechnic stunts and visual effects are dangerous and great care is required in their storage and use. The use, security and storage of explosives are regulated by the Control of Explosives Act 1991. These include blasting explosives, detonators, fuses, ammunition, propellants, pyrotechnics and fireworks.

The regulations also cover the use and storage of any 'restricted substances'. These are substances which can cause explosions when mixed together. Explosives are any substance which are UN Class 1 under the Classification and Labelling of Explosives Regulations 1983. Contravening licence requirements or provisions relating to explosives is a crown court offence. The penalty is two years' imprisonment, an unlimited fine or both.

In film and television work, producers should carry out a special effects risk assessment and a second one should be carried out by the stunt arranger/special effects technician and provided for the production management and the production health and safety office.

Note that under section 6 of the Health and Safety at Work Act comes a duty to make sure that any substance or effect has been tested for safety first and manufactured to avoid risks. As pyrotechnicians often design, make and supply their own effects, the obligations under section 6 should be read in conjunction with this chapter.

Producers should always follow the advice of the explosives expert. However check that they are full members of the Joint Industry Special

PYROTECHNICS, FIRE, SMOKE, FIREWORKS, BULLET HITS.

IAN ROWLEY
FOR
SPECIAL EFFECTS
Flamin' good effects since 1946.

COMPRESSED GAS EXPLOSIONS, ALL GASES INDOORS OR OUT, UNDERWATER.

ROWLEY WORKSHOPS LEEDS RODLEY LANE LEEDS LS13 1LB TEL: (WORK) 0113 257 4415 (MOBILE) 0374 611604

SPECIAL EFFECTS RISK ASSESSMENT

PRODUCTION COMPANY:	TITLE:	LOCATION/STAGE:	DATE:
YORKSHIRE TELEVISION	HOUR SPECIAL	STUDIO BURLEY ROAD	15 SEPT 98.

SPECIAL EFFECTS REQUIREMENTS: WOOLPACK INTERIORS EP 24 32 Sc 44-53.
CONTROLLED FIRE. FIREWORKS. SPONTANEOUS COMBUSTIONS. FLYING FIREWORKS

EQUIPMENT INVOLVED:

PURPOSE BUILT FIRE BAR RIG CUT INTO BAR TOP, COVERED WITH BAR TOWEL. FIRE BARS FITTED TO INTERIOR OF BAR SHELVING. MINITURE 12 VOLT SMOKE COIL AND IGNITION DEVISE. VARI-AC. CIRCUIT BREAKER, SUPPLY HOSES: FLASH TAPS. SET PIECE ON TRAY FOR SMOKE AND FLAME COMBUSTION TO NAPKIN. BATTERY AND FIRING BOX, SPRITZER. EXTINGUSHERS, PRESSURE PISTOL.

MATERIALS INVOLVED:

PROPANE: FLAMBAR N.5. FUME MASKS. LIGHTER FLUID. METHS PILOT. BUNGEE, LINE. BOXES OF DUMMY FIREWORKS FLAME PROOFED
* DUE TO ANNUAL HOLIDAYS OF THEATRICAL PYROTECHNICS SUPPLY OF SPECIAL FIRE WORKS FOR THIS EFFECT UNAVAILABLE UNTIL AFTER 8 SEPT. A SEPERATE ASSESSMENT TO FOLLOW A.S.A.P. *

ADVANTAGES OF USE:

GAS VENTED THROUGH BAR TOWER GIVES TOTAL CONTROL OF FLAME FOR ALL SHOTS. SET PIECE ON TRAY MAKES FOR QUICK RESET, FOR CANDLE BEING COVERED BY NAPKIN AND CANDLE BLOWING OUT FOLLOWED BY SPONTANEOUS IGNITION. ALL BAR AREA TO BE THOROUGHLY FIRE PROOFED AS WELL AS BAR TOWELS. FIRE IN THIS AREA CAN BE CONTROLLED WITH SPRITZER.

DISADVANTAGES OF USE:

RAPID HEAT BUILD UP. RAPID FUME BUILD UP. SEAT AREA FOR FIRE-WORK LANDING MUST BE STRIPPED OF ALL FOAM AND REPLACED WITH FIREPROOFED TIMBER SHAPE. CEILING CORNER WERE FIREWORK STRIKES TO BE REPLACED WITH PAINTED SUPERLUX.

POTENTIAL HAZARDS AND RISKS:

FUME HAZARD CARBON MONOXIDE AS WELL AS WASTE GASES FROM FIREWORKS
SECONDARY IGNITION OF SET.
FLAME AREA RESTRICTED TO BAR AREA, CEILING CORNER AND SEAT, BUT NOT ALL AT ONCE.
(THERE WILL BE NO FREE FLYING PYROS)

RECOMMENDATIONS:

SET DIRECTLY UNDER EXTRACTOR TALK TO STUDIO MANAGER.
FLAMEPROOFED, ATTENDED AT ALL TIMES. FLAME ON ONLY WHEN CAMERA ROLLING. STOPPING TO VENTILATE IF CONDITIONS BECOME UNCOMFORTABLE. FULL FIRE COVER.

Ian. C. Rowley 7 SEPT 98.

ADDITIONAL INFORMATION:

THE ABSOLUTE MINIMUM FIREWORKS WILL BE USED TO CREATE THESE EFFECTS DUE TO THE HIGH FUME CONTENT AND TEMPERATURE

H.A. & C. ROWLEY LTD. 27 SCOTLAND WAY, HORSFORTH, LEEDS LS18 5SQ TEL: (OFFICE) 0113 258 5618 VAT REG. NO. 170 2826 77 COMPANY REG. NO. 800833
CERTIFIED MEMBER OF THE JOINT INDUSTRY SPECIAL EFFECTS GRADING SCHEME FOR PHYSICAL AND PYROTECHNIC TECHNICIANS. BECTU 76157

ALL PICTURES ARE VIDEO GRABS OF IAN ROWLEY'S OWN WORK. FULLY INSURED AT LLOYDS.

Figure H16.1 *An example pyrotechnic risk assessment.* © *Ian Rowley*

Effects Grading Scheme and that they carry the appropriate card for pyrotechnic and special visual effects. Explosive effects must be supervised by a pyrotechnic supervisors card holder and carried out by a senior technician or technician card holder. They should also have attended the accredited course organized by the Royal Military College of Science.

Pyrotechnicians must be licensed to keep explosives. The certificate is called a stored explosives certificate (acquire and keep licence) and lasts for three years. Quantities of fireworks greater than 2 kg must be kept in a licensed store or be stored in registered premises. Storage of over 25 kg of explosives requires annual registration by the local authority and the HSE. The licence to keep explosives is individual to the premises and if explosives are going to be stored on location then another keep licence must be issued for that place. This explosives certificate is not a certificate of competence to use explosives.

To handle explosives the pyrotechnician needs to acquire a second licence which is renewed annually. This cannot be transferred to anybody else. So only licensed handlers may sell or transfer quantities of explosives to each other. For overseas production companies, a licence holder must make a sponsored application on their behalf and will be responsible for the acquisition and handling of any explosives and pyrotechnics. Production companies who want to bring explosives in will need an import licence and similarly an export licence is required to take explosives out of the country. These must also comply with any transportation regulations and carriage requirements. A non-licensed person may not handle, store, transport or attempt to buy any explosives.

Employers must not knowingly employ a prohibited or non-licensed person to handle, store or control any explosive or restricted substance. Pyrotechnicians must also be licensed to carry explosives under the Transport of Explosives by Road Regulations. Stunt arrangers and special effects supervisors should also carry their own third party, public and employers insurance cover.

A condition of an explosives licence is that the substance is stored safely. For example a quantity of gunpowder may be held up to 15kg. It must be stored in a locked wooden box or receptacle which complies with the Explosives Act 1875 away from any possible ignition. The lid of any box should read 'danger – no smoking – no naked flame'. Any explosives must be safe and properly labelled. Advice on the quantity and safe storage should be obtained from the explosives officer of your local police force.

Any storage enclosure for explosives must be of fire resisting construction against an outside wall and vented to the open air. The storage area must be away from the public. Access and keys must be strictly controlled. The door should read 'danger no smoking' and a 9-litre water fire extinguisher should be hung outside the enclosure door.

Fireworks, maroons and flash powder should always be stored separately from percussion caps, safety cartridges, safety fuses and detonators.

Gunpowder, fireworks, safety detonators, small arms and nitropowder are all classified as lower risk explosive along with some pyrotechnics.

The storage of high explosives requires a special licence and strict conditions of safe storage and security are applied to the premises. The premises are licensed by the local authority and the HSE. The owner or operator of the premises must appoint an individual in charge of security and explosive safety.

Special effects technicians are at risk when handling and using special chemical effects and under the Health and Safety at Work Act must take into account the risk to others if something goes wrong as well as the initial risk to themselves. It is the proximity of the individual to the explosion that makes film and television pyrotechnic work so dangerous. The Health and Safety at Work Act 1974 dictates that the stunt or pyrotechnic effect must be managed properly and safely and a full risk written assessment must be carried out.

All pyrotechnics are potentially dangerous and should be used in accordance with the manufacturer's and supplier's instructions. In no circumstances should 'home-made' pyrotechnics be made or used. It is dangerous and illegal to make pyrotechnics without a manufacturer's licence.

The distance between the explosive effect and people is a crucial calculation to make. Another is the correct weight of explosive to use in relation to the safe distance; for example, pyrotechnics designed for outside use should never be used indoors.

The siting of pyrotechnic devices is important. They should never be sited near any entrance or exit, or near any potential inflammable material such as props, drapes and scenery. An assessment must be made regarding the correct siting of the pyrotechnic in relation to any audience, performers and staff. This will depend on the strength of the device and the area in which it is to be employed. The site should also always be visible to the operator and a calculation made about the height, amount of smoke and noise produced as this could have serious risk factors. For example the blast shattering adjacent glass structures and dislodging dust and rubble from older or derelict buildings. The smoke could obscure visibility for aircraft or the noise could be mistaken for a bomb or explosion by the emergency services.

The pyrotechnic must be correctly wired for a safe detonation, including a properly constructed firing box. The firing box must be controlled by a key isolating switch. This must be in the possession of the operator firing the device.

The electrical supply should never be direct from the mains but reduced current via a transformer isolated to BS 3535. The output should not exceed 110 V. If the output exceeds 55 V, a centre tapping must be earthed to limit the voltage to earth. This ensures that no dangerous voltages are present in the device or the leads to them but ensuring an adequate current from a domestic 13 amp supply. The transformer should be adequately rated to supply the necessary current for firing and should be protected against overload.

The mains supply to the transformer should be controlled by a double pole key switch which retains the key unless in the off position. An indicator light should show when the box is energized. The firing circuits should be controlled by double pole switches biased to the off position and connected to the pyrotechnic device by an insulated lead.

The following safety conditions should be observed:

- Before loading any pyrotechnic device all firing circuits should be in the off position.
- The mains switch should be off and the key withdrawn. If the box is battery powered then the battery must be removed before loading.
- When loading a pyrotechnic device it is essential that the flash box or other device is isolated by unplugging it.
- After loading the device the operator should turn their back to the device before reconnecting this local isolator.
- Before the effects are loaded the danger area around the devices should be clear of people and combustible material.

The device should not be fired until everyone in the immediate vicinity is in a safe position. If a delay is to elapse before firing, the key or battery should be withdrawn and kept by the supervisor until final checking for firing. The firing box should not be energized until immediately prior to firing.

The operator(s) should have a clear view of all effects and their danger areas and should only fire on cue if it is safe to do so. If the device misfires or appears not to ignite then the following action should be taken. The key and firing circuits must be turned off and any battery removed. The mains supply must be turned off and the lead disconnected from the firing box and the device must be left for at least fifteen minutes.

A pyrotechnic device which appears to have misfired may nevertheless have ignited and may fire without warning even after being disconnected. Therefore a safe time delay must elapse before approaching the device and placing it in a non-combustible container covered with dry sand and removed to the open air in a non-public area. The manufacturer should then be contacted to carry out safe disposal after quoting the batch and code number. Never pour water on to a pyrotechnic as they contain magnesium and metallic powders which will violently explode if covered with water or CO_2.

If you are firing maroons these must be placed in properly constructed bomb tanks. Warning signs should be placed on every side which read 'danger explosives keep clear'. 'No entry, danger explosive' signs must be placed across any entrance to the device site.

The aim of the pyrotechnic is to produce a visual effect. Therefore substitution of safe materials may give you the desired effect without the danger. But a real explosion may leave you with nothing to film and look wrong as well.

The number of crew or people involved should be kept to a minimum. Keep members of the public and non-authorized persons away by having a proper permit to work system, barriers and security. This controls access and the risk of somebody unauthorized walking across the location when an effect is triggered. Ensure sufficient wardens and floor managers to protect each entrance door and access point to prevent unauthorized access. Red warning lights must indicate no access permitted for a sealed set or closed location.

If possible use a remote camera to film the stunt. If not keep crew to a minimum and ensure their protection. One of the main reasons for effects accidents is poor communication. Make sure that all involved know the order of the effect and the common signals the supervisor or the arranger will use. All staff must be briefed on this with no confusion so that there is no risk of the effect starting accidentally and finishing too early. All involved should be properly briefed on the procedure and safety precautions in advance in writing backed up by an oral briefing by the expert prior to filming. If the stunt is changed then a fresh briefing is required.

All effects must be rehearsed first for safety until everybody knows what will happen and how. Use a remote trigger or ignition device with a locked key safety button so it can't be started accidentally. The pyrotechnic arranger must be an expert in the wiring and handling of detonators. All radios, mobile phones and communication devices must be switched off and not allowed on site for the duration of the setting up and firing of the pyrotechnic explosion, as radio waves can trigger detonators prematurely. Mobile phones have also recently been identified as a risk. The Royal Military College of Science and the television union BECTU have agreed a safe minimum distance of 20 metres for mobile phones and radios. Pagers which only receive and do not transmit are considered safe. The British standard for electrical apparatus in explosive gas atmospheres is BS EN 60079–10. The code of practice for the selection, maintenance and installation of electrical apparatus in explosive atmospheres is BS 5345. The approved standard for electrical apparatus is BS 5501. Further advice can be obtained from the British Approvals Service for Electrical Equipment in Flammable Atmospheres.

Make sure the stunt arranger, operator and crew have visual contact with each other and the location of the effect. When the filming begins check that the vicinity is clear and safe first and leave a sufficient time delay afterwards for heat and fire to cool down and any fumes or vapour to clear. The supervisor must give the all clear and no-one should encroach on the set until this has been given – indicated by a green light and communicated to everybody.

Effects supervisors and crew should wear the appropriate personal protective equipment. It is essential to wear ear protection because of the noise and eye protection from the flash. Gloves and head protection should also be worn to protect from heat and flying debris.

Make sure that adequate fire and first aid facilities are in place. Any crew should be positioned well back in safe parameters. An emergency procedure must be formulated in advance and put into practice swiftly if something goes wrong. The fire services should be informed in case the public thinks the explosion is an accident. They can also give advice and will stand by if necessary.

The police should also be told in case a member of the public mistakes a loud explosion for a terrorist action or gas explosion.

Simulated disasters such as blowing up or large fires must be notified in advance to avoid confusion with the real thing.

Special effects are designed to be contained and employed away from people in properly ventilated locations where a build-up will be less dangerous. Any risk assessment must take into account special proximity hazards such as panic to people or animals. This is a risk in programmes involving audiences, children or animals and where locations are close to circuses, farms, riding schools and zoos. Beware of the proximity hazards to schools and nurseries.

The smoke from an effect could cause a danger if it restricts visibility for cars, other vehicles, planes, trains and plant. Rising smoke can present risks to crews working on scaffold towers or MEWPs. Make sure that any smoke or vapour does not obscure access points, steps, or the edge of steep drops and waterways. For the carriage of explosives by air, special rules and regulations apply. Contact the Civil Aviation Authority Dangerous Goods Department on 01293–573800.

The vibration from an explosion or any effect can cause risks and damage by shattering glass and loosening roofing material. If the quantity is misjudged or a soil survey has not been made the vibration may trigger an earth collapse with a risk of damage to parked crew buses, cranes, MEWPs or scaffolds. This could also affect anyone working in a trench or confined space. Vibration can also cause ear damage and break underground service cables and pipes. A proper locator should be used to detect them first.

This is why the effects should be controlled and minimal amounts of substance used to prevent and control the risk of secondary fires or explosions. For example, from flying sparks or hot debris into the vicinity of LPG storage used by catering/heating or gas used for welding or compressed air or oxygen for tools. All inflammable set materials and wood should be removed a safe distance away.

Very often explosion effects are generated by specialist equipment such as silo blasters which simulate mayhem but don't actually reciprocate the damage or hazards of a real explosion. Sometimes it is safer to use simulated effects, trick photography or library footage rather than the real thing.

Any risk to an audience should be identified in the risk assessment and the audience told in advance of the effect. Never involve a member of the public or untrained person in the operation or proximity to a pyrotechnic or special effect.

The management and supervisors must make sure that the explosion or flash effect is designed with safety in mind. Under the Construction (Design and Management) Regulations it is an offence to make an effect which has not had safety factors built in. For example the materials must be fire and heat proof. The effect should be capable of being started or disarmed by remote control. The device must be electrically safe and installed with sealed contacts and with properly insulated wiring to prevent an accidental explosion. The gas used must be the safest possible and be properly carried, labelled and stored until required and then only used in the smallest quantity necessary.

Always substitute a dangerous fuel or chemical with a safer alternative. Explosive label classifications should comply with UN, NATO and UK standards. Explosives are usually UN Hazard Class 1 with a group letter. Packaging is brown with yellow lettering. Use a symbol seeker to identify any ammunition or explosive. Beware of any that have no markings. Do not handle them and call for advice straight away.

Explosives are divided into four classes:

1 lethal and high explosive
2 potentially lethal
3 dangerous contents
4 inert/safe contents.

The explosive effect must not present a hazard or risk to the operator or members of the public from the heat, flame, noise, smoke or residue. Any chemical or toxic substance used to produce the effect or produced by it should be notified and entered in the COSHH register and the

COSHH hazard information data sheets with information provided by the manufacturer, supplier and operator. Never mix chemicals from different batches. The manufacturer must specialize in supplying explosives and pyrotechnic chemicals for television and film use. Never use the local garage or be tempted to use petrol or gas.

Smoke effects

The HSE have produced specific guidance for film and television work which uses smoke and vapour effects. The information sheet is called Smoke and vapour effects used in entertainment, HSE Entertainment Sheet No. 3, ETIS(3).

There are two main ways of producing smoke and vapour. The first is fluid-based smoke machines. The second is solid carbon dioxide (dry ice) fog machines.

Smoke machines work on the principle of superheating an oil- or water-based chemical, atomizing the fluid and forcing the resulting smoke out of the front of the machine under pressure. These should only be operated in accordance with the manufacturer's written instructions in their safe use.

To produce dry ice effects, solid carbon dioxide blocks or pellets are immersed in hot water or steam so that clouds of white mist are produced at ground level propelled by fans or via ducts in the floor. Dry ice should be handled only with imperforate gloves having good thermal insulation as skin contact could cause severe burns. Carbon dioxide is an asphyxiate and high concentrations can present a life risk to the audience, performers and stage staff – especially those in pit areas and under stage areas. Following initial generation the vapours become invisible and the concentration of gas may be difficult to determine. If there is any doubt about the concentration present then a gas meter reading must be made to monitor oxygen and carbon dioxide levels before staff and audiences can safely use the area formerly affected.

The operator should be properly trained and the smoke or vapour given off must be non-toxic and comply with the COSHH Regulations. The owners of any premises must be notified in advance that a substance or chemical considered dangerous under the COSHH Regulations will be brought into the location. The substance should be properly labelled and stored in an appropriate fire-proof container locked and separate from any other hazard and the public. No smoking must be allowed with safety warning signs to indicate 'no naked flames' and 'highly flammable'.

The smoke or vapour given off must not obscure emergency gangways or fire exits. You must also be aware of the effect of any smoke or vapour upon any sprinkler system, fire detection devices or smoke detectors in the building concerned as these may be activated.

Producers and effects supervisors must make sure that the smoke or residue given off does not exceed maximum permitted exposure levels and occupational exposure levels laid down in EH40. On-site monitoring of the effect should be in place and any risks must be controlled and an assessment must be made of the smoke given off and of the substances used to produce it. For example glycol and liquid nitrogen are inflammable and give off toxic fumes. Consideration should be given to the exposure below limits to asthmatics, small children, the elderly and those with respiratory problems to identify anybody at risk. Any risks identified must be contained and controlled to safe levels and any suppliers or manufacturers should provide you with product information to make a proper assessment. Similarly manufacturers of any effects machines must supply you with proper operating and safety instructions.

You must also make sure that any operator is properly trained and experienced in the use of the effect and the operation must be properly supervised.

The safe way to carry out explosive and pyrotechnic stunts is to plan well in advance with the services of an expert and control the effect by safe materials and design. Then carry out the filming with the minimum number of people at a safe distance with expert supervision. Ensure good communication and emergency procedures.

Never cut corners or try to do it yourself as the only thing you will blow up is yourself or others, and your professional reputation will go up in smoke.

Further reading

Control of Explosives Regulations 1991, SI 1531, HSE, 1991, ISBN 0-11-014531-3.

List of Authorised Explosives, HSE, 1992, ISBN 0-11-886396-7.

Guide to the Classification and Labelling of Explosives Regulations 1983, HSE, 1983, ISBN 0-11-883706-0.

Control of Substances Hazardous to Health Regulations 1994, Approved Code of Practice, HSE, 1995, ISBN 0-7176-0819-0.

An Introduction to the Control of Explosives Regulations, HSE, IND(G)115.

Dangerous Substances – Classified and Authorised Explosives, HSE, 1994, ISBN 0-7176-0772-0.

Dangerous Substances – Classified and Authorised Explosives. Supplement No. 1 (Misc-039), HSE, 1996, ISBN 0-7176-1134-5.

A Guide to the Control of Explosives Regulations 1991, L10, HSE, 1991, ISBN 0-11-885670-7.

New Explosives Controls, HSE, IND(G)115L-C1000.

Suitability of Vehicles and Containers and Limits on Quantities for the Carriage of Explosives, HSE, ISBN 0-7176-1224-4.

Approved Requirements and Test Methods for the Classification and Packaging of Dangerous Goods for Carriage, HSE, ISBN 0-7176-1221-X.

Approved Requirements for Construction of Vehicles for the Carriage of Explosives by Road, HSE, ISBN 0-7176-12225-2.

Acquisition and Use of Explosives by Historical Societies, HSE, ISBN 0-7176-1622-3.

A Step By Step Guide to COSHH Assessment, HS(G)97, HSE, 1993, ISBN 0-11-886379-7.

Occupational Exposure Limits, EH40/92, HSE, ISBN 0-7176-1021-7.

Seven Steps to Successful Substitution of Hazardous Substances, HSE-HS(G)110, ISBN 0-7176-0695-3.

Smoke and Vapour Effects used in Entertainment, HSE Entertainment Sheet No. 3 ETIS(3).

Symbol Seeker, Reid Marketing, 60 Moor St, Ormskirk, Lancs L39 2AW, Tel: 01695–570595.

Code of Practice for Pyrotechnics and Smoke Effects, Association of British Theatre Technicians, ISBN 0-11-341072-7.

J. F. Whitfield, *A Guide to Electrical Safety at Work*, 1992, EPA Press.

Robin Garside, *Electrical Apparatus and Hazardous Areas*, 2nd edition, 1994, Hexagon Technology Ltd.

BASEEFA List 1996: Certified and Approved Explosion Protected Electrical Equipment, 9th edition, HSE, ISBN 0-7176-1091-8.

Establishing Exclusion Zones when using Explosives in Demolition, HSE, CIS45.

Risk from Mobile Phones: see *Stage, Screen and Radio*, July 1998 p. 23 and *Daily Mail*, Thursday 16 July 1998, pp. 1 and 2.

Equity Spotlight Register of Stunt Action Co-ordinators and Performers.

Pyrotechnics – Reducing the Risks, *Stage, Screen and Radio*, November 1997, pp. 10–13.

Leading the Field – Pyrotechnics Courses, *Stage, Screen and Radio*, July 1998, p. 23.

The Approved Classification and Labelling Guide, HSE, ISBN 0-7176-1726-2.

Contact organizations

Association of British Theatre Technicians
47 Bermondsey St, London SE1 3XT
Tel: 0171–403–3778

British Actors Equity Association
Guild House, Upper St Martin's Lane, London WC2H 9EG
Tel: 0171–379–6000

British Approvals Service for Electrical Equipment in Flammable Atmospheres
Harpur Hill, Buxton, Derbyshire SK17 9JN
Tel: 01298–28000

BECTU
111 Wardour St, London W1V 4AY
Tel: 0171–437–8506

Civil Aviation Authority
Aviation House, Gatwick, W. Sussex RH6 0YR
Tel: 01293–573800

The Institute of Explosives Engineers
Unit 48, Century Business Park, Hammond Close, Attleborough Fields,
Nuneaton, Warwickshire CV11 6RY
Tel: 01203–350846

The Royal Military College of Science
Cranfield University, Shrivenham, Swindon, Wiltshire CSN6 8LA
Tel: 01793–784455

The Health and Safety Executive Explosives Inspectorate Group
Magdalen House, Stanley Precinct, Bootle, Merseyside L20 3QZ
Tel: 0151–951–4741

Hazard 17: Fire

The legislation

The Fire Regulations and Fire Precautions Act 1971
The Fire Precautions (Workplace Amendment) Regulations 1999
The Fire Safety and Safety of Places of Sport Act 1987
The Fire Certificates (Special Premises) Regulations 1976
The Health and Safety at Work Act 1974
The Management of Health and Safety at Work Regulations 1992
The Occupiers Liability Act 1984
The Health and Safety (Safety Signs and Signals) Regulations 1996
The Workplace (Health, Safety and Welfare) Regulations 1992

The risks

- access
- asphyxiation
- burns
- chemicals
- death
- electricity
- explosives
- fuel
- inflammable material
- ignition sources
- scenery
- shock
- smoke
- smoking

Those most at risk

Everybody when a fire starts.

The film and television industry has many fire risks. These can be hazardous and life threatening. Fires can kill if they are not dealt with quickly. So fire risks should be identified and proper fire precautions should be put in place.

The main components for a fire to start are fuel, an ignition source and oxygen. If any one of these three is missing then a fire cannot start. So a fire prevention plan should concentrate on identifying where these risks are in your operation and preventing them from coming together. This will reduce the chances of a fire occurring.

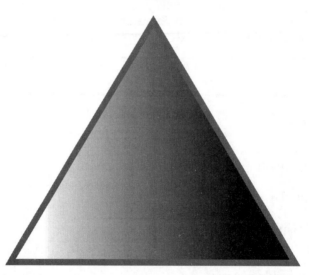

FUEL
Flammable gases
Flammable liquids
Flammable solids

OXYGEN
Always present in the air
Additional sources from
oxidising substances

IGNITION SOURCE
Hot surfaces
Electrical equipment
Static electricity
Smoking/naked flames

Figure H17.1   *Fire triangle.* Source: The Storage of Flammable Liquids in Containers, *2nd edition, 1998, HSE, HSG51, ISBN 0-7176-1471-9. © HMSO*

There are seven basic things that you must do:

1 Assess the fire risks in the workplace.
2 Check that a fire can be detected in a reasonable time and that people can be warned.
3 Check that people who may be in the building or location can get out safely.
4 Provide reasonable fire fighting equipment.
5 Check that those in the building know what to do if there is a fire. This includes fire drills and provision of proper fire safety signing.
6 Check and maintain your fire safety equipment.
7 Provide proper fire safety signs.

Identifying fire hazards and assessing the fire risks must be a priority for managers and producers. Fire risk means the risk of fire occurring and the risk to people in the event of a fire.

The Health and Safety at Work Act 1974 and the Fire Regulations cover the fire precautions which are intended to prevent the outbreak of a fire or to minimize the consequences should a fire occur.

Matters which come under the above include the storage of flammable materials, the control of flammable vapours, standards of housekeeping, safe systems of work, the control of sources of ignition and the provision of appropriate fire safety training.

The Fire Regulations and the amended Management of Health and Safety at Work Regulations 1992 place the following obligations on the employer, who is required to:

1 Carry out a fire risk assessment of the workplace.
2 This must include the fire risk to any employees, contractors, subcontractors, visitors and the public who may be affected by an outbreak of fire in the workplace.
3 The assessment must also include the risk to disabled and those with special needs for whom adequate provision must be made.
4 The significant findings of the risk assessment and the details of those at risk must be recorded if you employ five or more people.
5 Adequate fire precautions must be provided and maintained for the level of fire risk identified and the number of people employed.
6 Proper information, instruction and training must be provided by the employer for the employees and users of your workplace.

The fire risk assessment provides the basis on which decisions about the level and nature of the fire precautions required are made. It is the most important written document and should be undertaken properly and advice obtained from your local fire officer if necessary. There are five essential steps for carrying out a fire risk assessment. These are:

1 Identify potential fire hazards in the workplace.
2 Decide who might be in danger in the event of a fire and where they are situated. Can they escape in safety?
3 Evaluate the risks arising from the hazards and decide whether your existing fire precautions are adequate or whether more should be done to get rid of the hazard or to control the risks (e.g. by improving the fire precautions).
4 Record your findings and details of the action you took as a result. Tell your employees and others affected about your findings.
5 Keep the assessment under review and revise it when necessary.

There are six other legal duties which the employer must carry out:

1 You must nominate people to undertake special rules required under the fire emergency plan.
2 You must consult your employees (or their elected representatives or appointed trade union safety representatives) about the nomination of people to carry out particular roles in connection with fire safety and about proposals for improving the fire precautions, e.g. Who is the fire warden, fire safety officer or what are the new fire safety measures?
3 You must inform other employers who also have workplaces in the building of any significant risks you found which might affect the safety of their employees, and co-operate with them about the measures proposed to reduce and control those risks.
4 If you are not an employer but have any control of premises which contain more than one workplace, you are also responsible for ensuring that the requirements of the fire regulations are complied with in those parts you have control over.
5 You must establish a suitable means of contacting the emergency services and ensure that they can be called easily.
6 The law requires your employees to co-operate with you to ensure the workplace is safe from fire and its effects, and not to do anything which will place themselves or other people at risk.

Fire hazards can occur in base buildings, in buildings owned by others, in buildings which have been hired and in sets, stages and outside broadcast locations built for a specific purpose.

Any fire fighting strategy should concentrate on the following points. First, provide means for detecting fires and smoke. Second, give an alarm to everybody in the building and to the emergency services. Third, evacuate all the people safely via fire escape routes and exit doors to a designated evacuation point. Fourth, have a reliable way of accounting for all people who may be in the building.

Fifth, have the appropriate fire fighting equipment on hand to tackle any anticipated fire risk. Sixth, train staff in the use of fire extinguishers and evacuation procedures. Seventh, encourage a culture of fire precaution through the elimination of inflammable material, deposits of rubbish, storage of dangerous chemicals, use of faulty electrical equipment and prevention of smoking.

Eighth, keep a log of any dangerous substances stored. Nine, regular maintenance and fire checks. Lastly, hold regular fire drills, evacuation procedures and training days backed up by a quality supply of information about fire risks to all employees, subcontractors and visitors. Strong management and teamwork is needed to eliminate holes in fire precautions and to inform anybody who needs to know about fire safety. Fire safety is the responsibility of everybody – not just the management.

A key human factor in fires is a complacent attitude caused by familiarity of surroundings. But when fires start panic becomes a key factor, especially once the fire has taken hold. This false security can be dealt with by regular fire practice and panic can be dealt with by providing simple and relevant information about what to do if a fire is

Equipment	Period	Action
Fire detection and fire warning systems including self-contained smoke alarms and manually operated devices.	Weekly	Check all systems for state of repair and operation. Repair or replace defective units. Test operation of systems, self-contained alarms and manually operated devices.
	Annually	Full check and test of system by competent service engineer. Clean self-contained smoke alarms and change batteries.
Emergency lighting equipment including self-contained units and torches.	Weekly	Operate torches and replace batteries as required. Repair or replace any defective unit.
	Monthly	Check all systems, units and torches for state of repair and apparent working order.
	Annually	Full check and test of systems and units by competent service engineer. Replace batteries in torches.
Fire-fighting equipment including hose reels.	Weekly	Check all extinguishers including hose reels for correct installation and apparent working order.
	Annually	Full check and test by competent service engineer.

Note: Unless otherwise stated, the above actions can be carried out by the user. Manufacturers may recommend alternative or additional action. Further, more detailed information can be found in the relevant British Standards

Figure H17.2 *Fire equipment test schedule.* © HMSO

discovered. The distribution of fire fighting information can be backed up by training videos and talks from specialists from the emergency services and equipment supply companies.

For a list of approved fire equipment suppliers, read the Loss Prevention Council's Approved Guide 1998, ref. APS98.

The key to fire prevention is an effective fire hazards identification method backed up by a fire risk assessment plan. Employers must comply with the Fire Precautions (Workplace) Regulations 1997, which apply to the workplace of any employer. For the film and television business this means that any premises used for employment must have fire precautions.

The fire safety of any employees and members of the public is the aim, but what precautions should you have to implement?

Section 4 of the regulations states that in order to safeguard employees, 'a workplace shall, to the extent that is appropriate, be equipped with appropriate fire-fighting equipment and with fire detectors and alarms. Any non-automatic equipment so provided shall be easily accessible, simple to use and indicated by signs.' This means that every building has to have fire-fighting precautions and signs in order to comply with the regulations. These are some of the fire fighting precautions which you need to have. The level of precautions depends on if your building is classified as a, b or c.

Fire alarms

Early warning and detection provide crucial time for evacuation from fire. The first warning of a fire should be activation of the firm alarm as time is a crucial life saving factor with fire emergencies. The fire alarm signal must be clear and distinctive. This signal must override any other noise. This is crucial in workshop areas, noisy environments and areas where crew wear headsets. The audible warning should be backed up by a flashing visual signal. Fire alarms should conform to BS 5839.

Once the fire alarm is activated then the fire brigade must be contacted and the building evacuated without delay. Fire alarms should be tested at least once every week.

Smoke alarms

The effects of spreading smoke are fast and usually lethal so buildings should be fitted with smoke detectors and smoke alarms, especially in areas of high risk such as kitchens, stores and workshops. Fit smoke alarms and detectors conforming to BS 5839. Early warning and detection provide crucial time for evacuation and so prevent the risk of asphyxiation from deadly smoke.

Everybody should know what these alarm signals are. They should know what it is and what to do about it. There should be a clear evacuation procedure and assembly points. Access to buildings should be monitored so that it is easy to tell how many people are inside in the event of a fire emergency and fire assembly points are provided to check that everybody is safe. The location of these are indicated by fire signs.

Fire signs

One of the best ways of giving accurate information is the proper signing of fire escapes, fire doors, fire hazards and fire fighting equipment. All fire information signs should be large enough to be seen clearly. One of the main reasons for fire related injuries is the lack of proper information. All precautions and emergency procedures are useless if nobody knows about them. This is why proper signing is essential under the Workplace (Health, Safety and Welfare) Regulations 1992 and all staff should know what they mean.

The second part of the Health and Safety (Safety Signs and Signals) Regulations 1996 insist that all fire safety signs must contain a symbol from December 1998. Text only fire safety signs should have been replaced by this date.

Fire signs provide important fire safety information. Fire exit signs must be green and display the 'running person' pictogram. These should indicate the location of the fire exit supported by arrow directional signs to show the way to it. All fire exit signs should conform to BS 5499 and the Fire Safety Signs and Signals Regulations 1996 from 24 December 1998. The European harmonization of fire signs comes from EU Directive 92/58/EEC.

Figure H17.3 © *ARCO Ltd, reproduced by kind permission*

All fire equipment signs should be white pictograms on a red background and comply with BS 5499 Part 1 and BS 5378. These indicate the location of fire fighting equipment, fire alarms, fire hose reels and extinguisher locations.

Fire emergency signs and exits should also have battery or secondary illumination. No smoking and warning signs should be circular and outlined in red with a red line through the picture. These are prohibition signs which prohibit behaviour that is likely to result in a danger. Make sure that all staff and public understand these signs and the locations of the fire exits.

EN6   125 x 200
EN6PH
(Photoluminescent)

Figure H17.4 © *ARCO Ltd, reproduced by kind permission*

Fire exits

Fire moves extremely fast and smoke chokes quickly, so not knowing where the nearest emergency exit is can kill you. The Fire Precautions (Workplace) Regulations 1997 state that 'where necessary to safeguard the safety of employees in case of fire, routes to emergency exits from a workplace and the exits themselves shall be kept clear at all times.'

Never block or lock fire exits. Do not block emergency exits with cables and equipment. Do not prop open fire doors when transporting equipment as the passage of air will cause a fire to spread quicker.

All emergency routes and exits shall lead as directly as possible to a place of safety. The number, distribution and dimensions of emergency routes and exits shall be adequate having regard to the use, equipment and dimensions of the workplace.

They should also take into account the maximum number of persons that may be present in a building or set at any one time. Proper calculations must be made which allow for the total number of people who will be present. This calculation should include artists, actors, crew, performers, presenters, the public, subcontractors and visitors. The calculation will give you a total safe figure and this should never be exceeded. So fire regulations will place a strict limit on audience and visitors numbers for outside broadcast rostra, temporary audience scaffolding and studios. Advice on fire exit calculations can be found in the Building Regulations or in *A Guide to Fire Precautions in Existing Places of Entertainment and Like Places* (HMSO, 1990, ISBN 0-11-340907-9). Alternatively contact your local fire authority for help. Emergency exits shall open outwards in the direction of escape and shall not be so locked or fastened that they cannot be easily and immediately opened by any person who may require to use them in an emergency. All emergency exits and routes must be properly signed and provided with illumination and emergency lighting in the event of mains failure. These are all legal requirements but the measures required for fire fighting in each workplace can differ.

The regulations state that 'what is appropriate, is to be determined by the dimensions and use of the building housing the workplace, the equipment it contains, the physical and chemical properties of the substances likely to be present and the maximum number of people that may be present at any one time.' This recognizes that the fire-fighting requirements of a large film scenery construction workshop are going to be different from those of a small production office.

Fire extinguishers

From January 1997 all extinguishers should conform to European safety standard and BS EN 3 and be CE marked. All new extinguishers can retain a small colour panel for easy identification. The panel will indicate the contents by colour and a symbol will indicate the class of fires which the extinguisher may be used on.

There are four classes of fire:

- Class A: water, paper, cloth.
- Class B: flammable liquids and fats.
- Class C: flammable gases.
- Class D: electrical hazards.

There are four major types of new fire extinguisher:

1 Water or hydrospray – for wood/paper/fabric fires only. The panel colour is red. For Class A fires only. Do not use on electrical or chemical fires.

2 Foam spray (AFFF) – burning liquid fires only. The panel colour is cream. For Class A and B fires only. Do not use on electrical fires.
3 Dry powder – for burning liquid and electrical fires only. The panel colour is blue. For Class A, B, C and some electrical fires only (ideal for carrying in vehicles).
4 Carbon dioxide (CO_2) – for burning liquid and electrical fires only. The panel colour is black. For Class B and electrical fires only (ideal for computers, generators and lights).

NB halon (BCF) extinguishers were coloured green and were used for burning liquid and electrical fires only. However all halon extinguishers should have been replaced by 1999 as the CFCs they contain damage the environment.

Signs for fire extinguishers should be to BS 7863 to indicate the contents. Do not use the wrong type of fire extinguisher for a particular kind of fire. This can create a violent reaction or cause electrocution. Make sure all staff are trained in the correct extinguisher type to use and receive proper instruction on how to use them. Above all make sure that there are enough types of extinguisher for each category of fire risk and in sufficient quantity. All fire extinguishers should be properly serviced and maintained at least once a year in accordance with BS 5306 Part 3, 1985. Remember to provide fire extinguishers of the appropriate type in all your production vehicles and kitchens.

Other fire equipment

Fire blankets should be provided along with sand buckets (especially for chemical hazards). Ash trays, water buckets and fire hoses should also be provided. Fire hoses should conform to BS 5274. Never use fire fighting equipment for any other purpose. Fire fighting equipment should be regularly maintained and checked for vandalism. Where a significant fire hazard exists fire fighting equipment should be provided as a matter of course in all occupied buildings and at particularly hazardous locations such as storage areas, catering facilities, electrical grids, lighting maintenance areas, sets and public studios.

All fire fighting equipment must be safe in itself and regularly serviced and be correct for the task required. Consult leading fire equipment suppliers for the right equipment and training as the wrong equipment could effect your insurance cover. All fire fighting equipment must meet the BAFE (British Approvals for Fire Equipment) and FETA (Fire Extinguishing Trades Association) approval as well as BS EN 3 from January 1997. First aid precautions should include kits available to deal with major burns and staff trained to deal with burn injuries.

Fire prevention in base buildings

The fire-fighting needs for each building should be self-assessed individually and expert advice should be obtained from the fire-fighting authorities and leading fire prevention companies. This means making a fire risk self-assessment which managers, owners health and safety staff and producers should carry out together to evaluate the levels of fire risk and who it would affect. When this plan has been drawn up, it should be validated by the local fire brigade before implementation.

When drawing up a fire risk assessment plan questions to ask would be: What do we use this building for? What equipment do we have in it? What chemicals are stored in it and in what quantity? What heat sources and physical properties are used in it? Do the processes we are engaged in produce a fire risk? Once identified immediate action should be taken to control any fire risks. The fire action plan must be reviewed on a regular basis.

Fire wardens

Every building and location should have nominated appointed fire wardens who are experienced and competent. Factors which determine the choice of an appropriate person to have as a fire warden would be reliability, disposition and communication skills, plus adaptability and willingness to learn new techniques. Other personal qualities include somebody who can prioritize quickly and has the ability to cope with the stressful and physically demanding emergency procedures created by a fire.

Employers should give proper training to appointed fire wardens in basic fire fighting techniques by sending them on an approved fire wardens course for the level of risk. Staff should be sent on a fire extinguisher course and be given basic first aid training. Fire wardens and staff should be trained in the correct use of fire fighting equipment. It would be a risk to life if equipment is available and nobody knows how to use it.

Emergency fire drills should be held at least twice a year.

Every building should have a fire log book to report and record any incidents and accidents. There should be swift means of contact to the local fire services in the event of a fire emergency. The local fire authority should regularly inspect buildings every year for fire safety.

Base buildings with studios, offices, public stages and auditoriums are classed as public entertainment venues and must have a public fire safety certificate. The best guide to the regulations for places of entertainment is called *A Guide to Fire Precautions in Existing Places of Entertainment and Like Places* (HMSO, 1990, ISBN 0-11-340907-9). If you are working in a studio, set or auditorium, it is worth reading this first.

Fire certificates

Under the Fire Precautions Act 1971 a fire certificate is issued by the fire authority and is needed for any premises such as an office or workshop that employs twenty or more people or which employs ten or more people on any other floor than the ground floor including the basement. Fire certificates are also needed for any building which stores hazardous or explosive substances. For construction sites the Health and Safety Executive issues the fire certificate.

A fire certificate must be applied for on an official form by the occupier of the premises. It contains the address of the premises and the particular part of the building to which the certificate refers. It also has information about the use to which the premises is put and the quantities of chemicals stored.

Film premises such as major studios which store large quantities of chemicals and create lots of fire and explosive effects will have a special premises certificate with an individual requirement and special exemptions.

The ordinary fire certificate will contain the name and address of the owner of the premises and that of the occupier. Both the owner and the occupier will get a copy of the fire certificate with a master stored at the inspecting fire brigade. For multiple occupancy premises each occupier must possess a separate fire certificate.

On the back of the certificate is a plan of the building which will give the means of escape in the event of fire and the location of all fire exits. It will also detail any fire escape corridors, fire doors and fire escapes. It should also mark the location of the fire assembly point. It will also show the location of the nearest fire hydrants and water supply. It will also contain details of the fire alarm system including smoke detectors. It will tell you the location and details of emergency lighting. The fire certificate will also tell you the number, type and location of all fire extinguishers. It will also list any hazardous materials, inflammable materials or explosives stored on the premises.

A copy of the fire certificate must be kept on the premises and open to inspection at all times. The granting of a fire certificate involves the following legal obligations. The means of escape must never be obstructed. The fire alarm must be tested once a week and fire extinguishers checked, serviced and maintained regularly – at least once a year. The emergency lighting must be tested and checked every month, including the operation of any battery back-up supply. Regularly check batteries for corrosion and replace them at regular intervals.

Fire drills must be carried out at least twice a year and fire training must be carried out at regular intervals. Written records must be kept of all drills, training and tests in a fire log book. In any multi-occupied building a person must be nominated to be responsible for maintenance and testing of all fire equipment.

Fire certificates can also place limits on the number of persons in a building. Every studio has a specific limit of its own, separate from the building it is in. Floor managers should ensure that this limit is not exceeded. The fire certificate also places restrictions on the type and amount of inflammable material, explosive or hazardous substance that can be stored on the premises. Production managers and stores staff should ensure that this limit is not exceeded.

Occupiers must comply with the requirements of the fire certificate at all times. If any of the conditions are changed, for example by building work or the need to store extra substances, then the fire authority must be informed and will detail what work is necessary to issue an amendment or a new one. This is also necessary if the nominated fire equipment person changes.

If the fire authority inspect your premises and are dissatisfied with your precautions, equipment and arrangements, they can issue an improvement notice which specifies the required action within a time period. If they feel that there is a threat to life they can issue a prohibition notice which closes the building immediately until corrective actions to bring the precautions to the required standard are put in place.

When the fire authority is satisfied that the means of escape in case of a fire are adequate, the means for fighting fires are suitable and any process or storage is not dangerous they may exempt any building or part of it from the need for a fire certificate. A fire certificate is not necessary if the building employs less than twenty people in total and no more than ten people are employed on floors other than the ground floor. If ten or more people are employed on the first floor then it must have a fire certificate. If no hazardous, inflammable or explosive substances are stored some conditions may be relaxed.

However, under the Fire Precautions (Workplace) Regulations 1997 a building must still have adequate fire escapes and fire fighting equipment. If you feel your premises may need a fire certificate then you should apply to your local fire brigade headquarters and request a FP1/revised fire certificate application form.

Inherent fire hazards in base buildings

The main components for a fire to start are fuel, an ignition source and oxygen. If any one of these three is missing then a fire cannot start, so a fire prevention plan should concentrate on identifying where these risks are in your operation and preventing them from coming together. This will reduce the chances of a fire occurring.

Once a fire starts it can grow very quickly and spread from one source of fuel to another. As it grows the amount of heat it gives off will increase which can, in turn, cause other fuels to self-ignite. Removing potential sources of ignition can help to prevent a fire from starting. Fire prevention should begin by identifying these risks and keeping them separate. Potential ignition sources must be identified. For example, blow torches, aerosols, lighters, gas rings, gas heaters, lamps and lighting are all capable of producing heat, so they should be used, stored and situated with care as they present potential sources of ignition. They must be placed well away from any fire hazard. The identification and separation of sources of ignition and heat from potentially inflammable substances is a basic plank in constructing a fire risk assessment and building an effective prevention plan.

Identify any heat sources such as electricity, blow lamps, flame, hot pipes, lights and smoking. To reduce the fire risk to a safe level all chemicals, gases, fuel, paints and wood should be stored in separate compounds which are fire-proofed and cool. These should be a safe distance from any areas of main activity and kept locked in a hazardous substances cabinet. Dangerous substances should only be handled by competent and authorized staff. Only the minimum quantity required should be handled and stored, especially substances which are volatile upon contact with air or heat.

Locations of hazardous substances and chemicals should be properly identified with appropriate warning signs under the COSHH Regulations. The emergency services should be informed of any dangerous substances, chemicals or gases stored in large or dangerous quantities.

Storage of explosives must conform to the Control of Explosives Regulations 1991 with a proper site licence for storage. Information that the fire authorities would need in the event of a fire are how much you are storing, the chemicals' properties and a copy of the COSHH data sheet along with a plan of their storage location. It would also help to indicate the location of the nearest fire fighting equipment, water supply and emergency access point for fire fighting vehicles.

Smoking should be prohibited whenever possible, especially in restricted areas which contain inflammable materials. All carpets, costumes, wigs and scenery should be properly fire-proofed and stored in fire retardant boxes and store rooms. All film chemicals and tape should be controlled and stored in fire-proofed cabinets.

The storage of all inflammable liquids and gases is subject to the Highly Flammable Liquids and Liquefied Petroleum Gases Regulations 1972. Drums must conform to BS 814 and storage building and cupboards to BS 476. Storage cupboards must hold a maximum of 50 litres and be fire resistant for at least 30 minutes. Cylinders should be stored upright (unless the COSHH data sheet specifies otherwise) and strapped securely.

Tape and film stock storage areas carry a high fire risk and should be properly ventilated. Tape should be placed in fire security cabinets. The storage of antique nitrate film is strictly prohibited and confined to a specially licensed MOMI archive in Berkhampstead.

Canteens, costume stores, construction workshops, kitchens, vehicle maintenance bays, scenery construction areas, scenery stores, paint shops, model making areas, tape stores and laboratories are all inherently hazardous locations within broadcasting and film buildings.

However the fire risk factor of a building can dramatically increase by the introduction of dangerous chemicals, faulty equipment, dangerous processes and inexperienced people into your building.

Introduced fire hazards in buildings

Not all activities which contain a fire risk are inherent to the building. Some are introduced by regular visitors and subcontractors such as cleaning, building and maintenance operations. The fire risk assessment plan must take account of hazards produced by regular maintenance work, building work and routine cleaning. Controls should be introduced for bringing any chemicals, paint, petrol, electrical devices and inflammable material into base buildings. Fires have been started by blow torches and faulty electrical tools or accentuated by chemicals and accumulated rubbish. All inflammable materials and chemicals must be logged in and logged out of permanent buildings and locations. A book should be provided for the purpose to act as a COSHH register.

The introduction or storage of any dangerous chemicals or explosives should be notified to the emergency authorities including the local fire service. Establishing a signing system for access and exit will help to control regular work which requires hazardous items to be introduced and used in a building or set.

Producers and managers should also beware the casual introduction of any hazardous substances or fire risks by subcontractors or artists who may only visit for a short time for a specific purpose. For example actors, drivers, repair staff, stunt artists, location catering and visitors.

It should be clear by now that although the inherent fire risk can be assessed in permanent buildings used for film and television purposes they are not like steel plants or white collar offices where the function is regular and constant. The problem with the film and television business is of course the constant change in activities. We have to consider the new fire risk presented every time we introduce a new production. The danger factor can be increased dramatically by what we introduce as a result of production activity into a previously safe building or location.

Fire risk assessments must be done for each production and broken down again into each activity within that production so that controls are put in place which reflect the changing level of risk. The fire risk factor in production activity can therefore come from the fluctuating level and nature of what we use to do each job.

Fire hazards in other people's buildings

The fire risk assessment process is complicated further as we not only change the activities we undertake at base premises but we also undertake these varied activities in other locations as well. Film and television activity which take place outside the controls and confines of headquarters should also be included in your fire risk assessment.

So fire risks to include in your assessment would be the work conducted inside the premises of third parties and locations which are owned by other people. These can range from a stately home for a period fiction film to a steel plant for a documentary. The fire risks are not as familiar as base. The biggest risk here is unfamiliarity.

It is important to find out the fire risks in advance and obtain copies of the fire regulations and emergency procedures from the owners and operators of the buildings before any filming activity takes place. All relevant information about fire precautions in the building must be put on the call sheet and distributed to all those likely to be affected.

The owners and operators also have a legal responsibility for your fire safety so they should provide the same level of fire precautions and fire fighting equipment as you would expect at base and must provide visitors with all relevant information.

However you should always advise them of any activities and equipment you are going to introduce and use which would change or prejudice the quality of fire precautions already in place. For example, different types of fire extinguishers might be needed. Never turn a safe location into a dangerous one. Also consider if an increase in the number of people such as crew and cast into that location would compromise the quantity of existing provision of fire precautions. For example, the number of fire extinguishers required and the amount of emergency exits needed.

Fire hazards in temporary locations

As well as borrowing other people's buildings, we also construct a few of our own. A lot of film and television work takes places in temporary stages, sound stages and outside broadcast locations. So we not only have to consider the fire risks of permanent buildings but also those presented by short-term locations constructed for a particular production purpose. The safe design and construction of temporary locations come under the fire provisions of the Construction (Design and Management) Regulations 1992.

All sets must be built out of safe materials and flame proofed. Any deliberate fire hazards such as flame effects must be properly planned and supervised. They must be designed and carried out by an experienced person. Temporary fires must be contained on metal plates or trays to contain them. Any lights, candles or heat producing set features must be placed well away from drapes, curtains, costumes and wigs. Beware of fire risks if there is a need for smoking on set. The best way to prevent fire hazards from becoming high risk is to have regular liaison meetings between set designers, production managers, lighting crew, wardrobe and visual effects where potential for fire can be identified beforehand.

Identifying potential fire risks in advance is essential if temporary locations or venues are designed to accommodate an audience. The concern for public fire safety is critical and any temporary audience venues must apply for a fire inspection and hold a temporary fire certificate.

Architects, engineers, set designers and scaffolding contractors must comply with the regulations and design fire safety features in from the start. The best guide to the regulations for temporary venues is called *A Guide to Fire Precautions in Existing Places of Entertainment and Like Places* (HMSO, 1990, ISBN 0-11-340907-9). If you are going to film on a temporary set or stage it is worth reading this first.

Any fire risk in temporary venues must be controlled, separated and contained. Fire and smoke detectors must be installed along with a proper fire alarm signal. The provision of an emergency water supply separated from normal water supplies must be available. The biggest fire risk in temporary locations is access, design and safety. All locations must be designed with adequate means of escape in the event of fire. All fire doors should open outwards.

The size of fire doors and the width of fire escape corridors and pathways must be adequate for the number of people going to need them. The escape routes must be properly lit and marked. Fire escapes must be able to hold the weight of the maximum number of people who need to use them. Never design fire escapes or exits to run into other hazards such as blind alleys, vehicle access areas, roads, water and sudden drops. Make sure rubbish and debris are not stored in or adjacent to fire exits. No smoking signs must be put up and sand buckets and fire-proof bins provided. Fire exits and gangways should be regularly checked for obstructions and repairs.

Emergency access for fire fighting should be provided and clearly marked. These should be separate from emergency exit points so that in the case of an emergency incoming fire fighting vehicles have swift and easy access to fight the fire rather than fighting against escaping people. They should be kept separate and only used for emergencies. Make sure nobody can park in fire emergency assembly points, access roads or behind fire exits and emergency water hydrant locations.

Remember all emergency precautions are rendered useless if the fire fighting services cannot get in and those working in the location cannot get out. Fire precautions must be built in from the beginning and not as an afterthought. This is particularly necessary in the use of fire-proof construction materials and the safe supply of electricity and water. Stop valves must be installed for chemicals, fuel and gas.

Safety signs and lighting must be included along with the safe design and erection of scaffolding towers, sets and temporary rostra. This means that extra vigilance should be paid to fire risks when we shoot on temporary locations. Any fire risks should be identified in the planning stage and fire precautions built in from the start as part of the fire risk assessment plan.

The human factor as a fire hazard

The other factor which is so dangerous within film and broadcasting activity is the fluctuating number of people in a building or on location. As pointed out earlier, a requirement of the regulations is to know the maximum number of people present when assessing fire risks and the level of fire precautions necessary. In most work situations this is fairly easy as the maximum number of people in an office or factory remains pretty constant during working hours.

The working level on any film or television production however, can vary dramatically with the need for different numbers of actors, technicians and support staff. If the number of people working on a production increases, for example to shoot a crowd scene, then a fresh fire risk assessment must be made as the original one for a smaller number will be rendered invalid.

Producers should always be aware of the safe working numbers for studios and other locations and make extra fire precautions, paying particular attention to the number, size and location of fire exits and gangways. Fluctuating numbers of people involved during a production also means that you have many people who will be only acting a small part or be working on short-term contracts. Therefore they may not have been on set before and will not have much time to become acquainted with the fire emergency procedures and escape routes.

Freelance presenters or contributors may be unfamiliar with your building and location. Therefore special care must be taken to ensure that they are familiar with all fire fighting precautions before coming onto the site by sending them a copy of the fire precautions and procedures in advance with their contract.

The other human factor in film and television is the fire risks presented by audiences. The public are invited to witness production activity and to contribute to it. So producers must never exceed maximum studio numbers or invite too many people into a confined building. Entry should be by ticket to control numbers, and names should be checked upon entry and exit so that in the event of a fire a proper head count can be made.

The public audience will also be unfamiliar with the building and must be briefed on fire precautions, fire signals and the quickest means of evacuation. This should be provided on a laminated card when entering the building and reinforced by a briefing from the senior studio floor manager. Floor management staff, audience, stewards and marshals should all be trained in the safe and proper use of fire extinguishers and the fire evacuation procedures for audiences and the public. This should include how to deal with the needs of special individuals in an emergency.

Care should be taken if the audience has significant numbers of young, disabled or elderly members as this increases the risk factor in the event of a fire. Therefore proper crowd management and accommodation should always be provided for audiences and identified in the fire risk assessment plan.

Programmes such as *London's Burning* have deliberate fire hazards as an integral part of the programme content. Never use members of the public or untrained persons for fire scenes or live fire effects.

A production called 'The Priest and the Pirate' tried to use a bus driver to perform a fire eating stunt. Needless to say he was untrained and was badly burned. Afterwards the producers discovered that he had never done it before. The moral of the story is never play with fire. Any serious accidents or injuries caused by fire should be notified to the HSE under the Reporting of Injuries, Diseases and Dangerous Occurrences Regulations 1995 (RIDDOR) and the local fire authority.

Use a pyrotechnic supervisor and trained fire eaters for fire stunts. The stunts should be properly supervised and only carried out by a BECTU pyrotechnic card holder. Always check their credentials and get the advice of the local fire service or a television fire stunt expert. As a courtesy, inform the local fire authority about any stunts or effects which use inflammable or dangerous substances. This is to avoid confusion with a real fire. For dangerous work request a fire tender to stand by as a precaution. This will be a request for a special service and a charge will be made.

A health and safety method statement should be produced to deal with any assessed fire risk in base buildings, third party premises and temporary locations. This should lay out exactly what procedure to follow for any identified fire hazard and all staff, contractors or members of the public must be informed of its requirements. Any risk in productions from the use of fire or fire effects must be identified before any filming activity is undertaken to ensure it is carried out safely.

Further reading

J. F. Whitfield, *A Guide to the 16th edition IEE Wiring Regulations*, EPA, Press 1991 (Pocket Reference).

J. F. Whitfield, *A Guide to Electrical Safety at Work*, 1992, EPA Press.

Fire Safety: An Employer's Guide, HMSO, 1999, ISBN 0-11-341229-0.

Fire Safety – An Employer's Guide, HMSO, 1999, ISBN 0-11-341229-0.

Fire Precautions in the Workplace: Information for Employers about the Fire Precautions (Workplace) Regulations 1997, HMSO, ISBN 0-11-341169-3.

A Guide to Fire Precautions in Existing Places of Entertainment and Like Places, HMSO, 1990, ISBN 0-11-340907-9.

A Guide to Health, Safety and Welfare at Pop Concerts and Similar Events, HMSO, ISBN 0-11-341072-7.

Approved Document B: The Building Regulations 1991 – Fire Safety, HMSO, ISBN 0-11-752313-5.

John Ridley, *Safety at Work*, 4th edition, pp. 524–73, Butterworth-Heinemann, ISBN 0-7506-0746-7.

T. E. Marks, *Handbook on the Electricity at Work Regulations*, 2nd edition, 1994, William Ernest.

A. Smith, *The Handbook of Electrical Installation Practice*, 1996, Blackwell.

Fire Prevention Magazine, Fire Protection Association journal.

The Loss Prevention Council publishes many excellent detailed guides on all aspects of fire safety in the *Library of Fire Safety:*

- *Volume 1: Fire Safety Handbook*
- *Volume 2: Fire and Hazardous Substances*
- *Volume 3: Fire and Buildings*
- *Volume 4: The Management of Fire Safety*

Classification of Materials and Goods, CAE2, 1996.

Fire Protection of Stores Containing Hazardous Substances, CEA1, 1996.

Fire Risk Assessment – A Guide For Employers, FSB22, 1997.

Fire Safety Log Book, LB1, 1996.

Storage, Use and Handling of Common Industrial Gases in Cylinders (excluding LPG) RC8/1992.

Storage and Use of Flammable Liquids, RC20, 1990.

The following items are available from the Loss Prevention Council, Melrose Avenue, Borehamwood, Hertfordshire WD6 2BJ, Tel: 0181–207–2345.

- The Loss Prevention Council's List of Approved Fire and Security Products and Services 1998, Ref. APS98.
- *Guide to Fire Safety Signs*, Ian Jerome, FPA.
- The Loss Prevention Council Library of Fire Safety, Volume 4.

Fire videos available from John Burder Films, 7 Saltcoates Rd, London W4 1AR, Tel: 0181–995–0547: (1) The New Fire Extinguishers, (2) Fire at Work, (3) Extinguishing Fires in the Workplace.

Contact organizations

British Approvals for Fire Equipment and British Fire Protection
Systems Association (BFPSA)
48a Eden St, Kingston upon Thames, Surrey KT1 1EE
Tel: 0181–541–1950
Tel: 0181–549–5855 (BFPSA)

Chief and Assistant Fire Officers' Association
10–11 Pebble Close, Amington, Tamworth, Staffordshire B77 4RD
Tel: 01827–61516

Chubb Training Department
Chubb Fire Ltd, Chubb House, Sunbury on Thames, Middx TW16 7AR
Tel: 01932–77681

Fire Extinguishing Trades Association
48a Eden St, Kingston upon Thames, Surrey KT1 1EE
Tel: 0181–549–8839

Fire Protection Association
Melrose Avenue, Borehamwood, Hertfordshire WD6 2BJ
Tel: 0181–207–2345

Fire Research Station
Building Research Establishment, Garston, Watford WD2 7JR
Tel: 01923–894040

Fire Services College
Moreton in the Marsh, Gloucestershire GL56 0RH
Tel: 01608–650831

Institute of Fire Safety
PO Box 687, Croydon CR9 5DD
Tel: 0181–654–2582

Institution of Fire Engineers
148 Upper New Walk, Leicester LE1 7QB
Tel: 0116–255–3654

Hazard 18: Firearms and weapons

Ross Kemp shot. Star's lucky escape in gun drama on set.

The Sun, 29 October 1999, p. 1

The legislation

The Firearms Act 1968
The Firearms (Amendment) Act 1997
The Control of the Acquisition and Possession of Weapons EC Directive 91/477/EEC
The Control of Explosives Regulations 1991
The Classification and Labelling of Explosives Regulations 1983
The Road Traffic (Carriage of Dangerous Substances in Packages etc.) Regulations 1986

The risks

- being shot
- simulated action being mistaken for real crime
- a fake gun being mistaken for a real gun
- inexperience/lack of planning and supervision
- explosion of ammunition
- misuse of blanks

Those most at risk

Anybody on set/armourer/members of the public.

The safe use and security of firearms and weapons on a production or set should always be the responsibility of a supervising armourer. If the use of any weapon is contemplated in a production then the producer must identify this risk and use a qualified armourer to undertake a proper assessment before proceeding. A list of armourers may be obtained from BECTU's special effects grading scheme. Do not try and use ex-service personnel with no experience of film work.

The supervising armourer should be involved in the production planning from the script stage. They source, select and prepare any weapons including the correct ammunition. They also deal with any licensing requirements and liaise with production staff and actors. In the case of overseas productions they must obtain an export licence and a European firearms pass. Armourers also pack the weapons, arrange security, arrange airfreight packing and obtain an end user certificate. They will also liaise with local customs and security forces.

Note that under section 6 of the Health and Safety at Work Act comes a duty to make sure that any substance or effect has been tested for safety first and manufactured to avoid risks. As armourers often design and supply their own effects, the obligations under section 6 should be read in conjunction with this chapter.

The armourer or owner of the firearm should possess a current firearms certificate (section 1 for rifles and section 2 for shotguns) and have the correct insurance. The film industry has special status in firearms legislation so that a person taking part in the production of a film is allowed to hold a firearm without having a firearms certificate. However the supervising armourer must apply for and possess a current firearms licence for that type of gun. These last for five years.

The holder of a shotgun licence can hold multiple weapons once the reason to possess them has been granted. But for a section 1 weapon a separate application must be made for each new weapon unless they are approved at the original application. You can't just add more weapons on to a single licence.

A current firearms certificate is also needed for any gun or replica which, with conversion or modification, is capable of firing bullets. Replicas and totally disabled guns are exempt and do not require a licence. Blank ammunition does not require a certificate. But the possession of live ammunition does require a special firearms licence. The safe storage of ammunition (apart from shotguns) should be made with advice from the local police firearms officer.

Prohibited weapons such as hand guns and small arms come under section 5. Pump action firearms above .22 calibre are also prohibited weapons under section 5 of the Firearms (Amendment) Act 1997. This means that possession of such weapons are illegal.

A written application for authority to hold any prohibited weapons must be made to the secretary of state at the Home Office who will seek advice from the nearest chief constable of the police authority in which the applicant resides.

This is called an application for authority under section 5 to possess a prohibited weapon. You must apply to the Home Office Firearms and Explosives Section, Operational Policing Policy Unit, 50 Queen Anne's Gates, London SW1H 9AT, Tel: 0171–271–8977. Applications are free at the moment and take at least six weeks.

Productions or individuals who are planning to import weapons and guns into the country must apply for a visitors' firearm permit or a visitors' shotgun permit and possess a European firearms pass issued by the authorities in their home country.

Advice can be obtained from the firearms weapons licensing officer of the nearest police authority. Always notify any use of weapons in advance by writing to the superintendent of the local police and contact the local station to make a CAD entry. Twenty eight days' notice should be made to the firearms licensing officer of the police to get a temporary permit for any location filming involving arms.

Any firearms must have adequate security. Consult the firearm security leaflet published by the Home Office in 1992. All guns must be kept locked in a metal cabinet which is fixed to the floor and the wall. There must be no public access and the room must be alarmed. For any firearms or shotguns in excess of nine the store must be on an alarm that is monitored by a security company.

Any firearms being transported must be stored in a locked metal box fixed to the wall and chassis of the vehicle. This must be concealed and the container must be bolted. Any vehicle which contains a section 5 weapon must be fitted with a monitored alarm and a tracker device.

Prohibited weapons and ammunition should never be left unattended in vehicles during transportation. Similar security arrangements must apply to any store on location.

While on location the arms should be kept locked in a secure compound until they are needed. The box should be kept locked and only the qualified armourer should have the key. The armourer should carry out a risk assessment for their activity and they should supervise any stunt or effect.

The location area should be sealed off during filming with arms and controlled by a permit to work system to control access to the area. All access points should be secure and proper fire-fighting and first aid precautions should be in place.

Never point a loaded gun or blank at anybody and the person carrying out the stunt should have proper head and ear protection and a protective vest or jacket. Dispose of spent cartridges or ammunition safely. Keep all audience and crew to a minimum and if possible use a remote camera to film any firearms activity.

Firearms activity should be designed and managed safely under the direction of a qualified and experienced firearms expert or armourer. All involved should be properly briefed on the procedure and safety precautions in advance in writing backed up by an oral briefing prior to filming. If the stunt is changed then a fresh briefing is required.

Ammunition must be kept separate and secure in the minimum quantity necessary to carry out the stunt.

Figure H18.1　*From* Fast Food © *Vine International Pictures*

Producers should be aware that working with blanks can be just as dangerous. An armourer is still required. This is because an armourer has knowledge of ballistics and the safe distances of firearms. When a blank shell is fired it gives off a hot gas which can burn and the shell travels several feet. Also blanks can give off iron filings at high velocity which can blind and embed themselves under the skin – so in a sequence involving a blank firearm which requires a gun close to an actor then the safety implications are just as important as when dealing with 'live'.

A weapon which has been certified as incapable of firing ammunition is classed as a fake. But producers should be aware that it is an offence to carry or use a fake gun, starting pistol, flare gun or blank ammunition in a public place. So notice should always be made in advance to the police as simulated firearms activity can be mistaken for the real thing – especially the filming of simulated bank robberies, hold-ups and running with a fake firearm.

Simulated firearm or criminal activity has often been mistaken for the real thing by members of the public and police, even on private property. You could end up getting shot if mistaken by the police for a real criminal with a real gun.

It is an offence to brandish a fake firearm in public and producers and directors should be especially sensitive to the public and police reaction after the new gun laws in the wake of the Hungerford and Dunblane tragedies. Advice on the safe use of shotguns and weapons can be obtained from local gun clubs, shooting ranges and the police.

The British Association for Shooting and Conservation publishes its own shotgun safety code and their officers can give you advice.

Documentary and news crews should beware of firearms hazards if filming in volatile areas or while making programmes which may involve contact with people who carry arms such as insurgents, bodyguards, personal protection aides, arms dealers and the military.

Other weapons – including crossbows, historical guns and swords – should always be supplied by a qualified armourer and if possible should be made of plastic rather than metal. Care should be taken to avoid sharp points and edges which can damage eyes and hands. Any sharp surfaces should be blunted and smoothened. Actors should be instructed by an armourer in the safe use of any weapon and large fight scenes should be properly choreographed and controlled by a fight arranger or stunt action co-ordinator who is a full member of the Equity Stunt Register.

Fencing stunt arrangers must be grade 6 silver award from the Amateur Fencing Association in foil, sabre and epee. Any stunts employing weapons on horseback for historical dramas should be co-ordinated by a stunt arranger qualified in horse riding listed in the Equity Stunt Register.

Further reading

The Selection, Installation and Maintenance of Electrical Equipment for the Use in and Around Buildings Containing Explosives, HSE.

An Introduction to the Control of Explosives Regulations, HSE, IND(G)115.

Dangerous Substances – Classified and Authorised Explosives, HSE, 1994, ISBN 0-7176-0772-0.

Dangerous Substances – Classified and Authorised Explosives, Supplement No. 1 (Misc-039), HSE, 1996, ISBN 0-7176-1134-5.

A Guide to the Control of Explosives Regulations 1991, L10, HSE, 1991, ISBN 0-11-885670-7.

The European Firearms Pass, The Home Office Leaflet No. FA9, 1992.

Firearm Security, The Home Office, 1992.

Firearms – Permits for Visitors to Great Britain, Home Office Leaflet No. 12942/A, Home Office, J100191NJ-FA3.

Godfrey Sandys-Winsch BA (Cantab), *Gun Law*, 5th edition, Shaw & Sons, 1990, published in the UK, ISBN 0-7219-0363-0.

P.J. Clarke and J.W. Ellis, *The Law Relating to Firearms*, London: Butterworths, 1981.

Shotgun Safety Code, The British Association for Shooting and Conservation, reprinted 1986.

Contact organizations

The British Association for Shooting and Conservation
Marford Mill, Rossett, Clwyd, Wales LL12 0HL
Tel: 01244–570881

F8 Division
Room 543, The Home Office, 50 Queen Anne's Gate, London
SW1H 9AT
Tel: 0171–273–2343

Home Office Firearms and Explosives Section, Operational Policing
Policy Unit
50 Queen Anne's Gates, London SW1H 9AT
Tel: 0171–271–8977

The Institute of Explosives Engineers
Unit 48, Century Business Park, Hammond Close, Attleborough Fields,
Nuneaton, Warwickshire CV11 6RY
Tel: 01203–350846

The Royal Military College of Science
Cranfield University, Shrivenham, Swindon, Wiltshire CSN6 8LA
Tel: 01793–784455

The Department of Trade and Industry
Export Licensing Branch, Kingsgate House, 66–74 Victoria St, London
SW1E 6SW
Tel: 0171–215–8104

Hazard 19: First aid

The risks

- serious injury
- death
- insufficient training and equipment

First aid can save lives and prevent minor injuries from becoming major ones. First aid can also save lives by the administration of prompt attention if somebody falls ill or has an accident. Any delay can prove fatal but the provision of rapid first aid from a trained person can save life until a doctor, paramedic or ambulance can give assistance.

The Health and Safety (First Aid) Regulations 1981 and the new revised code of practice which came into force on 14 March 1997 requires employers to provide sufficient equipment and trained personnel to enable first aid to be given if employees are injured or fall ill at work.

Regulation 3 states that it is the duty of an employer to make provision for first aid: 'an employer shall provide, or ensure that there are provided, such equipment and facilities as are adequate and appropriate in the circumstances for enabling first aid to be rendered to his employees if they are injured or become ill at work.' and 'an employer shall provide, or ensure that there is provided, such a number of suitable persons as is adequate and appropriate in the circumstances for rendering first aid to his employees if they are injured or become ill at work.'

This means that sufficient first aid personnel and facilities should be available to give immediate assistance to any casualties and to summon an ambulance or other professional help. The extent of the first aid provision depends on the size and nature of the organization. The depth of knowledge and qualification required depends on the circumstances of each workplace. The attendance of a trained unit nurse or qualified paramedic on the set or location is always advisable.

The regulations insist on three things. First, a suitably stocked first aid container available at all places of work. Second, management must designate an appointed person to take charge of first aid operations. Third, management must provide information to employees on first aid arrangements. Producers must see that these regulations are carried out to provide adequate first aid at base sites and on location.

To do this managers and producers should carry out a risk assessment in accordance with the Management of Health and Safety at Work Regulations 1992 and identify those factors which might determine the size, scope and personnel required to cover first aid provision for their operation. Factors to consider would be:

1 The size and scope of the organization.
2 The number of different sites its activities occupy.
3 The number of workers, contractors and public present on the site.
4 The number of workers and contractors who may work away off site or alone for long periods.
5 The different workplace hazards and risks presented by the work.
6 The distance of the site or activity from immediate medical care and communication.

However a first aid container should always be available at base offices and workshops as well as in vehicles and on location. The location of it should be made known to everybody and it should be properly signed and maintained. The second part of the Health and Safety (Safety Signs and Signals) Regulations 1996 insist that all first aid safety signs must contain a symbol from December 1998. Text-only first aid safety signs should be replaced by this date. So first aid containers must be identified by a white cross on a green background.

The first aid container should be suitable for location, the type of risks involved and the number of people at risk. (Guidance Note 31 of the regulations suggest the minimum contents for a basic first aid container and Guidance Note 37 suggests the minimum for a travelling first-aid container.)

Producers should take into account the size of any audience, performers and actors as well as crew when assessing the size and nature of the first aid containers which need to be provided. If necessary they should seek advice from a competent supplier or from recognized first aid organizations.

Factors which would determine different first aid containers would include anybody working alone, anybody working with hazardous tools and chemicals, anybody working with electricity and anybody working in remote locations away from immediate emergency aid and facilities. In remote areas always inform the nearest mountain rescue service and contact the coastguard and air/sea rescue service. For an air ambulance these are operated by individual health trusts on lease from medical aviation services who can provide helicopter-based medical cover.

The need for these should be identified on a first aid risk assessment and the proper kit provided. Producers should also make sure that anybody working alone or at night still has access to the first aid container and has an emergency lone worker alarm or means of alerting others.

To comply with their responsibilities to train and provide first aid cover for staff, producers and managers must nominate an appointed person. An appointed person is someone appointed by an employer to take charge of an emergency first aid situation by phoning the emergency services. They are not necessarily a trained first aider so should not render first aid. In the absence of a trained first aider they may render emergency first aid only if they are properly trained to do so. Producers and managers should make sure that there is an appointed person for each location and building. They should also have one for each separate shift to maintain cover by an appointed person at all hours of work.

Obviously a small organization with comparatively low health and safety risks may not need a first aider but will need an appointed person. However, where the workforce is large or the work high risk then the number of appropriate first aiders and appointed people would increase. In this sense small film and TV businesses are more high risk than an office or a newsagent's on account of the risky nature of the work they do. This is especially true of factual film companies who might film in dangerous locations and fiction film companies where a lot of lighting, and pyrotechnics are used.

Where conditions of work are identified as dangerous – for example, working with heavy plant, dangerous machinery, electricity or chemicals – the first aid provision must be more comprehensive. First aid cover must be continuous (including holiday cover) and any first aiders must be trained in special procedures for the higher level of risk. A proper first aid room and more comprehensive facilities must be available and the

---

First-aid competencies

On completion of training successful candidates need to be able to apply the following competencies:

(a) the ability to act safely, promptly and effectively when an emergency occurs at work;

(b) the ability to administer cardio-pulmonary resuscitation (CPR) promptly and effectively;

(c) the ability to administer first aid safely, promptly and effectively to a casualty who is unconscious;

(d) the ability to administer first aid safely, promptly and effectively to a casualty who is wounded or bleeding;

(e) the ability to administer first aid safely, promptly and effectively to a casualty who:
   - has been burned or scalded;
   - is suffering from an injury to bones, muscles or joints;
   - is suffering from shock;
   - has an eye injury;
   - may be poisoned;
   - has been overcome by gas or fumes;

(f) the ability to transport a casualty safely as required by the circumstances of the workplace;

(g) the ability to recognise common major illnesses and take appropriate action;

(h) the ability to recognise minor illnesses and take appropriate action;

(i) the ability to maintain simple factual records and provide written information to a doctor or hospital if required.

Students will also be required to demonstrate knowledge and understanding of the principles of first aid at work, in particular of:

(a) the importance of personal hygiene in first-aid procedures;

(b) the legal framework for first-aid provision at work;

(c) the use of first-aid equipment provided in the workplace;

(d) the role of the first aider in emergency procedures.

Figure H19.1 *First aid competencies list.* © *HSE*

local emergency services informed of any dangerous processes, substances or chemicals present or introduced on site.

All base and location premises must have proper green safety signs (conforming to the Health and Safety (Safety Signs and Signals) Regulations 1996) giving details of the appointed person, how to contact them and emergency numbers to contact. The giving of proper first aid information is a requirement under the regulations and all staff should be provided with an emergency data sheet and a copy of the company's

Table 1 Suggested numbers of first-aid personnel to be available at all times people are at work, based on assessments of risk and number of workers. Where there are special circumstances, such as remoteness from emergency medical services, shiftwork, or sites with several separate buildings, there may need to be more first-aid personnel than set out below. Increased provision will be necessary to cover for absences.

Category of risk	Numbers employed at any location	Suggested number of first-aid personnel
Lower risk e.g. shops, offices, libraries	Fewer than 50	At least one appointed person
	50–100	At least one first aider
	More than 100	One additional first aider for every 100 employed
Medium risk e.g. light engineering and assembly work, food processing, warehousing	Fewer than 20	At least one appointed person
	20–100	At least one first aider for every 50 employed (or part thereof)
	More than 100	One additional first aider for every 100 employed
Higher risk e.g. most construction, slaughterhouse, chemical manufacture, extensive work with dangerous machinery or sharp instruments	Fewer than 5	At least one appointed person
	5–50	At least one first aider
	More than 50	One additional first aider for every 50 employed
	Where there are hazards for which additional first-aid skills are necessary	In addition, at least one first aider trained in the specific emergency action

Qualifications and training. Before taking up first-aid duties, a first aider must hold a valid certificate of competence in first aid at work, issued by an organization whose training and qualifications are approved by HSE. Information on local organizations offering training is available from HSE offices

Figure H19.1 *Continued*

health and safety rules. Any new employees or contract workers should be given a copy and any necessary information before coming on site and be given a proper induction to emergency procedures, first aid and health and safety policy.

Any premises where ten people or more at the same time are employed must keep an accident book under regulation 25 Social Security (Claims and Payments) Regulations 1979 which is kept for three years and any serious accident which requires hospital treatment or results in death or

Assessment of first-aid needs checklist

The minimum first-aid provision for each work site is:

● a suitably stocked first-aid container;
● a person appointed to take charge of first-aid arrangements;
● information for employees on first-aid arrangements.

This checklist will help you assess whether you need to make any additional provision.

Aspects to consider	Impact on first-aid provision
1 What are the risks of injury and ill health arising from the work as identified in your risk assessment?	If the risks are significant you may need to employ first aiders.
2 Are there any specific risks, e.g. working with: – hazardous substances; – dangerous tools; – dangerous machinery; – dangerous loads or animals?	You will need to consider: – specific training for first aiders; – extra first-aid equipment; – precise siting of first-aid equipment; – informing emergency services; – first-aid room.
3 Are there parts of your establishment where different levels of risk can be identified (e.g. in a university with research laboratories)?	You will probably need to make different levels of provision in different parts of the establishment.
4 Are large numbers of people employed on site?	You may need to employ first aiders to deal with the higher probability of an accident.
5 What is your record of accidents and cases of ill health? What type are they and where did they happen?	You may need to: – locate your provision in certain areas; – review the contents of the first-aid box.
6 Are there inexperienced workers on site, or employees with disabilities or special health problems?	You will need to consider: – special equipment; – local siting of equipment.
7 Are the premises spread out, e.g. are there several buildings on the site or multi-floor buildings?	You will need to consider provision in each building or on several floors.
8 Is there shiftwork or out-of-hours working?	Remember that there needs to be first-aid provision at all times people are at work.

Figure H19.2   *First aid needs check list. © HSE*

Aspects to consider	Impact on first-aid provision
9 Is your workplace remote from emergency medical services?	You will need to: – inform local medical services of your location; – consider special arrangements with the emergency services.
10 Do you have employees who travel a lot or work alone?	You will need to: – consider issuing personal first-aid kits and training staff in their use; – consider issuing personal communicators to employees.
11 Do any of your employees work at sites occupied by other employers?	You will need to make arrangements with the other site occupiers.
12 Do you have any work experience trainees?	Remember that your first-aid provision must cover them.
13 Do members of the public visit your premises?	You have no legal responsibilities for non-employees, but HSE strongly recommends you include them in your first-aid provision.
14 Do you have employees with reading or language difficulties?	You will need to make special arrangements to give them first-aid information.

Don't forget that first aiders and appointed persons take leave and are often absent from the premises for other reasons. You must appoint sufficient people to cover these absences to enable first-aid personnel to be available at all times people are at work.

What should the first-aid box or kit contain?

All establishments will need at least one first-aid box which should contain a sufficient quantity of suitable first-aid materials and nothing else.

In most cases these will be:

Item	First-aid boxes	Travelling first-aid kits
*Guidance leaflet *First aid at Work* (INDG4)	1	1
Individually wrapped sterile adhesive dressings (assorted sizes)	20	6

Figure H19.2 *Continued*

Item	First-aid boxes	Travelling first-aid kits
Sterile eye pads, with attachment	2	
Individually wrapped triangular bandages	6	2
Safety pins	6	2
Medium sized individually wrapped sterile unmedicated wound dressings (approx 10 cm × 8 cm)	6	
Large sterile individually wrapped unmedicated wound dressings (approx 13 cm × 9 cm)	2	1
Extra large sterile individually wrapped unmedicated wound dressings (approx 28 cm × 17.5 cm)	3	
Individually wrapped moist cleaning wipes (suggested minimum number)		6

* Available from HSE Books

Where tap water is not readily available for eye irrigation sterile water or sterile normal saline in sealed disposable containers should be provided. Each container should hold at least 300 ml and at least 900 ml should be provided.

FIRST-AID ROOMS

Do I need a first-aid room?

If you work in a high-risk industry, such as shipbuilding, chemical industries or large-scale construction, you should provide a suitably staffed and equipped first-aid room. The need for a first-aid room does not depend solely on the number of employees.

RECORDS

What records should a first-aider keep?

First-aiders should record all the cases they treat. Each record should include at least the name of the patient, date, place, time and circumstances of the accident and details of injury suffered and treatment given. The records should be kept in a suitable place, and should be readily available.

A written account should also be kept of first-aiders' certification dates, and the dates of additional, specific or refresher training.

Figure H19.2   *Continued*

serious injury involving an absence from work over three days must be reported under the Reporting of Injuries, Diseases and Dangerous Occurrences Regulations 1985.

Producers and managers must also make sure that there is a trained first aider. A first aider is someone who holds a current competency and training certificate in first aid skills from an approved training organization such as St John Ambulance. The certificate is valid for three years. The first aider is appointed by the employer to administer first aid at work. Separate specialists may be necessary for particularly hazardous work such as diving, electricity and chemicals.

Factors which determine the choice of an appropriate person to have as a first aider would be reliability, disposition and communication skills, adaptability and willingness to learn new techniques and training. The ability to prioritize and cope with the stressful and physically demanding emergency procedures is also important.

Courses can last anything from four hours to four days but managers must ensure that at least one first aider is on site or location at all working hours. This means that anyone working shifts, in small teams or by themselves must be trained as first aiders as they will be working outside or away from normal cover or first aid provision. On large sets or locations it is usually sensible to have a company nurse and doctor, with trained first aiders in each major section to provide a large trained permanent cover. Managers might also need to provide their trained first aiders with medical malpractice insurance, especially if they are dealing with big name stars or specialists.

Managers must also identify any group or individuals who may be at special risk and require specialist training or assistance such as elderly or young contributors, crews working on diving projects, climbing or caving in remote areas or filming riot situations. They should also provide contact information and communication for emergency rescue services, mountain rescue, lifeboat and air ambulance in case of a medical emergency in remote areas or a car crash.

Base managers and production managers should maintain an emergency contact sheet with phone numbers of local hospitals and the company doctor. It would be wise to also have on file for all staff, actors, subcontractors and artists details of NI number, NHS number, blood group, details of their doctor and information on any special medical conditions or medication. This is so that, in an emergency, accident or hospital situation, the staff on the scene can get access to medical records quickly and any vital information which could affect their treatment and type of drugs to use. Specialist cover will also be required if filming overseas.

Managers and producers should also be aware of the special risks for any staff who may be pregnant, or suffer from asthma or diabetes. Care should be taken to avoid them undertaking any heavy manual handling, sustained operation of VDUs, prolonged physical exertion or work involving moving or dangerous machinery. Staff who suffer from asthma should not be made to work in hot, dusty or confined situations. Similarly managers should identify anyone who suffers from claustrophobia, fear of heights, water or flying and not put them in that situation.

Managers and producers should also identify any special dietary requirements for medical, personal or religious reasons which may be provided in the location or base catering which must conform to food hygiene and environmental health regulations to prevent ill health or food poisoning. Lastly any programme with simulated emergency or medical content should take special care to inform the local police and real emergency services before filming in a public place to avoid confusion in the minds of the public with the real thing.

Further reading

The Health and Safety (First Aid at Work) Regulations 1981, Approved Code of Practice, HSE, ISBN 0-7176-1050-0.

Basic Anatomy – The Visual Dictionary of the Human Body, Dorling Kindersley, 1991, ISBN 0-8631-8700-5.

First Aid Manual, Dorling Kindersley, St John Ambulance and The British Red Cross Society, 1997, ISBN 0-7513-0399-2.

The following titles are available from Emergency Response Publications, 5 Shelly Court, South Zeal, Okehampton, Devon EX20 2PT, Tel: 01837–840102:

- A.C. Bronstein and L. Currance, *Emergency Care for Hazardous Materials Exposure*, 2nd edition, 1994, Code EME-8.
- Ian Greaves, Tim Hodgetts and Keith Porter, *Emergency Care, A Textbook for Paramedics*, Saunders, 1997, ISBN 0-7020-1975-5.
- *The Authorised First Aid Manual*, 7th edition, ISBN 0-7020-2345-0.

First Aid Training and Qualifications for the Purposes of the Health and Safety (First Aid) Regulations 1981, HSE, ISBN 0-7176-1347-X.

First Aid at Work – Your Questions Answered, HSE, IND(G)214L.

Basic Advice on First Aid at Work, HSE, IND(G)215L.

Health Information for Overseas Travel, HMSO, 1999 edition, ISBN 0-11-32-1833-8.

International Travel and Health, World Health Organisation, ISBN 92-4-158024-0.

Stuart A. Gray, *The First Aider's Pocket Companion*, Altman Books, 1995, ISBN 1-86036-000-9.

Ian Greaves, Peter Dyer and Keith Porter, *The Handbook of Immediate Care*, ISBN 0-7020-1881-3.

The Health Education Authority, Book Catalogue 1998, ISBN 0-7521-1125-6.

First Aid – The All Colour Guide to First Aid and Family Health, Marshall Cavendish.

The titles below are available from Loss Prevention Council, Melrose Avenue, Borehamwood, Hertfordshire, WD6 2BJ, Tel: 0181–207–2345.

- Infectious Diseases at Work, HSE12, 1994.
- Occupational Asthma, HSE13, 1995.

P.J. Teddy and P. Anslow, *The Pocket Guide to Head Injuries*, Gower Medical Publishing, 1999, ISBN 0-397-44569-5.
The Ship's Captain's Medical Guide, 22nd edition, 1999 (revised annually), Marine and Coastguard Agency, HMSO ISBN 0-11-551658-1.

Contact organizations

Ambulance Service Association
Room 519, Eileen House, 80–94 Newington Causeway, London SE1 6EF
Tel: 0171–972–2939

Association of Broadcasting Doctors
Sinalthorpe House, Ely, Cambridgeshire CB7 4SG
Tel: 01353–688456 (Peter Petts)

British Medical Association
BMA House, Tavistock Square, London WC1H 9JP
Tel: 0171–387–4499

The British Red Cross
9 Grovesnor Crescent, London SW1X 7EJ
Tel: 0171–235–5454

St John Ambulance
1 Grovesnor Crescent, London SW1X 7EF
Tel: 0171–235–5231

Health Education Authority
Trevelyan House, 30 Great Peter St, London SW1P 2HW
Tel: 0171–222–5300

Institute of Occupational Medicine
8 Roxburgh Place, Edinburgh EH8 9SU
Tel: 0131–667–4131

Loss Prevention Council
Melrose Avenue, Borehamwood, Hertfordshire WD6 2BJ
Tel: 0181–207–2345

Medical Indemnity Register
PO Box 838, London SW18 1PB
Tel: 0181–874–0403 (training and insurance)

Paramedic Rescue Services
Freepost (KT4337), West Molesey, Surrey KT8 2BR
Tel: 0181–642–7405

The Royal College of Nursing
20 Cavendish Square, London W1M 0AB
Tel: 0171–409–3333

The Royal Society of Health
38a St George's Drive, London SW1V 4BH
Tel: 0171–630–0121

The Society of Occupational Medicine
6 St Andrews Place, Regents Park, London NW1 4LB
Tel: 0171–486–2641

Hazard 20: Flying and airports

In June 1994 the actor Alan Tall was thrown from a Clydesdale horse during the filming of *Braveheart* after an RAF Tornado roared over the Glen Nevis film set. He was thrown from the horse which landed on top of him resulting in a broken pelvis.

Sunday Mail, 9 October 1994

In March 1983 a Yorkshire Television camera crew were killed when their Squirrel helicopter hit the mast of a ship while low flying over the River Humber.

Hull Daily Mail, 17 March 1983

On February 6th 1993 a stuntman plunged to his death. Ted Tipping fell thousands of feet into woods after his parachute failed to open during the stunt performed for the BBC 1 series 999.

The Times, 6 February 1993

On July 13th 1997 a nine year old boy was killed and three others injured when a Bell Jet Ranger helicopter hired by the TV charity Airborne crashed. It caught a wire fence during take-off and turned over bursting into flames.

The Sun, 14 July 1997

The legislation

The Air Navigation Order (General) Regulations 1993
The Civil Aviation Authority Air Navigation (No. 2) Order 1995
The Civil Aviation Act 1982
The Aviation Security Act 1982
The Licensing of Air Carriers Regulations 1992
The Rules of the Air Regulations 1996

The risks

- aerial stunts
- airports
- unsecured equipment
- unqualified air crew
- helicopter rotor blades
- low flying
- noise
- the weather

Those at risk

Air crew, animals, film crew, ground crew, the public.

Helicopters and plane licensing

Each aerial situation is different and so no summary can make up for the selection of an aviation company with many years' experience in filming work. Check with the CAA or look in Kay's *UK Production Manual 1999*. Producers should take care in their choice of aircraft operator as the quality of the pilot and the aircraft will rest on this decision. Always choose an aircraft operator who specializes in film and television work as this can save time and money. Since the choice of pilot and suitability of the aircraft is the responsibility of the contracted aircraft operator the importance of making the right choice cannot be stressed too much. Do not attempt to employ a private pilot or an inexperienced outfit to save money. This is illegal and is a false economy.

Light aircraft, charter aircraft and helicopters are used in film work for a variety of functions – for example to provide aerial camera mounts for aerial shots and as action vehicles. They can also be used for location finding, transport to locations and stunt work. Any aircraft operated for hire or reward is regulated by the CAA and must hold an aircraft operators certificate. This means that the operator must comply with CAA safety standards in the interest of the hirer.

Bona fide aircraft operators are properly insured, employ qualified pilots and possess the appropriate aircraft. They can advise you on the correct power and flexibility of the aircraft which you need for the job. They will also advise you on the type of camera, the number of crew you will need and the choice of camera mounts appropriate for your shoot.

In order to do this accurately you must brief your operator and pilot on what you intend to do so that they can give proper advice and draw up a risk assessment for the whole operation. Advance notice is essential and don't change your plans at the last minute unless this is essential for safe operation. If you do change your plans make sure that all those who are likely to be affected are notified and any crew are properly briefed before proceeding.

This information will then be made into a briefing plan for anyone involved in the filming. Do not change this plan once it has been agreed as your life may depend on it. Always provide the aircraft operator and pilot with a detailed shot list and a list of any equipment which you want to carry on the aircraft.

The operator and pilot will be looking at factors such as the weight of the equipment versus the power and capacity of the aircraft. They also need to know that you are not going to introduce any dangerous substances on to the plane such as pressurized containers, explosives or cylinders. They must check your communication equipment to make sure that it is CAA approved and on the correct frequency. This should not interfere with any equipment used by the aircraft or air-traffic control. Only one set of equipment is allowed. Certain types of radio equipment will not be allowed on aircraft. Check first. Mobile phones are not permitted under any circumstances on aircraft. The operator and pilot must approve of any equipment you plan to use. They must be informed if you are planning any stunts, low flying, parachuting or dropping anything from the plane onto the ground. Once they know these factors then a detailed risk assessment can be drawn up for your shoot.

The safety of aircraft in Great Britain is the responsibility of the Civil Aviation Authority who license aircraft operators and pilots.

The three major safety documents which you should check concern the aircraft operator, the plane and the pilot. Aircraft operators require a valid air operators certificate issued by the CAA which is always reviewed on a regular basis. Aircraft operators must also hold proper passenger liability insurance. Ask for a copy of their insurance certificate.

The aircraft requires an air worthiness certificate for the type of work which you require. There must also be adequate fire and first aid precautions in the plane or helicopter, especially if the aircraft is flying over water when extra safety regulations apply.

CAA air worthiness for planes and operators divides into four types:

(a) public transport – all commercial flying;
(b) aerial work – no passengers;
(c) private – no fee paying passengers;
(d) special permit.

Note that film work is considered fee paying so only public transport licensed aircraft are allowed for film and television work where passengers are carried such as the film crew. Anybody other than the air crew is legally considered as a passenger and they would only be covered by the public transport operators insurance. However for remote shots with only a flying crew, category b aircraft can be used.

Pilots must pass a strict medical examination and hold a valid CAA pilot's medical certificate, without which they cannot fly. This is the most important document to ask for as the failure of the medical will invalidate any pilot's licence. The strictness of the medical increases with the age of the pilot, the weight of the plane and the type of licence they hold. The medical certificate is reviewed from every 6 months to 2 years depending on these factors.

Pilots must also be trained in first aid. Production managers should also check the medical history and condition for anybody who is intending to fly for special conditions such as blood pressure or vertigo. The production company should also check with its own insurance brokers to obtain the correct cover for any employees, contractors and equipment being used in any aerial filming.

Check that your pilot is experienced in film work by asking for past job sheets. The pilot must also hold a CAA pilot's licence valid from ten years in the case of an ATPL to unrestricted in the case of a PPL. There are several types of pilot's licence:

CPLA – unrestricted commercial pilot's licence aircraft
CPLH – unrestricted commercial pilot's licence helicopters
PPLA – private pilot's licence aircraft
PPLH – private pilot's licence helicopters
BCPL – commercial pilot's licence
ATPLA – airline transport pilot's licence aircraft
ATPLH – airline transport pilot's licence helicopters.

Any aerial work undertaken as carriage for value consideration (i.e. for money!) means that the pilot must hold a valid unrestricted professional licence. For film work this means the pilot must hold a valid CPL or ATPL licence for either helicopters or a plane.

A person holding a private pilot's licence is forbidden to fly if the purpose is to collect material for commercial work such as film and television.

Requirement for pilot's briefing

The factors which pilots will brief you on before deciding if it is safe to fly are the weather, the wind speed and the visibility.

Figure H20.1   *Helicopter filming. © Castle Air Ltd*

They must also take extra precautions if the film work involves flying over water. If it does then helicopters should usually be twin engine. As single-engine helicopter operations over water for prolonged periods are very restricted, when flying over water everybody must wear life-jackets and appropriate life rafts should be carried. The aircraft or helicopter should be fitted with floats and buoyancy aids.

The pilots will also check any take-off and landing restrictions at your departure point and destination. Pilots will also check for any airspace requirements and flying restrictions from the Ministry of Defence. This is particularly important if you are planning to undertake low level flying in an aircraft or helicopter. Low level flying is anything below 1500 ft and your operator and pilot must have a special exemption to do so from the CAA. The pilot will need to take special precautions to avoid low level sorties from military aircraft and it is worth asking if a check has been made with the Royal Air Force to make sure.

Before you take off, the pilot must brief the air crew and passengers of any safety procedures and the emergency drill. This is a legal requirement under CAA regulations and the briefing takes the form of a list of features to watch out for and regulations which you must obey.

These will be printed on passenger briefing cards and a film industry safety sheet, backed up by a verbal briefing from the pilot. This will include information about communications, any hand signals and the location of lights, doors, safety belts and emergency exits.

Helicopter Safety Procedures:

1. Communication between ground and air shall be established at all times during the operation of the helicopter, using **one ground contact**.
2. The individual attached to the helicopter support truck shall be designated as the person to supervise safety around the helicopter.
3. No smoking within 50 feet of the helicopter.
4. Unless you are needed – remain at least 50 feet away from the helicopter.
5. Exercise extreme caution when working around helicopter – especially when helicopter engine is running. Leave and approach the helicopter from the front – with caution. At all times, keep your eyes and head forward.
6. Avoid rear and tail sections of helicopter at all times.
7. **Never** walk under tail section of helicopter.
8. Do not extend any equipment vertically into rotor blades – such as cameras, lights, sound booms, etc.
9. Carry all equipment parallel to ground within 50 feet of helicopter.
10. Pilots are the authorities concerning all helicopter operations – if you have questions, ask them.
11. **Never**, under any circumstances, throw anything such as grip tape, clothing, paper, etc. around the helicopter – whether it is running or not.
12. The landing area should be cleared of debris and, where necessary, wet down.
13. Protect your eyes as well as your equipment when helicopter is landing and taking off.
14. Plot plans and graphics will be prepared to locate landing area, intended flight paths, designated emergency landing sites, and location, as well as types, of explosives or squibs.
15. The pilot in command will have final approval as to aerial traverse and hovering positions of the aircraft.

All the above procedures are intended to conform with applicable laws and governmental regulations and in the event of any conflict, applicable laws and governmental regulations will prevail.

Figure H20.2   *Helicopter safety procedures diagram. © Castle Air Ltd*

Never smoke on an aircraft. Wear a flying suit as protection against the cold and a life-jacket if flying over water.

When approaching an aircraft or helicopter always follow the pilot's briefing and establish eye contact with the pilot before proceeding. Wear high visibility clothing so you can be seen at all times. The safe approach and departure is quite different for planes and helicopters. Approach prop aircraft and planes from the side, jet planes from the rear and helicopters from the front.

Approach or leave a helicopter in a crouched position. Helicopters can be approached rotors running but avoid walking anywhere near the tail rotor. Wear high visibility clothing so you can be seen and shield your eyes by wearing eye protection from any down draught.

Do not approach prop planes or jets until the engines have stopped and you are cleared to board. Avoid walking near the air intakes of jets and beware of jet blast. Wear ear protection if you are working near a prop plane, helicopter or jet.

One of the biggest risks in an aircraft or helicopter is the danger presented by loose equipment – especially in the event of a sudden manoeuvre or turbulence. Store any loose equipment in the safe lockers, especially tapes and batteries. Secure all loose equipment and camera equipment by mounts and safety clips to lines. If stunt flying is involved, particular attention must be paid to packing on board. All batteries, recorders and tapes must be tightly secured and always follow the safety briefing of the pilot.

Secure yourself against falling out and use a seat belt and a safety harness. All winches and chains should be regularly tested and checked for the maximum load you are intending to lift. If necessary employ a specialized winch operator.

Ground safety factors

There are also a number of ground safety factors to consider before filming from the air. The first is the provision of a flat safe landing area which is visible to the pilot. The flatness is crucial to helicopters and prop planes as the rotor blades can hit the ground on a slope or incline.

The size of the site will depend on the helicopter or plane. Helicopters can land in a much smaller space. However, the crucial factor in safe landing site selection is the safe approach and exit.

Location managers and the pilot should identify any adjacent hazards which could affect the safe approach of the aircraft such as tall buildings, sets, scaffold towers, cranes, pylons, masts and chimneys.

They should also beware of any electrical cables and any tall buildings, either in the flight path or on the landing field. Look out for any clusters of birds, either on the runway or adjacent to the landing field. They can be sucked in by air intakes and can fly up when disturbed by aircraft noise.

Access to the landing site should be restricted. For helicopters this should be at least 150 metres. Anybody who is working inside this area must attend the pilot's safety briefing and possess a permit to work. They should wear fluorescent clothing and wear eye and ear protection.

Beware of any loose items that could be affected by the down draught of helicopters and secure them. Keep all tools secured and carry them parallel to the ground. If the ground conditions are dry or loose, the landing area must be damped down. Always use a link engineer on the ground to co-ordinate and communicate between helicopter and the ground crew.

Only essential personnel should be allowed near the landing area. Essential ground support such as an engineer, fuel bowser, communications and fire precautions can be established with an air side permit to work system. Providers of aircraft fire protection services must be CAA licensed. Production managers should watch out for the introduction of boom poles, camera rig, cables, tripods, lighting, cranes, scaffolding and sets anywhere near the operations of an aircraft as these can damage wings or be drawn in by jet blast, prop wash or rotor down wash.

Producers should be aware of the risks caused by the noise of aircraft and helicopter filming operations to animals in nearby fields or those used directly in productions, especially the risk to horses and their riders from low flying.

Low flying and camera mounts

Producers and pilots must assess the risks of low flying over people and public roads. Access should be restricted to those taking part and the flying controlled from the ground by single radio communication.

The minimum flying height will change from rural to an urban location. Single engine helicopters are restricted to 1500 ft in built up areas and confined to the river corridor over central London. Twin-engine helicopters are restricted to 750 ft but your chosen aircraft operator can possess a CAA exemption for low flying down to 200 ft. The pilot will need to take special precautions to avoid low level sorties from military aircraft and it is worth asking if a check has been made with the Royal Air Force to make sure. Always choose an operator and pilot who have experience of low flying film work and who have an exemption to undertake low flying work. For CAA low flying exemption, telephone 01293–573540.

Single-engine helicopters cannot fly at night with passengers. In poor visibility they must fly IFR (instrument flying rules) and the pilot's decision about safe flying conditions must always be the deciding factor for the health and safety of everybody. The pilot will keep a constant check on the weather but ground crew should keep a watch for mist, low cloud and snow and inform any approaching aircraft.

When on the ground keep a special watch over the air temperature as ice on an aircraft can seriously change its flying capability from safe to dangerous especially in winter, at night and in remote locations. Helicopters are particularly prone to icing.

Figure H20.3 *(a) Helicopter nose mount. © Tyler Camera Systems Ltd*

Producers should also beware of the limit to filming time that maximum pilot flying hours creates. Maximum time must be built in to a safe schedule of work to allow enough time for re-takes and a safe return to the base. When working on remote locations, the fuel capacity and flying time of the aircraft must be greater.

GYROMOUNT

FOR FILM OR VIDEO

HELICOPTER POV:	SIDE (LEFT OR RIGHT)	FOCAL RANGE:	10 - 500 mm
MOVEMENT:	PAN, TILT (200°) & ROLL (60°)	MAX. CAM. WT.:	75 LBS.
STABILIZATION:	ACTIVE GYROS	SETUP TIME:	30 MIN.

On a boat deck (with splash gaurd installed).

In the belly of a T-28.

The Remote Control Unit includes a 5.5" Color LCD monitor, a joystick for Pan & Tilt and a knob for Roll. The stabilization of the Pan, Tilt & Roll axis can be rendered inactive at the push of a button (on any or all axis) allowing the Gyromount to also operate like a non-stabilized remote head (on the selected axis).

The Gyromount will soon be available for use in helicopters.

Tyler Camera Systems   14218 Aetna Street   Van Nuys, California 91401 • USA
(818) 989-4420   •   FAX   (818) 989-0423   •   www.tylermount.com

Figure H20.3   *(b) helicopter gyro-mount. © Tyler Camera Systems Ltd*

Helicopters have different safety requirements for single and twin engine types and producers should seek advice from their aircraft operator about these – especially for filming with the doors off – and the correct type to use for low flying and stunt work.

Production managers should build in to the schedule enough time when hiring aircraft to attach and detach camera rigs and mounts. Any

MIDDLE MOUNT II

FOR FILM OR VIDEO

TYLER camera systems

POINT-OF-VIEW:	SIDE (LEFT OR RIGHT)	FOCAL RANGE:	WIDE TO TIGHT
MOVEMENT:	PAN, TILT & ROLL (100°)	MAX. CAM. WT.:	60 LBS.
STABILIZATION:	FREE-FLOATING	INSTALL TIME:	30 MIN.

STC certified for *Bell* Jet Ranger / Long Ranger & *Eurocopter* Astar / TwinStar helicopters.

Tyler Camera Systems 14218 Aetna Street Van Nuys, California 91401 • USA
(818) 989-4420 • FAX (818) 989-0423 • www.tylermount.com

Figure H20.3 *(c) helicopter side mount. © Tyler Camera Systems Ltd*

alterations or attachments must be done by a CAA approved engineer.

Seek advice from your operator on a choice of the three main types of camera mount. These are rubber vibration mounts, balance mounts and gyro mounts. These can be internal or external to the aircraft, fixed or moving and can be placed or housed in the nose, the side or underneath the aircraft. Never attach a mounting to an aircraft without permission.

Always seek advice from your operator on the best type of mount to use. Production managers should supply advance information to the operator about the weight of the camera and the model so that the correct mount can be supplied.

Remote solutions and other aerial work

Avoid placing anybody in the air when you could use a remote camera system from the ground, especially to film low flying action. A remote hover-cam can sometimes be used for difficult shots where an aircraft could not go – for example in a tunnel or large pipe. They can work in situations where a larger aircraft could not go but they cannot shoot sound and present insurance risks in sequences involving actors. This is because the safety legislation for their use and the training for their operators is not as strict as an aircraft. So great caution should be exercised in the use of hover-cams and similar devices. For CAA rules and advice on model aircraft, telephone 01293–573525. Flying stunts by a PPL licence holder must be approved by a flying club senior instructor.

Balloons are also covered by safety rules. The operator must hold an air operators certificate even if the flight is free. You should plan your route with the pilot, making sure there are no power lines. The balloon pilot will brief you on safe landing procedures. A safety harness should be worn except when landing. All equipment must be secured within the gondola. Always check on the local weather before taking off and land if it deteriorates. Contact the CAA ballooning section, telephone 01293–573442.

Note that there have been 66 accidents involving balloons in the past ten years, in which one person has been killed and 51 seriously injured.

As a result of this, Parliament intends to introduce tighter safety standards for balloons in the near future.

Parachutists must be BPA members and hold an FAI class C licence. Parachutists holding a camera must be FAI class D. Use an automatic activation device to work the chute. Parachute jumps must be supervised by an advanced instructor. Parachuting safety and activity advice can be obtained from the CAA parachuting section, telephone 01293–573529.

Rules concerning microlight aircraft can be obtained from the BMAA British Microlight Aircraft Association. A microlight aircraft is no more than a two-seater with a maximum weight of 390 kg. The wing loading should not exceed 25 kg per square metre and the maximum fuel capacity should not exceed 50 litres. Microlight aircraft must possess a CAA airworthiness certificate and may only carry a passenger on a private flight but not for a fee or commercial purpose.

Obtain rules concerning gliders from the British Gliding Association (BGA). Check before hiring a glider that if you go as a second seat passenger that the glider carries second-seat insurance of £1m and third-party insurance of £1m.

The pilot must hold a glider pilot's certificate. These can be A, B, bronze and UK 750m diploma from the BGA or gold, silver and diamond from the FAI. Instructors must hold a British Gliders Association glider instructor's rating certificate. You must also check the maximum safe load rating of the glider you are going to use to make sure it is capable of carrying the combined weight of operator and equipment. The load plate is displayed inside the cockpit. If you want to use a remote camera and fix this to the nose cone or the wing tips then the installation must be approved and supervised by a British Gliders Association inspector.

Hang-gliding is regulated by the British Hang Gliding and Paragliding Association (BHPA). The pilot should be a member of the BHPA, who issue four kinds of licence: elementary pilot's certificate (EPC), club pilot's certificate (CPC-P1), cross country pilot's certificate (XCPC-P2) and the advanced pilot's certificate (APC-P3).

The hang-glider should be BHPA approved design. The seat harness and canopies must conform to CEN 136 standards. Never affix camera or mountings without checking with the designer or manufacturer as this can compromise the air stability. CAA advice on gliding, hang-gliding, microlights and airships can be obtained by telephoning 01293–573526.

Filming around airports

Always seek permission from the airport operator and give sufficient notice by writing in advance of what you want to film. For filming aircraft you should also get permission from the individual airline. Note that for filming airline desks, HM Customs areas and franchise retail outlets separate permission must be obtained for filming from the relevant manager as these are private and outside the control of the airport's administration. Restricted areas include security areas, HM Customs, the baggage reclaim hall and HM Immigration areas. The airport authority will usually co-ordinate with the regulatory authorities for these areas and with the individual airlines for you if proper notice is given. Note, however, that permission to film usually takes at least 24 hours to obtain.

Filming activity such as the recent documentary series about Heathrow Airport relies on the co-operation of very busy people to help things run smoothly. Therefore an initial visit and follow up meeting should help iron out any safety or security problems. When writing to the appropriate airport authority it helps them if you divide your request into three potential areas of activity as they each have their own safety and security requirements:

1 Terminal buildings and access roads. This is perimeter and non-airside activity.
2 Airside activity inside the terminal building. This is departure lounges, customs areas and internal buildings.
3 Airfield activity outside the terminal building. This means areas where aircraft operate such as the apron, hangars, stands and runways.

You will normally require separate permits and security passes for each area plus a separate pass for vehicles.

Try and divide your operations into these areas and give the following information. Fax the time, date and duration of the shoot; the specific locations which you would like to film; the size of the crew; their names and passport or driving licence numbers; the size, weight and type of equipment you are intending to use; and a list of contact numbers plus the minimum of £2m public liability cover. However, if you are planning to film outside then the insurance required will be much higher, especially if you are going airside and with vehicles. For example £10m for Humberside Airport and over £50m for a larger airport.

Once your activity has been approved then a film permit will be issued which must be carried at all times along with a copy of your insurance and individual identification. Separate permits are required to film in aircraft manoeuvring areas and on airside stands.

Any electrical items must be PAT-tested and protected by RCDs. The use of cables and lights should have a qualified electrician. The operation of lighting, tracking or barriers must be approved in advance. For example, lighting must not interfere with the airport lighting or be mistaken for landing lights or visual signals to an aircraft.

It is usually a requirement to use battery operated lights and equipment to avoid the need for cables. The trip hazards which these can present in a busy airport terminal are very high and should be avoided. The parking of any crew buses and live links vehicles must be approved by airport police and check that your communications do not interfere with those of the airport. The use of mobile phones and radios are unlikely to be permitted outside, particularly on parking aprons, in hangars and near fuel installations and tankers. A faxed plan of any large set-ups should help to identify any potential hazards.

Any filming that takes place inside the airside space or on the airfield itself must be accompanied at all times. Before filming starts the airport safety unit should give you a copy of their health and safety regulations which you must comply with at all times. Note that you will have two separate briefings and sets of rules to follow, one for the airport building and one for the aircraft active area.

Strict compliance with these rules must be made for your safety. Always remain within defined areas and do not wander or try to film in restricted or dangerous areas of the airport, especially in the airside fuel and security areas. Non-compliance with this may well lead to permission being withdrawn and a possible prosecution under the Air Navigation Order in exceptional circumstances.

You must also wear the appropriate protective clothing such as high visibility jackets, ear defenders and eye protection. Always have a spare crew member watch the back of the camera and sound operators as airports are full of fast moving and heavy objects such as trolleys and baggage trains. Take care of trip hazards on moving walkways and escalators and slip hazards on polished floors.

When filming near planes it is important to keep to a safe operating distance and beware of the noise hazards presented by aircraft engines. Wear appropriate ear protection and make sure that you can be seen by the pilot, especially at night. When wearing ear protection or when working in a loud environment it is important to ensure a separate visual system of communication to warn of any danger such as moving aircraft or service vehicles. Always avoid smoking in the airport, especially in fuel areas and near or inside aircraft. Keep to the designated safe areas. Finally don't leave your equipment or bags unattended. They may not be there when you come back.

Further reading

Air International (monthly), Key Publishing Ltd, Tel: 01780 755131.
Aeronautical Journal (monthly), Royal Aeronautical Society, Tel: 0171 4993515.
Flight International (weekly), Reed Business Information, Tel: 0181 652 3500.

The following titles are available from Westward Digital Ltd:

● Aircraft Fuelling, Fire Prevention and Safety Measures, Cap 74
● Aircraft Radio Equipment, Volume 1
● General Aviation Safety Information Leaflet
● Bob and Carol Howes, *The Ballooning Manual*
● Ken Stewart, *The Glider Pilot's Manual*
● Brian Cosgrove, *The Microlight Pilot's Handbook*
● Private Pilots Licence, Cap 53
● Rescue and Fire Fighting, Cap 605
● Safety Standards at Unlicensed Aerodromes
● United Kingdom Aerodrome Index, Cap 481

Tim Desbois, How to Use Helicopters & Aviation Insurance Guide. In *The Knowledge*, ISBN 0-863-824-13-7, Miller Freeman UK Ltd, Riverbank House, Angel Lane, Tonbridge, Kent, TN9 1SE, Tel: 01732 362666.

The following titles are available from Emergency Response Publications, 5 Shelly Court, South Zeal, Okehampton, Devon EX20 2PT, Tel: 01837–840102:

- Rick La Valla and Skip Stoffel, *Personnel Safety in Helicopter Operations: Helirescue Manual*, March 1988.
- Skip Stoffel and Rick La Valla, *Survival Sense for Pilots and Passengers*, 1986.

The International Civil Aviation Organization Publications Catalogue 1998.
The UK Aeronautical Information Publication 1998, 4 volumes.
Westward Digital Ltd Publications Catalogue 1998.
Kay's UK Production Manual 1999, ISBN 1-873987-16-1, Kay's Publishing, Pinewood Studios, Pinewood Road, Iver Heath, Bucks SL0 0NH, Tel: 01753 656844.

Contact organizations

Aerial Camera Systems Ltd
Shepperton Studios, Studios Rd, Shepperton, Middlesex TW17 0QD
Tel: 01932–564885

Airport Operators Association
3 Birdcage Walk, London SW1H 9JJ
Tel: 0171–222–2249

Bond Helicopters Ltd
Humberside International Airport, Kirmington, North Lincs DN39 6YH
Tel: 01652–688417

Bristow Helicopters Ltd
Aberdeen Airport, Dyche, Aberdeen AB21 ONT
Tel: 01224–723151

British Airports Authority
130 Wilton Rd, London SW1V 1LQ
Tel: 0171–834–9449

The BMAA British Micro Light Aircraft Association
Bullring, Deddington, Oxfordshire OX15 0TT
Tel: 01869–338888

The British Gliding Association
Kimberley House, Vaughan Way, Leicester LE1 4SE
Tel: 0116–2531051

The British Hang Gliding and Paragliding Association
The Old School Room, Loughborough Rd, Leicester LE4 5PJ
Tel: 0116–2611322

The British Parachute Association
5 Wharf Way, Glen Parva, Leicester LE2 9TF
Tel: 0116–2785271

Castle Air
Trebrown, Liskeard, Cornwall PL14 3PX
Tel: 01503–240543

Civil Aviation Authority
Civil Aviation House
45–59 Kingsway, London WC2B 6TE
Tel: 0171–379–7311

Civil Aviation Authority
Aviation House, Gatwick, W. Sussex RH6 0YR
Tel: 01293–573981
   Safety Regulation Group, Tel: 01293–567471
   Air operator's certificates, Tel: 01293–573399
   Pilot's licences, Tel: 01293–573498
   Ballooning, Tel: 01293–573442
   Gliding, hang-gliding, microlights, airships, Tel: 01293–573526
   Helicopters, Tel: 01293–573528
   Low flying exemption, Tel: 01293–573540
   Parachuting, Tel: 01293–573529

Civil Aviation Authority, Library and Public Information Centre
Aviation House, Gatwick, W. Sussex RH6 0YR
Tel: 01293–573725

Flight Logistics
Film & TV Aviation
Grip House Studios, Metropolitan Centre, 5–11 Taunton Rd, Greenford,
Middlesex UB6 8UQ
Tel: 0181–575–0528

Heathrow Airport Ltd
British Airport Authority Heathrow Public Affairs Department
Heathrow Point West, 234 Bath Rd, Harlington, Middlesex UB3 5AP
Tel: 0181–745–7224

International Civil Aviation Organization
999 University St, Montreal, Quebec, Canada H3C 5H7

Joint Aviation Authorities
PO Box 3000, 2130 Ka Hoofddorp, Netherlands
Tel: 0031–235679712

Medical Aviation Services
Gloucester Airport, Staverton, Cheltenham, Gloucester GL51 6SS
Tel: 01452–859999

RHH-Albert G Ruben (insurance brokers)
Braintree House, Braintree Rd, Ruislip, Middlesex HA4 0YA
Tel: 0181–841–4461

Rotary Wing
Ground Support Services, 157 Mosley Common Rd, Mosley Common,
Worsley, Manchester M28 4AH
Tel: 0161–799–6967

The Royal Aeronautical Society
4 Hamilton Place, London W1V 0BQ
Tel: 0171–4993515

Tyler Camera Systems Ltd
14218 Aetna Street
Van Nuys
California 91401
USA
Tel: 818–989–4420

Westward Digital Ltd
Publishers of Civil Aviation Authority and aeronautical books
37 Windsor St, Cheltenham, Gloucestershire GL52 2DG
Tel: 01242–235151

Hazard 21: Food and catering

The legislation

The Food Safety Act 1990
EU Directive, Hygiene of Foodstuffs 93/43/EEC
The Health and Safety (First Aid) Regulations 1991
The Fire Precautions (Workplace) Regulations 1997
The Workplace (Health, Safety and Welfare) Regulations 1992.

The risks

- contamination
- food poisoning
- fire risk

Those most at risk

Catering staff, employees, members of the public.

The Food Safety Act 1990 is the major legislation which food premises and providers must conform with. There are also regulations within this that deal with particular areas of food safety. The regulations are:

- The Food Labelling Regulations 1996
- The Food Premises Registration Regulations 1991
- The Food Safety (General Food Hygiene) Regulations 1995
- The Food Safety (Temperature Control) Regulations 1995

The film and television industry has contact with food hygiene in some important areas. These key areas are:

1 Film and television businesses operating their own canteens and restaurants where they prepare, cook and sell food for their own employees.
2 Film and television businesses providing kitchens or vending equipment in office and studios for the preparation or sale of food. This is either brought in by employees or supplied pre-packed by contractors (for detailed regulations on vending machines see *Industry Guide to Good Hygiene Practice: Catering Guide 1997*, Chapter 3, pp. 32–34).
3 Film and television businesses hiring mobile field kitchens, dining buses and mobile catering to productions on locations away from base premises (for detailed regulations on mobile vans see *Industry Guide to Good Hygiene Practice: Catering Guide 1997*, Chapter 3, pp. 28–31).
4 Film and television businesses providing or hiring hospitality as part of the promotional work of the production. This can happen in-house or externally in restaurants, marquees or dining suites. The scope can range from beer and sandwiches through to a last night party or formal awards dinner.
5 Film and television productions which have a food content or theme. This can range from specialist food and cookery programmes in the studio to film locations where food is prepared or eaten as part of the action.

Therefore food regulations can affect managers and owners of businesses with staff catering facilities, producers hiring mobile catering and buffets, organizers of production parties and specialist food programmes or films with food content in the script.

All these activities divide into those which take place on managed premises and those which happen off site or on the premises of others. So the responsibilities for the safe preparation, cooking and storage of food will operate in two ways. First, on the individual or company if they are direct providers of food for consumption and own the premises. Second, on the hirer or contractor to comply with the safe hygiene and food regulations themselves. In short this means that you must comply with the laws and regulations yourself or make sure that anybody who is providing food on their own site or who is contracted to you does the same. The way to comply is through a system of assured safe catering (ASC).

In both cases there is a legal responsibility to make sure that the food which is prepared and served must be fit and safe to eat and the areas used to store, prepare and cook it must be clean, hygienic and safe to work in.

Regulation 4.3 of the Food Safety (General Food Hygiene) Regulations 1995 states that, 'a proprietor of a food business shall identify any step in the activities of the food business which is critical to ensuring food safety and ensure that adequate safety procedures are identified, implemented, maintained and reviewed.'

This is a new legal requirement designed to make companies focus on the activities critical to food safety in their business and to find ways of controlling them. Under the Food Safety Act 1990 any food business or premises that fails to comply with hygiene or safety standards can be served by the local environmental health department with an improvement notice which requires action within 14 days to rectify any problems and take specified action to improve the operation. In extreme cases an emergency prohibition notice can be served which closes the named premises with immediate effect.

The best way to comply with legislation is to make a risk assessment at all the key stages of the food chain, from purchase through to consumption.

Once the risks have been identified a work method statement which sets out the right way to prepare, cook and serve food in a safe and hygienic way can be drawn up as part of the ASC. To do this catering managers, owners of food premises and chefs must first identify all the hazards which could be present at each stage of the food chain. A hazard is anything that could cause harm to the consumer. The three main food hazards are usually microbiological, chemical or physical. These are usually caused by neglect of food quality, temperature and cross-contamination from rodents, vermin or cleaning agents.

Managers of catering facilities must take steps to control and eliminate them in order to reduce the risk factor to acceptable levels. A work plan to identify them and achieve hygienic practice is called hazard analysis and critical control points (HACCP). The HACCP is a control plan for the food preparation process.

The key stages of food preparation hygiene are identified where controls are required to ensure food safety. The actions which you then take should be identified and carried out as company policy.

The HACCP plan should be drawn up and written down. The plan should be enforced by the management with the active participation of any staff involved in the stages of the food chain. Regular monitoring by managers must be backed up by improved training and spot checks to ensure vigilance and best practice.

Once in place the HACCP must be continually reviewed to keep up with new food products and the varied food situations that arise in the film and broadcasting industry. It is essential to do this as the legal implications of food poisoning to a major production or studio complex would be devastating.

The first point of the HACCP starts with food purchase. Any food which is bought or brought in should be either as fresh as possible or

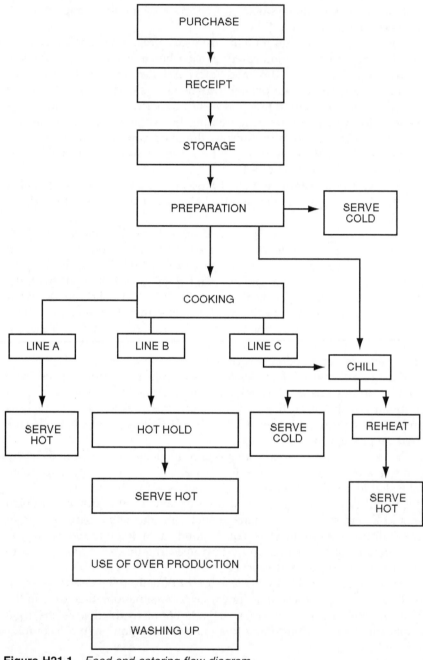

Figure H21.1   *Food and catering flow diagram*

properly frozen to guarantee best condition. Avoid buying food from poor quality suppliers. If necessary check the premises of potential suppliers to make sure that standards of health and hygiene are being complied with. Buying poor quality food is creating a potential hazard further down the food chain.

The second point of the HACCP is the delivery and receipt of the raw food. Things to look out for are broken packaging and dents, strange smells and poor colouring. Always check the use-by dates of any goods. Check tins to make sure that they have not blown. Check packets and boxes for holes or damage. Check the labels of frozen and fresh perishable goods to make sure that the contents are safe to use. Dry goods have best-before dates. Maintain the quality of catering food by date checking and proper stock rotation to ensure quality. Anything past the use-by or best-before dates should be thrown away as unfit for human consumption.

The standard of cleanliness of the delivery person and the vehicle may be a sign of the standards employed by your supplier. Specify the maximum temperature at delivery so that the food arrives to you in the safest possible condition and minimizes the time spent in transit.

Remember that once you have signed for and accepted food it is your responsibility to keep it safe. If you have any doubt about any supplied food get a second opinion before accepting it. The recommended maximum temperature which most operations work to is 5°C. Certain products can be stored at 8°C, so proper storage information should be obtained from the supplier or manufacturer.

Check the temperature on arrival especially in periods of hot weather. Record the goods into your purchase log with a record of any use-before dates, special storage instructions and a copy of the delivery note.

The third point of the HACCP is storage. Try to minimize the period that delivered goods are left at room temperature before storage. Separate raw foods from cooked. Do not store raw foods such as poultry, meat and fish above cooked foods in fridges. This is to avoid cross-contamination from dripping juices. Make sure that any refrigeration plant is properly serviced and defrosted. Check the storage temperature at regular intervals. Cooked and raw food should be stored separately at the correct maximum temperature of 5°C.

- Dry foods and fresh vegetables should be stored at least 45 cm off the ground in secure containers away from vermin and direct sunlight.
- Flour, nuts, bread, spices, etc., should be stored in secure bins or tins.
- All food should be covered and wrapped with correct labelling and stock rotation to ensure freshness and proper identification of contents.
- Do not store food adjacent to chemicals, animals, heat and sunlight.
- Use or dispose of stored food before the use-by date.

The fourth control point of the HACCP is preparation. Any surfaces and implements used for food preparation should be clean. Separate preparation surfaces must be used, one for raw food and one for cooked. Separate any equipment used for preparing different foods by colour coding them for raw and cooked. Also separate preparation surfaces and utensils for meat and vegetarian foods.

Anybody preparing food must have clean protective clothing. In some cases they should also wear a hat. They must have clean hands before touching any food. Separate raw and cooked foods during preparation and avoid prolonged exposure to room temperature as bacteria can multiply very quickly. Thaw any frozen food properly and check the temperature with a probe thermometer. Then cook the fresh ingredients as soon as possible.

The fifth control point of the HACCP is cooking. Wash and clean all vegetables and fruit. All cooking utensils should be clean. Use different

Step	Hazard	Control*	Monitoring
Purchase and delivery	Instrinsic contaminant (micro-organisms or foreign material)	Use reputable suppliers	Check delivery vehicles Check date codes, temperatures and condition of food
Storage	Bacterial growth further contamination (by micro-organisms, foreign material or chemicals)	Store at correct temperatures Cover/wrap foods Separate raw/cooked, high risk foods Stock rotation	Check temperatures Visual checks Check date marks
Preparation	Bacterial growth Further contamination	Limit time at kitchen temperatures Use clean equipment Good personal hygiene	Visual checks Cleaning schedules
Cooking	Survival of bacteria	Cook to centre temperature above 75°C	Check temperatures
Cooling	Growth of surviving spores Further contamination	Cool food rapidly. (Set a time period appropriate to dish). Refrigerate when cooled – below 5°C. Keep foods covered, where possible.	Check time and temperature

Figure H21.2   *Food preparation: hazard control points*

pans for raw and cooked food. Special care should be taken when cooking rolled joints, chicken and burgers so that the meat is cooked properly in the centre to at least 75°C for at least two minutes to kill off any bacteria. Other cuts of meat such as beef and steaks should be seared before cooking. Special care should be taken to prepare and cook certain kosher and hali food.

Change cooking oils and filters regularly and make sure that you follow the manufacturers cooking instructions for any given food product.

The cooking process is a key point to kill any surface bacteria and make sure that any food is safe and hygienic to eat. Fresh salad and vegetables should be cleaned and washed. Cooked food should be served immediately avoiding cross-contamination with raw foods.

The sixth control point of the HACCP is cooling. After cooking, food should be served straight away and not be allowed to stand in room

Step	Hazard	Control*	Monitoring
Chilled storage	Growth of bacteria Further contamination	Store at correct temperatures Cover/wrap foods/stock rotation Separate raw/cooked foods	Check temperatures Visual checks
Reheating	Survival of bacteria	Reheat to centre temperature above 75°C (In Scotland 82°C is required for some foods)	Check temperatures
Hot holding and service	Growth of bacteria Further contamination	Keep food above 63°C Use clean equipment Keep covered, where possible	Check temperatures Visual checks
Cold service	Growth of bacteria Further contamination	Keep cool or display for a maximum of 4 hours Use clean equipment Keep covered, where possible	Check temperature and time Visual checks

* Suggested controls in this chart are indicative of good practice and for some foods only. For example, some cuts of meat may have no significant contamination in the centre, and cooking to temperatures below 75°C (rare) is acceptable. They are not intended to be minimum compliance standards for all foods. Other foods or drinks may involve different handling or preparation steps. These will need to be analysed accordingly.

Figure H21.2 *Continued*

temperatures. Any food that is not going to be used at once should be chilled to below 5°C quickly and stored in a fridge until it is needed.

The seventh control point of HACCP is hot-holding. This means keeping any hot cooked food in proper heated trays at 63°C or above to maintain food quality. Only display small amounts and replenish when necessary to avoid prolonged display.

The eighth control point is reheating. Any reheated food should be heated to at least 75°C for a minimum of two minutes to kill any bacteria and stored during hot-holding at 63°C or above.

The ninth control point is proper serving of food. All food should be served on clean dishes. The staff who serve this food must be qualified in basic food hygiene. Staff should have clean clothes without pockets and avoid serving in gloves. Cold buffet food should be refrigerated at all times prior to serving. Do not let cold buffet food stand for extended periods at room temperature.

Food normally requiring temperature control may be kept above 8°C for a single period of 4 hours, to allow it to be served or displayed. After this period any food remaining should be thrown away. Only one tolerance period of service or display is allowed.

Avoid letting hot food cool down from 63°C to room temperature, which is an ideal breeding ground for bacteria and make sure that food remains covered until it is served. Use different tongs to serve vegetarian and meat products. Make sure the contents of dishes are properly labelled to warn those with special diet or religious needs to avoid eating products with nuts, pork, milk products, etc.

By identifying these key stages in the HACCP controls can be put in place all along the food chain from supply to consumption in order to achieve a safe and hygienic environment within the film and television industries. These standards should be in place within in-house food facilities and all contractors and caterers should comply with them.

These procedures will mean very little unless the actual kitchens are clean and hygienic and the staff are properly trained in these HACCP procedures. Management and head chefs must have proper HACCP training and qualifications in food hygiene supervision.

Any staff who serve or handle food should ideally possess at least one of two basic certificates: either the basic food hygiene certificate awarded by the Chartered Institute of Environmental Health Officers or the essential hygiene certificate awarded by the Royal Society of Health. Food handlers should be properly supervised by somebody who has gained a supervisors qualification such as the intermediate food hygiene certificate, while managers should possess the advanced food hygiene certificate. All chefs should possess the necessary qualifications including City and Guilds for the correct grade and level of responsibility. Staff should not work with food if they are feeling ill, especially with diarrhoea and vomiting. They should report this to their supervisor immediately.

All catering premises and food preparation and kitchen areas should have a proper supply of hot and cold water with a separate hand basin, towel, soap, nail brushes and drying facilities for catering staff. They should also have a separate changing area and toilet facilities under the Workplace (Health, Safety and Welfare) Regulations 1992. Employers should also possess adequate employers liability insurance for operating a business.

Any kitchen serving food to the public must be registered with the local authority under the Food Premises Registration Regulations 1991. They will be on the register of the local environmental health department and in some areas may require a licence as well. Mobile caterers must have a licence to sell and serve food on public roads and land.

Kitchens should be kept clean and the layout and design should reflect the number of people working in them and to make cleaning and hygiene as easy as possible. Kitchens should be properly lit with natural and artificial light. All drainage and refuse disposal facilities should be adequate. All ceilings, floors, walls and surfaces which come into contact with food should be well maintained and easy to clean and disinfect.

Food preparation surfaces should be separate for meats, fish, cooked and raw food with colour coded pans and utensils. Refrigeration facilities should be adequate for the size of the kitchen with separate units for uncooked and cooked products. Test the temperature of stored and held food at regular intervals and use a temperature log book to keep a regular record of safe storage temperatures. Storage bins and cupboards should be above floor level and airtight. Care should be taken to guard moving machinery such as mixers and slicers and prevent inexperienced staff from contact, while sharp knives should be kept in secure holders. In order to ensure kitchen safety, a proper risk assessment must be made for all operations and all staff must receive appropriate health and safety training. This should include fire precautions (especially for fat fires), first aid precautions, instruction in the safe use of machinery and safe working with knives, electricity and hot pans/surfaces. Personal protective equipment must be worn to protect hands, face and skin.

All wall surfaces should be ceramic or stainless steel with no damage or cracks in the surface. Any joins should have proper coving and all pipes and cables should be boxed in. All water, electrical and gas appliances should be safe and properly maintained. Ceilings should be suspended with proper ventilation to reduce heat to a safe working level otherwise hot working may apply. The air supply should also be filtered to remove dust, fats, oils and odours. There should also be adequate fly screens and pest control precautions including insect electrocutors. All cleaning chemicals should be stored away from heat and food.

Fire precautions should reflect the type and range of risks which might take place. For example smoke alarms, carbon monoxide detectors, microwave oven leakage detectors and fire extinguishers. Fire extinguishers must be adequate and appropriate for the types and scale of the fire risk; for example, there will need to be extra extinguishers to deal with hot fat fires. Chubb UK have brought out Fry Fighter™ which is an approved new extinguisher especially designed for kitchens.

Kitchens should also have first aid boxes including high visibility blue adhesive dressings. Staff with cuts or wounds should not be allowed to prepare food. All kitchens should have proper safety signs indicating locations of fire and first aid facilities. There should also be signs for dangerous machinery and hygiene requirements such as hand washing.

Mobile caterers and food vendors must have a licence to operate from the local licensing department of the council where they ply their trade. Reputable operators are usually members of the Mobile and Outdoor Caterers Association of Great Britain (MOCA) and can be found in trade directories such as *Kay's UK Production Manual 1999* and *International Production Directory 1999* (the 'white book'). The local environmental health office can advise you on any recent prosecutions and can undertake to inspect a contractor for you if required.

Any kitchen and catering operation must also comply with a number of other regulations. For example the site or kitchen must have a clean supply of water and a separate system of sanitation adequate for the amount of people. All refuse must be disposed of in a hygienic and safe manner, away from pests and vermin. Mobile units and kitchens should not be placed adjacent to rubbish tips, dumps, contaminated land or water.

Any cleaning chemicals must be stored away from food and their use recorded in compliance with COSHH regulations. Kitchens and catering activity also involves a lot of heat so beware of touching hot pans or placing equipment and cables on hot surfaces. Cooking with gas and having chemicals and paper waste in proximity means kitchens have a high fire risk. Proper fire precautions should be in place with the correct extinguishers, fire blankets, etc. Nobody should ever smoke in food preparation areas and kitchens. Staff should also be trained in fire fighting and first aid precautions.

In television programmes or film productions which involve food extra care should be taken to avoid food hazards. Any sets should be designed and built with health, hygiene and safety factors built in to comply with the CDM Regulations. Any gas or electrical supplies must be isolated and safe. Preparation surfaces must be clean and have separate units for raw and cooked foods. The surfaces must comply with catering hygiene regulations, being smooth and easy to clean. Storage for ingredients must be clean with separate containers for raw and fresh ingredients. All knives and moving machinery must be kept away from cables. Any electrical kitchen gadgets must be PAT-tested and safe. Sets and catering vehicles should always have suitable fire precautions for the type of activity undertaken.

Cooking should be done in real time and particular care should be paid to the temperature of any food. Cold food will rapidly get too hot under studio lights and deteriorate with the risk of infection. So producers and directors must be aware of the food hygiene risks presented by prolonged retakes in hot studios. For example utensils may have to be properly cleaned or replaced once food has been touched. If necessary have substitute or replacement food on hand for further shots to replace food that has deteriorated to unsafe temperatures. In hot locations you should have proper refrigeration and chilled containers to maintain safe cold food temperatures. An adequate supply of clean chilled water is also a good idea.

Hot food on location can get cold rapidly and requires adequate hot storage to ensure the correct safe eating temperature of 63°C or above. In extreme weather dining buses should be provided for the total number of cast and crew with adequate toilet facilities to ensure comfortable eating conditions and the welfare of all concerned with the production.

Ensure adequate rest breaks and meal breaks for productions and avoid alcohol consumption while filming. If necessary try simulating eating and drinking to avoid tasting food where a danger might occur. You could use substitute or artificial food for long shots or shoot all the close ups first. Lastly make a note of any special dietary or religious needs of production staff or crew who may be eating as this can offend or cause a medical condition especially when those concerned are very young or very old and so prone to bacteria and infection from food. Bon appetit!

Further reading

Industry Guide to Good Hygiene Practice: Catering Guide 1997, ISBN 0-900-103-00-0. Chadwick House Group Ltd, Chadwick Court, 15 Hatfields, London SE1 8DJ, Tel: 0171–827–5882.

EU Council Directive on The Hygiene of Foodstuffs 93/43/EEC, *Official Journal of the European Communities*, No. L 175/1, 18 July 1993.

SAFE (Systematic Assessment of Food Environment), British Hospitality Association, Queens House, 55–56 Lincoln's Inn Fields, London WC2A 3BH, Tel: 0171–404–7744.

Fire Safety in Catering Establishments, FSB32/1996, available from the Loss Prevention Council, Melrose Avenue, Borehamwood, Hertfordshire WD6 2BJ, Tel: 0181–207–2345.

Nicholas Johns, *Managing Food Hygiene*, 2nd edition, Macmillan, ISBN 0-333-65117-0.

Richard A. Springer, *Hygiene for Management*, 8th edition, Highfield Publications, 'Vue Pointe', Spinney Hill, Sprotborough, Doncaster, DN5 7LY.

David Edwards, *BBC Food Check,* ISBN 0-563-20789-2.

A Supervisor's Handbook of Food Hygiene and Safety, available from Royal Institute of Public Health and Hygiene, 28 Portland Place, London W1N 4ED, Tel: 0171–580–2731.

A Guide to The General Temperature Control Regulations, Department of Health pamphlet, reference G21/019 3561, 1P 500K Feb. 96 (02).

A Guide to Food Hazards and Your Business, Department of Health pamphlet, reference G21/020 3562, 1P 500K Feb. 96 (02).

Assured Safe Catering, Department of Health pamphlet, reference-G21/016 3323, 2P 270K Oct. 95 (02).

Assured Safe Catering, Department of Health, ISBN 0-11-32168-8. Available from HMSO, PO Box 276, London SW8 5DT, Tel: 0171–873–9090.

The HSE also publish a number of health and safety catering guides. The index reference is CAIS4 and all catering and food guidance pamphlets are indexed as 3.12 CAIS.

International Production Directory 1999 (the 'white book') ISBN 1-87449407-X, available from Inside Communications Ltd, Bank House, 23 Warwick Road, Coventry CV1 2EW, Tel: 01203–559658.

Kay's UK Production Manual 1999, ISBN 1-873987-16-1, Kay's Publishing, Pinewood Studios, Pinewood Road, Iver Heath, Bucks SL0 0NH, Tel: 01753 656844.

Contact organizations

British Examining Board in Occupational Hygiene
Suite 2, Georgian House, Great Northern Rd, Derby DE1 1LT
Tel: 01332–298087

British Pest Control Association
3 St James Court, Friargate, Derby DE1 1BT
Tel: 01332–294288

Her Majesty's Stationery Office
PO Box 276, London SW8 5DT
Tel: 0171–873–9090

The Chartered Institute of Environmental Health Officers (CIEH)
Chadwick Court, 15 Hatfields, London SE1 8DJ
Tel: 0171–928–6006

British Hospitality Association
Queens House, 55–56 Lincoln's Inn Fields, London WC2A 3BH
Tel: 0171–404–7744

Hospitality Training Foundation
International House, High St, Ealing, London W5 5DB
Tel: 0181–579–2400

Mobile and Outdoor Caterers Association of Great Britain (MOCA)
Centre Court, 1301 Stratford Rd, Hall Green, Birmingham B28 9AP
Tel: 0121–693–7000

National Britannia (Procheck Food Safety Advice)
Caerphilly Business Park, Caerphilly, Mid Glamorgan CF83 3ED
Tel: 012222–852000

Royal Institute of Public Health and Hygiene
28 Portland Place, London W1N 4ED
Tel: 0171–580–2731

The Royal Society of Health
38a St George's Drive, London SW1V 4BH
Tel: 0171–630–0121

Hazard 22: Hot work

On the set of *Lost in Space*, the temperature 40 or 50 feet up near the ceiling of the stage was 120 to 130°F. The lamps were too hot to hold without gloves.

Stage, Screen and Radio, June 1998, p. 20

The legislation

The Health and Safety at Work Act 1974
The Management of Health and Safety at Work Regulations 1992
The Workplace (Health, Safety and Welfare) Regulations 1992

The risks

- confined spaces
- lights
- studios
- lack of ventilation
- workshops

Those most at risk

Caterers, electricians, lighting crew, maintenance staff, plumbers.

Heat hazards can happen in the film and television industry in a variety of different ways. Some working environments are inherently hot – for example, a desert location or a catering unit kitchen – while in other locations we introduce heat as a result of the work we are carrying out – for example the introduction of lighting into a small space and the heat effects of studio lights in a grid area. Heat hazards can also be created by welding work and scenery construction. We can also film on the premises of third parties where hot work regimes will be in place, such as bakeries, boiler rooms, green houses, mines and power stations.

The Provision and Use of Work Equipment Regulations 1998 require that all tools, plant and machinery is maintained and safe, while the Workplace (Health, Safety and Welfare) Regulations 1992 insist that workplace environments are a safe working temperature. Hence, all heat creating tools such as lights should be checked for safety and heating systems in buildings should be adequate and safe.

At present there is no legal maximum work temperature but all hot work situations should be identified as a serious health risk. A risk assessment must then be made which should consider all activities, from routine base operations to special situations. Once this has been done, precautions can be put in place to protect the health and safety of any staff engaged in hot work.

The correct way to confirm the existence of potential hot work situations is to measure the temperature of the chosen work area. Do this at the same time of day and season as the intended action. This will give you an accurate measure and should be carried out before any activity is allowed. The measure of hot work situations is called wet bulb globe temperature (WBGT).

You should use a wet bulb thermometer to take a reading. This is a thermometer which has its bulb covered by a wet wick and you should use it to record ambient temperature. Multiply this reading by 0.7 to get your first figure. You should also take into account relative factors such as the level of humidity and the available air flow.

A second reading should then be taken from a globe thermometer. This responds to ambient temperate and radiant heat. A second reading should be made with this and multiplied by 0.3 to get your second figure.

The WBGT is the combined figure of the first and second readings added together. This figure or WBGT reading should be recorded and acts as the benchmark for hot work assessments. The length and level of precautions which you then take will depend on this reading.

Continuous work in WBGT conditions of 22°C or under are considered safe if the normal safety precautions are applied. However any work that takes place in a WBGT of 27°C or above is considered to come under the hot work regime. The identification of a hot work location must be recorded in the risk assessment and a hot work control system established by the management.

The management must ensure that the WBGT is monitored regularly in a hot work area once the total work time exceeds ten minutes. This must be carried out every five minutes and recorded in a log book.

Any staff who need to work in the area should be issued with a hot work permit. Access should be restricted to permit holders only, with entry controlled via a log-in point established for the purpose. Protective equipment regulations apply from this point. Cool rest areas should be provided with plenty of fluids available (not salt water). Any workers must be instructed in the correct replacement of fluid lost through perspiration as part of their training for hot work and in the recognition of heat stress symptoms. They should also be trained by the management in first aid, treatment for heat stress and emergency procedures.

Controlled work times must start from entry. If the monitoring detects a rise in the WBGT then the working time must be reduced accordingly. This could happen if lights are turned on or machinery is activated.

A safe system of work must be in place and a work method statement agreed and put in place before any job has begun. Fire and first aid precautions must be included along with any advice on which chemicals and gases must not be introduced into hot work areas as these can ignite or cause asphyxiation. Provide a list of approved tools and protective equipment. Confirm these arrangements in writing, backed up by a briefing from a supervisor to all concerned with the hot work.

Producers should ensure that staff working in hot work areas get proper rest periods according to the length of the work and the WGBT. Above 26°C degrees allow a minimum rest period of 20 minutes for 40 minutes work. At WBGT 29°C the rest should be 35 minutes for 25 minutes work. At WGBT 31°C the rest should be 50 minutes for 10 minutes work.

At temperatures above 31°C access should be for inspection purposes only. Any staff doing so must be under medical supervision of a trained nurse or doctor at the start of work to make sure that they are fit and suitable with a proper work/rest routine established. Once the chosen workers have been passed fit and the work/rest regime has been approved in writing then operational monitoring can be carried out by a trained first aider who has had appropriate additional training in heat stress treatment. The first aider must have access to a telephone to be able to contact more qualified medical personnel for advice at all times.

Apart from the WGBT another key factor to consider in hot work is the size of the space in which the work is being carried out. The more confined the space the hotter it will become so always refer to the hazard section on confined spaces for extra information. Remember the greater the number of people and the more lights and tools used then the faster the oxygen will be used up and the working temperature will rise quickly to unsafe and potentially dangerous levels.

Also consider that heat rises so identify any work that takes place over a hot environment such as a kitchen or boiler house. Check the location on building plans of any hot pipes for water and steam vents.

Hot work situations are created by roof spaces and ceilings which are confined and the high temperature is created through a combination of hot air rising from below, sunlight from above and magnified by insulation and hot water pipes.

A second key factor is the availability of fresh air or ventilation which can keep the temperature down and increase the comfort factor. This can reduce the temperature to a safe working level by reducing the effects of the heat. Another way of doing this is to wait until the heat source cools down by switching off lights or working when it is cooler rather than at midday.

A third key factor is to make sure that the work be done in such a way that entry into a hot environment is not necessary. This means substituting a potentially dangerous situation for a safer one.

If entry into a hot environment is deemed necessary then the working period should be kept to as short a length of time as possible. This means reducing the risk factor to the minimum exposure time and making sure that this is properly supervised.

It is also necessary for hot work risk assessments to consider the age and medical fitness of the workers in conjunction with the physical exertion that they will be asked to undergo. The greater the age and lack of fitness then the working time should be reduced or a fitter worker substituted, especially if the task is very strenuous. This is very important in work situations involving heavy machinery, power tools, manual handling and stress.

Workers undertaking hot work must be fit and healthy. They should be under 45 and have no previous heat illness, high blood pressure or skin disease. They should not be obese or taking any prescription or drugs, so producers or production managers should always consider the medical factors when selecting appropriate staff for a hot work environment and get them medically checked by a doctor if any doubt exists before starting.

Producers and managers who have requested work to be undertaken in hot areas must comply with the Personal Protective Equipment (PPE) at Work Regulations 1992 and provide adequate personal protective measures. The key to providing adequate personal protection is to identify first any hot work situations as part of the production risk assessment process. Any heat hazards should be identified and entered on the risk assessment sheet. Then identify which workers would be at risk and seek advice on the correct equipment to give them.

This can vary depending on the location and the type of risk. For example gloves should be provided for lighting crew to avoid burns from hot lights and cuts from sharp edges. Eye protection is needed to avoid damage from bursting bulbs. Note that any hot work involving asbestos or tented enclosures must have an emergency standby person waiting outside the airlock equipped with PPE in case of an emergency. Separate WGBT monitoring must be maintained for asbestos work.

In outdoor situations crew should be issued with sun glasses (minimum protection BS 2724 1987), hats and sun protection barrier cream factor 15 or above to guard against the effects of direct sun such as being dazzled, sun stroke and skin cancer.

Skin cancer has two main types: non-melanoma which is common among outdoor workers and malignant melanoma which can be fatal. Over 40,000 people are diagnosed with skin cancer every year in the UK, of whom 10 per cent will have malignant melanoma.

The risks from the sun in outdoor locations has recently received exposure from a study by the Health Education Authority. As the most powerful UV rays occur between 11a.m. and 3p.m. it is best to avoid scheduling excessive work in this period and insist on crew covering up and wearing protection. The risk from sun-induced UV light would be a particular risk in overseas locations such as Spain and California where the sun's strength is much greater.

In confined spaces protective suits and respiratory equipment may be needed. Suits should be coveralls and gloves must be long enough to cover the wrist area. Also consider the heat hazards for actors and presenters working in masks and costumes under lights – especially animal costumes and children's characters such as Mr Blobby and the Teletubbies which are very enclosed and hot.

Plenty of fluids and cool drinks should always be provided in hot outdoor locations and studios. Consider the effects of prolonged heat on any children, elderly people or animals. They may need extra protection and provision, especially if this involves travelling in excessive heat or extended periods of exposure and waiting in hot conditions. Assess the risks and seek advice about hot work if in any doubt.

Further reading

Hot Work, RC7/1994, available from the Loss Prevention Council, Melrose Avenue, Borehamwood, Hertfordshire WD6 2BJ, Tel: 0181–207–2345.
Hot Work at Docks: Health and Safety Precautions, HSE, DIS6.
A Critique of Recommended Limits of Exposure to UV Radiation with Particular Reference to Skin Cancer, HSE, CRR64, 1994, ISBN 0-7176-0728-3.

Contact organizations

European Foundation for the Improvement of Living and Working Conditions
Wyattville Rd, Loughlinstown, Co Dublin, Ireland
Tel: 351–204–3100

Health Education Authority
Trevelyan House, 30 Gt Peter St, London SW1P 2HW
Tel: 0171–222–5300

Loss Prevention Council
Melrose Avenue, Borehamwood, Hertfordshire WD6 2BJ
Tel: 0181–207–2345

The Royal Society of Health
38a St George's Drive, London SW1V 4BH
Tel: 0171–630–0121

Hazard 23: Human factors

TV's Airport star Jeremy Spake has been told to rest after suffering a suspected stroke. He was taken ill while driving to work. I'm told it was stress-related.

The Sun, 18 March 1999, p. 12

The legislation

The Health and Safety at Work Act 1974
The Provision and Use of Work Equipment Regulations 1998
The Reporting of Injuries, Diseases and Dangerous Occurrences Regulations 1995 (RIDDOR)
The Health and Safety (Consultation with Employees) Regulations 1996
The Management of Health and Safety at Work Regulations 1992
The Manual Handling Operations Regulations 1992
The Workplace (Health, Safety and Welfare) Regulations 1992
The Working Time Regulations 1998

The risks

- casualization
- inexperience
- lack of training
- lack of supervision
- long hours
- short notice
- stress
- working alone

Those most at risk

Art department, camera crews, freelance staff, make-up artists, permanent employees, single operators, trainees.

Since the beginning of the 1980s with the advent of greater competition, the broadcast and film industry has seen a shift in employment away from permanent positions towards short-term contracts and freelance status. While this has had a beneficial effect on the labour flexibility and share prices of production companies in the entertainment sector, this drift towards casualization has raised a number of human concerns for the health and safety of those working in the industry for the more exploitive companies.

The union BECTU has brought to the attention of its members a number of health and safety concerns created by new working patterns and demands. While the rate of fatalities and injuries to permanent employees has declined, the trend for freelance staff has increased with major injuries to self-employed workers rising by 18 per cent and fatalities by 28 per cent in 1984/5.[1]

Health and safety training

Workers in non-union companies are twice as likely to be seriously injured than those in workplaces with union health and safety reps and a joint union-management safety committee. UK workplaces which have union recognition are much more likely to have health and safety training.

Large workplaces are much more likely to have health and safety training than small firms. Public sector firms are more likely to get health and safety training than private sector firms. Men get more health and safety training than women. Full time staff get more health and safety training than part-time staff.[2]

This means that the broadcasting and film industry has more than its fair share of health and safety risks because the employers are often small-scale companies created for one production and the staff are recruited on a part-time or freelance basis. This means that they are often working with unfamiliar colleagues and in unfamiliar working environments. Moreover, these staff are unlikely to receive any formal health and safety training. In this context the importance of union membership becomes obvious as it can provide health and safety training, provide subsidy to attend health and safety courses and provide legal representation and negotiate compensation in the event of an accident. Attendance on BECTU, TUC or Skillset safety courses would help raise the awareness of freelances to health and safety issues.

Working hours

The working hours and conditions of the industry are another area of concern. Regular six-day working, buy-outs of rest days, unpaid lay-offs and poor scheduling result in a poor working environment and produce extra stress in the personal and family life of those working in the industry. The combination of excessive hours and stress can kill. A 19 hour day for ten days in not uncommon. This can create stress and tiredness which can result in an accident on set.

However, a greater number of injuries and fatalities have been as a result of car crashes while driving to or from work. There are no figures for this as they count statistically as road traffic accidents and not as workplace deaths or injuries. Therefore they would not be covered by employers insurance. Many people will know of somebody whom they have worked with who have lost their lives or been seriously injured when driving to or from work.[3] A simple reduction in the length of the working day and reducing the accumulated tiredness caused by lack of adequate breaks after travel would go a long way towards helping this dangerous situation. This is a topic which people are reluctant to talk about and for which no real figures exist at present.

Long working hours are endemic in the industry. For example, in *Spiceworld: The Movie*, the calls for actor Richard E. Grant were as follows: pick-up 6.45a.m., wardrobe 8a.m., make-up 8.15a.m., on set 9a.m.

For the drivers, wardrobe and make-up this meant leaving home at between 5.30a.m. and 6a.m. Then at the end of a long shoot day these people would be the last to finish and the last to get home late at night. These hours are being stretched and the stress increased by cuts to breaks and the practice of only paying for camera hours. For example all the hours of work before shooting starts and after it finishes are effectively unpaid. So a make-up artist with a 7a.m. start ready for shooting at 9a.m. and an 8p.m. finish from a 7p.m. wrap would only be paid from 9a.m. to 7p.m.

Buy-out clauses of working hours and overtime rates are increasingly used by some managers to limit unit costs and increase work flexibility. For example, *The Broker's Man*, shot in November 1997, asked crew to work an 11-day fortnight with technicians receiving no overtime and no pay over Christmas. The crew on *Spiceworld: The Movie* were issued with a contract which specified 'a working week shall consist of six working days in each seven day period and payments shall be inclusive of all overtime service including travel and prep/wrap time and to include specified extended days and bank holidays'.[4]

These new types of contracts contain rights buy-outs of overtime and the practice of Christmas hiatus where staff are effectively laid off in the middle of production with no pay for two weeks. Another factor which can increase the working day and the levels of stress is the practice of aggregation of working hours. For example if a technician signs up for a 60-hour week contract and only works 50 then they will be required to work a 70 hour week the following week for the same money.

Another concern is the stress caused by having two bases nominated in the contract. Staff are paid for travel from the nominated base to the location and return. By nominating a second base many miles away from the first but adjacent to another location the production company can save money by not paying the difference in time and miles between the two.

With cuts to drama budgets, increased competition and the need for 24-hour satellite television and breakfast TV, anti-social hours without extra payment are becoming more common. This is especially true of staff on soap operas which are being turned round quicker, shown more episodes per week and making extra 'specials' in order to attract ratings. The moves towards the maximization of revenue and the deterioration of working conditions in the industry is creating a wider gap between the budgets of many production companies and the health and welfare of their employees. This widening gap is clearly seen by the difference between industry practice to increase hours and cut breaks and the new welfare legislation called the Working Time Directive.

The Working Time Directive

From October 1998 the European Working Time Directive became law in the UK as the Working Time Regulations 1998. The regulations give entitlements to workers and place limits on employers. Traditionally working hours have been dictated by the terms and conditions of an employment contract rather than by law, so the hours an employee worked and the holidays which they received were down to their employer. Before October an employee in the UK had no general legal right to holidays including bank holidays. So any entitlement to leave was determined by the employer as well. However from October 1998 there are now new legal restrictions on the working time of individual employees including freelances.

These new regulations cover three areas of employment law: annual leave, rest breaks and weekly working hours. They also apply to all staff including temporary and part-time contract workers. The employee now has a legal entitlement to three weeks' paid annual leave.

All employees will also be entitled to minimum rest breaks and rest periods. For example where an individual's working day exceeds six hours they are entitled to a minimum rest break of twenty minutes.

All employees will also benefit from minimum rest periods of 11 hours in every 24-hour working period and an uninterrupted rest period of at least 2 days in every 14-day period. However for workers in agriculture, hospitals and the media, the conditions relating to leave and rest periods will not apply.

The new regulations regarding weekly working hours do apply which mean that no employee can be forced to work more than an average of 48 hours a week. Working time is defined as the period of time when a worker is working at his employer's disposal carrying out activities or duties at their behest or instruction. It covers all individuals who have entered into or work under a contract of employment or 'any other contract whether express or implied whether oral or in writing'.

This 48-hour working week must be actual for the first 17-week period. This means that for the first 17 weeks the hours cannot be averaged out, for instance by working more in the first three weeks and less in the others. Employers can no longer front-load working hours so that production staff are working a 60-hour week for three weeks of filming.

Secondly the practice of not counting off-camera time as working time will be illegal as the person employed is still working and being asked to carry out work. This could be good news for over-worked freelance staff and short-term contract workers in the film and television industry. This entitlement will not apply to family businesses or managers.

Employers must keep accurate and up-to-date records of their employees working time and will be committing a criminal offence if they breach any obligations under the new regulations. However if an employee states in writing that s/he does not wish to be bound by the directive then its terms do not apply. This could well see employment contracts in the film and television industry being drawn up in the future with exclusion clauses inserted. Employees in non-unionized companies may also come under pressure to waive their rights under duress or the need for job security. However, they can withdraw that permission and withdraw from opting out of the agreement if they give seven days' notice in writing. It will remain to be seen how much relief the implementation of the Working Time Directive gives to the high stress levels of employees.

Stress

Stress at work is fast becoming endemic as the growing impact of long hours, increasing work loads, job insecurity and flexible hours impacts on the work force. The department of health has estimated that stress causes six million working days to be lost each year at a cost of £5 billion to the economy. Individual companies also lose around 6 per cent of total payroll costs because of workplace health problems, of which stress is now the most significant factor.

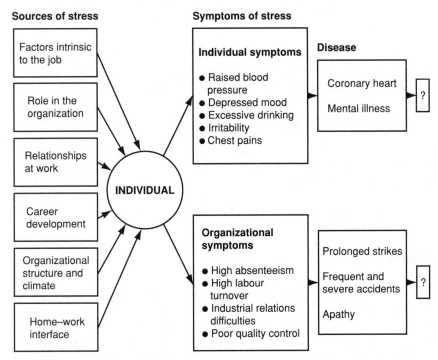

Figure H23.1 *Stress diagram*

Stress is now the fastest growing area of claims against employers. Many employers do not have an effective system for reporting and managing stress for their employees. This failure to communicate could lay organizations and their insurers open to costly legal action for injuries if the employer has not taken sufficient care to eliminate potential risks. This has become such a problem that a new scheme for managing workplace stress has been designed by the Association of Insurance and Risk Managers to protect companies from potential claims.

Stress has now been recognized as the biggest occupational health problem and the HSE has issued new guidelines for employers to cut down on stress.[5,6]

The main causes of stress have been endemic to the film and television business for a long time. These include working to deadlines, short notice, flexible hours, unsocial hours, lack of breaks, inadequate rest periods, excessive travel after long periods of work and casualization. Studies by the Manchester School of Management estimate that two-thirds of stress absence has been caused by workplace bullying. Overworked and stressed managers having to implement downsizing and cost efficiency are causing excessive psychological stress to those affected by their decisions on a daily basis. Secondly managers are more pre-occupied with trying to implement fresh changes than checking health and safety.

Stress can also have an effect on the physical health of employees. The Manchester School of Management report looked at the health effects of long weekly working hours which included fatigue, headaches, heart disease, eye strain and the resulting inability to sustain a healthy lifestyle with an increase in smoking, drinking and poor diet. Passive smoking is also detrimental to health.

Workplace stress will also impact on families causing family break-ups, arguments and divorce. A stressed worker is likely to be less efficient and has a raised risk of having an accident either at work or when travelling. The most commonly held solution is to change the work situation by varying the workload, the work plan and schedules.

Freelances

Freelance working is so prevalent in the film and television industry that a special health and safety leaflet has been produced by the HSE in conjunction with the Joint Advisory Committee for Broadcasting and Performing Arts.[7] The stress factors of being self-employed such as finding work and paying for equipment and tax leave little time for consideration of health and safety. Ironically it is freelances who are most in need of it and yet have the least time to catch up on and obtain training and advice about health and safety.

Many employers are now stipulating health and safety qualifications or special certificates for certain jobs before they will engage someone on a contract. In other words the freelancer is being made responsible for their own health and safety training. On top of this they must also have their own insurance including public, third-party and employers liability cover. This must cover anybody who is working for them as the freelancer has legal health and safety obligations to anyone they employ or subcontract.

They must draw up risk assessment plans for work which they are in charge of or supervise, as well as being responsible for the competence and supervision of any employees and subcontractors working for them on a production.

This duty under the Management of Health and Safety at Work Regulations 1992 includes a duty to pass on information about the work such as how to safely handle hazardous substances and the safe operation of tools, plant, vehicles and equipment. A work method statement must be drawn up and implemented. Anybody working for you must also be given the proper personal protective equipment and given sufficient health and safety training.

Working alone

As well as being responsible for others one of the biggest risk factors for the freelancer can be that of working alone, which for many in the film and television industry is a fact of working life. This means that you have no-one to watch your back and that you are left responsible for your own welfare. For example, anybody working by themselves must take precautions for alerting somebody if they have an injury or accident. This places a premium on good communications and extra first aid precautions for freelances working in isolated locations and by themselves at night (see Hazard 12: Dangerous terrain and Hazard 26: Night operations and bad weather).

The typically long and irregular hours involved in television and film work will prove extra demanding on single workers who have nobody to cover for them and who will have no time for rest breaks. Single news operators are especially at risk as they have no cover for driving to and from location (in the era of twin crews, the sound or lights operator became the spare driver and halved the workload).

The single operator will also fall foul of the Manual Handling Operations Regulations 1992. These impose an overriding duty to avoid lifting heavy equipment. So the single operator should assess the risks and make suitable arrangements to reduce lifting equipment to an acceptable level. As a standard two-lamp lighting kit can weigh 19 kg and a broadcast camera even more, the practical implementation of this for news crews working to deadlines and reacting to sudden events is very difficult and many sustain slip, trip and fall injuries and will often sustain long-term damage to their backs. One only hopes that the advent of lighter DV and digital cameras will help to relieve the single operator burden of acting as driver, sound recordist, lighting engineer, rigger, electrician and reporter's minder.

Further guidance on camera operations can be obtained by reading in conjunction with this section the HSE guidance for camera operations.[8]

When management make an assessment of workers at risk from being alone they should not only consider those who have to work in confined, dangerous, remote and underground locations but also those who deal with dangerous activities and substances. Extra health and safety precautions should apply to those working with chemicals, electricity, explosives, height, machinery and plant. This is because the likelihood of serious injury would be greater if an accident happens. Therefore extra communication, first aid, fire, guarding, protective equipment and warning signs should apply. Lone workers should always carry lone worker alarms and make check ins at regular intervals to confirm their well being, with an action plan of rescue or assistance in place in the event of injury or accident.

Lone worker assessments must take into account those who work in laboratories, projection rooms and transmitter masts. Similar consideration must be given to those who work alone in offices and workstations such as accounts, computer operations, editors, graphics and researchers who run the risk of eye strain damage from VDUs and display screens. Workers who use these by themselves forget to take rest breaks and risk damaging their eyes (for more detailed information see Hazard 32: Visual display screens).

The emphasis for making risk assessments for lone workers must be put on planning and being able to foresee sudden or long-term health and safety risks. Precautions must be put in place before the activity begins.

A pre-requisite to any solo activity must be a briefing from management about the nature of the works and the risks involved. This will take the form of a work plan which takes into account the following factors:

1 A clear definition of responsibilities for managing the work and identifying any hazards in advance by a site visit and recording a written risk assessment.
2 A clear idea of who will supervise the work and check that it is safe.
3 A clear written statement of any advance precautions to be taken specifying the correct tools for the job and the personal protective equipment that must be worn.
4 A clear written statement of emergency procedures including communication, evacuation, fire, first aid and rescue provisions. This should include the reporting of accidents and fire evacuation.
5 A clear work method statement specifying what is to be done, who with (if anyone), who is in charge, how the job is to be done, how long it will take, what time of day or night, checks made about the weather, and the implementation of a permit to work regime. A clear identification of any hazardous substances, with instructions provided about safe storage, use and health monitoring.
6 A clear indication of restrictions on working times and the recording of hours undertaken.
7 A clear provision for welfare such as drinks, food and toilets. Safe design and ergonomics of plants, systems and machinery.

8 Extra vigilance must be used, especially when last-minute changes to work plans or sudden reductions in team size send somebody out by themselves.
9 In these cases it helps to have someone with experience as the activity will be unsupervised. Therefore an assessment must be made of the most suitable and experienced person for the job. If none exists, hire in help or supervision and provide proper training.

To try and prevent accidents the main human factor to take into account is the competence and experience level of anybody selected to carry out a job of work. Similarly the greatest risk factor is inexperience.

At the end of the day competence is the determining factor. For example, the task to be performed could involve filming underwater or from a helicopter. It would be relatively easy to find somebody who was an experienced diver or pilot. However it would be much harder to find a diver or a pilot who was specifically competent in film and television work and who was aware of the risks and how to avoid them.

The selection of an expert is crucial to the success and safety of any job. The more complex the job, the more competent the person needs to be. For example, never involve members of the public or inexperienced people to undertake stunts. This might seem like common sense but this is far less common than you would suppose. So do not be tempted to take risks and employ someone who is inexperienced and incompetent to carry out dangerous and specialized tasks. Use a qualified pyrotechnic supervisor, stunt arranger or specialized camera operator. This will not only be safer but will also be quicker and save you shooting time in the long run.

If you have staff who are inexperienced then it is essential to identify them and provide proper training and supervision for any activity which you ask them to undertake. The selection of a properly qualified and experienced trainer or supervisor is essential. With cuts to education and training budgets and the increase in freelance employment there is always a tendency for budget conscious management to select according to price rather than ability. This is a false economy and can result in a dangerous situation of somebody trying to carry out a risky task for which they have little experience under pressure of time. The end result could well be an accident or serious injury.

Through proper supervision and training, inexperienced and initially incompetent workers can become experienced and competent in safety – without putting others at risk from a situation they should not be in. If you doubt your ability to undertake a task get a second opinion or bring in specialized advice for a safe shoot.

Notes

1 *Stage, Screen and Radio*, February 1997 p. 21.
2 Phillip Beaumont and Richard Harris, *Health and Safety Training in the EU*, OSH, April 1998.
3 For cases of this see *Stage, Screen and Radio*, November 1994 p. 9; November 1997 p. 23; and June 1998 p. 19.
4 *Stage, Screen and Radio*, Dec 1997/Jan 1998 p. 10.
5 *Stage, Screen and Radio*, May 1998, pp. 10/11.
6 Seumas Milne, Job insecurity leads to stress epidemic, *The Guardian*, 15 January 1999. Stress at Work: A Guide for Employers, HSE, ISBN 0-7176-0733-X. Stress Research and Stress Management – Putting Theory to Work, HSE, ISBN 0-7176-0684-X.
7 Facts for Freelances, HSE-IND(G)217L C100, 1996.
8 Camera Operations on Location: Guidance for Managers and Camera Crews on News Gathering, Current Affairs and Factual Programming, 1997, HSE-HSG169, ISBN 0-7176-1346.

Further reading

Health and Safety Law – A Trade Unionists Guide, Labour Research Department, 78 Blackfriars Rd, London SE1 8HF.

The Working Time Regulations 1998, HSE, ISBN 0-11-079410-9.

Camera Operations on Location. Guidance for Managers and Camera Crews on News Gathering, Current Affairs and Factual Programming, HSE, HSG169, ISBN 0-7176-1346-1997.

The Management of Health and Safety at Work Regulations 1992, Approved Code of Practice, HSE, L21, ISBN 0-7176-0412-8.

The Provision and Use of Work Equipment Regulations 1992, Guidance on Regulations, HSE, L22, ISBN 0-7176-0414-4.

The Manual Handling Operations Regulations 1992, Guidance on Regulations, HSE, L23, ISBN 0-7176-0411-X.

The Workplace (Health, Safety and Welfare) Regulations 1992, Guidance on Regulations. HSE, L24, ISBN 0-7176-0413-6.

The Personal Protective Equipment at Work Regulations 1992, Guidance on Regulations. HSE, L25, ISBN 0-7176-0415-2.

The Health and Safety (Display Screen Equipment) Regulations 1992, Guidance on Regulations, HSE, L26, ISBN 0-7176-0410-1.

The Health and Safety (Consultation with Employees) Regulations 1996, Guidance on Regulations, HSE L95, ISBN 0-7176-1234-1.

Taking Action on Stress at Work: A Guide for Employers, HSE, HS(G)116, 1995, ISBN 0-7176-0733-X.

Stress Research and Stress Management – Putting Theory to Work, HSE, ISBN 0-7176-0684-X.

Facts for Freelances, 1996, HSE, IND(G)217l C100.

Working Alone in Safety, HSE, IND(G)73rev, ISBN 0-7176-1507.

Passive Smoking at Work, HSE, IND(G)63rev, ISBN 0-7176-0882-4.
Preventing Asthma at Work, HSE, L55, ISBN 0-7176-0661-9.
Good Health Is Good Business: An Employer's Guide, HSE-Misc-130.
Safety Representatives and Safety Committees ('the brown book', 3rd edition) Approved Code of Practice and Guidance on the Regulations, HSE-L87, ISBN 0-7176-1220-1.
Health and Safety at Work: Know Your Rights, TUC, ISBN 1-85006-102-5.
The Hidden Workplace Epidemics, free leaflet published by the TUC.
Organisational Interventions to Reduce Work Stress: Are they Effective? A Review of the Literature. CRR193, ISBN 0-7176-1625-8.

Contact organizations

Advisory Conciliation and Arbitration Service
Brandon House, 180 Borough High St, London SE1 1LW
Tel: 0171–210–3613

Association of British Theatre Technicians
47 Bermondsey St, London SE1 3XT
Tel: 0171–403–3778

British Actors Equity Association
Guild House, Upper St Martin's Lane, London WC2H 9EG
Tel: 0171–379–6000

BECTU
111 Wardour St, London W1V 4AY
Tel: 0171–437–8506

European Foundation for the Improvement of Living and Working Conditions
Wyattville Rd, Loughlinstown, Co Dublin, Ireland
Tel: 351–204–3100

Ergonomics Society
Devonshire House, Devonshire Square, Loughborough, Leics LE11 3DW
Tel: 01509–243904

Faculty of Occupational Medicine
6 St Andrew's Place, Regent's Park, London NW1 4LB
Tel: 0171–487–3414

Health Education Authority
64 Burgate, Canterbury, Kent CT1 2HJ
Tel: 01227–455–564

The Industrial Injuries Advisory Council
A4, 6th floor, The Adelphi, 1–11 John Adam Street, London WC2N 6HT
Tel: 0171 9628066

Institution of Occupational Safety and Health
The Grange, Highfield Drive, Wigston, Leicester LE18 1NN
Tel: 0116–257–1399

International Ergonomics Group
School of Manufacturing and Mechanical Engineering
The University of Birmingham, B15 2TT
Tel: 0121–414–4233

The International Stress Management Association
South Bank University LPSS, 103 Borough Rd, London SE1 0AA
Tel: 01702–584025

London Hazards Centre
Interchange Studios, Dalby St, London NW5 3NQ
Tel: 0171–267–3387

National Asthma Campaign
Providence House, Providence Rd, London N1 0NT
Tel: 0171–226–2260

National Back Pain Association
The Old Office Block, Elmtree Rd, Teddington, Middx TW11 8ST
Tel: 0181–977–5474

Occupational and Environmental Diseases Association
Mitre House, 66 Abbey Rd, Bush Hill Park, Enfield, Middx EN1 2QH
Tel: 0181–360–8490

Public Concerns at Work
42 Kingsway, London WC2B 6EN
Tel: 0171–404–6609

Repetitive Strain Injury Association
Chapel House, 152–156 High St, Yiewsley, West Drayton, Middx UB7 7BE
Tel: 01895–431134

Robens Institute of Industrial and Environmental Health and Safety
University of Surrey, Guildford GU2 5XH
Tel: 01483–259203

Stress at Work
14 Albion Place, Northampton NN1 1UD
Tel: 01604–259770

The Trades Union Congress TUC
Congress House, Great Russell St, London WC1B 3LS
Tel: 0171–636–4030

Hazard 24: Lasers and radiation

The legislation

The UK Ionising Radiation Regulations (Revised)
The Ionising Radiation Regulations 1985
The Ionising Radiation (Outside Workers) Regulations 1993
The Radioactive Substances Act 1993

The risks

- eye damage
- fire
- explosions
- mobile phones
- skin damage

Those most at risk

Actors, laser technicians, musicians, pregnant staff, the public.

Lasers

The laser is a light amplifier which is capable of generating an intense parallel beam of coherent light. Lasers come in different strengths and are classified according to BS EN 60825. The level of risk will vary according to the class you use: the main risk from strong lasers is skin or eye damage. General purpose safety glasses offer no protection. Eye protectors must be suitable for the type of laser used. Stronger laser beams could also damage camera lenses if the beam is pointed at a camera.

The risk from lasers in film and television work has increased with their use in medical and defence research, light entertainment, medical programmes, music concerts, outside broadcasts and special effects. Laser beams can be visible, ultraviolet or infrared so they are often invisible to the naked eye. Never look directly at a laser or point one at somebody else. Lasers should always be labelled correctly to determine the level of safety precautions required. The level of laser hazard can be reduced by the use of a lower class of laser (this reduces its capability to injure), the correct training and selection of the operator (reducing the human error) and the selection of a proper controlled environment for its use including mounting and enclosure.

However, the potential for eye or skin damage will depend on the wavelength and strength of the laser and the duration of the exposure. This can vary very greatly depending on the class of laser as the range available is very wide so the risk factor from laser work can vary accordingly from very low to high. In other words not all laser work is high risk and not all laser work carries the same degree of risk.

The most usual damage would be photokeratitis (inflammation of the cornea) or conjunctivitis (inflammation of the conjunctiva) from ultra-violet rays (100 nm–400 nm). The symptoms are painful and similar to welder's flash or snow blindness. Eye damage from visible radiation (400 nm–780 nm) takes the form of burns or blind spots. Stronger infrared rays (780 nm–1 mm) can cause cataract formation (similar to glass blower's or furnaceman's cataract).

If you are planning to use a laser in a production then the choice, installation and safe use of the laser should be undertaken by a qualified expert. The laser equipment must be operated to comply with safety standard BS EN 60825–1 1994 and the maximum permitted exposure levels. By May 2000, the European Council Directive 96/29 Euratom on the protection of workers and the public from the dangers of ionizing radiation will be adopted and will result in an updating of the current regulations.

The use of lasers in public performances may also come under the licensing agreements for that venue or area. So make sure you check with the local authority first for any restrictions. Laser radiation is subdivided into ionizing and non-ionizing radiation. More powerful ionizing radiation is produced by gamma and X-ray radiation. In ionizing radiation the energy is strong enough to move electrons from one atom to another. Less powerful non-ionizing radiation is produced by ultaviolet, infrared and microwave lasers. This works with the reduced energy exciting electrons within an atom without splitting or moving them. In other words ionizing radiation is further up the spectrum and much stronger than non-ionizing radiation.

The use of lasers should be identified in the initial production planning stage and included as part of the programme risk assessment.

Safe working practice should take into account the safety of the operator, the safety of the public, provision of adequate warning signs and personal protective equipment. The laser must be suitable and safe for the task required and the operator must have training. Specific training to the appropriate level is required for operators of class 3a, 3b and class 4 lasers. Safe operating instructions for lasers and the provision of eye/hand protection must be identified and provided by the management. Under the Personal Protective Equipment At Work Regulations 1992 British CE standard eye protection must be used for work with class 3b and 4 lasers.

Class 3b lasers must have key control, a beam stop device, an audible or visual fail safe emission warning signal and an interlock built in as design safety features. Class 3b and class 4 lasers should have laser protective enclosures. Medical supervision of laser operators and medical precautions for laser accidents might also be necessary. Make sure that your production insurance covers the use of lasers.

Production operations employing lasers above class 3a must also have a designated laser safety officer.

You should also seek advice on the correct laser for your intended use and you must make sure that the laser operator is experienced for that type of work. Some local authorities may also have special conditions relating to laser displays in the licensing agreements for public performance venues or outside broadcasts.

Lasers are usually either continuous wave or pulsed mode and the danger factor would come from the intensity of the light or the radiation produced by the laser. This can be ultraviolet or microwave. Laser products are classified according to strength as follows:

- Class 1: Inherently safe, low-power lasers.
- Class 2: Low-power devices emitting visible radiation which the eye can protect itself against by blinking.
- Class 3a: Medium-power lasers which should not be viewed directly or through a telescope, microscope, prism or camera lens.
- Class 3b: Medium-power lasers which require detailed control measures including the appointment of a laser safety officer as direct beam viewing is always hazardous.
- Class 4: High power lasers whose use is very hazardous and require extreme caution as these cause direct skin burns and could constitute a fire hazard.

Do not point any laser effect at people such as actors, audiences, presenters or crew. Make sure that the set or stunt situation has no reflective surfaces such as mirrors, glass, metal, etc. It is the responsibility of the set designer under the Construction (Design and Management) Regulations 1994 to assess this risk and take it into account when designing the set. The stunt co-ordinator or pyrotechnic supervisor must take responsibility for the safe design and management of any effect or stunt involving a laser.

In April 1997 the British Entertainment Laser Association (BELA) was formed by companies in the entertainment sector who were concerned about the safe operation of lasers. They plan to develop a working code of practice for all members involved in laser work to minimize the risk of injury. They will also establish a helpline to advise on safety related issues.

Enforce safety rules for hazardous laser work. Any work involving lasers should always be identified as part of the production planning process and a proper risk assessment should be carried out before any production activity with lasers commences so that the proper precautions and personal protection measures are in place before filming starts.

Mobile phones

Non-ionizing radiation hazards can come from use of low-level devices over long periods of time. Some now consider mobile phones to be a health and safety concern after recent studies by the Defence Establishment Research Agency.

In April 1999 it was reported that entrepreneur Richard Branson has warned his staff over the danger of mobile phones (*Occupational Safety and Health Risk Watch*, April 1999, p. 13). The effects of prolonged exposure to blasts of microwave signals from mobile phones has raised more questions than answers about their safe use over a prolonged period of time.

A number of court cases have been brought including one by a scientist specializing in radioactivity who claimed that people using a mobile phone for more than twenty minutes at a time were putting their health at risk. He tried unsuccessfully to sue a mobile phone supplier for not issuing health warnings (*Occupational Safety and Health Risk Watch*, October 1998).

Court cases so far have not met with success as experts maintain that the level of microwave energy is too low to impair health (see *Independent on Sunday*, 25 November 1998 and 1 November 1998 p. 12; also *Guardian Education*, 23 March 1999, p. 9). It could be another one of those health scares or it could be a long-term risk to health. If found to be true then the use of mobile phones in production communications would have to be identified as a potential hazard to health. Damage will only become obvious in the long term. A Department of Health study on the health effects of mobile phones is due to be published by Bristol University shortly and this may help to clarify the situation.

A feature on mobile phone risks by Nick Cook in RoSPA *Safety Express* April 1999, p. 13 quotes Dr Michael Clark of the NRPB who casts doubt on the health scares and who believes that the risks are minimal. Another risk comes from using them while driving.

Leading safety organizations including RoSPA and road agencies are campaigning to ban the use of mobile phones while driving. This will include use of 'hands free' equipment as the conversation alone can prove a distraction to the driver. Guidance to avoid the use of mobile phones while driving has now been included in the new Highway Code.

Radiation

This type of long-term risk from low level radiation may also come from the use of microwave ovens for catering and kitchens by catering staff and crew. Ultraviolet radiation may also be a risk when used in display lighting and LEDs.

Other risks from microwave waves would be to links and transmitter staff who have to work with microwave links and transmitters. A risk assessment should be made for staff working with this equipment.

The Ionising Radiation Regulations control the use of radioactive substances and X-ray machines. Any areas where the statutory dose limits may be exceeded are designated as controlled or supervised areas. For radiological protection advice and before working in areas containing ionizing radiation you must consult a radiation protection advisor. S/he should have a certificate of competence to practice and advise in radiation protection which is valid for five years.

There were also post-graduate radiological protection courses which are now being replaced by specific NRPB short courses for radiological protection advisors.

The safety for such areas is controlled by the radiation protection advisor backed up by a radiation protection supervisor. Anybody working in controlled areas must comply with a written system of work which can be shown to limit their exposure to potential radiation hazards.

Employers and operators of these premises also have a duty to inform female employees of the possible hazard to a foetus from exposure to ionizing radiation. The health of workers involved in ionizing radiation must be monitored and a record kept on a special form – the F2067 Ionising Radiation Health Record.

Film and television workers who have to work or visit the workplaces of other organizations or employers which contain a radiation hazard come under the Ionising Radiation (Outside Workers) Regulations 1993. So they must be issued with an approved radiation pass book (available from HMSO). This contains calculations made about the total exposure time of any worker plus the daily dose limits entered by the employer. The pass book should also record the entry time and exit time from the controlled area. Anybody asked to work in a controlled area should be given a copy of the safety regulations, be briefed properly on the safe working practices and be provided with proper personal protective equipment.

Ionizing radiation can produce higher level hazards. Areas where you could encounter these risks include proximity to nuclear powered submarines, reactors and ships. Radar from communication equipment in defence establishments and ships can also generate significant radiation hazards. Hospital scanning devices and medical locations may also generate radiation for X-ray radiology, radiotherapy and nuclear medicine. Camera crews should beware of the NMR magnetic risks in hospitals. Exposure to this in scanning areas could seriously damage any metal equipment such as cameras. Precautions should also be taken before filming in X-ray areas. Damage to your eyesight is one hazard – and it could also wipe your tape.

Any establishment where significant radiation work is carried out must have a radiation protection advisor appointed under the Ionising Radiation Regulations 1995. Seek advice from them first before trying to film. Never try to enter any radiation area without authority. Current radiation exposure limits are regulated by EC Council Directive 96/29/Euratom and the Radioactive Substances Act 1993.

All sites which use radioactive material must be licensed and hold a certificate of registration. Camera crews filming in nuclear sites or radioactive areas would have to comply with safety procedures for personnel in controlled areas. The standard BNFL procedures to be followed are:

1 The person in question must have completed a radiological protection course, or as visitors would be accompanied, full-time by an approved person.
2 A hard hat and a change of clothes or a pair of coveralls must be provided and must be worn.
3 A pair of socks and a pair of controlled issued shoes must be issued and worn.
4 Cosmetics must not be applied in controlled areas, no food or drink may be consumed, nor is smoking or the taking of snuff permitted.
5 Avoid touching things unnecessarily. Do not bite fingernails or put fingers in your mouth, ears, nose or eyes.

6 Film badges or other dosimeters are issued and worn in approved locations.
7 People in controlled areas must wash their hands thoroughly before and after using the lavatory.
8 People leaving controlled areas must observe the correct changing room procedures to prevent the spread of contamination. Having left their shoes at the 'barrier' they should remove their outer garments before thoroughly washing their hands and entering the IPM machine. (If contamination is present the location will be identified. The machine will not allow the person to enter 'clean' areas, and they must return to the washing/shower area and either wash off the contamination, or call for specialist assistance to do so.)

In addition to these general guidelines film crews should also take the precautions of:

1 Having all lenses monitored before entering a controlled area. (Many lenses are coated with a radioactive protective finish. The monitoring procedure when leaving a controlled area would be unable to discriminate radioactively coated lenses from contamination picked up whilst in the controlled area.)
2 Applying protective tape to tripod bases, equipment boxes and any goods or equipment that may be put onto the ground or floors whilst in controlled areas. This can be stripped off at the changing room when leaving the controlled area.
3 Making sure that once all the equipment has been thoroughly monitored by the BNFL safety staff, you retain the monitoring certificate. (You may be asked to produce it when leaving the site.)

For advice about filming inside nuclear establishments, information concerning the level of risk and the precautions to be taken, contact the radiation protection advisor via the press office of the establishment concerned. Note that new ionizing regulations are due out around 2000. This should include the mandatory legal requirement for a radiation protection advisor.

Further reading

The Journal of Radiological Protection, quarterly.
The Institution of Lighting Engineers, Code of Practice for Use of Lasers and Other Decorative Lighting in Public Places.
Working With Radiation, BNFL, M43/35M/193
BS EN 60825: Safety of Laser Products, Part 1, 1994, British Standards Institution.

The Ionising Radiation Regulations 1985, Approved Code of Practice, HSE, COP23, 1988, ISBN 0-11-883978-0.

The Protection of Persons Against Ionising Radiation Arising from any Work Activity, HSE, L58, 1994, ISBN 0-7176-0508-6.

The Protection of Outside Workers Against Ionising Radiation, HSE, L49.

The Ionising Radiation (Outside Workers) Regulations 1993, Approved Code of Practice, 1993, ISBN 0-7176-0681-3.

The Radiation Safety of Lasers Used for Display Purposes, HSE, HS(G)95, 1996, ISBN 0-7176-0691-0.

Controlling the Radiation Safety of Display Laser Installations, HSE INDG 224.

Ionising Radiation Health Record, HSE, F2067, ISBN 0-7176-0816-6.

The Dispersion of Releases of Hazardous Materials in the Vicinity of Buildings, HSE, CRR70, 1995, ISBN 0-7176-0887-5.

Radon in the Workplace, HSE, INDG210.

Working Group on Ionising Radiations 1993/4, HSE, 1995, ISBN 0-7176-0927-8.

Documents of the NRPB: Occupational, Public and Medical Exposure, Volume 4, 1993, ISBN 0-85951-361-0.

Diseases Induced by Ionising and Non-Ionising Radiation, CM-4280, Industrial Injuries Advisory Council, ISBN 0-10-142802-2.

Health Effects Related to the Use of Visual Display Units, Volume 5, 1994, ISBN 0-85951-376-9.

Kitchen, R., *The Radiation Safety Handbook*, Butterworth-Heinemann, Oxford, 1993, ISBN 0-7506-1712-8.

Safety of Laser Products, Part 3: Guidance for Laser Displays and Shows, Draft IEC.825.3, British Standards Institution.

Council Directive 96/29 Euroatom, 13th May 1996, Laying Down Basic Safety Standards for the Protection of the Health of Workers and the General Public Against the Dangers Arising from Ionizing Radiation. *Official Journal of the European Communities*, LL59/L, 29th June 1996.

NRPB At A Glance Series – Non-Ionising Radiations/Radon/Radio Waves.

Health Surveillance of Persons Occupationally Exposed to Ionising Radiation: Guidance for Occupations – Physicians, International Atomic Agency, ISBN 92-0-103898-4.

Low Doses of Ionising Radiation: Biological Effects and Regulatory Control, IAEA, ISBN 92-0-102698-6.

Contact organizations

The Association of University Radiation Protection Officers
c/o Christine Edwards, Faculty of Science, University of Central Lancashire, Corporation St, Preston, Lancashire PR1 2HE
Tel: 01772–893488

The British Entertainment Laser Association
Twinffrwd House, Llansor, Caerleon, Gwent, NP18 1LS
Tel: 01275–395052

British Standards Institution
389 Chiswick High Rd, London W4 4AL
Tel: 0181–996–9000

The Environment Agency
Waterside Drive, Almondsbury, Bristol BS34 4UD
Tel: 01454–624400

British Nuclear Fuels plc
Pelham House, Calderbridge, Cumbria CA20 1DB
Tel: 019467–28987

H and M Scientific Consultants Ltd
PO Box MT27, Leeds LS17 8QA

The Institute of Radiation Protection
64 Dalkeith Rd, Harpenden, Herts AL5 5PW
Tel: 01582–715026

Institution of Lighting Engineers
Lennox House, 9 Lawford Rd, Rugby, Warwickshire CV21 2DZ
Tel: 01788–576492

Lighting Industry Federation
Swan House, 207 Balham High Rd, London SW17 7BQ
Tel: 0181–675–5432

The National Radiological Protection Board (NRPB)
Chilton, Didcot, Oxfordshire OX11 0RQ
Tel: 01235–831600

Performing Services Association
Hawks House School Passage, Kingston upon Thames, Surrey KT1 3DU
Tel: 0181–392–0180

The Professional Lighting and Sound Association
7 Highlight House, St Leonards Rd, Eastbourne, E. Sussex BN21 3UH
Tel: 01323–410335

Society of Radiographers
2 Carriage Row, 183 Eversholt St, London NW1 1BU
Tel: 0171–391–4500

The Society for Radiological Protection
148 Buckingham Palace Rd, London SW1W 9TR
Tel: 0171–823–4971

Hazard 25: Manual handling and lifting

The legislation

The Health and Safety at Work Act 1974
The Manual Handling Operations Regulations 1992
The Provision and Use of Work Equipment Regulations 1998
The Reporting of Injuries, Diseases and Dangerous Occurrences
Regulations 1995 (RIDDOR)

The risks

- back strain
- repetitive strain injury
- slips, trips, falls

Those most at risk

Camera crew, cleaners, costumers, hairdressers, hire staff, riggers,
grips, lighting crew, make-up artists, repair staff, scenery staff,
stores staff.

The Manual Handling Operations Regulations 1992 affect anyone
involved in carrying or lifting. Handling and lifting injuries account for
over a quarter of all reported accidents. These are estimated to cost

industry £1.26 billion every year and are the most common workplace injury. The average handling injury is estimated to average 20 days off work, so for producers the identification of manual handling risks should be a priority.

The film and television business involves a lot of portable equipment where the weight can vary from a small torch to a large generator. The variety of locations and terrain which you encounter in film and television work presents a different risk every time. Moving loads from one place to another is an integral part of the business. But apart from base premises a fresh assessment must be made every time the location and nature of the load changes.

Employers must identify situations which require manual handling and have a legal duty to avoid hazardous lifting and carrying operations. They can do this by carrying out a manual handling risks assessment. This means identifying any part of the production process where carrying or lifting will occur. Then through proper training and the correct use of equipment the manual handling risk can be reduced to a safe working level.

Once identification of the lifting hazards has been made then a work method statement can be produced which sets out how the risks will be tackled. Since handling and lifting happens every day it makes sense to ingrain good practice into regular routines.

The first step is to eliminate and reduce the amount of handling and lifting which people have to undertake by buying proper equipment. Assisted lifting is a lot safer and production companies should make lifting and moving equipment available for all operations. Provide barrows and trolleys for moving equipment around locations and from stores to vehicles.

Very often it is light objects which are carried incorrectly that cause injuries so the use of equipment to move even light loads can significantly reduce the risks on a daily basis. Identify the points in your everyday operations where equipment must be moved and cover these first. For example, from an equipment store to a vehicle. Once base buildings have been covered you can then move on to identifying manual handling and lifting problems on location.

Film and television sets should be assessed for risks in the same way as your office. Break down operations into sequences and spot where lifting or handling is required. For example, moving lights or scaffolding. Again fill these loopholes by providing assistance equipment that will lighten the load such as forklifts and stair lifters. These should be provided where the need is identified and proper training given in their use.

One way of improving handling is to make sure that vehicles are fitted with the correct tailgates at waist height and that vans and trucks are fitted with hoists. Another is to make sure that awkward stairs and steps are replaced by smooth ramps in buildings and sets to reduce the risks from trips and falls while carrying.

Film and television work often takes place in buildings which belong to other people. So before setting out as part of the production planning process you should obtain as much information about any handling or lifting risks which are inherent to the proposed location. Obtain as much information as you can from a site visit backed by plans and telephone enquiries.

Things to look out for are the distance you may have to move equipment – for example, from the car park to the building. Try and park as near as possible to unload by arranging access beforehand. Do you need a trolley and a barrow to assist you? Walk the route that equipment will be taken and check for steps, uneven surfaces and restricted doorways. Choose an alternative route if the shortest is not safe and build the moving time into your shooting schedule.

If you are filming in basements or above ground level check for easy access methods such as delivery hatches and lifts to avoid moving equipment up or down stairs. If necessary bypass stairs by constructing a temporary hoist to gain access to roof level or in extreme cases use a helicopter to move objects in a safer way. Never exceed the safe working weight of lifts, hoists and lifting ropes.

There are manual handling situations where it will be necessary for staff to undertake lifting and moving without mechanical assistance. Producers and managers must take steps to ensure that these operations do not result in accident or injury to those who have to do this. There is no legal weight limit that a person is forbidden to lift so the safest course to choose is to avoid lifting anything heavy without assistance. Team lifting can reduce a serious risk to a safe one. Waiting for help can eliminate the risk from a hasty action. This is especially advisable on productions with lots of crew but a light budget.

Managers and producers must also assess the suitability of the person to the task required. This means fitting the job around the strengths and weaknesses of your staff. Never ask anybody to lift or handle objects who is ill or untrained. A crew of young people trained in manual handling can move more than an elderly crew who are not. Select staff to move and lift on their physical strength and ask weaker people to move lighter objects. But always remember that the incorrect movement of a light object can cause more damage than a heavy object lifted in the right way.

So managers should send any staff who are engaged in lifting or moving on a proper manual handling course to learn safe lifting techniques. RoSPA provide a manual handling and risk assessors certificate and other manual handling courses.

A course will teach you proper kinetic lifting. The closer the centre of gravity of the load can be kept to that of the body the easier, more natural and safer the lift. So position your feet the right distance apart and lift with a straight back. Avoid stoop lifting.

Always bend the knees not your back. This is especially important as awkward and large shaped objects can cause more injury than the weight if tackled in the wrong way. Hand hooks or lifting aids should be used for unwieldy objects.

The majority of injuries in film and television are bad back injuries caused by repetitive lifting of tripods, cameras and lights in the wrong way over a prolonged period of time. Early retirement with bad backs is especially common for ENG crews who have to move quickly without taking into account the long-term damage this can cause. Always seek to use safer ways of working that avoid repetitive and damaging lifting routines.

For example, redesign and plan your work activities to eliminate lifting hazards and reduce weight. This can be done in a number of ways. Redesign equipment stores so that heavy items are kept at waist height, which eliminates bending or stretching. Store the lightest equipment nearer the ceiling and provide steps to avoid over-reaching. Store the most frequently used equipment in the most accessible place which is nearest to the dispatch point. Avoid high stacking of items.

Designers and location managers can help by constructing sets and stages with access factors considered so that loads are not carried up steps or over long distances. If a task involves the repetitive movement of a large quantity of equipment try and reduce the task to a safer proportion. Designers can help by building safety factors into props and sets by the use of lighter materials, proper handles and wheels.

Managers can help reduce loads by obtaining supplies in the same quantity but in smaller size containers which reduce the individual weight of each lift. Several smaller trucks can be safer than one large load as breaks can be scheduled to allow for proper rest. Production managers should always ask if there are ways to make the task lighter and easier through good logistics and scheduling of operations. Tasks can be made safer by reorganizing and reducing the operation to a safe working level with enough staff and equipment to perform it.

Directors should avoid excessive takes which involve actors or crew in repeatedly strenuous lifting or carrying sequences, either directly in the action or as a result of it. Try to avoid moving or lifting in bad conditions such as rain and at night which increase the risks of slips and trips. Ensure that all lifting and carrying operations are properly lit and staff wear high visibility vests which can be seen by drivers of trucks and fork lifts. This precaution is very necessary for lifting and carrying operations near busy roads, airports and railways.

Staff engaged in lifting or moving should wear proper protective equipment. The back support belt must be issued to all staff engaged in manual handling and lifting operations. Steel capped boots to protect the feet and gloves to protect the hands from sharp edges and spills must be worn. Staff lifting in loading bays or high storage areas should wear hard hats for head protection from falling objects, especially if the movement involves working at height.

Management can reduce the risks involved in manual handling and lifting by identifying the weight of each case and carton. Proper labelling can help staff identify heavy and high risk objects so that they can seek assistance. Flight cases can be built and designed for safe lifting with proper handles and carrying straps. If necessary, wheels should be attached or they should fit onto a trolley for moving. If no easy carrying is possible then use a mechanical aid or get extra help.

Safe manual handling and lifting in the last resort rests on reliable information being given to staff who have been asked to undertake these operations. Obtain information from suppliers about the weight and packaging of the load you are receiving. If necessary specify how you would like it to be made up. Always allow enough time for the job to be carried out safely and use staff who are properly trained in manual handling and lifting. Give them the proper equipment to carry out the task and provide enough people for the task at hand. Identify any risks in advance and make sure all carrying and lifting operations are properly supervised at all times by an experienced and qualified person.

Further reading

The Manual Handling Operations Regulations 1992, HMSO No. 2793, 1992.

Manual Handling – Solutions You Can Handle, HSE, HS(G)115, 1994, ISBN 0-7176-0693-7.

Getting to Grips with Manual Handling – A Short Guide for Employers, HSE, IND(G)1431 1993.

The Manual Handling Operations Regulations 1992, Approved Code of Practice and Guidance, HSE, L23, 1992, ISBN 0-7176-0413-6.

Manual Handling. Guidance on the Regulations, HSE-L23, ISBN 0-7176-2415-3 (revised 1999).

Pascal Don, Staying Safe on Location Filming, *Safety Management*, November 1997, pp. 12–15.

IPAF Guide to MEWPs, International Powered Access Federation, 1994.

Code of Practice for the Safe Use of Lifting Equipment, Lifting Equipment Engineers Association.

Rider Operated Lift Trucks. Operator Training, Approved Code of Practice and Guidelines, HSE COP 26, ISBN 0-7176-0474-8.

Safety in Working with Lift Trucks, HSE, HS9(G)6, 1993, ISBN 0-11-886395-9.

Getting to Grips with Manual Handling, *Safety Management*, November 1997, pp. 32–37.

Manual Handling Guidance Update, *RoSPA Safety Express*, March/April 1999, p. 12.

Manual Handling, The Facts. Available from Safety Videos, Tel: 01492–531811.

Contact organizations

Association of Loading and Elevating Equipment Manufacturers
Ambassador House, Brigstock Rd, Thornton Heath, Surrey CR7 7JG
Tel: 0181–665–5395

British Industrial Truck Association Ltd
Scammell House, 9 High St, Ascot, Berkshire SL5 7JF
Tel: 01344–623800

British Standards Institution
389 Chiswick High Rd, London W4 4AL
Tel: 0181–996–9000

Performing Services Association
Hawks House, School Passage, Kingston upon Thames, Surrey KT1 3DU
Tel: 0181–392–0180

Construction Industry Training Board (CITB)
Health and Safety Development, Bircham Newton, King's Lynn,
Norfolk PE3 6RH

Health Education Authority
Trevelyan House, 30 Great Peter St, London SW1P 2HW
Tel: 0171–222–5300

Institute of Occupational Medicine
8 Roxburgh Place, Edinburgh EH8 9SU
Tel: 0131–667–4131

International Powered Access Federation
PO Box 16, Carnforth, Lancashire LA6 1LB
Tel: 01524–781393

Lifting Equipment Engineers Association
Waggoners Court, The Street, Manuden, Bishop's Stortford, Herts
CM23 1DW
Tel: 01279–816504

The National Back Pain Association
The Old Office Block, Elmtree Rd, Teddington, Middx TW11 8ST
Tel: 0181–977–5474

Institute Of Logistics
Douglas House, Queens Square, Corby, Northants NN17 1PL
Tel: 01536–205500

International Powered Access Federation
PO Box 16, Carnforth, Lancashire LA6 1LB
Tel: 01524–781393

National Association of Lift Makers
33/34 Devonshire St, London W1N 1RF
Tel: 0171–935–3013

St John Ambulance
1 Grovesnor Crescent London SW1X 7EF
Tel: 0171–235–5231

Hazard 26: Night operations and bad weather

The risks

- bad visibility
- extreme weather
- inadequate protective equipment
- injury and exposure
- moving vehicles
- lifting and manual handling
- slips, trips and falls

Those most at risk

Camera crew, lighting crew, actors, presenters, the public.

Night time operations in film and television work increase the health and safety risk of normal activities by adding extra danger factors to potentially dangerous production operations. The lack of visibility increases the chances of an accident. This risk is especially high from any production activity combining moving vehicles or machinery with crew and actors. For example, the risk factor of working in the vicinity of airports, docks, railways, roads and water becomes a lot higher as these situations combine fast moving vehicles at night with production staff concentrating on a job. There is a much higher risk of somebody getting hit. There is also the added risk of somebody falling into water and not being seen. So visibility must be a priority with any night operations, together with extra security to prevent theft and intruders. Overnight vandalism to tools and machinery can cause accidents to your crew and to the intruders themselves in some cases.

This need for extra visibility means that producers and managers should provide extra precautions and protective equipment. The first precaution to take is to inform the operators of third-party premises that you will be filming at a particular location and at what time. This is so that supervisors and operators of vehicles and machinery can alter their routines to take account of your activities by slowing down as they approach your zone of action – for example trains or cranes.

You should take extra care to cordon off your zone of work with fluorescent tapes and emergency lights similar to a roadworks zone at night. This is so a protection zone for your production is established which you can work within and which other people can see and avoid. Then make sure that this area is properly lit by bright lights and that a secondary emergency lighting system will automatically cut in the event of mains or generator failure.

However, be aware that a brightly lit area in an unusual place might create problems for local residents. Bright lights incorrectly used and badly shaded could dazzle motorists. Brightly lit areas could also create havoc near an airfield and confuse pilots with disastrous results. Similarly, rail companies have special rules regarding lights shining near railway tracks to avoid confusion with signals. It is usual to specify first what you need to film, then safe, fenced-off locations may be provided trackside and airside as part of the permit to film and crews will be accompanied by safety staff at all times. High visibility clothing and hard hats must be worn and look-outs posted to give advanced warning for train movements, trucks, airport vehicles and fork-lift trucks.

Make sure that all local residents, landowners and the police are informed in advance. Try to keep disturbance to a minimum and ensure extra site security, including proper fences, at night.

If the production activity requires the movement of equipment or vehicles, try and avoid any major lifting or hazardous vehicle situations such as car stunts during night time. If you have to, confine these activities to cordoned off zones and vehicle lanes designated for the purpose and restrict access to a minimum number of people to do the job. To make operations safer, double the amount of supervisors and look-outs who have no other function than to make sure that operations are conducted safely and that crew are protected and warned of any danger.

All moving vehicles should be properly lit and emit an audible warning on approach or manoeuvre. Any staff working at night must be seen and be able to see. Management must equip them with high visibility jackets and vests, with bright hard hats. They should also be equipped with emergency torches and lamps to see in the dark and to warn others of their presence. These battery lights are also needed as emergency cover in the event of any main lighting failure on the site.

Remember that the further north, the further into winter and the higher you go increases the risks from cold and exposure at night as the temperature can drop quickly to dangerous levels. This is particularly true of exposed locations such as airfields, coastline, mountains, moors, rooftops and deserts.

Similarly fog, rain and snow can turn an apparently benign evening location into a lethal one, combining cold and poor visibility. So always take these factors into account when filming at night. They dramatically increase the risks involved. Always check the weather forecast before setting out to film at night, especially at sea or at exposed locations.

Monitor the air temperature so that you can stop if it gets too cold. The majority of accidents at night happen because people are not prepared, are often inexperienced and do not wear or carry the right protective equipment. Crew working at night have often been working extended hours and so tiredness increases the risk factor. So make sure that schedules are realistic to allow for tiredness. Remember that moving and setting up equipment is slower and lighting set ups can take longer at night.

All participants, including actors, crew, presenters and the public, must be issued with warm protective clothing, including jackets, hats and gloves. Management must increase the welfare facilities and breaks during night work by scheduling more rest periods and providing better rest facilities, including hot meals and drinks.

There is a very high risk to staff who are required to drive at night after an extended working day or who have to drive in the early morning after working most of the night. A lot of accidents in the film and television business have happened to staff who are driving at night or after prolonged night work. This can effect studio crews, security staff and editors as well as eng. crews and location crews. Road accidents are classed as RTAs so they never appear on statistics for film and television accidents. But the high incidence of these types of accident indicate that managers and producers should do more to prevent staff from driving at night and driving after night work by scheduling better rest periods and offering accommodation.

Producers and managers should always seek advice about special night working involving flying at night, explosives and stunts. Bad weather, especially in winter, can create night time conditions and productions should take extra precautions and adopt night time working practices and enforce safety rules for exposed conditions. The need for night work should always be identified as part of the production planning process and a proper risk assessment should be carried out before any production activity at night commences so that the proper precautions and personal protection measures are already in place.

Further reading

Wilkerson, Bangs and Hayward, *Hypothermia, Frostbite and Other Cold Injuries*, code HYP1. Available from Emergency Response Publications 5 Shelly Court, South Zeal, Okehampton, Devon EX20 2PT, Tel: 01837–840102.

Contact organizations

Production Managers Association (CoPACT)
45 Mortimer St, London W1N 7TD
Tel: 0171–331–6000

Production Services Association
Hawks House, School Passage, Kingston upon Thames, Surrey KT1 3DU
Tel: 0181–392–0180

Hazard 27: Noise

The legislation

The Noise at Work Regulations 1989
The Environmental Protection Act 1990
The Control of Pollution Act 1974

The risks

- subsidiary accidents
- hearing damage
- stress
- tinnitus

Those most at risk

Floor managers, gun experts, pyrotechnic engineers, scenery woodwork and metal workers, studio crew, eng. crew, sound mixers,
anyone exposed to extreme sound.

The HSC have estimated that some 2m UK workers are at risk from
excessive noise and that 30 per cent of industrial workers have some
work related hearing loss. In the film and television industry sound can
seriously damage the health of employees. Employers, managers and
producers must take action to assess, control and prevent noise risks.

Noise risks have two major forms. First, exposure to a sudden extreme burst of sound such as gun fire or an explosion. Second, prolonged exposure to harmful levels of sound over a period of time from machinery, vehicle noise, music or headphones. The total amount of noise exposure over the whole working day is called the 'daily personal noise exposure'.

The health risks of noise cause damage to the ear, causing deafness, tinnitus and loss of balance. Hearing loss is measured by audiometry which tests the threshold of hearing. A difference of 20 dB(A) or more indicates serious hearing loss. The provision for audiometry tests in the UK is very poor but it is a reliable way to prove hearing loss. The damage to hearing is caused by the intensity of the sound and its duration.

The safety risk of work related deafness comes from the stress it can cause. It is also dangerous as those affected become unable to hear a warning of an imminent danger. Risks from noise can occur on location and at base buildings, so most staff are potentially affected.

Symptoms of a noisy environment include having to shout to communicate with somebody very near to you, or, when you leave a work area, finding that you have difficulty hearing or your ears are ringing. This can cause long-term damage to the ear and induce deafness and tinnitus. Occupational deafness is classed as an industrial disease.

The employer must measure noise levels in all areas of the workplace as part of the risk assessment process. The employer must make decibel meters and noise meters available to take measurements and the standard used is BS 4142. All sound level and integrating sound level meters must conform to IEC 61672. Dosemeters must conform to either EN 61252 1995, BS EN 61252 1997 or IEC 1252 1993. Sound calibrators must conform to BS 7189 1989 or IEC 1988. Type 3 sound level meters are not suitable for noise assessments. All sound meters must be inspected, repaired and tested in accordance with BS 7580 Parts 1 and 2.

The figure used is the level of noise at the ear, not the source of the sound. Note that noise damage does not operate in an even way. For every increase of 3 dB(A), the noise level doubles and the exposure time must be halved. In other words a sound level of 87 dB(A) is twice as noisy as 84 dB(A), while 90 dB(A) is ten times the intensity of 80 dB(A).

There are three noise action limits which are legal requirements for employers. The first action level is 85 dB(A), the second 90 dB(A) and the peak action level equivalent to 200 pascals/140 dB(A) (see noise action level table, Figure H27.2). If the measured noise levels go above these action levels, the employer must put precautions in place and take action.

The first action they must take is to supply information. The employer must warn you of any noise danger and explain how you can avoid the risk. If the noise level exceeds 85 dB(A) then written records of this noise

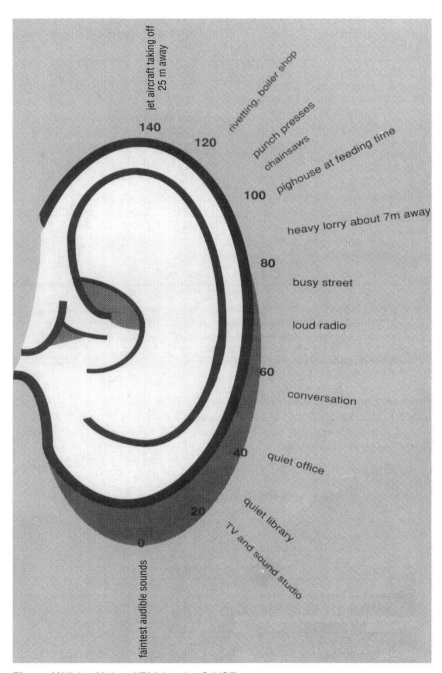

Figure H27.1 *Noise d(B)A levels. © HSE*

Action required where $L_{EP.d}$ is likely to be: *(see note 1 below)*	below 85 dB(A)	85 dB(A) First AL	90 dB(A) Second AL
EMPLOYERS' DUTIES **General duty to reduce risk** Risk of hearing damage to be reduced to the lowest level reasonably practicable (Reg 6)	■	■	(2) ■
Assessment of noise exposure Noise assessments to be made by a competent person (Reg 4)		■	■
Record of assessments to be kept until a new one is made (Reg 5)		■	■
Noise reduction Reduce exposure to noise as far as is reasonably practicable by means other than ear protectors (Reg 7)			■
Provision of information to workers Provide adequate information, instruction and training about risks to hearing, what employees should do to minimise risk, how they can obtain ear protectors if they are exposed to between 85 and 90 dB(A), and their obligations under the Regulations (Reg 11)		■	■
Mark ear protection zones with notices, so far as reasonably practicable (Reg 9)			■
Ear protectors Ensure so far as is practicable that protectors are: – provided to employees who ask for them (Reg 8(1)) – provided to all exposed (Reg 8(2)) – maintained and repaired (Reg 10(1)(b)) – used by all exposed (Reg 10(1)(a))		■ ■	 ■ ■ ■
Ensure so far as reasonably practicable that all who go into a marked ear protection zone use ear protectors (Reg 9(1)(b))			■ (3)
Maintenance and use of equipment Ensure so far as is practicable that: – all equipment provided under the Regulations is used, except for the ear protectors provided between 85 and 90 dB(A) (Reg 10(1)(a)) – ensure all equipment is maintained (Reg 10(1)(b))		■ ■	■ ■

Figure H27.2   *Employers' noise duty table. © HSE*

Action required where $L_{EP.d}$ is likely to be: (*see note 1 below*)	below 85 dB(A)	85 dB(A) First AL	90 dB(A) Second AL
EMPLOYEES' DUTIES **Use of equipment** So far as practicable: − use ear protectors (Reg 10(2)) − use any other protective equipment (Reg 10(2)) − report any defects discovered to employer (Reg 10(2))		■ ■ ■	■ ■ ■
MACHINE MAKERS' AND SUPPLIERS' DUTIES **Provision of information** Provide information on the noise likely to be generated (Reg 12)		■	■

NOTES: (1) The dB(A) action levels are values of daily personal exposure ($L_{EP.d}$).
(2) All the actions indicated at 90 dB(A) are also required where the peak sound pressure is at or above 200 Pa (140 dB re 20 μPa).
(3) This requirement applies to all who enter the zones, even if they do not stay long enough to receive an exposure of 90 dB(A) $L_{EP.d}$

Figure H27.2 *Continued*

assessment must be kept and the work area must be designated an ear protection zone. Any identified noise risk must be properly indicated by safety signs warning of the danger and should read 'danger ear protection zone'.

Other signs should enforce mandatory action which instructs what personal protective equipment you must wear such as ear plugs or ear defenders. These must be provided individually to all employees and must be worn in all ear protection zones. Staff must comply with all instructions regarding ear protection. All ear protection must be CE marked and conform to BS 6344. However, note that ear protectors are only any good if they are being used at all times when working in ear protection zones. If they are worn for seven hours out of eight the protection factor declines to 75 per cent. To avoid this, rotate noisy jobs between staff and keep to short working periods. Enforce breaks and establish acoustic refuges where staff can take ear protection off to rest.

The employer has a duty to reduce the noise levels to a safe working level. Ear protection should not be used as a cheap substitute for real noise reduction measures. Management must take steps to muffle machines and insulate them to reduce noise levels. Silencers can be fitted along with anti-vibration devices. They can buy silent running machines such as generators and the quietest possible model to replace old noisier machines.

Human factors to consider are moving the machine away from people or taking the people away from the machine. This can be done by placing barriers and the use of controls situated behind protective screens. Other measures you can take include keeping the number of people exposed to a noise hazard to a minimum. Another is to limit the time exposure to the noise by having strict restrictions on working time. The higher the noise level, the less exposure time should be allowed. Note that guidance is available from Code of Practice, Reducing the Exposure of Employed Persons to Noise 1972.

Ear protection is required to guard against sudden loud noises. Gun experts and pyrotechnic operators should wear ear mufflers and plugs to guard against loud firing and explosion sounds. This type of sudden noise risk also applies to workers who use cartridge tools and compressed air.

Ear protection is also necessary for staff exposed to constantly high levels of noise. For example, woodworkers, metal workers, scenery construction workers and vehicle maintenance staff are all exposed to loud levels of noise. Their working areas should be ear protection zones.

Location staff should also beware of noise risks from the activities in third-party premises such as shipyards, steelworks, foundries and assembly lines where noise levels are very high. Building sites, airports and roads are other areas where this is also true. The owners and operators of these premises should issue visiting staff and contractors with ear protection and staff intending to work on a noisy location should be issued with ear protection before setting out.

Noise risks can come from tools and equipment used in film and television work, especially air tools, compressors, generators and power tools. For example, the noise level of a generator is 117 dB(A), a forklift truck 101 dB(A), air tools 100 dB(A), circular saw bench 107 dB(A) and cranes 119 dB(A). The manufacturers and suppliers of such equipment have a legal duty to provide information on the noise which they produce. Check this information and provide it to anyone operating these tools.

Remember that you can cause noise pollution to people living adjacent to location sites by producing excess noise. This is a prosecutable offence under the Control of Pollution Act 1974 and the Environmental Protection Act 1990, so try and restrict noisy work to set periods of the day and use silent generators protected behind earth barriers and deflectors. Always ask yourself if you would find it acceptable and act accordingly.

Some noise risks in film and television work can be identified as being very obvious. For example, the risk from loud popular music or orchestras in outside broadcasts, location concerts or studio programmes. The noise levels can get very high and ear protection must be provided for crew.

However, some noise risks are more long term but can be extremely damaging to the hearing. These risks are less obvious because the sound is confined by earphones or headsets. Studio sound mixers and location sound mixers use headsets every day. Constant daily exposure to sound can in the long term cause ear damage. This can also happen to camera operators, autocue operators and floor managers who work on studio talkback systems as part of their everyday work. A high risk group are sound recordists and sound assistants. Headsets and ear pieces should have regulators built in that cut out and filter noise above a safe working level. However the long-term effect of this type of exposure in the film and television business has had very little attention paid to it and further research could well produce many cases of work induced deafness. Concern about this issue can be extended to any workers in film and television who have had to use communications and telephones on a long-term, repetitive basis as part of their work such as enquiry staff, switchboard operators, lines bookings staff and communications engineers.

Noise risks also produce problems of communication. For example, misunderstanding instructions because the noise level was too high. This can have a serious effect on health and safety since it becomes impossible for anyone involved in a noisy situation to hear a spoken warning of an impending danger such as a falling object or a moving vehicle. Alternative visual means of communication must be established and clearly understood before work commences.

Figure H27.3 *Courtesy Yorkshire Television Limited*

Noise hazards in film and television work should always be identified as part of the production planning process and a proper risk assessment should be carried out before any production activity involving noise commences. Identify areas where sudden noise can take place and where long-term noise levels are very high. Then the proper precautions and personal protection measures can be put in place before filming begins.

Further reading

A Survey of Sound Levels at Pop Concerts, HSE, CRR35, 1991, ISBN 0-11-885995-1.
Assessment of Compliance with the Noise at Work Regulations 1989, HSE, RP36, 1994, ISBN 0-7176-0798-4.

Attitudes Towards Noise as an Occupational Hazard

- Volume 1, 1993, HSE, ISBN 0-11-882128-8
- Volume 2, 1993, HSE, ISBN 0-11-882128-8
- Volume 3, 1993, HSE, ISBN 0-11-882133-4.

Hearing Protection in the Construction Industry, HSE, CIS30.
Introducing the Noise at Work Regulations – A Brief Guide, 1993, HSE, INDG75L (Rev).
Listen Up – Advice to Employees, HSE, INDG122, ISBN 0-7176-0962.
Noise at Work – Advice to Employees, HSE, INDG99, ISBN 0-7176-0962.
Noise in the Workplace – A Select Bibliography, HSE, 1990, ISBN 0-11-885577-8.
Noise and the Foetus – A Critical Review of the Literature, HSE-CRR 3, 1994, ISBN 0-7176-0728-3.
The Noise at Work Regulations 1989, HSE, 1989, ISBN 0-7176-0454-3.
Reducing the Exposure of Employed Persons to Noise, Code of Practice, 1972.
Steemson, J., Noises Off, *Occupational Safety and Health*, Jan. 1988, Vol. 18, pp. 36–39.
Noise and Hearing Loss: London Hazards Centre Fact Sheet, *The Daily Hazard*, No. 38, March 1993, p. 3.
Noise at Woodworking Machines, Woodworking Information Sheet No. 13, The Woodworking National Interest Group, 14 Cardiff Rd, Luton, Beds LU1 1PP.
R. Taylor, *Noise*, Penguin Books, 1970.

Contact organizations

Audiometry tests can be obtained from:

British Society of Audiology
80 Brighton Rd, Reading, Berkshire RG6 1PS
Tel: 01734–660622

British Standards Institution
389 Chiswick High Rd, London W4 4AL
Tel: 0181–996–9000

The Association of Noise Consultants
6 Trap Rd, Guilden, Morden, Nr Royston, Herts SG8 0GE
Tel: 01763–852958

The London Hazards Hearing Project
c/o The London Hazards Centre Ltd, Interchange Studio, Dalby Street,
London NW5 3NG
Tel: 0171–267–3387

Hazard 28: Outside broadcasts

In 1986 Michael Lush died during rehearsals for the BBC pro-gramme *The Late, Late, Breakfast Show*. He was suspended 120 ft above the ground and was meant to spring free and abseil down the elasticated rope. The rope snapped and he fell more than 70 ft to his death.

The Times, 6 February 1993

The legislation

The Health and Safety at Work Act 1974
The Lifting Operations and Lifting Equipment Regulations 1998
The Management of Health And Safety at Work Regulations 1984
The Construction (Design and Management) Regulations 1994
The Fire Precautions (Workplace) Regulations 1997
The Food Safety (General Food Hygiene) Regulations 1995
The Food Safety (Temperature Control) Regulations 1995
The Health and Safety (First Aid) Approved Code of Practice 1997
The Workplace (Health, Safety and Welfare) Regulations 1992

The risks

- access
- access platforms
- catering
- cranes
- crowds
- electricity
- fire
- height

- manual handling
- the public
- violence
- the weather

Those most at risk

Camera people, OB crews, eng. crews.

As outside broadcasts are outside the first factor to consider in any risk assessment is the weather. A change in the weather can turn a benign location into a lethal one. Outside broadcast locations are especially vulnerable to bad weather.

Make sure the site surface is safe in the event of rain with proper drainage and protection. Check that all emergency access and exits have solid roadways and will not become a sea of mud if it rains. A sudden temperature rise can turn the lifting and moving of equipment into a hot and risky operation. So always keep a track on the long-term weather forecast and get regular updates from the local weather centre or coastguard.

Remember that the further north, the further into winter and the higher you go increases the risks from cold and exposure. Similarly fog, rain and snow can turn an apparently safe location into a dangerous one combining cold and poor visibility. Accidents happen in poor conditions, due to bad planning and lack of advance preparation. Warm protective clothing must be available to staff operating exposed camera positions on cranes and scaffold towers. It is important to keep a check on weather factors which will affect access platforms and those working from rooftops and cranes, such as fog, ice, snow and rain.

Temperature monitoring is advisable for workers on exposed camera positions in order to detect danger from frostbite or hypothermia caused by wind chill. A zero temperature can become −15°C and lower if the weather is cold and the working platform is higher in the air. For every 10 ft in the air the temperature decreases rapidly and the wind chill factor increases. For example a ground temperature of 10°C will become 0°C in a 20 mph wind. Wind speed must be measured from the roof top or platform top by a hand held anemometer and checked on the Beaufort scale.

High winds can have a dramatic effect on the stability of cranes. The maximum excepted wind speeds for operation are: tower cranes 45 mph, crawler cranes 31 mph, mobile cranes 22 mph. However the wider the load, the less working margin for error – so with a wider load these figures should be reduced.

High winds also affect the stability of mobile access work platforms. The maximum speed that a platform can operate at is generally accepted as 28 mph. The higher the platform, the greater the windspeed. At 20 m the wind speed can be 50 times greater than at ground level. Camera crew and operators must wear warm protective equipment including gloves, a hard hat and a warm coat. They must be secured by a safety harness and equipment must be attached by safety lines to prevent falls or dropping equipment when working at height or in high winds.

The wind force can be accentuated by the following factors: proximity to airports, passing aircraft and helicopters, high sided vehicles and the dangerous wind funnelling effects of tall buildings. A 15 metre gap should be maintained between the working platform and any structures.

In some cases the wind speed between high sided buildings can double so great caution should be exercised and a wind speed test carried out for any outside broadcast work at height involving filming from cranes, MEWPs, rooftops and scaffolds.

Producers should also take account of the risk from heat when operating outside broadcasts during periods of extremely hot weather. Producers should ensure that staff get proper rest periods according to the length of the work. Above 26°C allow a minimum rest period of 20 minutes for 40 minutes work. The temperature on top of scaffold towers, roofs and cranes should be monitored. At temperatures above 31°C access should be for inspection purposes only and operatives should be medically monitored as this constitutes dangerous hot work.

Staff should be issued with a work permit to control hot work. Staff working in heat must get proper rest periods in a cool area and must be provided with plenty of fluids but not salt water.

Night work on outside broadcasts

Outside locations are often exposed and become doubly dangerous at night. So visibility must be a priority with film and television operations at night.

Take extra care to cordon off your zone of work with fluorescent tapes and emergency lights similar to a roadworks zone at night. This is so an illuminated protection zone is established which you can work within and which other people can see and avoid – particularly moving vehicles.

Try and keep night time disturbance to local residents to a minimum and inform the police and local landowners of your intentions. Make sure that your production area is brightly lit and that a secondary emergency lighting system will automatically cut in in the event of mains or generator failure.

Try to avoid the movement of equipment and vehicles at night. Confine equipment operations to cordoned off zones and vehicle movements to special vehicle lanes designated for the purpose. All moving vehicles should be properly lit and emit an audible warning. Restrict access to a minimum number of people to do a job. But to make night work safer, double the amount of supervisors and lookouts who have no other function than to make sure that operations are conducted safely and that crew are protected and warned of any danger, especially during lifting work and stunts.

Staff working outside at night must be seen and be able to see. So management must equip them with high visibility jackets and vests, with bright hard hats. They should also be equipped with emergency torches and lamps to see in the dark and to warn others of their presence.

Working outside at night increases the risk of cold and exposure, especially during the winter months. The temperature can drop quickly to dangerous levels. This is particularly true of exposed locations such as airfields, coastline, mountains, moors, rooftops and deserts. Check the weather forecast before setting out to film at night, especially at sea or at exposed locations. Monitor the air temperature so that you can stop if it gets too cold.

The majority of accidents at night happen because people are not prepared, and do not wear or carry the right protective equipment. All participants including actors, crew, presenters and the public must be issued with warm protective clothing including jackets, hats and gloves.

Crew working at night have often been working extended hours and tiredness increases the risk factor. Make sure that schedules are realistic to allow for tiredness. Remember that moving and setting up equipment is slower and lighting set-ups can take longer at night.

Management must increase the welfare facilities and breaks during night work by scheduling more rest periods and providing plenty of hot food and drinks. Budget for accommodation and taxis so that tired staff do not take risks by driving home after night work on outside shoots.

Access and logistics

Before you set off to an outdoor location check what the weather is going to be like. Take a proper map, compass, GPS, flares, food, drink, waterproof torch and protective clothing. Take a coat that is visible, waterproof and warm, as well as boots and a hat. Make sure your vehicle is roadworthy and insured with a winch, tow rope, spare petrol, jump leads, water and a first aid kit. Always take some good means of communication.

When making your outside broadcast risk assessment always consider problems of logistics. Take a good map and work out how long it will take to get there and get back. Allow time for delays such as roadworks and build travel time into your schedule.

Also consider problems of access. Always include a plan of your intended location and mark on it key information such as the nearest parking spot. This is essential for any vehicle with lots of equipment which needs to be as close as possible to reduce manual handling and communication problems. Park your scanner van with permission of the local police and make sure that all cables run in ducts and do not cause a trip hazard on pavements and access points.

If you have to enter a building or a site, check the maximum vehicle width and the maximum vehicle height you can use safely. Check for any clearance problems such as low slung cables and arches. Look and see if the site is level and is suitable for parking heavy vehicles and lifting operations.

Separate site entrances must be made and kept clear for emergency vehicle access only. No car parking should be allowed close to the site and emergency exits must be entirely separate from emergency access lanes and active vehicle entrances. The site should be designed properly so that in the event of an emergency members of the public and staff can exit quickly and safely while incoming emergency services can get instant access without risk.

Avoid locations with only one exit or entrance point if you are going to have a substantial amount of equipment or large numbers of people on site. This could be a death trap in the event of a fire and access to confined locations should be restricted to the minimum number of essential staff. Avoid working in narrow or confined locations.

When making your location risk assessment check for any manual handling problems. Can you move equipment round the site easily and will you have to bring trolleys, barrows and lifting equipment? If you will need extra help to move your equipment make sure this problem is identified.

Outside broadcasts often take place in temporary locations established for the purpose which have a public audience to consider as an extra safety factor. The design and management of such sites fall under the Construction (Design and Management) Regulations 1994.

This means that the designers, managers and operators of temporary public locations should design and manage the site to prevent any risk to audience health and safety. Precautions must include fire, first aid measures and electrical safety. The best guide to the regulations for outside temporary venues is called *A Guide to Fire Precautions in Existing Places of Entertainment and Like Places* (HMSO, 1990, ISBN 0–11–340907–9). If you are going to film on a temporary set or stage it is worth reading this first. There must be a sufficient number of fire wardens and fire extinguishers for the total numbers present (not just the audience). Fire extinguishers must be provided to cover the types of fire risk, the total number of people present and to cover each fire escape route. Fire wardens must be trained in fire evacuation procedure and the proper use of fire extinguishers. All fire extinguishers should be CE marked and rated at BS EN 3 from January 1997.

Fire exits should be clearly marked. All fire signs should be on a red background and comply with BS 5499 Part 1 and BS 5378. These indicate the location of fire fighting equipment, fire alarms, fire hose reels and extinguisher locations. All fire exit signs are green and yellow and should conform to BS 4599 and EU Directive 92/58/EEC. All fire information signs should be large enough to read clearly and be placed on luminant backgrounds.

Fire exits should be checked regularly for rubbish or obstructions. Never obstruct fire exits with cables or equipment. Gangways and exits should be wide enough to allow quick exit for the size of the audience in the event of a fire emergency. Gangways, corridors and exit points must be properly indicated by signs. The exit routes and safety signs must be illuminated and provided with emergency back-up lighting in the event of a mains failure.

When an audience is admitted the management should ensure that enough ushers and floor management supervisors are available and are properly trained in emergency procedures. They should all be given a copy of the company's health and safety policy and any special regulations for the temporary location. Special chaperoning and extra ushering must be provided for any blind, deaf, elderly or young members of the audience.

There should also be a sufficient number of trained first aid wardens (Health and Safety (First Aid) Regulations 1981) and sufficient first aid equipment available. St John Ambulance should be consulted about the right precautions and may be present along with a doctor if special risks are anticipated. The First Aid at Work Regulations 1981 oblige employers to make sure that the staff are properly trained in first aid and that the kits are right for the task. So ensure that your crew are properly trained in first aid and emergency procedures.

Outside broadcast work will have electricity driven from a generator or taken from a convenient external supply. So electrical supplies and equipment should be properly installed and maintained by a qualified electrician. The Electricity at Work Regulations insist that any supply is safe to use and appropriate for the task. The National Inspection Council for Electrical Installation Contracting (NICEIC) has an approved list of 10,500 contractors who undertake electrical installation work to IEE wiring regulations.

Never cross, connect or touch three-phase supplies. Always try and use stepped down low voltage 110 V equipment and cordless 55 V tools. Try to avoid equipment which is 240 V mains. If you do, such equipment must be fitted with circuit breakers rated at 30 mA with no time delay. This is to protect the user in the event of a damage to the cable or a fault with the supply.

All portable electrical equipment must be PAT tested and fitted with the correct fuse. Before attaching any cables check damage and cuts, check plugs and fittings for cracks and damage. Always test the sockets with a power tester before plugging anything in.

Electrical supplies should be routed away from vehicle lanes and public access points in ducts or conduits. Terminals and switches should be secure and isolated from the public. Keep cables out of the reach of audiences and the radius of moving equipment. Lights must be attached by safety chains and have safety gauzes. An adequate electrical back-up supply should cut in on a trip in the event of generator or mains failure. A battery operated emergency lighting supply should also be installed (see Hazard 15: Electricity).

Food and water

Mobile caterers and food vendors for outside broadcasts must have a licence to operate from the local trading standards department of the council where they ply their trade. Reputable operators are usually members of the Mobile and Outdoor Caterers Association of Great Britain (MOCA) and can be found in trade directories such as Kay's and the white book. The local environmental health office can advise you on any recent prosecutions and can undertake to inspect a contractor for you if required.

The operator must possess public liability insurance cover and possess at least basic qualifications in food handling and hygiene. Proper fire precautions should be in place with the correct extinguishers, fire blankets, etc. Nobody should ever smoke in food preparation areas and kitchens. Hot food on location can get cold rapidly and requires adequate hot storage to ensure the correct safe eating temperature.

The kitchen must have a clean supply of water and a separate system of sanitation adequate for the amount of people. All refuse must be disposed of in a hygienic and safe manner, away from pests and vermin.

Cleaning chemicals must be stored away from food and their use recorded in compliance with COSHH Regulations. Do not place equipment and cables on hot surfaces. Do not use the catering electricity supply to power your equipment or use kitchens as cold weather refuges. Proper dining buses must be provided for the total number of cast and crew.

There should be three totally separate water supplies on outside location: one which is safe for drinking water and catering, one which is for emergency and fire use and one which is for toilet and sewerage use. The sewerage and toilet arrangements must be large enough to cope and cater for men, women and disabled people, with separate facilities for crew, performers and catering. They must be cleaned and comply with public health and environmental regulations. The storage of the waste must comply with COSHH and the disposal of the waste must comply with the disposal of hazardous waste and water pollution regulations and not simply flushed into the nearest drain or stream.

Camera equipment and lighting

Care should be taken that no risk to the audience will arise from camera or cable placements. Check that no risk exists from falling or faulty equipment. Lights and suspended equipment should be secured by clamps and safety chains. Safety nets should be suspended and attached to catch falling tools, equipment or staff. Lighting stands should be well secured with proper safety chains and weights. To prevent them falling they should be secured. If they do fall then this should be allowed for by an adequate free fall area which protects the public and any participants.

Camera positions in audience locations must be safe with no risk from height, movement or electrical supply. There should always be safe access and exit points for crew in the event of an emergency. Camera positions should have proper guard rails and edge protection in case of falling equipment.

Check the weight restrictions of cranes, access platforms and scaffold towers and do not overload them with too much equipment or too many people. If you are working at height on outside broadcasts, secure any equipment with safety lines and make sure operators have a safety harness when conducting work. Warning signs should read 'danger working at height'.

Camera positions should be barrier protected and secure from public access. The audience should be protected well back behind barriers and make sure that they are clear from any extended cranes/jibs or moving dollies. Barrier protected runs should be made for flying arms or Steadicam operations with no public access.

Always film action, stunts and performances behind guard rails and protective barriers. Extend the distance between the action and the audience or crew to establish a safe working zone. Crew and invited audiences should also be protected from noise hazards produced by equipment. Noises over 85 dB(A) require ear protection under the Noise at Work Regulations. Stroboscopic or laser effects are especially dangerous to epileptic people and can damage eyesight. Special care should be taken on drama shoots to inform the public that the activity you are going to film is a simulated activity. For example firearm or criminal activity has often been mistaken for the real thing by members of the public and police, even on private property. Special advice should be taken regarding any pyrotechnic explosion or stunt. (For safe use of cranes, see Hazard 11 and scaffolding, Hazard 29.)

Public violence

Outside broadcast work for news and current affairs can often bring with it the risk of violence. The level of risk should be identified first on a proper recce or by a reliable local contact on the ground. In other words the risk of violence should be assessed before filming in the production planning stage. Key figures here are the heads of news gathering, commissioning editors and producers who have the information first and take the decision for filming to begin. As they control the activity they must be responsible for deciding if it is safe to proceed and what precautions to take.

The best aid to safety on the ground is keeping up-to-date information about the situation and being able to react quickly to unfolding events which may change a previously safe location into a very dangerous one. You should always ensure that you have good local knowledge and an escape route if trouble develops.

It is also possible to encounter violence when filming on locations such as housing estates and at sports grounds. The most common risk is the threat of violence from people who do not want their activities recorded on film. If you do get attacked then withdraw quickly.

Very often during a riot or civil disturbance the threat could also come from the forces trying to prevent protest who do not want their activities shown in a bad light. An assessment should be made about what side of the fence physically you are going to film from and from what source or direction the threat of violence is likely to come. Will it come from the authorities, their opposition or both?

Try to film from concealed positions which are above the street level and which give a safe but excellent vantage point. If this is not possible, keep your recording equipment hidden or use miniature or hidden cameras. If by filming you may endanger yourselves or escalate a dangerous situation, withdraw quickly. If necessary form a broadcasting pool with other agencies and share footage from one source to minimize the risk.

As outside broadcast work is outside the confines of base safety precautions, extra planning is needed to inspect potential sites in advance. Gather as much information as you can from site owners and operators. Obtain copies of their health and safety measures. Try to brief your crew before leaving base and supply them with the equipment they need to do the job and proper personal protective equipment. Give them information about any specific health and safety risks on location and try and allow for extra equipment, communications and welfare as you are outside and away from base.

Further reading

British Standards Institute, 389 Chiswick High Rd, London W4 4AL:

- BS 7121 Part 1, 1989 For The Safe Use of Cranes.
- BS 7171 Mobile Elevating Work Platforms.

CPA, The Inspection and Testing of Elevating Work Platforms, available from the Construction Plant Hire Association, 52 Rochester Row, London SW1P 1JU, Tel: 0171 6306868.

EC, European Standard for Mobile Elevating Work Platforms, PR-EN 280.

Cris Hannam, *An Introduction to Health and Safety Management for the Live Music Industry*, Production Services Association Pocket Book Volume 1, 1997, ISBN 0-9530914-06.

HSE, *A Guide to Fire Precautions in Existing Places of Entertainment and Like Places*, HMSO, 1990, ISBN 0-11-340907-9.

A Guide to Health, Safety and Welfare at Pop Concerts and Similar Events, HMSO, ISBN 0-11-341072-7.

Electrical Safety at Places of Entertainment, HSE, GS(50), 1991, ISBN 0-11-885598-0.

Workplace Health, Safety and Welfare Workplace Regulations 1992, Approved Code of Practice and Guidance, HSE, L24, 1992, ISBN 07176-0413-6.

Health and Safety in Construction, HS(G)150, HSE Books, 1996, ISBN 0-7176-1143-4.

Safety in Working with Power Operated Mobile Work Platforms, HSE, HS(G)19.

Safety at Powered Operated Mast Work Platforms, HSE, (G)23.

Safety with Mobile Elevating Work Platforms: Industry Survey and Accident Review, HSE, 3.37 SIR46.

Avoidance of Danger from Overhead Electric Lines, HSE (G)GS6.

Avoiding Danger from Underground Services, HSE (G)G47.

Construction Sheet No. 19, The Safe Use of Mobile Cranes on Construction Sites.

A Guide to the Lifting Plant and Equipment (Records of Test and Examinations etc.) Regulations 1992, HSE.

Safety in Broadcasting Sports Events, HSE, ETIS 1-C100.
Mobile Crane Operator's Safety Guide, CITB, revised 1994, (book, CJ502).
Safe Start – Construction Site Safety Handbook, GE 707, CITB, 1995, ISBN 0-902-02974-6.
IPAF Guide to MEWPs, International Powered Access Federation, 1994.
Lifting Equipment Engineers Association, Code of Practice for the Safe Use of Lifting Equipment.

Contact organizations

Alimak Ltd
Northampton Rd, Rushden, Northants NN10 9BW
Tel: 01933–410400

Guild of Location Managers
37 Woodeaves, Northwood, Middx HA6 3NF

Peter Hurd & Son Ltd
English St, Hull HU3 2BT
Tel: 01482–227333

International Powered Access Federation
PO Box 16, Carnforth, Lancashire LA6 1LB
Tel: 01524–781393

Lesters TV and Film Services
Lane End Rd, Sands, High Wycombe, Bucks HP12 4HG
Tel: 01494–448689

Lifting Equipment Engineers Association
Waggoners Court, The Street, Manuden, Bishop's Stortford, Herts CM23 1DW
Tel: 01279–816504

National Inspection Council for Electrical Installation Contracting (NICEIC)
Vintage House, 37 Albert Embankment, London SE1 7UJ
Tel: 0171–582–7746

Prefabricated Aluminium Scaffold Manufacturers Association Ltd (PASMA)
PO Box 1828, West Mersea, Essex CO5 8HY
Tel: 01206–382666

Production Managers Association (CoPACT)
45 Mortimer St, London W1N 7TD
Tel: 0171–331–6000

Production Services Association
Hawks House, School Passage, Kingston upon Thames, Surrey KT1 3DU
Tel: 0181–392–0180

Hazard 29: Scaffolding and heights

Telly star Gary Olsen was rushed to hospital after high winds brought a lighting rig crashing down on top of him. The rig was bent double by a freak gust of wind and hit him on the head. He needed stitches to a head wound.

The Sun, 28 January 1998

The legislation

The Construction (Design and Management) Regulations 1994
The Health and Safety at Work Act 1974
The Construction (Health, Safety and Welfare) Regulations 1996
General Access Scaffolds 1982

The risks

- cold
- falls
- falling objects
- head injuries
- poor construction
- wind speed

Those most at risk

Camera crew, lighting staff, riggers.

The HSE and BECTU's London production division had a meeting on 3 October 1996 which identified working at heights as one of the major risks of the film and television industry. As a result, in April 1999, the HSE brought out a new advice sheet on this subject – Entertainment Sheet No. 6, Working at Heights in the Broadcasting and Entertainment Industries. This should be read in conjunction with this chapter.

Scaffolds are used either for access or as working platforms. Location risk assessments should highlight the need for safe working platforms and making sure that filming activity at height is not entertained unless stringent precautions have been taken. Working at height is defined as 2 metres or above.

A sensible precaution would be to ask if the shot can be obtained in another way. For example, filming from a nearby building or the use of a MEWP could be quicker and safer. Scaffolds in film and television work are used to provide structures for attaching scenery and providing temporary audience accommodation as well as working platforms for cameras and lighting in films, outside broadcasts and sports events.

A scaffold is a structure made up of tubular members, poles, friction clamps and timber. Scaffolds must be built to BS 5973, 1993. Prefabricated aluminium towers have different regulations which will be covered later in the chapter.

Note that under section 6 of the Health and Safety at Work Act 1974 it is the duty of any person who erects or installs any article for use at work to ensure that it is erected and installed in a way that, when used, it is safe and without risk to health and safety. The best way to do this is to use a competent contractor experienced and qualified in film and television scaffolding requirements.

All rigging and scaffolding installation and repair work must be properly supervised and the riggers and scaffolders who carry out the work should be CITB qualified and experienced. They should also appear on the Screen Industry Training and Apprenticeship Committee (SITAC) register as advanced scaffolders and riggers. To qualify for an SITAC advanced riggers ticket takes nearly two years and the rigger is then qualified for film and television work. There is also a trainee and intermediate grade. SITAC members carry a record book.

It is advisable to use a SITAC rigger as they will have film specific experience of, say, putting a rig on a car or erecting a safe working platform for stunts over the edge of a tall building. They can also contract and supervise other riggers to do the work but must carry their own insurance.

The risk at working at height can come from a number of different areas. The most simple risk is that of falling objects such as tapes, cables and production equipment. Falling sharp objects can inflict fatal injuries by a rapid gain in velocity so make sure your crew wear adequate head protection. Steps should also be taken to protect those below by securing yourself and any equipment by sufficiently strong secure lines and safety harnesses. This is a particular risk if production work overhangs or is adjacent to a public streets. Warning signs should be placed below and should read 'danger working at height' to indicate that a risk exists and nobody should walk underneath. Also create a safe exclusion zone to protect third parties.

Any rope work should be carried out by and supervised by a card carrying member of the Industrial Rope Access Trade Association (IRATA) or a qualified mountaineer or steeplejack. All rope must be tested and be suitable for the task and the weight.

Make sure that all tower scaffolds and constructions are safe before attempting to use them. They should be erected and dismantled by a qualified and competent contractor. The scaffold should be the right type for the intended work activity. There are five major types:

1 putleg
2 independent
3 birdcage
4 mobile tower constructed with tubes fittings and wheels
5 mobile tower with system or proprietary ready-made sections designed and supplied by the contractor.

Scaffolds are used for general access, for towers and as working platforms.

It is essential that any scaffolding is erected by a licensed and authorized contractor. Any scaffold construction must be inspected every seven days. You should be given a seven-day scaffold inspection report by the contractor. However the scaffold must be re-inspected after any adverse weather, changes in ground conditions, or any structural alterations. The contractor should supply a handover certificate (form F91) indicating that the structure has been designed and built safely.

The scaffold construction should also have a green scaffolding tag indicating it has been inspected and the safe working load. The Scafftag labelling system will give you the contact name and number of the scaffolding contractor. It will also tell you when the scaffold was erected and by whom. The Scafftag will also tell you when it is due for a new inspection.

A green Scafftag and edge caps should indicate that it is safe. If it has not got these do not use it. Check with the constructor first. A red tag or edge caps indicates that it is still being built or has not been inspected and passed for use.

There should be no access allowed to a partially constructed or dismantled scaffold. Warning signs should be in place and barriers

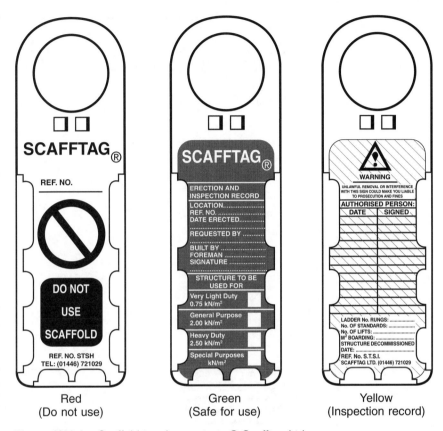

Figure H29.1 *Scaffold tagging system. © Scafftag Ltd*

erected to deny access until the work is completed. Scaffolds should be built with proper internal ladders and hoists for equipment. It is vital to ensure good access and quick egress in the event of an emergency. The internal ladders and exits must be constructed safely and secured.

The timber boards should be in good condition and strong enough for the intended weight. Double guard rails at least 910 mm above the edge and toe boards at least 150 mm high should be fitted to all working areas to prevent falls of personnel and equipment. If necessary, fit a safety net and barrier as well for extra protection. If working on a sloping roof of more than 10 per cent, fit catch barriers with two 430 mm boards and guard-rails with toeboards. All poles should have edge caps for protection. Warning signs should be placed below and should read 'danger working at height' to indicate that a risk exists and nobody should walk underneath. Also create a safe exclusion zone to protect third parties.

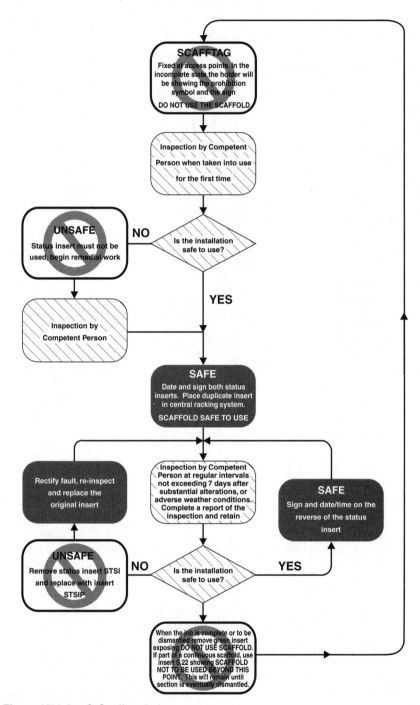

Figure H29.2   © *Scafftag Ltd*

The design of the scaffold will depend on the task in hand and the weight which the scaffold has to support, including staff and equipment.

The scaffold must be built out of proper materials in accordance with HSE GS42 guidance notes. Beware of any scaffold that is not braced or tied and built with rusty, bent or defective tubes. The scaffold should be able to support the intended weight and not be blown over or topple. Wheel mounted tower scaffolds with four square standards must be tied to an external wall.

The design of the scaffold must take into account the design of the frame and adequate ties. You should also check the foundations to make sure that the surface is hard, level and can support the weight. Most accidents with scaffolds happen because it was only a short job so corners were cut. It was not very high and looked safe but it was built by an inexperienced person with no supervision and no safety system was in place for its use.

Key questions to ask before deciding which scaffold to use include: What is it to be used for? Access, vantage point or for a specific job? Will it be used as a working platform and what weight will it need to support, including equipment and people? Do you need to use a scaffold at all?

The designer should then know what materials will be needed and how many working platforms to construct. Access and egress ladders will be planned and the foundation must be strong enough to support the weight. The ground conditions must be checked and the site investigated to see if the scaffold can be tied or will need outriggers. The correct bracing and clamps must be used. The designers and erector must be qualified and competent. The scaffold will then be checked for safety before it is used and inspected every seven days for safety.

It is important to keep a check on weather factors which will affect either the scaffold or the safety of those working on it. For example fog, ice, snow and rain. Always make sure staff have proper personal protective clothing as the wind chill factor can be dangerous.

High wind is a special risk. This should be measured from the working platform top. The wind force can be accentuated by the funnelling effects of high buildings. In some cases the wind speed between high-sided buildings can double so great caution should be exercised and a wind speed test carried out. The wind speed is also greater according to the height of the working platform. The higher the platform, the greater the wind speed can be.

Site suitability is a key safety factor for building scaffolds. The structure must be built on a hard level site. Checks must be made for anything which would affect soil stability such as hard frost, excessively dry conditions or heavy rain. The scaffold feet must be wide enough and implanted properly. Never construct a scaffold close to power lines and cables, working cranes, the edge of an excavation or a steep drop.

Scaffold towers can also come ready-made from aluminium sections. Manufacturers and suppliers of prefabricated aluminium tower suppliers of any proprietary scaffold systems should be members of PASMA. Such scaffolds should be built and designed in accordance with BS 1139 Part 3 1994 (HD1004) and European standard EN 4711.

Aluminium tower scaffolds should always be tied to a permanent structure and weighted to avoid toppling or being blown over. The maximum height of aluminium tower scaffolds should be three and a half times the base inside and three times the base outside.

Erectors of prefabricated aluminium scaffolding towers should have passed a PASMA course. You should always check the supplier's licence. The rigger must show a PASMA certificate and produce their identity card before operations begin. Never use an unqualified or inexperienced operator. For further information consult the PASMA operator's code of practice.

Further reading

A Guide to Fire Precautions in Existing Places of Entertainment and Like Places, HMSO, 1990, ISBN 0-11-340907-9.

European Harmonisation Document HD 1004.

Managing Construction for Health and Safety, The Construction (Design and Management) Regulations 1994, Approved Code of Practice L54, HSE, 1995, ISBN 0-7176-0792-5.

Managing Crowd Safety in Public Venues, HSE, CRR53/1993, ISBN 0-71760708-9.

General Access Scaffolds and Ladders, HSE CIS49.

Tower Scaffolds, HSE, CIS10, 1997.

Tower Scaffolds, HSE, 1987, GS 42, ISBN 0-11-883941-1.

Entertainment Sheet No. 6, Working at Heights in the Broadcasting and Entertainment Industries, HSE.

The Personal Protective Equipment at Work Regulations 1992, A Guide to the Regulations, HSE, ISBN 0-7176-0415-2.

Cris Hannam, *An Introduction to Health and Safety Management for the Live Music Industry*, 1997, Production Services Association Pocket Book Volume 1, ISBN 0-9530914-06.

Contact organizations

Construction Industry Training Board (CITB)
Health and Safety Development, Bircham Newton, King's Lynn, Norfolk PE3 6RH

Industrial Rope Access Trade Association (IRATA)
235 Ash Rd, Aldershot, Hants GU12 4DD
Tel: 01252–33631

The National Association of Scaffolding Contractors
18 Mansfield St, London W1M 9FG
Tel: 0171–580–5404

National Federation of Master Steeplejacks and Lightning Conductor
Engineers
4d St Mary's Place, Lacemarket, Nottingham NG1 1PH
Tel: 01159–558818

Prefabricated Aluminium Scaffold Manufacturers Association Ltd
(PASMA)
PO Box 1828, West Mersea, Essex CO5 8HY
Tel: 01206–382666

Production Services Association
Hawks House, School Passage, Kingston upon Thames, Surrey KT1 3DU
Tel: 0181–392–0180

The Professional Lighting and Sound Association
7 Highlight House, St Leonards Rd, Eastbourne, E. Sussex BN21 3UH
Tel: 01323–410335

The Screen Industry Training and Apprenticeship Committee (SITAC)
c/o BECTU, 111 Wardour St, London W1V 4AY
Tel: 0171–437–8506

Hazard 30: Scenery and props

In October 1997 construction manager Roy Evans died aged 61 from work related fibrosis alveolitis.

Stage, Screen and Radio, October 1997, p. 10.

The legislation

The Control of Substances Hazardous to Health Regulations 1994 (COSHH)
The COSHH (Amendment) Regulations 1996
The Chemicals (Hazard Information and Packaging for Supply) (Amendment) (No. 2) Regulations 1999 (CHIP 99 (2))
The Construction (Design and Management) Regulation 1994
The Health and Safety at Work Act 1974
The Highly Flammable Liquids and Liquefied Petroleum Gases Regulations 1972
The Manual Handling Operations Regulations 1992
The Management of Health and Safety at Work Regulations 1992
The Provision and Use of Work Equipment Regulations 1998

The risks

- chemicals
- dermatitis
- dust
- fire
- lifting
- solvents
- noise
- unguarded machinery

Those most at risk

Carpenters, painters, scenery construction workers, welders, woodworkers.

Scenery designers have a legal responsibility to design scenery that is safe. Hazardous materials should not be used. Safety and health considerations must also apply to the construction and preparation of sets and scenery. The construction of sets and scenery are covered by the Construction (Design and Management) Regulations (CDM Regulations) which insist that any built construction should be properly designed with safety features built in.

Note that under section 6 of the Health and Safety at Work Act comes a duty to make sure that any substance or effect has been tested for safety first and manufactured to avoid risks. As props makers and scenery designers often design and supply their own props and scenery the obligations under section 6 should be read in conjunction with this chapter.

Handling weight and falls

To comply with the Manual Handling Operations Regulations 1992 all scenery and constructions must be capable of being lifted and carried safely either by machine or person power. They should be fitted with handles and secure lifting points for chains or ropes. All scenery movements must be carried out by appropriate lifting and carrying machines.

All cranes, ropes, chain and forklifts must comply with the safety requirements and the operators must be properly trained (see Hazard 11: Cranes, hoists, lifts and access platforms). Any manual lifting must comply with the regulations (see Hazard 25: Manual handling and lifting). The team selected to do the moving must be trained in lifting techniques, be provided with the proper equipment and be of adequate size and fitness for the job. All carrying, lifting and installation must be properly supervised after a risk assessment has been made by experienced riggers and stage hands.

The potential weight of scenery must be considered, taking into account the load bearing potential of the floor and the ceiling suspension system. Designers and installers must take account of the potential risks from falling or loose scenery. All scenery should be prevented from falling by scaffold, wires, rigging, weights and props.

If sets are outside then the effect of adverse weather and wind speed should be considered and, if inside, the effects from heat and movement – especially clearance factors from studio doors and lighting grids inside and from electric cables outside. All sets and scenery must be properly designed, built and installed to prevent sudden falls or collapse – especially any prop or set which is suspended at height or very heavy.

Electricity

All sets, scenery and props must be wired properly for safety taking into account the Electricity at Work Regulations 1989 and the 16th edition IEE Wiring Regulations. All wiring, switches and power supplies must be installed properly and be safe to use. All electrical installations should be safety tested prior to use by an experienced electrician and the risk of any electrical fires identified and removed.

All electrical power tools should be 110 V or used with a step-down transformer. Tools must be protected by an RCD and regular checks made on the safe condition of plugs, connectors and cables (see Hazard 15: Electricity).

Fire risks

Designers and scenery construction workers must take fire risks into account when constructing scenery and sets. All wood and material must be flame proofed and treated with flame retarding paints. Standards include wood BS 476, Part 7 class 1; fibreglass BS 476 Part 7 class 1; drapes BS 5687 Part 2; carpets BS 4790; and all hay, straw and peat must be fire retarded.

The biggest risk involves upholstery and furniture coverings. In domestic situations such fires are responsible for 40 deaths and 413 non-fatal injuries per 1000 product fires. Recent research has shown that up to 90 per cent of such fires can be prevented by the use of effective fire retardants. However fire retardants can cause skin irritation and dermatitis so great care should be exercised in applying them. Advice should be taken as some countries in Europe have expressed concerns about the safe use of fire retardants and claim that there are potential significant risks to human health and the environment. There could be a possible health risk from the use of fire retardant substances. If in doubt, consult the supplier.

Set makers should also avoid the risk of explosion from direct heat sources such as sunlight, electrical sparks and welding activities during construction. Scenery and drapes must not come into contact with fire lamps or flame effects when used in studios.

All construction and preparation areas must have smoke alarms and detectors conforming to BS 5839. Early warning and detection provide crucial time for evacuation. Fire extinguishers must conform to European safety standard BS EN 3 marked CE. These new extinguishers will be coloured red with a small coloured panel indicating the contents.

The selection and provision of fire extinguishers is crucial for construction and preparation areas. Managers should take into account the range of fire hazards present and provide the correct extinguishers for wood, chemical and electrical fires. When deciding the number of units required managers must assess the quantity of materials so that sufficient exist to tackle potential fires. Staff should be trained in their use and the storage locations clearly marked. Hose reels, sand buckets and sprinklers should also be provided where appropriate.

Management must also ensure that adequate first aid facilities are provided. This is especially important for preparation areas which carry a higher risk of serious injury from high voltage electricity, power tools, machinery and hazardous substances. So the size and content of first aid kits should reflect the potential injuries. The location of these should be clearly marked and staff trained in their use.

Fire precautions for chemicals and hazardous substances

Managers must make sure that proper fire prevention precautions are in place with the correct extinguishers and sand buckets. All fire fighting equipment must be safe in itself, regularly serviced and correct for the task required. All sets, scenery, props and drapes must be fire proof. Any structures made must not have large quantities of hazardous substances; the COSHH and CHIP 99 (2) regulations apply to the materials used in scenery preparation and construction.

No smoking should be allowed in preparation areas and wood must be stored away from inflammable materials and chemicals. Beware of the explosion risk from concentrations of dry wood dust in saw shops and construction bays. This would be increased by dry weather and spillages of paint and thinners. In the event of a chemical spillage prevent access until the area is safe. Anybody entering must wear protective equipment including gloves, boots, suits, eye protection and respiratory masks. Then spread Rench-Rapid or similar absorbent to soak up any oils or chemicals. The residue and waste should be disposed of safely and the area checked for fumes before access is permitted.

Toxic substances

Any harmful substance has to be properly labelled and marked under the COSHH, CHIP 99 (2) and Health and Safety (Safety Signs and Signals) Regulations. So employers should make sure that any hazardous substance which is introduced by suppliers or contractors is properly labelled with square orange warning signs to indicate a COSHH health hazard. The main classifications are:

1 explosive
2 irritant
3 highly flammable
4 harmful
5 oxidizing
6 toxic
7 corrosive.

The storage of all inflammable liquids and gases is subject to the Highly Flammable Liquids and Liquefied Petroleum Gases Regulations 1972. Drums must conform to BS 814 and storage building and cupboards to BS 476. Storage cupboards must hold a maximum of 50 litres and be fire resistant for at least 30 minutes. Cylinders should be stored upright (unless the data sheet specifies otherwise) and strapped securely.

Use proper chemical resistant pallets and make sure the surface is level. LPG should never be stored in rows of more than six. Never store gas which is heavier than air on raised platforms or near ditches, drains, pipes, sewers or water courses (for further information see *The Storage of Flammable Liquids in Containers*, HSE HSG51, ISBN 0-7176-1471-9).

Paint

Do not store hazardous chemicals such as white spirit or paraffin etc. in inappropriate containers such as coffee jars or similar. Use the correct sealed container and the correct label for identification. Careful thought should be given to the storage of large amounts of paint, thinners and spirits. These should be kept cool and separate.

Care should be taken when mixing paints or chemicals to ensure that the resulting preparation is not inflammable or toxic.

Chemicals known as teratogens and fetoxins should not be used by pregnant workers as these can cause serious birth defects. Chemicals which contain these substances must be labelled toxic to reproduction. These include art materials such as lead and cadmium which have special safety regulations and solvents such as benzene and toluene. Anybody suffering from respiratory disease including asthma and hay fever should not use paints based on isocyanates. Always consult the manufacturer's safety data sheet and a copy of the paint manufacturer's personal advice code.

Chemicals which can cause allergic reactions are labelled sensitizing. All chemicals should have a warning label, a packaging label and be accompanied by a safety data sheet with product safety information.

Any chemicals supplied must be on the European approved supply list. The chemical hazards section from the product information of paints and thinners must be read and any risk of contact dermatitis identified from paints, soaps and cleansers. Proper hand protection and barrier cream must be worn to protect painters' hands (see *Essentials of Skin Management. A Practical Guide to the Creation and Maintenance of an Effective Skin Management System*, C.L. Packham, Limited Edition Press, 633 Liverpool Rd, Southport PR8 3NQ, ISBN 8-5988-045-2).

When paint spraying the operatives must wear proper protective suits and respiratory systems. The spray shed must be properly ventilated. This means proper provision of a clean air supply coming in and extraction for removal of spray residue, fumes and solvents out. Any waste disposal and extraction must comply with COSHH Regulations 1988, the Environmental Protection Act 1990 and the Control of Pollution Act 1974.

Fibreglass has been used for many years in sets, scenery, props and models. It is polyester based and gives off bad fumes which can be explosive. This has led to rising insurance costs as the risks from solvents and fumes became clearer. The use of a safer substitute such as jesmonite is recommended. Avoid the use of asbestos, cadmium and lead. Special regulations control their use and these products have legal maximum exposure levels. Care should also be taken when handling or cutting glass.

Care should be taken when using either air tools or compressed air. Operatives should be fully trained in their safe use. Checks should always be made for damaged hoses and connectors before switching on. Always wear eye protection BS 2092–1 and never point an air tool or air line at your eye or at somebody else.

Metalwork and welding

Scenery construction can involve metalwork and welding. This must take place in a well ventilated area away from hazardous chemicals, cylinder storage and inflammable materials. Proper fire precautions should be in place and all fabricators must adhere to a hot working regime.

Welding can be either electric arc welding or gas welding. For electric arc welding operatives must wear fixed face shields or a welding helmet to BS 1542 Part 3 fitted with glare filters to BS 679. For gas welding operatives should wear goggles to BS 1542 Part 2 fitted with filters to BS 679. This is to prevent spark damage and welder's flash.

For electric arc welding only operatives who are competent and fully trained should carry out such work. The welder and helper must wear personal protective clothing including an adjustable welding helmet, leather cape with sleeves, leather gloves, leather apron, spats, safety shoes or boots.

The welding area must be protected by a portable screen or drapes. All welding equipment should be regularly inspected and serviced by an authorized competent person. The service should be written down and the record kept on file. Before any welding begins inspect the equipment for defects. Report any straight away and do not use the equipment until it is safe to do so.

Beware of electrical hazards. Ensure that the electrode holder is insulated and free from exposed metallic fittings which could cause contact. Do not place the electrode holder on metal objects and disconnect the supply if the holder is to be left for any length of time. Ensure all the connections and cables are fitted correctly and well housed. Check for exposed wire cables and that the cables forming the welding circuit have the same current carrying capacity. Always use a strong earth or return lead clamp or a satisfactory bolting arrangement.

For gas welding and burning equipment only personnel who are competent and trained should use oxygen acetylene equipment. They should wear eye and hand protection. Before use ensure that the equipment including hoses, connectors and cylinders are in good condition. Report any defects and do not use faulty equipment.

Always ensure that the gas cylinders are secured to prevent accidental displacement. Do not attempt to fill one cylinder from another or mix gases in a cylinder. Do not place cylinders near a heat source such as a blow torch or heater. Do not smoke near welding gas. Do not allow cylinders of oxygen to come into contact with grease or oil. Do not lubricate valves or fittings or use any jointing lubricants. Do not hang clothes in such a way as to obscure equipment or regulators.

Regulators

Before connecting regulators to cylinders always 'crack open' the cylinder valve or line valves. Always open cylinders and line valves gradually. Do not open cylinders or line valves when pressure is exerted by the adjusting screw being screwed in. When closing down shut the cylinder valve before slackening the adjusting screw while there is pressure in the rubber tubing and the blowpipe valve is closed. Anti-flashback arresters must be in use with all oxygen/acetylene equipment.

Hoses

All hoses used for gas welding and cutting should conform to BS 5120, 1975. Jubilee clips must not be used – only proprietary clips. Inspect all hoses daily to ensure that they are free from cuts, scratches, burns or tears. Protect hoses at all times from sharp edges, falling metal, moving plant and sparks. Always use red hoses for acetylene and other fuel gases and blue hoses for oxygen. Never interchange hoses. When removing the hoses from the blowpipe they must be removed completely from the tailpiece.

Blowpipes

Always make sure that gases are flowing from the blowpipe nozzle before applying a light. In the event of a backfire, turn off both gases quickly but always the oxygen first. Ensure you have the correct nozzle for the type of fuel you are using. If the blowpipe gets hot after backfiring, it should be plunged into a bucket of water with the oxygen flowing slowing from the nozzle. If after this the blowpipe still backfires, have it replaced.

Wood

Carpenters and woodworkers should be aware of dust hazards, especially when constructing large-scale sets and rostra from soft wood. One particular hazard that has recently been identified is the amount of fine dust and formaldehyde fumes given off by working with MDF (medium-density fibreboard), described by Ray Lockett of BECTU as the asbestos of the 1990s.

MDF

The risk from MDF only became clear when workers with prolonged exposure to it began to fall ill. As dust related diseases take 20 years to develop, the risk from a product that is 25 years old will only now start to be seen. Normal procedures would recommend that masks and respiratory equipment should be used with proper ventilation. Dusts masks should be CE/EN149 with an FFP3 filter.

MDF fibres, however, are very small and pass through normal dust masks, while the UK recommended exposure level for formaldehyde, at 2ppm, is 20 times higher than Europe or the USA. Proper masks and improved dust extraction in workshops would help to reduce the risk but this costs money. The formaldehyde gas given off is colourless and is emitted after manufacture for several months. The solution here is to buy MDF which is bonded with safer resins. Again this is more expensive. So in a climate of tight financial controls the outlook for rapid improvement in the risk from MDF is not good.

Woodworking machines – guards, noise levels

The use of woodworking machines is covered by the Woodworking Machine Regulations 1974 and The Safe Use of Woodworking Machinery – Provision and Use of Work Equipment Regulations 1998. Notices containing a summary of the regulations must be displayed on a placard in any workplace were woodworking takes place. The most common machines are circular saws and planing machines. Particular attention should be paid to the training and safe operation of these machines as they are responsible for 65 per cent of the accidents caused by woodworking machines. The woodworking regulations set out strict requirements for guarding machines.

Twelve types of machine are specified by the regulations.[1] These machines must have proper start/stop buttons and be protected by guards and cages to prevent injury from moving parts and cutting surfaces. Never attempt to clean or adjust a machine when it is switched on or moving. Never wear loose clothes, belts, ties or scarves and always wear protection for head, ears, eyes, feet and hands.

Other safety factors to consider are compliance with the Noise at Work Regulations 1989. Machines must be muffled to reduce noise levels and all operatives must wear proper ear protection. They should also wear protection for eyes, hands and feet. Any defects to machines must be reported immediately and the machine stopped until safe to use.

Operatives must be properly trained before being allowed to operate any woodworking machine and any work must be properly supervised. Training must include instruction in any type of equipment which the operative will have to use, including the safe methods of working and the use of guards. Instruction must emphasize the danger of the machines and ensure familiarity with the Woodworking Machine Regulations.

Operatives must also comply with age restrictions, being over 18 unless they have completed an approved course (certificate of approval no. 1 F2469, no. 2 F2472).

The regulations cover the use of portable handtools which are also regulated by the Provision and Use of Work Equipment Regulations and the Electricity at Work Regulations. This means that all operatives of handtools must be properly trained and the equipment provided must be safe to use.

The working shop must have a level floor which is not inclined or slippery. The working space must allow clear and unobstructed operation of the machines and must have proper artificial lighting which illuminates the machine without glare to the operator.

When woodworking machinery is in use the temperature should not fall below 13°C and should be kept at 16°C. If the temperature rises above this then procedures for hot working must be put in place. All operatives must wear suitable dust masks. All premises where woodworking takes place must be properly ventilated and each machine should have an LEV fitted. This means proper provision of a clean air supply coming in and extraction for removal of dust and dirty air out. Any dust produced must be kept away from the vicinity of camera operations as it will damage the lens. Sawdust is inflammable and should be separated from heat sources such as lights. Any waste disposal and extraction must comply with the COSHH Regulations 1988, the Environmental Protection Act 1990 and the Control of Pollution Act 1974.

Note

1 Those covered are: circular saws, band saws, grooving machines, planing machines, chain saws, mortising machines, tenoning machines, vertical spindle moulding machines, routing machines, multi-cutter moulding machines, trenching machines, boring machines and automatic and semi-automatic lathes.

Further reading

G. Stevens and A. Mann, Risks and Benefits of Flame Retardants in Consumer Products, University of Surrey study for the DTI. Available from the DTI, Room 432, 1 Victoria St, London SW1H 0ET.

W. Chapman, *Workshop Technology, Volume 1*, 5th edition, 1972, ISBN 0-7131-3269-8, *Volume 2*, 4th edition, 1972, ISBN 0-7131-3272-8, Edward Arnold.

A.C. Davis, *The Science and Practice of Welding, Volumes 1 and 2*, 10th edition, 1993, ISBN 0-5214-3566-8, Cambridge University Press.

Turner, Janice, MDF: The Asbestos of the 90s, *Stage, Screen and Radio*, October 1997, pp. 10–12.

Howell, Jeff, Are we playing with fibre? (Article on the MDF risk) *Independent on Sunday*, 28 September 1997, p. 9.

Clearing the Air – A Guide to Controlling Dust and Fume Hazards, Rapra Technology Ltd, Shawbury, Shrewsbury, Shropshire SY4 4NR, Tel: 01939–250383.

Managing Construction for Health and Safety – The Construction (Design and Management) Regulations 1994, Approved Code of Practice, L54, HSE, 1995, ISBN 0-7176-0792-5.

A Step by Step Guide to COSHH Assessment, HSE, 1993, HS(G)97, ISBN 0-11-886379-7.

The Chemicals (Hazard Information and Packaging for Supply) (Amendment) (No. 2) Regulations 1999, HSE, HSE(G)126, ISBN 0-7176-0857-3.

The Approved Supply List, 5th edition, HSE, ISBN 0-7176-1725-4.

The Approved Supply List, Information Approved for the Classification and Labelling of Substances and Preparations Dangerous for Supply, HSE, L76, ISBN 0-7176-1116-7.

The Approved Classification and Labelling Guide, 4th edition, HSE, ISBN 0-7176-1726-2.

Respiratory Protective Equipment – Approved List, HSE, ISBN 0-7176-1036-5.

Respiratory Protective Equipment – A Guide for Users, HSE, ISBN 0-7176-1198-1.

Michael McCann, *Health Hazards Manual for Artists*, 4th edition, Nick Lyons Books, 1994, ISBN 0-941130-06-1.

Monona Rossol, *The Artist's Complete Health and Safety Guide*, 2nd edition, Allworth Press, 1994, ISBN 0-927629-10-0.

The Electricity at Work Regulations 1989, HSE, ISBN 0-11-096635-X.

Electricity at Work, Safe Working Practices, HSE, G85, ISBN 0-7176-0442-X.

Protection Against Electric Shock, HSE, GS23, ISBN 0-11-883583-1.

Electrical Safety In Arc Welding, HSE, PM64, ISBN 0-11-883938-1.

Welding Review International magazine.

Welding and Metal Fabrication magazine.

Electrical Safety at Places of Entertainment, HSE, GS50, ISBN 0-11-885598-0.

The Safe Use of Woodworking Machinery – Provision and Use of Work Equipment Regulations 1998 as Applied to Woodworking Machinery, Approved Code of Practice and Guidance, HSE, L114, ISBN 0-7176-1630-4.

Woodworking Machines Regulations – Encapsulated Version, HSE, ISBN 0-7176-07828.

Training Woodworking Machinists, HSG83, HSE, ISBN 0-11-886316-9.

Nick Rudkin, *Machine Woodworking*, 1998, Arnold, ISBN 0-340-61423-4.

Personal Protective Equipment at Work Regulations 1992, HSE, L23, ISBN 0-7176-0801-8.

The Safe Use of Compressed Gases in Welding, Flame Cutting and Allied Processes, SG139. HSE, ISBN 0-7176-0680-5.

The Control of Exposure from Welding, Brazing and Similar Processes, HSE, EH55, ISBN 0-11-885439-9.

Contact organizations

BECTU
111 Wardour St, London W1V 4AY
Tel: 0171–437–8506

British Ceramic Confederation
Federation House, Station Rd, Stoke on Trent ST4 2SA
Tel: 01782–744631

British Constructional Steelwork Association Ltd
4 Whitehall Court, Westminster, London SW1A 2ES
Tel: 0171–839–8566

British Standards Institution
389 Chiswick High Rd, London W4 4AL
Tel: 0181–996–9000

British Textile Technology Group
Shirley House, Didsbury Rd, Manchester M20 2RB
Tel: 0161–445–8141

British Woodworking Federation
Broadway House, Tothill Street, London SW1H 9NQ
Tel: 0171–222–1522

Ceram Research (Ceramic Research)
Queens Rd, Penkull, Stoke on Trent, Staffs ST4 7LQ
Tel:01782–845431

Construction Industry Training Board (CITB)
(Health and safety development, Gordon Eagle/Dave Mason)
Bircham Newton, King's Lynn, Norfolk PE3 6RH
Tel: 01553–776677

Dustraction Ltd
PO Box 75, Manderville Road, Oadby, Leicester LE2 5NE
Tel: 0116–271–3212

Fabric Care Research Association Ltd
Forest House Laboratories, Knaresborough Rd, Harrogate HG2 7LZ
Tel: 01423–885977

Jesmonite Technologies Ltd
The Old School, Stanton Lacy, Near Ludlow, Shropshire, SY8 2AE
Tel: 01584–856–585

National Federation of Painters and Decorating Contractors
18 Mansfield St, London W1M 9FG
Tel: 0171–580–5404

The Paint Research Association
8 Waldegrave Rd, Teddington, Middx TW11 8LD
Tel: 0181–977–4427

Production Services Association
Hawks House, School Passage, Kingston upon Thames, Surrey KT1 3DU
Tel: 0181–392–0180

The Screen Industry Training and Apprenticeship Committee (SITAC)
c/o BECTU, 111 Wardour St, London W1V 4AY
Tel: 0171–437–8506

Solvents Industry Association
Magnolia House, Bromley Rd, Frating, Colchester CO7 7DR
Tel: 01206–252268

The Welding Institute (TWI)
Abington Hall, Abington, Cambridge CB1 6AL
Tel: 01223–891162

Hazard 31: Sports grounds

On 25th March 1997 Granada TV were ordered to pay £327,000 plus costs after a make-up artist's career was ended as a result of being knocked over by a 6 ft 3 in, 17-stone wrestler carrying out a pre-arranged but unannounced scuffle. The artist was knocked over as the wrestler ran off the set.

Stage, Screen and Radio, April 1997, p. 17

The legislation

The Fire Safety and Safety of Places of Sport Act 1987
The Health and Safety at Work Act 1974
The Lifting Operations and Lifting Equipment Regulations 1998
The Management of Health and Safety at Work Regulations 1992
The Manual Handling Operations Regulations 1992
The Noise at Work Regulations 1989
The Safety of Sports Grounds Act 1975

The risks

- access platforms
- cranes
- heights
- lifting
- noise
- vehicles
- violence

Those most at risk

Camera crews, the public, riggers.

The HSE have issued an information sheet entitled Safety in Broadcasting Events. This reflects the level of concern at the risks that are present in sports grounds. The risk can come from the proximity of the sport itself to the production operations. Then there is the risk introduced by the production team. Then there is the risk presented by the proximity of both to crowds and the public.

The close proximity of a sport to production operations can be dangerous, especially when filming motor sport or high speed events. Camera operators may not have time to escape from moving vehicles which crash off the course due to adverse conditions or driver error. Then there is the risk of an 80 kg prop forward crashing into touch, or the high speed cricket ball. The closer the action to the touchlines and camera positions, the higher the risk from contact with a heavy or fast moving object.

The best means of protection is separation of the event from the production operation behind protective barriers, and, as a last resort, crew identified as being at risk should wear personal protective clothing. Another means of separation and risk reduction is to use a remote camera on a flying arm or track.

Another problem is caused by lack of proper access. For example, could a crew get out of the way in the event of an accident? Access to commentary and camera positions was often up a rickety ladder to a crow's nest affair on top of a main stand or lighting column. This presented a high risk because there was only one way out in the event of a fire or an emergency evacuation situation such as a bomb scare. Also the means of escape was slow and often more danger to life and limb than the emergency.

Following the Bradford and Hillsborough disasters, exit safety in the event of a fire or an emergency became an issue. When performing an initial site visit, location managers and engineering managers must check for ease of escape from production positions. Checking for rubbish, blocked exits, narrow corridors and emergency lighting.

The stadium owners or operators should brief you on the safety rules of the stadium and of the fire and first aid procedures. This includes provision of information such as the sound of the fire alarm, the location of fire exits, the location of evacuation assembly points and the location of the nearest fire fighting equipment. Staff should also be briefed on the location of the first aid post and the location of any ambulance.

Production vehicles and equipment must not block fire exits, emergency exits or access routes for emergency vehicles.

Risks can also be introduced by the nature of the production operations themselves. A lot of heavy equipment will have to be moved from trucks to locations inside the stadium. All such moving will come under the Manual Handling Operations Regulations 1992. Lifting teams must be trained in safe procedures and sufficiently fit people must be chosen for the job. Mechanical assistance such as trolleys and forklifts must be provided for heavy loads and the trucks should be equipped with hoists. Any physical problems such as narrow gangways, steps, stairs or slippery surfaces must be identified and alternative access used which may have easier access and a lift.

All moving and lifting operators must be qualified. Drivers and operators of forklifts should have passed an RITB course for industrial work and a CITB course for construction work. Forklifts must be powerful enough for a safe working load and should have a warning light or siren to warn others when it is moving. This applies equally to any cranes used for lifting equipment or to provide vantage positions.

Lorry mounted crane operators should have a CITB CTA construction plant operators licence. You should always check the driver's licence before operations begin. Never use an unqualified or inexperienced driver. Since January 1998 all crane drivers have had to pass a new EU standard test.

The cranes themselves must be correctly taxed and insured. All paperwork and examination certificates must comply with BS 7121 Part 2 for the inspection, testing and examination of cranes. You should check that the crane operator or contractor can supply a test and examination certificate F96. Always check the duty chart in the cab which is specific to each crane. This gives vital information such as the SWL, maximum extension of the arm and the emergency controls to use in case of a power failure.

Each crane must have a valid HSE inspection and test certificate. The certificate is valid for four years and carries details of the crane's owner, maker, type, date of manufacture, identification number, registration number, maximum radius and safe working load. The crane should also be tested every 14 months.

The owner/operator should also supply a 14 month insurance test certificate for a lifting machine or appliance. Any chains or lifting gear attached should be examined every six months with a certificate issued: a separate lifting gear inspection certificate is needed to check that all the chains, hooks and tackle are in safe working condition before operations begin.

The automatic indicator should be regularly tested and the owner/operator/contractor or hirer/supplier must give you a valid handover certificate to indicate that the crane is in safe working condition. A separate certificate is required for passenger hoists. This will be needed for any crane which will lift and be used as a working camera or lighting platform.

Before commencing any lifting operations always check that the crane you have hired and the chains for lifting will be of sufficient power and strength to take the load which you intend to place on it.

Any operations employing mobile access platforms must conform to the legal requirements and follow the safety regulations, operating instructions, safe working loads and licensing requirements. Always check that the insurance and liability cover of the crane, access platform and forklift truck company is sufficient for a public arena and will cover crowds.

All lifting equipment operations and scaffold structures must be sufficiently far away from adjacent risks such as power cables and floodlights. They must also avoid any sudden or rapid movement which might scare animals involved in sporting events or police horses.

Staff will be operating at height, either rigging equipment or operating it. A proper risk assessment for working at height must be made. Special attention must be made for securing equipment properly from vibration and wind. All working platforms including cranes, access platforms and scaffolds must have safety rails and be fitted with edge protection so that the operators and equipment cannot fall out.

Management must check on the weather and make sure that lifts, hoists and cranes are not operated in adverse weather conditions, especially high winds. Snow and ice may render the working platforms unsafe. Staff must be provided with extra warm clothing including face and hand protection. They should also wear personal protective clothing including safety boots, fluorescent jacket, hard hat and safety harness. They should also wear a safety belt and an extra lifeline. Management must also ensure that operatives are in constant two-way communication with the ground operator in case of an emergency or sudden deterioration in the weather.

All temporary scaffolding must be supplied and built by SITAC trained riggers and must be safe to use. The design of scaffold structures must take into account the maximum load they will be required to support, including personnel and equipment. Extra support and clamps may be required for vibration protection from crowd movement and high winds.

Suspended lighting must be properly secured against wind and vibration with proper locking clamps and safety chains. All scaffold towers and lighting stands must be constructed on a firm solid base and either attached to a solid structure or else fitted with outriggers.

Any cables must be in good condition with sealed connectors to keep out rain and ground water. All generators and link vehicles must be in good working condition and provided with barriers to separate them from the public.

Similarly, flying arms, remote cameras and Steadicam operations must be provided with free runs separate from the public. Any equipment movement must have sufficient clearance from barriers, cables and structures. Fixed camera positions should be protected by buffer bags and situated behind barriers or permanent structures.

Mobile cameras must keep a safe distance from the touch line or arena. The usual safe distance is 2 metres although this might increase for more dangerous motor sports. Operators of mobile cameras with cables must be accompanied by a minder to control the safe position of cables in relation to the event, the structures and the public. The second person can also watch the back of the operator as their pair of eyes. This is especially handy in the event of stray animals, out of control vehicles or crowd violence.

Camera crews filming sports events are at risk from crowd violence as they could become targets when things turn nasty or if they are perceived to be gathering potential evidence. These days the risk can also come from the players and the dug outs. Further guidance can be found in ETIS 2, Violence to Workers in Broadcasting. If a risk is identified then a fast means of escape is essential along with the use of personal protective equipment such as a hard hat.

The noise of crowds can be excessive in itself and cause talkback and communication systems to be turned up to high levels. The risk of ear damage must be identified to comply with the Noise at Work Regulations 1989. If levels exceed 89 dB(A) then protective action must be taken including the use of ear protection such as high fidelity ear plugs and sound excluding headphones.

Further reading

Safety in Broadcasting Sports Events, HSE Entertainment Sheet No. 1, ETIS-1.
Health and Safety at Motorsport Events: A Guide for Employers and Organisers, HSG112, ISBN 0-7176-0705-4.
The Safety at Work Regulations 1992, Approved Code of Practice, HSE, ISBN 0-7176-0412-8.
Noise at Work, HSE, ISBN 0-7176-0454-3.
Violence to Workers in Broadcasting, HSE Entertainment Sheet No. 2, ETIS-2.

Contact organizations

Football Association
16 Lancaster Gate, London N2 3LW
Tel: 0171–262–4542

Football League
Edward Seventh Quay, Navigation Way, Preston, Lancs PR2 2YF
Tel: 01772–325800

The National Association of Scaffolding Contractors
18 Mansfield St, London W1M 9FG
Tel: 0171–580–5404

Rugby Football Union
Rugby Rd, Twickenham, Middx TW1 1DS
Tel: 0181–892–2000

Sports Council
16 Upper Woburn Place, London WC1H 0QP
Tel: 0171–273–1500

England and Wales Cricket Board
Lords Cricket Ground, London NW8 8QZ
Tel: 0171–432–1200

All England Tennis and Croquet Club
Church Rd, Wimbledon, Surrey SW19 5AE
Tel: 0181–944–1066

Hazard 32: Visual display screens – office computers and editing equipment

---

The legislation

The Provision and Use of Work Equipment Regulations 1998
The Management of Health and Safety at Work Regulations 1992
The Health and Safety Display Screen Equipment Regulations 1992

The risks

- back strain
- eye strain
- repetitive strain injury

Those most at risk

Editors, graphics journalists, office workers, PAs, secretaries, studio staff.

If you use a VDU or display screen as a significant part of your work then you will come under the Display Screen Equipment Regulations 1992 – especially those who are highly dependent on VDUs or have little choice about using them as part of their work. This includes temporary workers and the self-employed who may use the workstation of their client. The definition of a user is someone who normally uses a VDU for continuous spells of an hour or more at a time. It includes people who have to transfer information quickly to and from the screen or who need to apply high levels of attention or concentration.

In the film and television business this would include temporary office workers, bookings staff, researchers, administration staff and graphics operators. With the increased use of computers the risks from poor set-up or over-use of display screens can apply to most staff.

Editors are particularly at risk with the widespread use of non-linear editing systems and the intensity of the task they perform. Similarly journalists and studio staff must use keyboards and use display screens for the majority of their work under pressure of deadlines. In other words the longer the hours spent at a screen and the more intense the work then the risk of eye strain and RSI becomes greater.

Employers must make an assessment of any staff who work with display screens and ensure that the equipment is set up properly to minimize discomfort. Display screens must be assessed for health and safety risks and should meet the minimum requirement for workstations.

Managers must also ensure that work routines allow for proper rest periods away from the screen and that regular eye tests are conducted to monitor the health of staff who work with display screens. The health risks fall into three areas: musculoskeletal discomfort, eyestrain and stress.

Physical discomfort and RSI

Common physical problems include backache, neck/shoulder ache and repetitive strain injury. The physical layout of your workstation can be improved to minimize physical strain. For example, you should sit upright rather than slouching. Take time to sit comfortably. Good posture can be helped by the use of an adjustable chair. This should support your arms, back and thighs so that your feet are flat on the floor and your arms are in a relaxed position with a 90° bend at the elbow.

Ensure that your neck is not bent too far forward as this puts strain on your back and neck muscles. If your neck is bent too far forward you may get headaches, backache and neckache which leads to tension, stress and tiredness. Position your screen so that you are looking down slightly.

Upper limb disorders can also be caused by prolonged and intensive keying with a forceful action. Try to reduce the pressure you put on the keys and take regular short breaks before you get tired. Make sure your keyboard does not stick and that you can rest your wrists in front of the keyboard. Keep your upper arms relaxed at the side of your body and your lower arms and wrists straight while typing.

Report any symptoms of stress or discomfort. Repetitive strain injury or RSI is a term employed for various strains and pains in the upper arms and the back and is associated with working with display screens. The term, first used in 1992, presents difficulties in defining repetitive and then employing the word injury to symptoms which are intermittent. Recent research on RSI divides into two camps: one which thinks the causes are physical and mechanical, the other which thinks the causes are located in the brain which gets confused with demands for too many quick repetitive movements characteristic of today's computerized work.

It is difficult to find reliable recent figures for the number of people affected by upper limb disorders. However female workers develop this condition more than men as they are more likely to use keyboards for everyday work tasks. Pace your work load and rotate tasks which require intense use of the keyboard. Scribes had suffered from a similar condition centuries before the invention of the computer!

Eyestrain

Users of visual display screens can also suffer eye strain as well as physical problems associated with intense use of keyboards. Symptoms include sore eyes and problems with focusing. You should ensure that your workstation is properly lit and with minimum glare. Try and avoid working with your workstation screen in front of a window. Use a window blind and use a screen which has a filter built in or a positive polarity screen which gives you dark characters on a light background.

It helps to keep your screen clean from dust and apply anti-static cleaner regularly. Adjust the contrast and brightness of your screen so that it is comfortable. Focusing problems are caused by repetitively having to focus on the screen and then back to written sheets you are taking information from. It helps to use a document holder positioned at the same height and distance as your screen to reduce eye strain.

If you are a user of a visual display screen then you have a legal right to a free eye, eyesight or vision screening test. Major employers will do this by giving you a referral letter to an optician or by arranging for workers to be tested. Eyesight and eye tests detect an injury or damage to the eye. A vision screening test will indicate whether there is any significant problem with your eyesight. The test must be conducted by a qualified optician and where any defect is identified you must be informed and referred for a full sight test.

You are entitled to request an eye test when you first become a user, then at regular intervals or if you experience symptoms of eye strain. Any corrective measures such as spectacles or contact lenses you need specifically for display screen work must be provided by your employer.

The prescription will be to provide eye protection solely for working with display-screen equipment (DSE).

The standard for display screen operators is set by the Association of Optical Practitioners. This means that the operator must satisfy the following criteria:

- The ability to read N6 at a distance of $\frac{2}{3}$ metre down to $\frac{1}{3}$ metre.
- Monocular vision or good binocular vision.
- No central (20°) field defects in the dominant eye.
- Near point of convergence normal.
- Clear ocular media.

The best way to avoid eye strain is to rotate your work with non-screen tasks and vary your routine. Take short breaks to rest your eyes from the screen and to move around. Short frequent breaks of five minutes help to rest your eyes. Always rest before your eyes become tired.

Deliberate rest breaks from display screen work and periodic changes of activity to your work pattern must be part of the safety measures provided by your employer. The employer must also provide information about the correct set-up and safe use of your workstation and the entitlement to eye tests. In other words you should be trained to use it properly, and, as work equipment provided by the employer, it must be set up properly to minimize any health and safety risks.

To do this, management must appoint workstation assessors to recognize risky workstation layouts, environments and working practices. The assessors will also perform a risk assessment on each workstation with a checklist of points to inspect. Any adjustments and improvements can then be implemented. The regulations cover the ergonomic features that all workstations must have (the deadline for inclusion of these features was 1996). This includes design of furniture, the VDU hardware, software and accessories. A checklist would include the following points.

The display screen
1 Is the display screen image clear?
2 Is it damaged?
3 Does it need cleaning?
4 Is the image free from flicker or movement?
5 Does the screen colour need adjusting?

Does the brightness or contrast require adjustment?
1 Can the screen swivel and tilt for better posture?
2 Is the screen free from glare and reflections?
3 Do you need an anti-glare filter?
4 Does the lighting require improvement?

The keyboard

1 Is the keyboard tiltable?
2 Is there enough space to rest hands in front of the keyboard?
3 Do the keys function properly?
4 The operator's hands should not be bent at the wrist.
5 The operator's fingers should not be stretched.
6 The keyboard should be separate from the screen.
7 Is there enough distance between the monitor and the keyboard?
8 Is the keyboard glare free?

The furniture

1 Is the work surface large enough for the monitor, keyboard and documents?
2 Can the printer and file storage be placed elsewhere?
3 Is the surface glare free?
4 Is the chair adjustable, supportive and comfortable?
5 Is the user sitting correctly with horizontal arms and eyes level with the VDU case?

Posture

1 Are the operator's feet flat on the floor?
2 Is the back of the chair supported by the floor?
3 Is the back straight and the user relaxed?
4 Are there any obstructions under the chair?
5 Are the chair arms supportive?

Workstation environment

1 Is there enough room to change position and vary movement?
2 Is there sufficient light?
3 Is the light too bright?
4 Is the workstation away from heaters?
5 Is the workstation away from noisy printers and photocopiers?
6 Is the ventilation and air-conditioning adequate?
7 Does the computer give out too much noise and heat for the space?

Software

1 Is it the proper software for the job?
2 Is the operator trained to use it?
3 Is the storage sufficient?

Beware of exaggerated claims and misinformation from suppliers of products that are supposed to reduce risks but don't. For example unnecessary radiation filtering devices, over elaborate adjustable tables and tinted VDU spectacles.

With the increasing use of computers and digital equipment the risks from visual display equipment are set to become the biggest source of health and safety hazards in the film and television industry. The spread of non-linear editing is one area which managers will have to monitor closely. However, almost everybody will use a display screen of some sort and employees should exercise their right to a free eye test.

Freelances should also arrange to get their eyes tested regularly and make sure that workstations are properly set up to comply with the display screen regulations. Potential users of visual display screens who suffer from epilepsy or are pregnant are not thought to be at any significant risk. However they should be identified and allowed to seek medical advice and if necessary given tasks that do not require significant use of display screens.

Further reading

The Management of Health and Safety at Work Regulations 1992, Approved Code of Practice, L21, HSE, ISBN 0-7176-0412-8.

The Provision and Use of Work Equipment Regulations 1998, Guidance on Regulations, L22, HSE, ISBN 0-7176-0414-4.

The Health and Safety Display Screen Equipment Regulations 1992, Guidance on Regulations, L26, HSE, ISBN 0-7176-0410-1.

VDUs: An Easy Guide to the Regulations, HSG 90, HSE, ISBN 0-7176-0735-6.

Working with VDUs, HSE, ISBN 0-7176-0814-X.

VDU Workstation Checklist, HSE, ISBN 0-7176-0804-2.

Dr Richard Pearson, The Keyboard Menace, *The Guardian*, 9 March 1998, p. 55.

Roger Dobson, Finger Trouble – RSI, *The Guardian*, 27 April 1999, pp. 12–13.

David Travis and Tanya Heasman, Display Screen Equipment Health Problems: User Based Assessments of DSE Health Risks, CRR 198/98, ISBN 0-7176-1647-9.

Contact organizations

The Association of Optical Practitioners
90 London Rd, London SE1 6LN
Tel: 0171–261–9661

Repetitive Strain Injury Association
Chapel House, 152–156 High St, Yiewsley, West Drayton, Middx UB7 7BE
Tel: 01895–431134

Hazard 33: Water

The legislation

The Dangerous Substances in Harbour Areas Regulations 1987
The Dock Regulations 1988
The Health and Safety at Work Act 1974
The Maritime and Aviation Security Act 1990
The Merchant Shipping (Life-Saving Appliances) Regulations 1986
The Merchant Shipping Act 1995
The Personal Protective Equipment (PPE) at Work Regulations 1992
The Provision and Use of Work Equipment Regulations 1998

The risks

- cables
- cranes
- cold
- drowning
- electricity
- pollution
- swift current
- tides
- Weil's disease

Those most at risk

Anybody near or on water.

Health and safety in inland and inshore waters are covered by the Health and Safety at Work Act 1974. Three-quarters of drownings occur in inland water rather than at sea. These accidents happen in canals, lakes, pits, ponds, rivers and reservoirs. Water accidents are caused by misjudgement and misplaced bravado. People used to leisure swimming in a swimming pool are unprepared for the hazards of fresh running water. They misjudge it and assume it is safe. Then they are caught out by one or a number of factors such as the depth of water, the speed and strength of the current, underlying hazards such as weed and pollution and most of all by the cold temperature of the water. Quite simply, they are out of their depth and are caught unprepared.

The risk factors can be reduced if they are understood to apply to any type of water and sufficient planning and preparation is made to make sure that the correct health and safety precautions are in place. A preliminary site visit followed by a risk assessment can identify most of the hazards backed up by advice from experts and a safe system of water work.

The most basic precaution is to find out how many of the crew and anybody involved in the production can swim. This is so those most at risk can be identified and replaced by people who can swim if necessary.

The second is to check on their medical condition as the shock of sudden immersion in cold water can kill. Anyone at risk should be prevented from taking an active role near water. If necessary extra supervisors must be used who have strong swimming and lifesaving qualifications backed up by emergency medical care in the event of an accident. This should include a qualified first aider trained in resuscitation.

The best way to prevent accidents is to separate the production activity from the water, making sure that nobody works near the edge or can fall in. Protective barriers must be used to prevent access to water and emergency netting behind this if the barriers are visually undesirable. Warning signs should indicate 'danger deep water'.

To prevent anybody falling in, a fall arrest harness to BS 1397 should be worn by anybody working near water. If they slip and fall the arrest will prevent them from being immersed.

If anybody does fall in the water the main risk comes from sudden loss of body temperature. Sea temperatures range from 7°C in the winter to 16°C in the summer. Survival time would be 1–2 hours for an average person in everyday clothing. However in freezing temperatures and rough weather this figure would be halved. Fresh water can reach freezing point and can be much colder than sea water. The effect on anybody falling in would be dramatic on skin temperature, circulation and breathing. Continued heat loss after three minutes' immersion brings about hypothermia symptoms resulting in loss of consciousness. This means that immediate rescue is necessary.

The production site should have a drowning alarm that can be activated if somebody falls in the water. They should be equipped with a drowning alarm which gives off a loud noise and an emergency flash strobe.

This is so that the victim can be located quickly especially at night. To prevent rapid loss of body temperature everybody at risk should wear a survival suit or wet suit which will allow more time for rescue and prevent deterioration. They should also be wearing a safe inflatable life-jacket to BS 3595 and at least a flotation jacket or visible work vest.

The four standards for life-jackets are:

1 N50/EN393: These are for buoyancy aids and are only for use by good swimmers in sheltered water, where help is close at hand. They will not hold the face of an unconscious wearer clear of the water. They are also unsuitable for children.
2 N100/EN395: These are life-jackets for use in inland waterways and relatively sheltered waters. These will not turn unconscious wearers face up if they are heavy.
3 N150/EN396: These are suitable for use in all waters. These will turn most unconscious wearers face up unless they are wearing heavy foul weather clothing.
4 E275/EN399: These are for use in offshore and extreme conditions. These will turn the unconscious wearer face up in water under almost all circumstances, even if the wearer is dressed in heavy protective clothing. Reputable manufacturers include Secumar and Stearns. This helps preserve body temperature and keeps you afloat with your head supported. A hard hat should also be worn to prevent head injury when falling in.

If somebody falls into the water then the production management must have allowed provision for their rescue. Lifelines of 30 metres or more with a buoyant rescue quoit must be on hand in case of a rescue and sufficient life rings for the number of people at risk. These can be thrown to aid the buoyancy and rescue of anyone who falls in.

If production operations demand either diving, immersion in water or working next to fast flowing and tidal water then a standby rescue boat must be provided to rescue anybody who falls in. The operator of the craft must be qualified and insured, with an assistant trained in life-saving. This allows one person to navigate and the other to effect a rescue. The boat must be seaworthy and must be power driven with a fixed self-starting motor of sufficient capacity to run against fast currents. The boat should carry distress flares, a first aid kit, life-buoys and grab lines.

Another basic precaution is to test the water before filming for pollution and toxic substances. This is especially true of deep water near old industrial mills, chemical works or canals. Beware also of agricultural pollution in water courses. A test can be carried out by a National Rivers Authority laboratory and will identify any contamination. A particular risk is contamination of water by rats', dogs' and cattle urine which causes Weil's disease. This is contracted by swallowing or inhaling contaminated water and is potentially fatal. The symptoms are red eyes, fever, headaches and muscle ache.

A water contamination risk assessment should always be carried out. Weil's disease is often known as leptospirosis (HSE INDG84, AIS5, AIS19). The risk of this should be fully assessed, especially in water near disused buildings and sewers. Always look out for droppings and other signs of vermin. If necessary call in a specialist pest contractor to remove the vermin as exposure to them constitutes a high risk to the health and safety of employees and a breach of the Environmental Health Act. Weil's disease is a named reportable disease under the Reporting of Injuries, Diseases and Dangerous Occurrences Regulations 1985. Make sure all your staff have had recent polio and tetanus jabs.

Any staff entering the water must be free of cuts and abrasions. They must also wear a dry suit for protection and a face mask as Weil's disease can enter via the eyes. Do not swallow any water and shower immediately after coming out from the water before smoking or eating.

If you work with electricity take care that all equipment is powered down with a step-down transformer to 110 V and protected by residual current devices. All electrical equipment must be intrinsically safe and try to use battery powered equipment whenever possible.

Take special precautions when working in swimming pools and other public areas which have water hazards. Beware of submerged electric cables when conducting boat movements or media diving operations. Also beware of dangers below the surface such as waste outlets, intakes, sharp metal, fishing cages and trawl lines.

If you plan to film in a harbour you should obtain permission to film from the harbour master, in docks from the dock master and in ports from the port authority manager. You should follow the port or dock safety code which will include the compulsory wearing of personal protective clothing such as hard hats, visibility vests and life-jackets. If you are building any scaffolding and working over water then you must follow the construction industry training board guidance for working over water and comply with the port authority regulations.

When working in a dock, port or waterway you must check in advance for potentially dangerous ship movements especially if working in the water. You must also check for water surges from the opening and closing of weirs, locks and sluices, many of which will be automatic. You should also check with the coastguard and port authorities for tide times. A special factor here is the difference in levels between high and low tide and how fast this happens. This will dictate the time you have to work at a safe level.

Tide times are especially important if you are filming on a promenade or beach. High tide could present high waves coming over the top of a promenade, transforming a safe shoot into a dangerous one. Similarly, beware of getting caught on isolated rocks or beaches by a fast incoming tide, especially near steep cliffs which give no means of escape.

Figure H33.1

Lookouts should be posted and wrap times must take into account how long it will take to return to safety. Health and safety at sea is regulated by the Maritime Safety Agency and the MCA (Maritime and Coastguard Agency). The coastguard and rescue authorities should always be informed of your location and adequate provision made for emergency communication and escape. Always carry distress flares, life-jackets and some form of location device so you can be found quickly and easily in the dark.

If you are filming at night always inform the coastguard and harbour authorities as your lights may be mistaken for navigation lights or distress signals. Also consider that in conditions of poor visibility it may be necessary to carry some emergency device by which you can be heard and post extra advance lookouts to warn of oncoming shipping.

When the use of a captained vessel is commissioned, the captain must check on the weather and tidal conditions. They are also responsible for the safe navigation of the ship. Your life and those of others depends on the selection of a competent and experienced skipper. This means that they must hold a valid master's ticket for the class of ship and operating waters.

For small boats within 20 miles of the coast a RYA/DTP coastal skipper (motor) is required. This is a class 3/4 licence. For small boats within 60 miles of the coast a yacht master (off-shore) licence is required. This is a category 2 licence. For up to 150 miles off-shore a yacht master category 1 licence is required. For large vessels and ocean going craft an unrestricted skippers licence is needed. The skipper should also have passed a medical examination and possess a medical fitness certificate. They must also have a radio operator's certificate.

Skippers must have experience of local waters and tidal conditions. All vessels must be properly insured to carry passengers and have a valid certificate of seaworthiness from the Department of Transport. Small charter vessels must have a small commercial vessels certificate.

Small vessel skippers must have a DTP boatman's licence and have passed an approved engine and navigation course including radio work. Yacht skippers must have passed a RYA yacht master's exam as well as courses on navigation and communications.

All ships and vessels must comply with the DTP and Maritime Safety Agency regulations for that class of vessel. This relates to the type of radio equipment, radar and type of safety equipment required.

The ship must also be equipped with distress flares, life-belts, life-jackets and life-boats or life-rafts. It must also have adequate radar, echo sounder and communications systems.

When engaging a diver you should always check on their credentials and make sure they are qualified to do what is required of them. Always try and engage a shipping company and skipper that has particular experience of providing them for film and television work. For example, as working platforms for underwater wildlife filming or as period reconstructions of maritime action.

As film work often involves simulations or reconstruction of action, producers must inform the police, harbour authorities and coastguard if any of the following are contemplated as part of the action:

- The firing of rockets or distress flares.
- The firing of maroons, firearms or explosives.
- The use of fire, smoke or toxic emissions.
- The simulation of maritime accidents, drowning, sinkings, disasters or invasions that might in any way be mistaken for genuine events either by the authorities or members of the public.

When working near water always wear high visibility clothing and keep a regular check on members of the production crew. Be careful of parking production vehicles near slipways and quayside when unloading. Beware of moving vehicles such as fork-lifts, lorries and railway trains. Also be aware of hazards overhead such as crane movements and containers. Avoid slipping hazards, such as oil, and tripping hazards, presented by mooring lines and supply cables.

Further reading

International Code of Safety for High Speed Craft, Marine and Coastguard Agency, HMSO, ISBN 0-11-552084-8.

The Code of Practice for the Safety of Large Commercial Sailing and Motor Vessels, HMSO, ISBN 0-11-551911-4.

Safety in Docks – The Docks Regulations 1988, Approved Code of Practice with Regulations and Guidance, HSE, COP25, ISBN 0-7176-1408-5.

A Guide to the Dangerous Substances in Harbour Areas Regulations 1987, HSE, HSR27-ISBN 0-11-883991-8.

The Safety of Small Commercial Motor Vessels, A Code of Practice, 3rd edition, 1998, ISBN 0-11-551185-7.

The Safety of Small Workboats and Pilot Boats, A Code of Practice, HMSO, ISBN 0-11-552006-6.

The Ship's Captain's Medical Guide, 22nd edition, Marine and Coastguard Agency, ISBN 0-11-551658-1.

Maritime Journal (monthly), The Maritime Journal Ltd, Tel: 01329 825335.

The titles below are available from Emergency Response Publications, 5 Shelly Court, South Zeal, Okehampton, Devon EX20 2PT, Tel: 01837–840102.

- David S. Smith, *Water Rescue*, ref: WAT1.
- Ray Slim, *Swiftwater Rescue*, ref: ZSWI.

Contact organizations

Associated British Ports
150 Holborn, London EC1N 2LR
Tel: 0171–430–1177

British Waterways Board
Willow Grange, Church Rd, Watford, Herts WD1 3QU
Tel: 01923–226–422

The British Canoe Union
John Dudderidge House, Adbolton Lane, West Bridgford, Nottingham NG2 5AS
Tel: 01159–821100

Bureau Veritas
British Central Office, Capital House, 42 Weston St, London SE1 3QL
Tel: 0171–403–6266

Coastguard Agency
Bay 1/17a Spring Place, 105 Commercial Rd, Southampton, Hampshire
SO15 1EG
Tel: 01703–329401
(will give you details of local MRCC, MRSC or coastguard)

The Environment Agency
Waterside Drive, Almondsbury, Bristol BS32 4UD
Tel: 01454–624400

The Institute of Leisure and Amenities Management
Ilam House, Lower Basildon, Reading, Berks RG89 9NE
Tel: 01491–874800

The International Maritime Organization
4 Albert Embankment, London SE1 7SR
Tel: 0171–735–7611

Lloyd's of London
100 Leadenhall St, London EC3A 3BP
Tel: 0171–709–9166

The Maritime and Coastguard Agency
Spring Place, 105 Commercial Rd, Southampton, Hants SO15 1EG
Tel: 01703–329100

The Marine Land and Liability Division
Department of Transport, Ashdown House, 123 Victoria St, London
SW1E 6DE
Tel: 0171–890–5307

The National Federation of Charter Skippers
Peper, 88 Harow Rd, Godalming, Surrey GU7 2PN
Tel: 01483–417782

The Ports Safety Organisation
Room 220, Africa House, 64–78 Kingsway, London WC2B 6AH
Tel: 0171–242–3538

The Professional Boatman's Association
Lynora, West Charleton, Kingsbridge, Devon TQ7 2AE
Tel: 01548–531678

The Royal National Lifeboat Institution Headquarters
Public Relations Office, West Quay Rd, Poole, Dorset BH15 1HZ
Tel: 01202–671133

The Royal Yacht Club
RYA House, Romsey Rd, Eastleigh, Hants SO50 9YA
Tel: 01703–627400

Square Sail Shipyard Ltd
Charlestown Harbour, St Austell, Cornwall PL25 3NJ
Tel: 01726–70241

Trinity House (shipping safety and regulation)
Trinity House Lane, Kingston upon Hull HU1 2JG
Tel: 01482–324956

Water UK (formerly the Water Authorities Association)
1 Queen Anne's Gate, London SW1H 9BT
Tel: 0171–344–1844

Appendix 1: Licences and Forms

Sample copies of some of the following licences and forms can be found on the Focal Press web site:

http://www.focalpress.com/companion/0240515315

Hazard 2: Animals
Certificate of Registration for a Performing Animal

Hazard 3: Asbestos
Licence to Work With Asbestos Form ASB2a
Notification of Work With Asbestos Form ASB5
Application for Licence to Carry Out Work With Asbestos
Contents of an Air Monitoring Report

Hazard 5: Building and construction sites
Site Inspection Report
Notification of a Project

Hazard 7: Children
Licence for Training a Child

Hazard 10: Confined spaces, including caving and mines
Permit to Work in a Confined Space
Longannet Colliery Filming Safety Rules
RJB Filming Safety Rules

Hazard 11: Cranes, hoists, lifts and access platforms
Work Platform Handover Certificate
CTA Plant Instructor Card
CTA Plant Operator Card
Safety Awareness Course Certificate CSNo74
PAL/IPAF Powered Access licence
Safe use of Cranes Course Certificate BS7121
Factory Overhead Cranes Certificate
Six Month Lifting Gear Inspection Certificate
Wire Rope Test and Examination Certificate F87
Lifting Appliance Weekly Inspection Sheet F91

Crane 12 Month Test Certificate L3
Four Year Test and Examination of Crane Certificate F96
Fork-lift Truck Basic Training Certificate
Fork-lift Truck Refresher Course Certificate

Hazard 14: Diving and underwater

ADC Membership Certificate
HSE Notice of Particulars of a Diving Contractor
Diving Contractor's Insurance Certificate
Specification of a Diving Contract
Diving Contractor's Risk Assessment
Certificate of Appointment of a Diving Supervisor
Diver's Part 1 Training Certificate
Diver's First Aid Training Certificate
Diver's Medical Fitness Certificate
Diver's Log Record
Diver's Chainsaw Certificate
Diver's Underwater Inspection Certificate
Diver's Offshore Survival and Fire-fighting Certificate

Hazard 16: Explosives and pyrotechnics

Application for an Explosives Certificate COER 1/2
Certificate to Acquire and Keep Explosives COER 3
Licence to Transport Explosives by Road
Joint Industry Pyrotechnic/Physical Technician Card
Cranfield University Explosives Course Certificate
Pyrotechnic Course Certificate

Hazard 17: Fire

Application Form for a Fire Certificate
A Fire Certificate
Receipt for a Fire Certificate
Fire Drill Requirements
Fire Precautions Required
Emergency Lighting Test Log
Fire Alarm Test Log
Fire Detector Test log
Fire-fighting Equipment Test Log
Fire Drill Record Log Sheet
Fire Safety Instruction Log Sheet

Hazard 18: Firearms and weapons

Application for a Firearm Certificate F101
Reference for a Firearm Application F125

Firearm Certificate F102
Ammunition Certificate
Application for a Shotgun Certificate F103
Shotgun Certificate F104

Hazard 19: First Aid
First Aid Basic Certificate
Appointed First Aid Qualification Certificate

Hazard 20: Flying and airports
CAA Air Operators Certificate
Air Operators Insurance Certificate
CAA Transport Pilot's Licence, Helicopters
CAA Pilot's Medical Certificate
Gliding Airworthiness Certificate
Gliders Pilot Certificate

Hazard 21: Food and catering
Registration of a Food Premises
Food Emergency Prohibition Notice
Food Improvement Notice
Basic Food Hygiene Certificate
Intermediate Food Hygiene Certificate
Advanced Food Hygiene Certificate
Essential Food Hygiene Certificate
Food Hygiene Awareness Certificate
Essential Food Hygiene for the Food Industry Certificate
Certificate in Food Health and Safety
Certificate in Food Hygiene Management
Diploma in Food Hygiene Management
Diploma in Food Health and Safety Management

Hazard 29: Scaffolding and heights
PASMA Course Certificate
Scaffold Inspection Report
Scaffold Handover Certificate
SITAC Trainee Card
SITAC Basic Card
SITAC Advanced Card

Hazard 32: Visual display screens – office computers and editing equipment
DSE Referral letter for an eye test
DSE Eye Test Report

Appendix 2: Addresses of HSE offices

South West
Inter City House
Mitchess Lane
Victoria Street
Bristol
BS1 6AN
Tel: 0117 988 6000

South
Priestley House
Priestley Road
Basingstoke
Hants
RG24 9NW
Tel: 01256 404000

South East
3 East Grinstead House
London Road
East Grinstead
West Sussex
RH19 1RR
Tel: 01342 334200

London North
Maritime House
1 Linton Road
Barking
Essex
IG11 8HF
Tel: 0181 235 8000

London South
1 Long Lane
London
SE1 4PG
Tel: 0171 556 2100

East Anglia
39 Baddow Road
Chelmsford
Essex
CM2 0HL
Tel: 01245 706200

Northern Home Counties
14 Cardiff Road
Luton
Beds
LU1 1PP
Tel: 01582 444200

East Midlands
5th Floor, Belgrave House
1 Greyfriars
Northampton
NN1 2BS
Tel: 01604 738300

West Midlands
McLaren Building
35 Dale End
Birmingham
B4 7NP
Tel: 0121 607 6200

Wales
Brunel House
2 Fitzalan Road
Cardiff
CF2 2SH
Tel: 01222 263000

Marches
The Marches House
Midway
Newcastle-under-Lyme
Staffs
ST5 1DT
Tel: 01782 602300

North Midlands
1st Floor, The Pearson Building
55 Upper Parliament Street
Nottingham
NG1 6AU
Tel: 0115 971 2800

South Yorkshire and Humberside
Sovereign House
110 Queen Street
Sheffield
S1 2ES
Tel: 0114 2912300

West and North Yorkshire
8 St Paul's Street
Leeds
LS1 2LE
Tel: 0113 283 4200

Greater Manchester
Quay House
Quay Street
Manchester
M3 3JB
Tel: 0161 952 8200

Merseyside
The Triad
Stanley Road
Bootle
L20 3PG
Tel: 0151 479 2200

North West
Victoria House
Ormskirk Road
Preston
PR1 1HH
Tel: 01772 836200

North East
Arden House
Regent Centre
Gosforth
Newcastle-upon-Tyne
NE3 3JN
Tel: 0191 202 6200

Scotland East
Belford House
59 Belford Road
Edinburgh
EH4 3UE
Tel: 0131 247 2000

Scotland West
375 West George Street
Glasgow
G2 4LW
Tel: 0141 275 3000

Appendix 3: UK health and safety organizations

The Law Society Accident Line
50 Chancery Lane, London WC2A 1SX
Tel: 0500–192939

Broadcasting, Entertainment, Cinematograph and Theatre Union
(BECTU)
111 Wardour St, London W1V 4AY
Tel: 0171–437–8506

British Safety Council: National Safety Centre
70 Chancellors Rd, London W6 9RS
Tel: 0181–741–1231

British Standards Institution
BSI Standards, 389 Chiswick High Rd, London W4 4AL
Tel: 0181–996–7111

Hazards Forum
1 Great George, St London SW1P 3AA
Tel: 0171–839–9971

Industrial Injuries Advisory Council
A4 6th Floor, John Adam St, London WC2N 6HT
Tel: 0171–962–8066l

Institute of Risk Management (IRM)
Lloyd's Avenue House, 6 Lloyd's Avenue, London EC3N 3AX
Tel: 0171–709–9808

Institution of Occupational Safety and Health (IOSH)
The Grange, Highfield Drive, Wigston, Leicester LE18 1NN
Tel: 0116–257–1399

London Hazards Centre Ltd
Interchange Studios, Dalby St, London NW5 3NQ
Tel: 0171–267–3387

The Loss Prevention Council
Melrose Avenue, Borehamwood, Herts WD6 2BJ
Tel: 0181–207–2345

National Examination Board in Occupational Safety and Health
(NEBOSH)
NEBOSH House, The Grange, Highfield Drive, Wigston, Leicestershire
LE18 1PP
Tel: 0116–288–8858

Royal Society for the Prevention of Accidents (RoSPA)
Edgbaston Park, 353 Bristol Rd, Birmingham B5 7ST
Tel: 0121–248–2000

Royal Society of Health (RSH)
38a St George's Drive, London SW1V 4BH
Tel: 0171–630–0121

Safety and Reliability Society
59 Piccadilly, Manchester M1 2AQ
Tel: 0161–228–7824

Skillset
91–101 Oxford St, London W1R 1RA
Tel: 0171–306–8585

Trades Union Congress (TUC)
Congress House, Great Russell St, London WC1 B3LS
Tel: 0171–636–4030

Appendix 4: Safety books, magazines, posters and videos

Safety books and magazines

BECTU, *Stage, Screen and Radio* (bi-monthly), (Broadcasting, Entertainment, Cinematograph and Theatre Union).

British Safety Council, *Safety Management* (monthly).

Croner's Health and Safety Manager, Croner Publications Ltd, Croner House, London Rd, Kingston-upon-Thames, Surrey KT2 6BR, Tel: 0181–247–1175.

The Health and Safety at Work Brief, Locksley Press Ltd, Freepost 3044, London EC1B 1PN.

Hazards at Work, TUC, Congress House, Great Russell St, London WC1 B3LS, Tel: 0171–636–4030.

The Health and Safety Survival Guide, Terry Brimson, McGraw-Hill, 1995.

Institution of Occupational Safety and Health, *The Safety and Health Practitioner* (monthly).

Office for Official Publications of the European Communities, 2 Rue Mercier, L2985, Luxembourg, Tel: 352–499281.

Principles of Health and Safety at Work, Allan St John Holt, IOSH Publishing, 5th edition, ISBN-0–901–357–219.

RoSPA – Safety Express (bi monthly).

RoSPA – Occupational Safety and Health (monthly).

RoSPA – Occupational Safety and Health Bulletin.

The RoSPA Handbook of Health and Safety Practice, Jeremy Starks, Pitman, 4th edition, 1994.

RoSPA Health and Safety Guides:

1 Human Factors
2 Health and Safety Law
3 Management Systems
4 Occupational Health
5 Office Safety
6 Safety Technology

The Safety Audit, Roger Saunders, Pitman, 1994.

Safety at Work, John Ridley, Butterworth-Heinemann, 4th edition, 1994.

Tolley's Health and Safety at Work Handbook, The British Safety Council.

Safety posters

The British Safety Council, Direct Marketing Department, British Safety Council Sales Ltd, 70 Chancellors Rd, London W6 9RS, Tel: 0181–600–5576.

Safety videos

John Burder Films, Tel: 0181–995–0547.
List of videos, HSE, Misc 110.
Safety Videos Ltd, 18 Wynnstay Rd, Colwyn Bay, Conway LL29 8NB, Tel: 01492–531811.

Appendix 5: European safety organizations

The European Foundation for the Improvement of Living and Working
    Conditions,
Wyattville Rd, Loughlinstown, Co Dublin, Ireland
Tel: 353–1-204 3100

Office for Official Publications of the European Communities
2 Rue Mercier, L2985 Luxembourg
Tel: 352–499281

Euro Info Centres

Belfast
Euro Info Centre
Ledu House
Upper Galwally
BT8 4TB
Tel: 01232 491031

Birmingham
European Business Centre
75 Harborne Road
Edgbaston
B15 3DH
Tel: 0121 455 0268
Fax: 0121 455 8670

Bradford
West Yorkshire Euro Info Centre
Mercury House, 2nd Floor
4 Manchester Road
BD5 0QL
Tel: 01274 754262
Fax: 01274 393226

Bristol
Euro Info Centre
Business Link West
16 Clifton Park
Clifton
BS8 3BY
Tel: 01179 737373
Fax: 01179 745365

Burgess Hill
Euro Centre Sussex
Greenacre Court
Station Road
Burgess Hill
RH15 9DS
Tel: 01444 259259
Fax: 01444 259190

Cardiff
Wales Euro Info Centre
UWCC Guest Building
PO Box 430
CF1 3XT
Tel: 01222 229525
Fax: 01222 229740

Exeter
Euro Info Centre Southwest
Exeter Enterprises Ltd
Reed Hall
University Of Exeter
EX4 4QR
Tel: 01392 213085
Fax: 01392 264375

Glasgow
Euro Info Centre Ltd
Franborough House
123 Bothwell Street
G2 7JP
Tel: 0141 221 0999
Fax: 0141 221 6539

Hull
Euro Info Centre
Brynmor Jones Library
University of Hull
Cottingham Road
HU6 7RX
Tel: 01482 465940
Fax: 01482 465488

Inverness
Euro Info Centre North of Scotland
20 Bridge Street
IV1 1QR
Tel: 01463 720560
Fax: 01463 715600

Leicester
Leicester Euro Info Centre
10 York Road
LE1 5TS
Tel: 0116 2559944
Fax: 0116 2553470

Liverpool
Euro Info Centre North West
Liverpool Central Libraries
William Brown Street
L3 8EW
Tel: 0151 298 1928
Fax: 0151 207 1342

London 1
Euro Info Centre
33 Queen Street
EC4R 1AP
Tel: 0171 4891992
Fax: 0171 4890391

London 2
Euro Info Centre
Mitre House
177 Regent Street
W1R 8DJ
Tel: 0171 734 6404
Fax: 0171 734 0670

Maidstone
Kent European Information Centre
Springfield
Kent
ME14 2LL
Tel: 01622 6941090
Fax: 01622 691418

Manchester
Manchester Euro Info Centre
Churchgate House
56 Oxford Street
M60 7BL
Tel: 0161 237 4020
Fax: 0161 236 9945

Newcastle upon Tyne
Euro Info Centre
Great North House
Sandyford Road
NE1 8ND
Tel: 0191 2610026
Fax: 0191 2221774

Norwich
Euro Info Centre
   East Anglia
112 Barrack Street
NR3 1UB
Tel: 0345 023114
Fax: 01603 633032

Nottingham
Euro Info Centre
309 Haydn Road
NG5 1DG
Tel: 0115 9624624
Fax: 0115 9856612

Slough
Thames Valley Euro Info Centre
Commerce House
2–5 Bath Road
Berks
SL1 3SB
Tel: 01753 577877
Fax: 01753 524644

Southampton
Southern Area Euro Info Centre
Civic Centre
SO14 7LW
Tel: 01703 832866
Fax: 01703 231714

Staffordshire
Staffordshire European Business
   Centre
Commerce House
Festival Park
ST1 5BE
Tel: 01782 202222
Fax: 01782 274394

Telford
Shropshire and Staffordshire Euro
   Info Centre
Trevithic House
Stafford Park 4
TF3 3BA
Tel: 01952 208213
Fax: 01952 208208

Appendix 6: Production safety forms

COMPANY SAFETY DECLARATION
HEALTH & SAFETY AT WORK ACT 1974

TO   :   ALL MEMBERS OF THE CAST AND CREW

DATE   :

PRODUCTION :

1. The Company recognises as a primary responsibility its statutory obligations for the safety and well being of all its employees and other persons at locations where company business is being carried out. In fulfilling this responsibility the company will act, so far as is reasonably practicable, in accordance with Section 2 HASAW Act 1974, to ensure the health, safety and welfare of all persons, including persons not employed by the company who may be affected thereby:

BY: a) the provision of plant and systems at work that are safe and free from health risks
      b) arrangements for ensuring safety and absence of risk to health in connection with the use, handling, storage and transport of articles or substances.
      c) the provision of such information, instruction, training and supervision as is necessary to ensure the health and safety at work of all the employees.
      d) the maintenance at every location under the management's control in a condition that is safe and free from risk.
      e) a provision of a working environment that is safe and free from risks to health with adequate facilities and arrangements for the welfare of employees at work.

2. All employees of the company under Section 7 of HASAW Act, 1974 have a responsibility for their personal safety and also have a duty of care to their fellow employees. Each employee's responsibilities includes:

      a) the duty to comply with the safety instructions and directions laid down by their management.
      b) a duty to use properly the means and facilities provided for safety and health at work.
      c) a duty to refrain from the wilful misuse or interference with anything provided in the interests of health, safety and welfare and any actions that might endanger him/herself or others.
      d) the duty of all employees in authority to ensure that the necessary safety instructions are given

3. (PRODUCTION COMPANY NOMINATED PERSON i.e. THE HEALTH AND SAFETY OFFICER is the executive responsible to the production company for the effective implementation of the Health and Safety Policy during the production. He/She will co-ordinate all health and safety procedures and ensure with Heads of Departments that the relevant codes of practice and all statutory provisions are adhered to.

4. (PRODUCTION COMPANY) will bring to the notice of its employees the Health and Safety Policy of third party when the Production Company is using production facilities at a third party location.

5. It shall be the company's duty to conduct undertakings in such a way as to ensure, so far as is reasonably practicable, that persons not in the company's employment who may be affected thereby, are not exposed to risks to their health and safety.

6. ALL ACCIDENTS must be reported to the Production Office and an accident report must be completed and handed to the Health and Safety Officer for onward transmission to the HSE under the reporting of Injuries, Diseases and Dangerous Occurrences Regs 1995.

PRODUCTION SAFETY FORM

COMPANY

The Company recognises as a primary responsibility its statutory obligations for the safety and well being of all its employees and other persons at locations where company business is being carried out. In fulfilling this responsibility the company will act, so far as is reasonable practicable, in accordance with Section 2 HASAW Act 1974, to ensure the health, safety and welfare of all persons, including persons not employed by the company who may be affected thereby:

"Employees must safeguard so far as is reasonably practical,
the health, safety and welfare of the people who work for them"

Health and Safety at Work Act 1974

The purpose of this form is to help identify hazards and ensure appropriate steps are taken to minimise risks in order to protect the health and safety of company employees and anyone connected with the production.

COMPANY

PRODUCTION

LOCATION

PRODUCER

DIRECTOR

DATES

SIGNED

This form must be completed and safety measures implemented before any production activity is undertaken

PRODUCTION SAFETY FORM

UNIVERSITY/COLLEGE

The University/College recognises as a primary responsibility its statutory obligations for the safety and well being of all its employees and other persons at locations where university/college business is being carried out. In fulfilling this responsibility the university/college will act, so far as is reasonably practicable, in accordance with Section 2 HASAW Act 1974, to ensure the health, safety and welfare of all persons, including persons not employed by the university/college who may be affected thereby:

"Employees must safeguard so far as is reasonably practical, the health, safety and welfare of the people who work for them"

Health and Safety at Work Act 1974

The purpose of this form is to help identify hazards and ensure appropriate steps are taken to minimise risks in order to protect the health and safety of university/college employees and anyone connected with the production.

PRODUCTION

LOCATION

STUDENT NAMES

YEAR

COURSE

DATES

TUTOR APPROVED

This form must be completed and safety measures implemented before any production activity is undertaken

HAZARD IDENTIFICATION

The hazards listed below can be encountered during production. They have to be identified before filming commences. When a hazard has been identified you must now perform a risk assessment. The producer should assess whether the risk is high, medium or low, and take appropriate action to minimise the level of risk. The health and safety of production members and the public must be protected by the establishment of a safe and controlled working environment.

HAZARD IDENTIFICATION	IS THE HAZARD PRESENT?	
	Yes	No
Action Vehicles		
Agriculture		
Animals		
Asbestos		
Audiences and Groups		
Building & Construction sites		
Chemicals & hazardous substances (children)		
Churches & Village Halls		
Civil Unrest/Riot & War Zones		
Confined Spaces and Underground		
Cranes/Hoists, Fork Lifts and Access Platforms		
Dangerous Terrain		
Derelict Buildings & Land		
Diving & Underwater Filming		
Electricity, Lights & Cables		
Explosives & Pyrotechnics		
Extreme Weather Conditions		
Fire		
Firearms/Weapons		
First Aid		
Flying/Airports		
Food and Catering		
Hot work		
Human Factors		
Lasers & Radiation Safety		
Machinery		
Manual Handling/Lifting		
Night Operations		
Noise		
Outside Broadcasts		
Props Making		
Protective Equipment		
Restricted Access		
Roads/Driving		
Scaffolding & Working at Height		
Scenery Construction		
Special Effects		
Special Needs		
Sports Grounds		
Stunts		
VDU's & Computers		
Water Safety		
Working Overseas		
Other		

RISK ASSESSMENT

The producer should now assess whether the risk is high, medium or low, and take appropriate action to minimise the level of risk involved. The health and safety of production members, contractors and the public and anybody at risk must be identified by establishment of a safe and controlled working environment

HAZARD IDENTIFICATION	RISK ASSESSMENT		
	Low	Medium	High
Action Vehicles			
Agriculture			
Animals			
Asbestos			
Audiences and Groups			
Building & Construction sites			
Chemicals & hazardous substances (children)			
Churches & Village Halls			
Civil Unrest/Riot & War Zones			
Confined Spaces and Underground			
Cranes/Hoists, Fork Lifts and Access Platforms			
Dangerous Terrain			
Derelict Buildings & Land			
Diving & Underwater Filming			
Electricity, Lights & Cables			
Explosives & Pyrotechnics			
Extreme Weather			
Fire			
Firearms/Weapons			
First Aid			
Flying/Airports			
Food and Catering			
Hot work			
Human Factors			
Lasers & Radiation Safety			
Machinery			
Manual Handling/Lifting			
Night Operations			
Noise			
Outside Broadcasts			
Props Making			
Protective Equipment			
Restricted Access			
Roads/Driving			
Scaffolding & Working at Height			
Scenery Construction			
Special Effects			
Special Needs			
Sports Grounds			
Stunts			
VDU's & Computers			
Water Safety			
Working Overseas			
Other			

RISK REDUCTION

ACTION RECORD FORM

ACTION TAKEN	Producer signed and date

Ensure all fire and first aid precautions are identified.

Eliminate significant risks from chemicals, display screens, electricity, food and catering, lighting, lifting, water and working at height.

Clearly identify any expert help required and specialized equipment needed.

Attach site plans, photographs and documents where necessary.

EMERGENCY PROVISION

FIRE PRECAUTIONS

Location

Name of Fire Officer

Telephone

FIRST AID

Location

Name of Nominated First Aider

EMERGENCY ARRANGEMENTS

Details

COMMUNICATIONS

Vital Telephone Nos:

DANGEROUS CHEMICALS

Name

Supplier's Name

Date Sheet required   Yes/ No

Quantity

Location

CONTRACTOR ASSISTANCE FORM

CONTRACTOR 1

Name

Address

Liability Cover:

Cert. No.

Risk Assessment
Received:

Yes/No

Details of Service
Provided

CONTRACTOR 2

Name

Address

Liability Cover:

Cert. No.

Risk Assessment
Received:

Yes/No

Details of Service
Provided

CONTRACTOR 3

Name

Address

Liability Cover:

Cert. No.

Risk Assessment
Received:

Yes/No

Details of Service
Provided

CONTRACTOR 4

Name

Address

Liability Cover:

Cert. No.

Risk Assessment
Received:

Yes/No

Details of Service
Provided

PERSONAL PROTECTIVE EQUIPMENT FORM

PRODUCTION NAME:

LOCATION:

PRODUCER:

DATES: TEL NO:

Equipment	Required		Quantity	Issued to
	Yes	No		
Adverse Weather Clothing				
Barrier Cream				
Chemical Protection				
Communications				
Ear Protection				
Face Mask				
Face Protection				
Face Shield				
Fall Arrest Devices				
Fire Extinguishers				
First Aid Kit				
Gas Detector				
Gloves				
Head Protection				
Hidden Services Probe				
Laser Protection				
Life Jackets				
Respiratory Protective Equipment				
Safety Footwear				
Safety Goggles				
Safety Harness				
Smoke Alarms				
Visibility Clothing				

Collected by _____   Returned by _____

Signed _____   Signed _____

Date _____   Date _____

Appendix 7: Training organizations

CYFLE, Caernarfon
Gronant
Penralt Isaf
Caernarfon
LL55 1NW
Tel: 01286 671000

CYFLE, Cardiff
Crichton House
11–12 Sgwar Mount Stuart
Cardiff
CF1 6EE
Tel: 01222 465533
Fax: 01222 463344

MMTC
Studio 11
Nottingham Fashion Centre
Huntingdon Street
Nottingham
NG1 3LF
Tel: 0115 9930151

NIFC
21 Ormeau Avenue
Belfast
BT2 8HD
Tel: 01232 232444

PIRS
5th Floor
45 Mortimer Street
London
W1V 7TD
Tel: 0171 8306600
Fax: 0171 8306611

Scottish Screen
249 West George Street
Glasgow
G2 4QE
Tel: 0141 3021761
Fax: 0141 3021715

Skillset
91–101 Oxford St
London
W1R 1RA
Tel: 0171 3068585

Skillnet SW
59 Prince Street
Bristol
BS1 4QH
Tel: 0117 9254011

YMTC
40 Hanover Square
Leeds
LS3 1BQ
Tel: 0113 2944410
Fax: 0113 2944989

Index

 **Focal Press**

http://www.focalpress.com

Visit our web site for:

- The latest information on new and forthcoming Focal Press titles
- Technical articles from industry experts
- Special offers
- Our email news service

Join our Focal Press Bookbuyers' Club

As a member, you will enjoy the following benefits:

- Special discounts on new and best-selling titles
- Advance information on forthcoming Focal Press books
- A quarterly newsletter highlighting special offers
- A 30-day guarantee on purchased titles

Membership is FREE. To join, supply your name, company, address, phone/fax numbers and email address to:

USA
Christine Degon, Product Manager
Email: christine.degon@bhusa.com
Fax: +1 781 904 2620
Address: Focal Press,
225 Wildwood Ave, Woburn,
MA 01801, USA

Europe and rest of World
Elaine Hill, Promotions Controller
Email: elaine.hill@repp.co.uk
Fax: +44 (0)1865 314572
Address: Focal Press, Linacre House,
Jordan Hill, Oxford,
UK, OX2 8DP

Catalogue

For information on all Focal Press titles, we will be happy to send you a free copy of the Focal Press catalogue:

USA
Email: christine.degon@bhusa.com

Europe and rest of World
Email: carol.burgess@repp.co.uk
Tel: +44 (0)1865 314693

Potential authors

If you have an idea for a book, please get in touch:

USA
Terri Jadick, Associate Editor
Email: terri.jadick@bhusa.com
Tel: +1 781 904 2646
Fax: +1 781 904 2640

Europe and rest of World
Christina Donaldson, Editorial Assistant
Email: christina.donaldson@repp.co.uk
Tel: +44 (0)1865 314027
Fax: +44 (0)1865 314572